D1760000

ISBN 0-19-929006-7
9 780199 290062 >

Journal of Semitic Studies Supplement 12

STUDIES IN ISLAMIC AND MIDDLE EASTERN TEXTS AND TRADITIONS

IN MEMORY OF

NORMAN CALDER

edited by
G.R. Hawting, J.A. Mojaddedi and A. Samely

Published by Oxford University Press
on behalf of the University of Manchester

2000

Great Clarendon Street, Oxford OX2 6DP

Oxford University Press is a department of the University of Oxford.
It furthers the University's objective of excellence in research, scholarship,
and education by publishing worldwide in

Oxford New York

Athens Auckland Bangkok Bogotá Buenos Aires Calcutta
Cape Town Chennai Dar es Salaam Delhi Florence Hong Kong Istanbul
Karachi Kuala Lumpur Madrid Melbourne Mexico City Mumbai
Nairobi Paris São Paulo Shanghai Singapore Taipei Tokyo Toronto Warsaw

with associated companies in Berlin Ibadan

Oxford is a registered trade mark of Oxford University Press
in the UK and in certain other countries

Published in the United Kingdom
by Oxford University Press, Oxford

First published 2000

A catalogue for this book is available from the British Library

Library of Congress Cataloguing in Publication Data
(Data available)

ISSN 0022-4480
ISBN 0-19-929006-7

Subscription information for the *Journal of Semitic Studies* is available
from

Journals Customer Services
Oxford University Press
Great Clarendon Street
Oxford OX2 6DP
UK

Journals Marketing Department
Oxford University Press
2001 Evans Road
Cary, NC 27513
USA

Printed by the Charlesworth Group, Huddersfield, UK, 01484 517077

Table of contents

Acknowledgement

The editors are very grateful to Judith Willson, editorial assistant of the *Journal of Semitic Studies* from 1994 to 1999, for her help in producing this volume.

Abbreviations

AH	Anno Hegirae
AIUON	*Annali, Istituto Universitario Orientale di Napoli*
AO	*Acta Orientalia*
AOAT	*Alter Orient und Altes Testament*
art.	article
b	in front of a tractate name: tractate of the Babylonian Talmud (Bavli)
Bartholomae	C. Bartholomae, *Altiranisches Wörterbuch*, Strasbourg 1904
Borger	R. Borger, *Akkadische Zeichenliste,* Kevelaer/Neukirchen–Vluyn 1971
BJRULM	*Bulletin of the John Rylands University Library of Manchester*
BSOAS	*Bulletin of the School of Oriental and African Studies*
ch.	chapter
EI1	*Encyclopaedia of Islam*, 1st edn, Leiden 1913–38
EI2	*Encyclopaedia of Islam*, 2nd edn, Leiden 1960–
fol.	folio
FJB	*Frankfurter Judaistische Beiträge*
GAL	C. Brockelmann, *Geschichte der arabischen Litteratur,* Leiden 1937-49
GAS	F. Sezgin, *Geschichte des arabischen Schrifttums*, Leiden 1968–
GLECS	*Comptes rendus du Groupe Linguistique d'Études Chamito-Sémitiques*
GVG	C. Brockelmann, *Grundriss der vergleichenden Grammatik der semitischen Sprachen*, Berlin 1908–13
HTR	*Harvard Theological Review*
JAAR	*Journal of the American Academy of Religion*
JAL	*Journal of Arabic Literature*
JAOS	*Journal of the American Oriental Society*
JBL	*Journal of Biblical Literature*
JESHO	*Journal of the Economic and Social History of the Orient*
JJS	*Journal of Jewish Studies*
JJTP	*Journal of Jewish Thought and Philosophy*
JRAS	*Journal of the Royal Asiatic Society*
JSQ	*Jewish Studies Quarterly*
JSS	*Journal of Semitic Studies*
JSSS	Journal of Semitic Studies Supplements
l.	line
Labat	R. Labat, *Manuel d'épigraphie akkadienne* , Paris 1948
Lith.	Lithography
m	in front of a tractate name: Mishnah tractate
m.	mort
mB.B.	Mishnah tractate Bava Batra
mB.Q.	Mishnah tractate Bava Qamma
mBer.	Mishnah tractate Berakhot
mEd.	Mishnah tractate Eduyyot
mGiṭ.	Mishnah tractate Giṭṭin
MGWJ	*Monatsschrift für Geschichte und Wissenschaft des Judenthums*
mḤal.	Mishnah tractate Ḥallah
MIDEO	*Mélanges de l'Institut Dominicain d'Études Orientales*
mMak.	Mishnah tractate Makkot
mNaz.	Mishnah tractate Nazir
mNed.	Mishnah tractate Nedarim
mQid.	Mishnah tractate Qiddushin
mSoṭ.	Mishnah tractate Soṭah
mTer.	Mishnah tractate Terumot
mYev.	Mishnah tractate Yevamot
n. d.	no date

n. p.	no place
NBSS	Th. Nöldeke, *Neue Beiträge zur semitischen Sprachwissenschaft*, Strassburg 1910
Nyberg	H. S. Nyberg, *A Manual of Pahlavi*, 2 vols, Wiesbaden 1964, 1974
OLA	Orientalia Lovaniensia Analecta
PRU	*Les Palais Royal d'Ugarit*
r.	with folio number: recto
r.	with year: reigned
rev.	revised
RFSEI	*Revue de la Faculté des Sciences Économiques d'Istanbul*
RS	Ras Shamra
s. d.	sans date
sh.	shamsi (solar year)
tr.	translated
ult.	last line(s)
v.	voir
v.	with folio number: verso
WO	*Welt des Orients*
y	in front of a tractate name: tractate of the Palestinian Talmud (Yerushalmi)
ZDMG	*Zeitschrift der Deutschen Morgenländischen Gesellschaft*
¶	paragraph

Norman Calder (1950-1998)

Norman Calder
21 March 1950–13 February 1998

Stefan Sperl (School of Oriental and African Studies)

Knowing the dead, and how some are disposed:
Subdued under rubble, water, in sand graves,
In clenched cinders not yielding their abused
Bodies and bonds to those war's chance saves
Without the law: we grasp, roughly, the song.[1]

When I visited Norman Calder for the last time I asked him, as usual, about his opinion on an issue that had begun to preoccupy me. It involved the nature of poetry written under the impact of persecution and exile. Sitting in a waiting room of a Manchester hospital he engaged in an animated conversation during which he told me about the poetry of Geoffrey Hill whom he considered 'the best living English poet'. A few days later a letter arrived, dated 10 February 1998, with notes on an elegy by Hill dedicated to the Jews of Europe. The following are his comments on the first four lines which are cited above:

> *Knowing the dead, and how some are disposed*: It is tempting to read the word *some* there as equivalent to they, so that the whole sentence is about the dead (and acquiescence in a iambic pattern pushes this reading: *and HOW some ARE disposed*). The words after the colon then tell us about the dead: *subdued under rubble*, etc. It is a reading that will not be driven away (for the dead are certainly disposed of, scattered, even dispossessed and dis-poised – the poet makes that word work hard) but the word *some* calls out for a stress and a different referent. Some – of the survivors surely – are disposed in a particular manner, they have a certain disposition or inclination. The words after the colon now describe their disposition, not in truth but in metaphor: *in clenched cinders not yielding their abused / Bodies and bonds to those whom war's chance saves / Without the law*. Outside of Moses' law: the chance of war has saved the non-Jew; and the Jews (some of them), in clenched cinders, reliving the suffering of their people, are not inclined to yield their suffering ...? Knowing the dead (but how?) and how some are disposed (some) – presuming to know so much: *we grasp, roughly, the song*. That is, we have a rough and approximate grasp of the song. Or is it that, presuming to know so much, we seize and grasp the song roughly and violently – do an injustice based on the arrogant claim to know the dead and how some are disposed. Or do we grasp the song as we might grasp a nettle, roughly, with violence, because there is no other way to get our hand on this?

The remarkable sense of observation displayed in the above paragraph is, I believe, characteristic of Norman's entire *oeuvre*. With him, sensitivity to the finest nuance of a text never remains just that but leads to the discovery of new fields of vision which

[1] Geoffrey Hill, *Collected Poems*, London 1985, 30.

change the meaning of it as a whole. In this case, noticing the ambiguity in the word *disposed* makes him reveal in these four lines an extraordinary meditation upon the relationship between victims and survivors, the living and the dead.[2] I could not have hoped for a richer, more thought-provoking answer to the query I had approached him with.

My first memory of Norman also involves his reading skills, though in a rather more light-hearted setting. It dates back to the autumn of 1969 when we were attending elementary Arabic language classes at the Oriental Institute in Oxford. Asked to read their sentences aloud, the students in the class would pause after every word as they struggled with the unfamiliar sounds. Norman approached the task with gusto, determined to read his sentences at break-neck speed. To everyone's amusement his intrepid efforts sometimes ended in disaster, but the rest of us all realized that this red-haired, bespectacled young man with an air of distance about him was someone to be reckoned with.

I believe we started talking because we were both, in very different ways, outsiders in Oxford. Being German, I had difficulty in understanding the English way of making conversation and found it hard to strike up a relaxed relationship with my fellow students. Norman, born in Buckie, a remote fishing town in the Scottish Highlands, had had his own experience with communication problems. When he moved to Dunstable with his family at the age of eleven he found that the children in his new school failed to understand his Scottish accent. For the better part of a school year he hardly talked to his class mates and I recall that he attributed his early search for companionship in books to this experience.

In Oxford, Norman noticed the difficulties I was having and proceeded to make me aware that communicating through allusion and understatement has its own value and charm. I remember in particular his assertion that much warmth and mutual acknowledgement can be detected in the many ways English people comment upon the weather. Depending on the inflection of the speaker's voice, 'grey day today isn't it' could, he said, communicate as affectionate a welcome as a firm handshake and a broad smile in another setting. These conversations did much to help me adapt to the country that was to become my chosen home and marked the beginning of a friendship which lasted nearly thirty years.

Despite being passionately interested in his studies and obtaining a first class honours degree in Arabic and Persian, Norman's mind was not set on a career in scholarship. He was eager to leave the university environment and thought of a range of different options he could embark upon. The seminal experience Oxford provided to both of us, however, was that of being brought face to face with a long tradition of

[2] The interpretation of the poem by Ricks (which Norman mentions) also notices ambiguity in the word 'disposed' but fails to explore it (see C. Ricks, *The Force of Poetry*, Oxford 1984, 291).

learning of which Norman would ultimately choose to become a part. Two of our teachers were, I believe, particularly influential in this respect: Freddy Beeston, the Laudian Professor of Arabic and Richard Walzer, Reader in Greek and Arabic Philosophy, who had officially retired at that time but was still busy teaching.

Walzer, born in Berlin in 1900 and of Jewish descent, was the living embodiment of an intellectual quest undaunted by ethnic, cultural and religious divides. He had studied Greek in Germany, Arabic in Italy as a refugee and then came to Oxford where he introduced his students to the transmission of Greek learning from antiquity to Islam and thence to Christian Europe. In doing so he felt a sense of kinship with the Oxford philosophers of medieval times who, as he often pointed out, knew their classical sources principally through Arabic translations.

If Walzer seemed to hold the key to an unbroken tradition stretching back, through the prisms of three monotheist religions, all the way to Plato and Aristotle, the real impact he had on us as students came from his personality which exhibited, in the words of Alan Bullock, 'a serenity of mind undisturbed by either rancour or resentment'.[3] Indeed, his kindness and gentle sense of humour belied the loss of his family members in the Holocaust. It was as though his scholarly ability to listen attentively to so many differing voices over the centuries had imparted him with a larger sense of vision that could transcend even personal tragedy.

Scholarship in Walzer then appeared to be more than just a profession. It seemed to hold the promise of a greater good, of a moral force that could be distilled from the cumulative human efforts inherent in the great traditions of learning. It is perhaps for this reason that Norman and I, both in Oxford and for some years thereafter, often talked about the question whether 'to become like Dr Walzer' was a desirable goal to strive for. The answer differed somewhat every time and the discussion often turned into a joke; then the issue was forgotten. With hindsight I now see that Norman followed Walzer's footsteps to a remarkable extent.

Professor Beeston, the other great figure of our student days, represented a younger though for us no less meaningful tradition than Walzer. It was that distinctly British fascination with Arabia and the Arabic language which made echoes of Doughty, Burton and T. E. Lawrence resonate in his sonorous readings of Arabic poetry and classical prose. His singular philological erudition, combined with his first-hand knowledge of, and evident love for, the flora and fauna of the desert, made his teaching of pre-Islamic poetry especially memorable. As for so many of his students, the *Muʿallaqa* by Labīd which Beeston later described as 'one of my favourite Arabic

---

[3] A. Bullock, "Richard Walzer", in S. M. Stern, A. Hourani and V. Brown (eds), *Islamic Philosophy and the Classical Tradition: Essays Presented by his Friends and Pupils to Richard Walzer,* Oxford 1972, 2.

poems and one which I have long studied'[4] became an indelible part of our mental fabric.

In my case his teaching awakened an abiding interest in the classical Arabic ode or *qaṣīda* which was to lead me to a doctoral thesis on the subject. Many of my ideas were, however, developed in conversation with Norman, who was no less taken by the *qaṣīda* which he called 'a kind of perfected parable of life'. While his published work hardly touches on poetry he developed his own theory on the much debated question of the coherence of the *qaṣīda* form and, in particular, on the meaning of the seemingly enigmatic juxtaposition of personal love and public praise in the panegyric ode. He very aptly saw the two parts not as 'discordant halves but as explorations of one theme, namely love ...'. As so often with Norman, scholarly exchanges shifted into humorous flights of fancy. One example is the following *qaṣīda* parody of his which freely plays upon echoes from Labīd's ode:

> See the sand, stop and cry a little for it reminds me of a place where there was no sand between John O'Groats and Land's End, not far from Wales or Ireland. There I watched one day while the beloved packed and left and the lampposts and the street cars and the fabled towers, shimmering in a mirage stole away from the railway platform. And the platform too stole away. (The arrows of fate never miss their mark!) Thus in a strong plane in bumpy weather I crossed the Pacific and the Atlantic, Europe and Africa – Asia was on the right hand, where the red-leafed Acerbus sprouts. See! where men coupling have brought forth foals in the valleys of the mountains. Soon to the mountains of Yemen – on the right hand – where the summer stars give rain, belting across the horizon; the clouds stretching – so it seems – from Australia in the West to Stornoway and Skye. Then in a swift charter to Cairo with pubs and clubs and brothels. Never a morning – and the sun rises clear every morning, coming up in the east and dying in the west – but I will drink a clear draught. And so, on to the Friend ...

The above appears in a letter Norman wrote during his middle eastern interlude, when, for a period of four years after gaining his first degree, he taught English in Iran and Saudi Arabia. While he did not, to my knowledge, cross the Pacific and the Atlantic at that time he certainly travelled all over the Middle East, perfected his spoken Arabic and Persian and established that indispensable, living relationship with the culture he had chosen to study.

Our paths crossed again in 1976 when Norman, after much hesitation, decided to join the School of Oriental and African Studies in London in order to embark on a doctoral thesis. Suitably, he was assigned perhaps the most inspiring, but also, as some would say, the most daunting pair of supervisors the Middle East Department in SOAS could muster: Anne K. S. Lambton and John E. Wansbrough. The imprint of the former is evident in several articles Norman published on Imāmī Shīʿī jurisprudence, which was also the subject of his thesis. It is Wansbrough, however, who was to prove the

[4] A. F. L. Beeston, "An Experiment with Labīd", *JAL*, 7 (1976), 2. Michael Gilsenen's tribute to Beeston also mentions his teaching of Labīd (see "A Personal Introduction" in A. Jones [ed.], *Arabicus Felix Luminosus Britannicus. Essays in Honour of A. F. L. Beeston*, Oxford 1991, iv).

single most decisive influence upon Norman's future research. Since he was also my supervisor at the time I was privileged to witness the beginning of this intellectual relationship at close hand.

Wansbrough, though American by birth, was, from the point of view of his scholarly pursuits, the heir of a different domain. As remarked by Yapp, 'something of the Grand Central European tradition was known to embellish his speech and pen'[5] – except that this legacy went much beyond embellishment. The works of Goldziher, Schacht and Nöldeke, coupled with the insights of literary historians such as Auerbach and Curtius, provided the framework for his own inquiries into the origins of Islam, and their example was a regular point of reference in his teaching. No less important for the development of his distinct approach was his affinity to literature in general and, to my surprise, to German literature in particular.[6] Indeed, Wansbrough's literary erudition must be seen as an integral part of his scholarly outlook in that the latter permits no fundamental distinction between literary, historical or religious texts; the reality conveyed in all of these is seen to be first and foremost a literary construct and thus to be analysed as such. This approach, through which Wansbrough reached the startling insights for which his work has become famous, fell on particularly fertile ground with Norman Calder. The latter shared with his mentor an equal passion for, and knowledge of, literature, in particular the tradition of the European novel which, for both of them, reached a point of culmination in Thomas Mann's *Joseph and his Brothers*.

Furthermore, it may not be amiss to note that their interest in the study of religion was undoubtedly nurtured by their Roman Catholic background, which is another element they had in common. It does not, however, noticeably impinge upon the nature of their scholarly inquiry, which emphatically approaches Judaism, Christianity and Islam as a single tradition marked by a shared though divergent salvation history, the message of which is accessible only through assiduous study of literary texts. As stated by Norman with characteristic irony, 'to know God it is reading skills that are required'.[7]

The scholarly technique Norman developed under the influence of his teachers has yielded rich results, which are exemplified most impressively in his *Studies in Early Muslim Jurisprudence*.[8] Here he demonstrates how literary analysis can, by

[5] M. Yapp, "Professor J. E. Wansbrough", in *In Honour of J. E. Wansbrough*, Special Issue of *BSOAS*, 57 (1994), part 1, 2.

[6] Wansbrough's obituary of his teacher Paul Wittek mentions their 'shared affection for German literature' and acknowledges his debt to him 'for an appreciation of George and Musil, whose works I began twenty years ago to read with fresh and inspired guidance', see *BSOAS*, 42 (1979), 138.

[7] N. Calder, "History and Nostalgia: Reflections on John Wansbrough's *The Sectarian Milieu*", in H. Berg (ed.), *Islamic Origins Reconsidered: John Wansbrough and the Study of Islam*, Special Issue of *Method and Theory in the Study of Religion: Journal of the North American Association for the Study of Religion*, 9-1, Berlin 1997, 49. This seminal article which is both a statement of allegiance and critical evaluation gives much insight into Norman's approach to Wansbrough's scholarship. For a detailed review see J. A. Mojaddedi, "Taking Islam Seriously: The Legacy of John Wansbrough", *JSS*, 45 (2000), 109-14.

[8] Oxford 1993.

giving insight into the historical evolution of a literary tradition, reveal a picture of the evolving social reality which has given rise to it. What makes this possible is the strict observance of 'the methodological imperative that only after analysing the texts in relation to their own time should they be used as sources of earlier history' (p. 199).

The substance of the work lies in the type of analysis undertaken. The reader is treated to meticulous dissections of the structural fabric of individual texts which in some cases reveal unexpected fault lines and stylistic layers and, in others, an equally remarkable degree of stringency and coherence. This is combined with a no less painstaking examination of the evolving meanings of technical terms, an issue to which Norman also devoted several of his scholarly articles. From this careful attention to detail a wider picture emerges that is not without surprises: early Muslim legal texts are the product of the third century AH and reflect the urban practice of the Fertile Crescent and North Africa, not tribal Arabia. Key elements habitually presumed to be the sources of the law, in particular Qurʾānic sanction, prophetic example and Arab Bedouin custom, are shown to have been integrated into the system not at the beginning but at the end of its formative period.

This picture, rich in implications for our understanding of early Islamic history, adds a new dimension to Wansbrough's earlier findings which are largely based on non-legal texts. Of equal if not greater significance, however, is another outcome of Norman's approach to this type of material. Reading legal texts first and foremost as literature allows him to give adequate attention, for the first time perhaps, to their purely aesthetic properties, which are shown not to have been ancillary or secondary features but which became, increasingly, a driving force in the elaboration of the tradition as a whole. Far from being a grey and utilitarian discipline, Muslim jurisprudence emerges under his scrutiny as a remarkable form of sacred verbal art, bearing witness to 'the intrinsic delight of the juristic task' (p. 222) and revealing 'a patterned beauty that appeals as instantly to the intellect as a Persian carpet does to the eye' (p. 243).

These outstanding features are, moreover, not limited to the legal texts of the early period. The entire classical tradition of *fiqh* up until the nineteenth century displays, in his view, an unbroken chain of continuity, vitality and creativity which brought about what he called 'the greatest intellectual and literary achievements of Muslim religious thought'.[9] Such an assessment is, of course, diametrically opposed to received opinion which has long viewed Islamic and Arabic literary culture, from the late Middle Ages onwards, as subject to increasing stagnation because of its deliberate adherence to traditional forms of thought and expression. In Norman's view, however, the assumption that such adherence reflects 'decline, decay, and ankylosis is the product of a failure (or simple absence) of reading on the part of Western scholars' (p. 64).

---

[9] "History and Nostalgia", 62.

The last major task Norman engaged in was an attempt to remedy this situation. With the help of a two-year grant from the British Academy he intended to produce a study of the genres and social function of Muslim juristic literature from 400/1010 to 1300/1883. Considering the many tomes which need to be examined to cover such a long period this enterprise can only be described as monumental, even for someone who seems to have developed the ability to read texts of *fiqh* as though they were novels. He was not able to complete this great undertaking but left behind four chapters which are enough to provide a telling insight into the complex relationship between the law as an idealized system and its manifestation in social practice. They are currently being edited for publication by his colleague Colin Imber.

Norman not only excelled as an author of scholarly research but also proved himself to be a gifted teacher, an activity to which he devoted the lion's share of his time, first at Leeds and, from 1980 onwards, at Manchester University. Having acquired the technical skills of language teaching during his years in the Middle East helped him to develop a structured and professional approach to the subject and it comes as no surprise that while in Manchester he 'modernised the teaching of Arabic, and persuaded his colleagues to reform the middle eastern studies teaching programme'.[10] His most important contribution, however, was probably in the field of post-graduate supervision, about which his colleague Philip Alexander wrote the following:

> He supervised some 20 post-graduate students, most of whom came from the Middle East or the wider Islamic world. There was potential for deep conflict in the meeting of his own, radical western approach to Islam and the more intellectually conservative attitudes of his Muslim students. That this tension remained creative rather than destructive, is a tribute to his tact, patience and humour, and to his students' ready perception that he had their interests at heart.[11]

What may well also have helped to make this delicate exercise in cross-cultural communication a success is the nature of Norman's approach to his subject. Both as a scholar and as a teacher he was able to provide an interpretation of the Islamic tradition which, while being in many ways at variance with orthodox opinion, does not diminish it but asserts its individuality and creativity in a manner which dispels long-held prejudice and betrays a profound degree of empathy. In the fraught dialogue between Islam and the West Norman clearly had a vital contribution to make and his early death is an inestimable loss.

'We grasp, roughly, the song'. The ambiguity and dread Norman perceived in this phrase of Geoffrey Hill strangely conveys something of the reaction I felt at the

---

[10] P. Alexander, "Norman Calder: A Fresh Look at Islam's Origins", in *The Guardian*, London, March 18, 1998, 24 (Obituaries).
[11] *Ibid.*

news of his illness. I will always remember the moment when he first told me that something was amiss. It was one morning over breakfast at the Sherlock Holmes Hotel in Baker Street where he was staying while attending a conference in London. There was as yet no word of cancer but an ominous feeling filled the air. Months later, when the worst fears were confirmed, began a new phase in our friendship. He showed me that inspiration, good cheer and wit can co-exist with terminal illness and daily pain. Like many of those who visited him at the time I was astonished to find myself leaving him with a sense of elation rather than sadness, enrichment rather than loss.

That enrichment will stay with us. As illustrated by the appearance of this volume in his memory, the verses by Eliot he cited at the end of his reflections on the nature of literary history apply to him now in a different but no less poignant way:

> We die with the dying:
> See they depart and we go with them.
> We are born with the dead:
> See they return and bring us with them.[12]

[12] T. S. Eliot, "Little Gidding", in *The Complete Poems and Plays*, London 1969, 197, as cited by N. Calder in "History and Nostalgia", 71.

Published works of Norman Calder

Books

Studies in Early Muslim Jurisprudence, Oxford: Clarendon Press, 1993

Classical Islam: A Sourcebook of Religious Literature (jointly edited with J. A. Mojaddedi and A. Rippin), London–New York: Routledge, in preparation for 2001.

Four Studies in Islamic Law, edited by C. Imber, Oxford: Oxford University Press, in preparation for 2001.

Articles and published papers

"Judicial authority in Imāmī Shīʿī jurisprudence", *BRISMES Bulletin*, 6 (1979), 104–8.

"*Zakāt* in Imāmī Shīʿī jurisprudence, from the tenth to the sixteenth century A.D.", *BSOAS*, 44.3 (1981), 468–80.

"Accommodation and revolution in Imāmī Shīʿī jurisprudence: Khumaynī and the classical tradition", *Middle Eastern Studies*, 18.1 (1982), 3–20.

"*Khums* in Imāmī Shīʿī jurisprudence, from the tenth to the sixteenth century A.D.", *BSOAS*, 45.1 (1982), 39–47.

"*Ikhtilāf* and *ijmāʿ* in Shāfiʿī's *Risāla*", *Studia Islamica*, 58 (1983), 55–81.

"The significance of the term *imām* in early Islamic jurisprudence", *Zeitschrift für Geschichte der Arabisch-Islamischen Wissenschaften*, 1 (1984), 254–64.

"Friday Prayer and the juristic theory of government: Sarakhsī, Shīrāzī, Māwardī", *BSOAS*, 49.1 (1986), 35–47.

"The *saʿy* and the *jabīn*: some notes on Qurʾān 37:102–3", *JSS*, 31.1 (1986), 17–26.

"Legitimacy and accommodation in Ṣafavid Iran: the juristic theory of Muḥammad Bāqir al-Sabzavārī (d. 1090/1679)", *Iran: Journal of the British Institute of Persian Studies*, 25 (1987), 91–105.

"From Midrash to scripture: the sacrifice of Abraham in early Islamic tradition", *Le Muséon: Revue d'études orientales*, 101.3–4 (1988), 375–402.

"*Ḥinth, birr, tabarrur, taḥannuth*: an inquiry into the Arabic vocabulary of vows", *BSOAS*, 51.2 (1988), 214–39.

"Doubt and prerogative: the emergence of an Imāmī Shīʿī theory of *ijtihād*", *Studia Islamica*, 70 (1989), 57–78.

"The *Ummī* in early Islamic juristic literature", *Der Islam*, 67.1 (1990), 111–23.

"The *Qurrāʾ* and the Arabic lexicographic tradition", *JSS*, 36.2 (1991), 297–307.

"*Tafsīr* from Ṭabarī to Ibn Kathīr: problems in the description of a genre", in G. R. Hawting and Abdul-Kader A. Shareef (eds), *Approaches to the Qur'ān*, London–New York: Routledge, 1993, 101–40.

"The *Barāhima*: literary construct and historical reality", *BSOAS*, 57.1 (1994), 41–51.

"Exploring God's Law: Muḥammad b. Aḥmad b. Abī Sahl al-Sarakhsī on *zakāt*", in Chr. Toll and J. Skøvgaard-Petersen (eds), *Law and the Islamic World, Past and Present*, Copenhagen: Det Kongelige Danske Videnskabernes Selskab, 1995, 57–73.

"Al-Nawawī's typology of muftis and its significance for a general theory of Islamic Law", *Islamic Law and Society*, 3.2 (1996), 137–64.

"Law", in S. H. Nasr and O. Leaman (eds), *History of Islamic Philosophy*, London–New York: Routledge, 1996, ii, 979–98.

"History and nostalgia: reflections on John Wansbrough's *The Sectarian Milieu*", in H. Berg (ed.), *Islamic Origins Reconsidered: John Wansbrough and the Study of Islam*, Special Issue of *Method and Theory in the Study of Religion: Journal of the North American Association for the Study of Religion*, 9.1 (1997), 47–73.

"The limits of Islamic orthodoxy", in F. Daftary (ed.), *Intellectual Traditions in Islam*, London: I.B.Tauris, 2000, 66–86.

"The *ʿUqūd rasm al-muftī* of Ibn ʿĀbidīn", *BSOAS*, 63.2 (2000), 215–28.

Entries in encyclopaedias

"Abū Dāwūd al-Sijistānī", "Abū Ḥānīfa", "Abū Yūsuf", "al-Bukhārī", "Ibn Ḥanbal", "Ibn Ḥazm", "Ibn Māja", "Ibn Taymiyya", "Mālik ibn Anas", "Muslim ibn al-Ḥajjāj", "al-Nasāʾī", "al-Shāfiʿī", "al-Shaybānī", "al-Tirmidhī", in J. R. Hinnells (ed.), *Who's Who of World Religions*, London: Macmillan, 1991.

"Ghayba", "Ḥillī, ʿAllāma ibn al-Muṭahhar", "Law: legal thought and jurisprudence", "Marjaʿ al-taqlīd", in J. L. Esposito (ed.), *Oxford Encyclopedia of the Modern Islamic World*, New York–Oxford: Oxford University Press, 1995.

"Law, Islamic philosophy of", in E. Craig (ed.) *Routledge Encyclopedia of Philosophy*, London–New York: Routledge, 1998.

"Sharia law", *Microsoft Encarta Encyclopaedia* (British edition), 1998.

"Feqh", in E. Yarshater (ed.), *Encyclopaedia Iranica*, ix, New York: Bibliotheca Persica Press, 1999.

"al-Sarakhsī", "sharīʿa", "al-Ṭaḥāwī", "taḳlīd", "uṣūl al-fiḳh", in *Encyclopaedia of Islam*, 2nd edn, Leiden: E. J. Brill, ix (1997); x (2000).

Jewish tradition in early Islam
The case of Enoch/Idrīs*

Philip S. Alexander (University of Manchester)

The Isrāʾīliyyāt

Muslim and non-Muslim scholars alike have long recognized the presence in early Islamic sources, starting with the Qurʾān itself, of a substantial body of Jewish tradition. This Jewish tradition, or Isrāʾīliyyāt as it has sometimes been called,[1] has provoked intense interest and debate.[2] Where did it come from? What does it say about the relationship between Judaism and Islam during Islam's formative period? Why was this material taken over into Islam, and how has it been used?

The problem of the Isrāʾīliyyāt is complicated, more complicated than is sometimes supposed. It is not just a case of direct borrowings from the Hebrew Bible. These might be easily enough explained, if the early Muslims had access to translations of the Bible, which is not unlikely, since very early renderings of parts of the Hebrew Bible into Arabic, done by Syriac Christians from the Greek, are attested. There were also Jewish converts to Islam, possibly even within the circle of the Prophet, some of whom may have been rather learned in Judaism, and may have had access to the Bible in its original Hebrew. However, even when clearly retelling biblical stories, as for example in Sūrat Yūsuf, the Isrāʾīliyyāt are seldom straightforward Bible. When we read them closely, it becomes obvious that the Muslim authors or their sources have reworked the biblical tales and included all sorts of details which suggest that they knew Midrash, the post-biblical Jewish tradition of Bible exegesis as well. We also find elements in the Isrāʾīliyyāt which are not derived from the Bible, but which are demonstrably Jewish in origin. There are elements which we may strongly suspect are Jewish in origin, but for which we cannot now find a Jewish source. And some elements even seem to presuppose forms of Judaism which it is now impossible to identify precisely or to document.

---

* I offer this essay, which lies somewhat outside my métier, as the memorial of a long dialogue with a dear friend. We discussed the issues raised here over endless cups of coffee, and I know he would have disapproved of my conclusions. But he would have relished the argument. 'As iron sharpeneth iron, so a man sharpeneth the countenance of his friend.'

[1] I use Isrāʾīliyyāt not in any negative sense, but simply as a convenient designation for all those elements in the Qurʾān, Tafsīr and *ḥadīth* which have clear parallels in Jewish sources. This corresponds to the older use of the word by Islamic writers. Today, however, the term is sometimes felt by Muslims to be pejorative.

[2] See, for example, A. I. Katsh, *Judaism in Islam: Biblical and Talmudic Backgrounds of the Koran and its Commentaries*, New York 1954; H. Speyer, *Die biblischen Erzählungen im Qoran*, 1961 (repr. Hildesheim 1971); H. Schwarzbaum, *Biblical and Extra-Biblical Legends in Islamic Folk-Literature*, Walldorf-Hessen 1982.

To analyse properly the Isrāʾīliyyāt requires an almost exhaustive knowledge of the Jewish tradition. It is only by reading the Muslim sources closely against this tradition in all its fullness and complexity that we can begin to understand them correctly – what has been taken over more or less unchanged, and what has been altered and given a new meaning. And it is only when we compare the Muslim sources comprehensively with the Jewish that we can identify those cases where the Jewish source is no longer extant, or where an otherwise unknown form of Judaism is apparently presupposed. Few have had the knowledge of both the Jewish and the Muslim traditions to make such a comparison.

The study of the Isrāʾīliyyāt, like almost everything else in Muslim–Jewish relations, has been bedevilled by politics. This point can be illustrated from the work of the nineteenth-century German Jewish scholar Abraham Geiger, who wrote one of the pioneering studies of the subject, entitled *What did Muḥammad Take from Judaism?*[3] This remains to the present day a useful essay, but one should not miss its polemical sub-text. Geiger suggests that Islam was a derivative religion, which took all its good ideas from Judaism. But, in fact, Islam was not the only target that Geiger had in his sights. When he wrote there were very few Muslims in western Europe to be offended by his remarks. Rather, he was taking a sly dig at Christianity. Later he was to make the attack on Christianity explicit, and to argue that all the noblest ethical and religious insights not only of Islam but of Christianity as well were ultimately derived from Jewish Pharisaism of the Second Temple period. Geiger was writing at a time when Jewish emancipation and Jewish Reform were burning issues in Germany, and in retrospect it is clear that his scholarship was influenced and compromised by his political agenda.[4]

It would be futile to get involved in this argument now, especially since it is based on a profoundly mistaken premise. All religions – Judaism included – have always used whatever antecedent traditions were to hand. Judaism drew heavily on Islam in the Middle Ages, particularly, though not exclusively, on the Kalām. That does not delegitimize Judaism, any more than Islamic use of Jewish tradition delegitimizes Islam. What is so impressive about the Isrāʾīliyyāt, and decisively refutes any charge of plagiarism, is the creativity which the Muslim writers show in using the Jewish tradition, and the profound transformations which it undergoes at their hands. Indeed, the way in which the Isrāʾīliyyāt are normally characterized, as 'borrowings', misconstrues the subtle inter-textual relationship between the Jewish and

[3] *Was hat Mohammed aus dem Judenthume aufgenommen?*, Baden 1833. The book was originally a prize essay submitted to the University of Bonn at the suggestion of Georg Freytag. It earned for Geiger a doctorate from Marburg. The English translation by F. M. Young, *Judaism and Islam*, Madras 1898, was reprinted by Ktav, New York in 1970. Though he argued that Islam was derivative, the generally respectful and objective tone of Geiger's work marked a welcome advance on the unrelenting vilification of Islam typical of Christian scholars in his day.

[4] See Susannah Heschel, *Abraham Geiger and the Jewish Jesus*, Chicago–London 1998, 50–75.

the Islamic sources. The changes which we find in the Islamic texts are of precisely the same order as those we find already *within* Jewish tradition. If we were to identify say in Shir ha-Shirim Rabba a reworking of a tradition which is attested earlier in Bereshit Rabba we would not naturally speak of Shir ha-Shirim Rabba as *borrowing* from Bereshit Rabba. We would be more inclined to model the relationship in terms of an ongoing, dynamic and developing tradition. But why should this model be rejected when we find similar processes at work in Islamic texts? The traditions flow uninterrupted across the boundaries between the two religions. This has profound implications. It suggests that, from one perspective, at the earliest stages which concern us here, we are not in fact dealing with two clearly demarcated religions and to impose such a distinction is anachronistic. Earliest Islam can be quite properly regarded as a form of Judaism.[5] We face the same problem with early Christianity, which, when it emerged, was even more clearly a form of Judaism, and which continued and developed Jewish tradition in a remarkably dynamic fashion.

There is one final preliminary point which needs to be made. In discussing the problem of the Isrāʾīliyyāt the assumption is sometimes too readily made that the borrowing went only one way – from Judaism to Islam. This is manifestly incorrect. There are clear examples where Islamic elements, or what appear to be distinctively Islamic developments of Jewish tradition, have been taken over into Jewish Midrash. There is evidence that already in the seventh and eighth centuries Jewish and Muslim scholars were interacting in significant ways. The mass appropriation of the Kalām by Saadya in the ninth century did not come out of the blue. This point is well illustrated by the strange Jewish Midrashic text known as Pirqei de-Rabbi Eliezer, Islamic influences on which have long been recognized.[6]

The Matter of Enoch

It is unhelpful to talk about the Isrāʾīliyyāt in terms of generalities. Each concrete case throws up its own peculiarities, and a lot more detailed examples will have to be fully worked before we will find ourselves in a position to make well-founded universal

---

[5] Or of Christianity, though that is not my concern here. I am not trying to revive the old polemical *canard* that Islam is simply a Jewish or Christian heresy. I am speaking purely as a historian in tradition-historical terms. However, it should be noted that at a popular level the boundaries between Judaism, Christianity and Islam have sometimes become very blurred. In mixed communities in the Middle East, especially in rural areas, where Jews, Christians and Muslims have lived side by side peacefully for long periods of time, each group can participate in the others' religious practices and venerate the others' saints. A kind of common, popular religion emerges, despite the displeasure of the religious leaders, who have a vested interest in maintaining separation. See on this the 1999 Oxford DPhil dissertation of Joseph Waleed Meri, "Sacred Journeys to Sacred Precincts: The Cult of Saints among Muslims and Jews in Mediaeval Syria".

[6] See B. Heller, "Muhammedanisches und Antimuhammedanisches in den Pirke R. Eliezer", *MGWJ*, 69 (1925), 47–54; M. Ohana, "La polémique judéo-islamique et l'image d'Ishmael dans Targum Pseudo-Jonathan et dans Pirqe de Rabbi Eliezer', *Augustinianum*, 15 (1975), 367–87; J. Heinemann, *Aggadah and its Development*, Jerusalem 1984, 181–99, 242–7 [Hebrew].

statements. In the present essay I shall attempt to explore the problems of the Isrāʾīliyyāt by taking one particular Jewish tradition – about the patriarch Enoch – and investigating how it was developed in early Islamic sources. In addition to illustrating a particular tradition-historical approach to this material, I want to address the concrete questions of why this tradition was taken over, who was responsible for appropriating it, and what light Muslim use of it throws on the relationship between Judaism and Islam.

Enoch, who lived, according to the biblical history, before Noah's Flood, had one of the most illustrious careers in post-biblical tradition of all the biblical heroes. The literature about him, and, allegedly by him, in the pre-Islamic period, is very extensive. In fact the only biblical figure to match Enoch's standing in the post-biblical period is Moses the lawgiver of Israel. It is possible that Enoch was deliberately set up, at least in some circles, as a rival to Moses, and as offering an Enochic as opposed to a Mosaic paradigm of Judaism. Yet, curiously, the biblical basis for this elaborate development is exiguous in the extreme. Enoch is mentioned in the Bible in only eight verses, as part of a dry-as-dust genealogy (Gen. 5:18–25):

> And Jared lived a hundred and sixty-two years and begot Enoch: and Jared lived after he begot Enoch eight hundred years, and begot sons and daughters: and all the days of Jared were nine hundred and sixty-two years and he died. And Enoch lived sixty-five years and begot Methuselah. And Enoch walked with God after he begot Methuselah three hundred years, and begot sons and daughters: and all the days of Enoch were three hundred and sixty-five years: and Enoch walked with God: and he was not; for God took him. And Methuselah lived a hundred and eighty-seven years, and begot Lamech.

Lurking in this rather matter-of-fact statement is a claim which intrigued later commentators, and which they were to exploit to the full in order to develop the figure of Enoch: 'And all the days of Enoch were three hundred and sixty-five years; and Enoch walked with God, and he was not, for God took him'. The language is mysterious. One feels instinctively that something is being hinted at which one has not been told. What does it mean that Enoch 'was not, for God took him'? Another figure in the Bible – Elijah the prophet – was said to have been 'taken' by God, and in Elijah's case this 'taking' meant taking up to heaven, without dying (2 Kgs 2:5). So in post-biblical Jewish tradition Enoch ascends to heaven without dying, and plays an important role in the heavenly world. And since he never died some asserted that he would come back from heaven to earth at the end of time to take a key role in the events surrounding the Day of Judgement. And what does the verse mean by saying that 'Enoch walked with God'? The word for God here in the Hebrew, *ʾelohim*, sometimes means 'angels'. So, some claimed, Enoch communicated with the angels and received from them revelations about the workings of the cosmos and about the future history of the world. And what is the significance of the period of Enoch's life on earth – 365 years, the number of days in the solar year? And what are the meanings of the names in this passage? Enoch's father's name Jared seems to come from the Hebrew verbal root *yarad*, 'to descend'. He was so called, said some, to commemorate an important event that happened during his lifetime, the descent of the angels known as the Watchers from heaven to earth. And so on. The text proves to be a lot more promising that at first reading one might think.

It is impossible to do justice in brief compass to the rich post-biblical, pre-Islamic traditions about Enoch that were based on this passage, but let me try and summarize what I have expounded at length elsewhere.[7] It is possible to see the post-biblical tradition about Enoch within Judaism as going through three overlapping phases. In the first there was a strong tendency to exalt Enoch. That exaltation reaches its culmination in the sixth century in the effective deification of Enoch: he becomes a second God. The second phase develops in reaction to the first and attempts to denigrate Enoch, to argue that he was really no better than he should have been, that he did not ascend to heaven and was not a revealer of secrets. The third phase adopts a mediating position between these two extremes. Enoch was someone special, and he was taken up miraculously to heaven, but it is futile to speculate on the heavenly phase of his existence. Rather, we should concentrate on his earthly life as a righteous man, and as the embodiment of the virtues of the philosopher-king. By the Middle Ages all three competing images of Enoch were current in Jewish literature.

Enoch seems to have begun his spectacular career some time in the Persian period, probably in the early fourth century BCE. He was used by a group of educated Jews at that time to domesticate within Israel a body of new 'scientific' doctrine about the workings of the cosmos, particularly the movements of the heavenly bodies and the functioning of the calendar. They chose Enoch as the patron of this new science, attributing it to him and claiming that it had been revealed to him by the angels. Enoch, who began life as a Scientific Sage, was soon transformed into a Preacher of Righteousness. He was seen as having stood for justice against the wicked generation who lived on the earth before Noah's Flood. He warned them of the inevitable consequences of their wickedness and he was taken to Paradise by God as a witness that God had acted justly in bringing upon the world the cataclysmic destruction of the Flood. He was also involved in the judgement of the Watchers, the angels who descended to earth in his days, and who ended up misbehaving with human women and fathering Giants. And, it was claimed, Enoch would return to earth at the end of history to assist in the final divine judgement of humanity. All these ideas are found in

[7] See my essay "From Son of Adam to Second God: Transformations of the Biblical Enoch", in M. E. Stone and T. A. Bergren (eds), *Biblical Figures outside the Bible*, Harrisburg, PA 1998, 87–123. Further, J. C. VanderKam, *Enoch: A Man for All Generations*, Columbia, SC 1996.

the so-called First Book of Enoch and, with slight variations, may also be found in the Book of Jubilees 4:15–28.

The First Book of Enoch is a composite work, and in its latest strata, the so-called Similitudes of Enoch which date from the end of the first century CE, an important development takes place. Whereas the earlier strata of 1 Enoch had carefully maintained the position that Enoch did not leave the earth (he was translated to Paradise, which lies on the same terrestrial plane as ourselves, at the eastern edge of the habitable world), nor did he physically ascend into heaven, in the Similitudes he *does* go up to heaven, and in the process appears to be transformed into an angelic being, who is called the heavenly Son of Man. What is only a rather cryptic suggestion in the Similitudes is clearly articulated in the almost contemporary text known as the Second Book of Enoch. In this work Enoch quite clearly ascends bodily into heaven and in the process is physically transformed into an angel. This line of development was to reach a dramatic culmination some five centuries later in the Third Book of Enoch. There Enoch's physical transformation is described in graphic detail. He becomes not just any angel, but the highest archangel of all who goes by the name of Metatron. Metatron, astonishingly, bears the title 'The Lesser YHWH', and God leaves in his care the running of the universe, retiring into the impenetrable fastness of the upper heavens. What we are witnessing here is nothing less than the deification of Enoch. Enoch's deification as Metatron gave him a new lease of life, which continued vigorously in the medieval Jewish mystical tradition of the Qabbalah. Metatron becomes one of the names of the manifest God, as opposed to the hidden God, the Undefined or Ein Sof. The position taken here is even more extreme than in 3 Enoch. In 3 Enoch, Metatron (transfigured Enoch) is an angel – the highest angel maybe, bearing the ambiguous name of Lesser YHWH, but still, arguably, outside the godhead. In some strands of the Qabbalah, however, Metatron appears to have been absorbed into the Godhead, and to have become identified with the manifest God.[8]

It is hardly surprising that there was a strong orthodox reaction to these developments, which were deemed offensive on two fronts. First, they seemed to compromise monotheism, by setting up a second God. Or else they could be construed as breaching one of the fundamental principles of theism, namely that there is an unbridgeable ontological gap between the being of God and the being of his creatures. Second, Enoch threatened the supremacy of Moses. He had lived before Moses, and there is more than a hint that his followers regarded his revelations as being at least on a par with those granted to Moses. Thus the tendency arose to

---

[8] For these developments see D. Abrams, "The Boundaries of the Divine Ontology: The Inclusion and Exclusion of Metatron from the Godhead", *HTR*, 87 (1994), 291–321.

denigrate Enoch. This denigration of Enoch is classically expressed in the great rabbinic commentary on Genesis known as Bereshit Rabba (25:1):

> *And Enoch walked with God, and he was not, for God took him* (Genesis 5:24). Rabbi Ḥama the son of Rabbi Hoshaʿya said: [*And he was not* means] that he was not inscribed in the scroll of the righteous but in the scroll of the wicked.
>
> Rabbi Aivu said: Enoch was a hypocrite acting sometimes as a righteous, sometimes as a wicked man. Therefore the Holy One, blessed be He, said: 'While he is righteous I will remove him.'
>
> Rabbi Aivu also said: He judged him on New Year, when he judges all the inhabitants of world.
>
> Heretics asked Rabbi Abbahu: We do not find that death is mentioned in the case of Enoch? How so?, he inquired. They said: *Taking* is mentioned here and also in connection with Elijah: *Do you know that today the Lord is taking your master away from you?* (2 Kgs 2:5). If you stress the word *taking*, he answered, then *taking* is mentioned here, while in Ezekiel it is said, *Behold, I take away from you the desire of your eyes [with a plague]* (Ezek. 24:16). Rabbi Tanḥuma observed: He answered them well.
>
> A matron asked Rabbi Yose: We do not find death stated of Enoch. Said he to her: If it had said, *And Enoch walked with God*, and no more, I would agree with you. Since, however, it says, *And he was not, for God took him*, it means that he was no more in the world, *for God took him [in death]*.

The position mediating between these two extremes arose in the Middle Ages. It is found, for example, in the retelling of the biblical story in the *Sefer ha-Yashar*, a work composed in the twelfth century, possibly in southern Spain, which may show traces of Islamic influence in its depiction of Enoch as the ideal philosopher king. In *Sefer ha-Yashar*, while it is acknowledged that Enoch was taken up into heaven, a veil is drawn over his heavenly existence. Instead all the emphasis is placed on describing his life as a righteous man on earth.

Ṭabarī's Transformation of Enoch

It is against the background of this Jewish tradition regarding Enoch, which I have lightly sketched in, that we must read the early Islamic literature. What was the fate of Enoch in Islam? I shall focus the discussion on Ṭabarī's *History*, i, 166–79.[9] Ṭabarī is very useful for our present purposes, because he was an assiduous encyclopaedist and managed to collect together most of the early Islamic traditions about Enoch into a single more or less coherent story. There is much that could be said about his very rich account, but space allows me to highlight only the salient points.

It is obvious that Jewish sources lie behind at least part of what Ṭabarī has to say: he openly acknowledges as much himself by mentioning among his informants 'the people of the Torah', and 'someone knowledgeable in the Torah'. I do not think

[9] Ṭabarī, *History* (ed. M. J. de Goeje), Leiden 1879, i, 166–79; tr. F. Rosenthal, *The History of al-Tabari*, Albany, NY 1989, i, 336–48.

Ṭabarī could have written what he has written in this section of his *History* without having read the Bible itself, or having been told its straightforward narrative, and deriving from it his basic chronological framework. Yet it is equally clear that he must also have had access, either directly or indirectly, to a tradition of Jewish commentary on the Bible. It is interesting to note that even where Jewish sources are being used what comes out in Ṭabarī is not quite what we find in the Jewish tradition. Ṭabarī and his Muslim informants seem to have made the Jewish material their own, and in the process transformed it into something new. Note, for example, the allusion to the tradition about the Giants: 'Their children were godless tyrants. They were given large stature, supposedly thirty cubits tall' (i, 167). I know of no Jewish text which asserts, as Ṭabarī does here, that the Giants were the children or grandchildren of Lamech (Ṭabarī's text is not quite clear on this point). Rather, in early Jewish tradition the Giants were the offspring of the Fallen Angels and human women, the reason for their great size being that they were the monstrous issue of a sexual union that was contrary to nature. Ṭabarī does not mention the myth of the Fallen Angels, but he provides an alternative story which seems, as I shall argue presently, to presuppose a knowledge of that myth.

The myth of the Fallen Angels was based on Gen. 6:1–2, 'And it came to pass, when men began to multiply on the face of the ground, and daughters were born unto them, that the sons of God saw the daughters of men that they were fair; and they took them wives of all that they chose'. According to the earliest Jewish Enochic literature, the 'sons of God' here are angels, who descended to earth in the time of Jared, Enoch's father – an event alluded to, as we noted earlier, in Jared's name, which can be derived from the Hebrew verb 'to descend' – and who coupled with human women, producing giant children. Ṭabarī, however, tells a rather different story, or rather two closely related stories. First, in i, 168 he states that the 'sons of God' are the righteous descendants of Seth who lived in the mountains. When reports reached them that the ungodly sons of Cain were enjoying themselves with all kinds of musical instruments down on the plain some of them went down to join in the festivities, in defiance of the admonitions of righteous Jared. As a result they married some of the daughters of Cain, and were corrupted by them. 'They became very much engaged in iniquity', says Ṭabarī, and 'wickedness and' – horror of horrors – 'wine-drinking spread'. Then in i, 168 Ṭabarī reports a slightly different version of this tale:

> According to Ahmad b. Zuhayr – Musa b. Isma'il Dawud, meaning Ibn Abi al-Furat – 'Ilba' b. Ahmar – 'Ikrimah – Ibn 'Abbas, reciting this verse of the Qur'an (addressing women): 'And do not display your finery as in the first Jahiliyyah!' [Q33:33] and commenting on it as follows: It was the period between Noah and Idris [!] and it was a thousand years. There were two tribes (*baṭn*) of Adam's descendants. One of them dwelled in the plain, and the other in the mountain. The mountain men were handsome, and the mountain women

ugly, while the women of the plain were beautiful, and the men ugly. Iblis came to one of the inhabitants of the plain in the form of a young man and hired himself out as his servant. Iblis invented something like the flutes used by shepherds but produced with a sound, the likes of which people had not heard before. When those around them heard about it, they took turns going to them and listening to it. They established a yearly festival where they assembled, arranging for the women to display their finery to the men – he continued – and for the men to come down to them. One of the mountain people intruded upon them during that festival of theirs. He saw the beauty of the women and, going back to his companions, told them about it. They moved down to live with the women, with the result that wickedness appeared among the women. This is [meant by] God's word: 'And do not display your finery as in the first Jahiliyyah!' (tr. Rosenthal).

These two stories illustrate graphically how tangled and complex the antecedents of Ṭabarī's text may be. The idea that the sons of God in Genesis 6 are the righteous sons of Seth and that they descended from a holy mountain to the plain to have intercourse with the wicked daughters of Cain is not, as far as I am aware, found in any mainline Jewish source. In fact, although within the rabbinic tradition there was a tendency from the mid-second century CE onwards to interpret 'sons of God' as righteous *men*,[10] there seems to be a positive avoidance of identifying them with the line of Seth, probably with good reason: certain Gnostics – taking up earlier Jewish tradition – glorified the Sethites, and this may have made this tradition suspect in rabbinic eyes. Rabbinic interpreters reacted towards the glorification of Seth, just as they reacted towards the glorification of Enoch, and opposed it because it was associated with heterodox groups.[11] However, Ṭabarī's tales are very closely paralleled in the Ethiopic Book of Adam and Eve and in the Syriac Cave of Treasures.[12] The Ethiopic Book of Adam and the Syriac Cave of Treasures are clearly related at this point, and it is reasonable to suppose that one is dependent on the other, but I can see no way of deciding for certain in which direction this particular borrowing went. However, we can be reasonably confident that the basic story is pre-Islamic, and that there is no possibility that it was Islam which actually engendered this tradition. The core of the Adam traditions which lie behind the Ethiopic Adam Book (though not this story about the Sethites) can be traced all the way back possibly to a Hebrew work of the first century CE.[13]

[10] See my essay, "The Targumim and Early Exegesis of 'Sons of God' in Genesis 6", *JJS*, 23 (1972), 60–71.

[11] For a useful summary of early traditions about Seth see J. D. Turner, "The Gnostic Seth", in Stone and Bergren, *Biblical Figures*, 33–58

[12] See S. C. Malan, *The Book of Adam and Eve, also called the Conflict of Adam and Eve with Satan*, London 1882, 133–41 (ii, 20–22); E. A. Wallis Budge, *The Book of the Cave of Treasures*, London 1927, 84–98. Further C. Bezold, *Die Schatzhöhle*, Leipzig 1883–8, i, 13–18 (translation); ii, 56–76 (Syriac and Arabic texts).

[13] See further G. A. Anderson, "Adam and Eve in the 'Life of Adam and Eve'", in Stone and Bergren, *Biblical Figures*, 7–32. In tracing the history of the Adam traditions the Ethiopic Book of Adam and Eve has been rather neglected. A thorough investigation of this work is long overdue. Malan, *Book of Adam and Eve*, p. vi, suspected, with good reason, that the Ethiopic was derived from an Arabic version. The Cave of Treasures also circulated in Arabic, so it is possible whoever compiled the

There are three other points which I would like to make about this highly instructive example. First, since the Ethiopic Book of Adam and Eve and the Syriac Cave of Treasures are Christian texts, we might be inclined to posit a Christian as opposed to a Jewish source for this element in Ṭabarī. However, we should be very cautious about making too sharp a distinction between 'Jewish' and 'Christian' in this type of material. There are unquestionably Jewish sources for both these Christian works, and in any case Christians and Jews in late antiquity shared a huge fund of traditions about the *Heilsgeschichte* of Old Testament times and broadly subscribed to the same grand narrative. This narrative is best treated as 'common' and the urge to label bits of it as distinctively 'Jewish' or 'Christian' resisted. Second, from a cursory reading just of Ṭabarī, without regard to the antecedent tradition, one might be inclined to identify especially these stories within his rich and varied text as 'folksy' in character, and might, therefore, suppose that they were drawn from popular oral tradition. However, we can, as I have indicated, identify potential *literary* sources for them, and when we analyse the stories closely against the earlier tradition they turn out to be learned and to betray strong exegetical traits. The dichotomy between 'popular oral' on the one hand and 'learned literary' on the other, which seems to be implied by some of the more recent analyses of early Islamic tradition, particularly of the Isrāʾīliyyāt, is problematic. All the traditions in this section of Ṭabarī with which we are dealing appear on close inspection to be learned and are best explained as having been transmitted across a very narrow bridge from one intellectual élite to another. In other words, they have come about by contact between scholars, rather than from some general diffusion of stories by popular story-tellers. Third – to return to a point which I touched on earlier and to show how learned the stories are – I think a case can be made out for seeing these stories, both in Ṭabarī and in the Christian sources, as having been originally framed precisely with the intention of displacing the story of the fall of the angels. The idea that angels can have sexual intercourse with women is problematic theologically and puzzled some early scholars.[14] Some therefore took the term 'sons of God' as referring not to angels but to righteous humans and the 'descent' alluded to in Genesis as descent from a mountain and not from heaven. It is the motif of 'descent' which gives the game away. It is found only in the Bible, hidden away in the etymology of the name Jared. But the name Jared would probably never have been linked to the idea of descent in the first place but for the interpretation of 'sons of God' as angels. However, though rejecting any reference to angels later scholars still felt obliged to propose an alternative understanding of the name: hence descent from a mountain. The mountain is nowhere to be found in the

original of the Ethiopic Book of Adam and Eve knew an Arabic version of the Cave of Treasures. However, there is also much material in the Ethiopic text which is not in the Cave of Treasures and some of this overlaps with the Latin, Greek, Slavonic, Armenian and Georgian Adam books.

[14] See, for example, the rationalistic explanation of what it meant in Testament of Reuben 5:6.

biblical text. It may, however, be a remote transformation of the idea, found in 1 Enoch, that when the angels first came to earth they alighted on Mount Hermon.[15]

Ṭabarī portrays Enoch, very much in the spirit of the Jewish Enochic literature, as a bringer of culture and revealer of secrets, as the inventor of writing, and as the author of books. But there are also elements in his account which probably have non-Jewish sources. Thus the claim that Enoch/Idrīs was 'the first to cut and sew clothes' (i, 173), an assertion which is found also in Masʿūdī and Ibn Khaldūn,[16] and which turned Idrīs into the patron saint of tailors, is probably not Jewish in origin. I do not know of it in pre-Islamic Jewish sources. Later Qabbalists claimed that Enoch was a cobbler, 'who praised God with every stitch he made'.[17] There must, surely, be some connection between Enoch the Cobbler and Enoch the Tailor, both trades which involve the use of the needle.[18] The balance of probability favours the conclusion that the Jewish tradition has here borrowed from the Islamic and not *vice versa*. It is clear, I would suggest, that Ṭabarī is no slavish imitator of the Jewish tradition, nor a plagiarist, but rather he was making out of the fabric of the diverse traditions which were to hand something quite new and original.

Ṭabarī's text, then, is deeply learned, and multiple and quite diverse sources stand behind it. It is likely that he consulted Jewish scholars. After all, he lived in Baghdad at the same time as the great Jewish scholar Saadya, the head of the Rabbinical Academy of Sura in Baghdad, who immersed himself in contemporary Islamic learning. One of the most astonishing elements to find in Ṭabarī is the name ʿAdna or Edna for the wife of Enoch's son Methuselah, and Batanush as the name for the mother of Noah. Neither of these names is found in the Bible, and in the extant Jewish literature, as far as I am aware, they occur together only in one other place, the Book of Jubilees.[19] How could Ṭabarī have got hold, either directly or indirectly, of a

15 1 Enoch 6:6.

16 Masʿūdī, *Meadows of Gold* (ed. Pellat), i , 73; Ibn Khaldūn, *The Muqaddima*, v 2, 26 (tr. Rosenthal, 317, 367–8).

17 See L. Ginzberg, *Legends of the Jews*, Philadelphia 1968, v, 166, quoting Yalqut Re'ubeni, Gen. 5:22 (27a end). Ginzberg comments: 'I venture to suggest that instead of Enoch, Methuselah should be read, as this is very likely based on the fact that the numerical value of מתושלח בן חנוך corresponds to the value of the words הוא היה תופר בנעלים, "he made shoes"'. But this is surely far-fetched. Ginzberg does not seem to have known the Islamic parallels.

18 Note how Masʿūdī, *Meadows of Gold* (ed. Pellat), i, 73, simply says that Enoch 'invented sewing and the use of the needle', which would cover both tailoring and shoe-making.

19 Jubilees 4:27–28: 'And in the fourteenth jubilee Methuselah took a wife, ʿEdnah the daughter of ʿAzariel, his father's brother's daughter, in the third week, in the first year of the week, and he begot a son and called him Lamech. And in the fifteenth jubilee, in the third week Lamech took a wife, and her name was Betenos, the daughter of Barachel, his father's brother's daughter; and in this week she bore him a son, and he called him Noah, saying, "The one who will comfort me for my trouble and all my work, and for the ground which the Lord has cursed."' Ṭabarī, *History*, i, 177, 'As I was told by Ibn Ḥumayd – Salamah – Ibn Isḥaq, when Enoch's son Methuselah was 137 years old, he married ʿAdna [Edna], the daughter of ʿAzraʾil b. Abushil b. Enoch b. Cain b. Adam. She bore him his son Lamech. Methuselah lived 700 years after the birth of Lamech. (Several) sons and daughters were born to him. The total length of Methuselah's life was 919 years. Then he died. When Lamech b. Methuselah b. Enoch was 187 years old, he married Batanus[h], the daughter of Barakil b. Mehujael b. Enoch b. Cain

tradition that is attested in Jewish sources only in a text written about 1,150 years before his time, and which was apparently unknown to later Judaism? There are a number of possibilities. Some Jews may, in fact, have known the Book of Jubilees in Ṭabarī's day. An early tradition actually records that Saadya found a Book of Jubilees in the library of the Sura Yeshivah, but since it reveals nothing of the book's content we cannot be sure whether it was a version of the work we now know under this name[20]. There is also evidence that Syriac Christianity was acquainted with the traditions of the Book of Jubilees: they are reflected in the Syriac Cave of Treasures literature and in the Book of the Bee. Ṭabarī may also have drawn on popular traditions about Enoch that were circulating in Iraq in late antiquity. The Manichaeans preserved one of the early Enochic texts, the so-called Book of Giants, a version of which was also transmitted through rabbinic channels in Midrash Shemḥazai and ʿAzaʾel.[21] Enoch is mentioned in the Aramaic magical bowls from Iraq, which date from the Sasanian period.[22] Ṭabarī's sources of information in this case were various. We should not assume that simply because an element in his writings is basically Jewish in origin, it must have come to him directly from a Jewish source.

From our analysis it should be obvious that Ṭabarī is bringing over, quite consciously, a considerable body of non-Islamic tradition into Islamic scholarship. It is instructive to observe how he attempts to root this alien wisdom in the Qurʾān. Note how he finds an allusion to the Books of Enoch in Q87:18f.:

> Some assumed that God sent Idrīs [that is Enoch, as we shall see presently] to all the people of the earth living in his time. He gave him the combined knowledge of the men of the past, adding to it thirty scrolls. This is [meant by] God's word: 'This is in the first scrolls, the scrolls of Abraham and Moses'. He continued: By 'first scrolls' are meant the scrolls that were revealed to Adam's son Hibat Allāh (Seth) and to Idrīs ... (i, 174; tr. Rosenthal).

Of course Ṭabarī is forcing the words of the Qurʾān, which are most decidedly not referring to the Books of Enoch, but his exegetical opportunism, deployed in the service of validating an alien tradition, will surprise no one acquainted with rabbinic Bible exegesis.

The more important way in which Ṭabarī links the Enochic traditions to the Qurʾān is through the identification of Enoch with Idrīs. Idrīs is mentioned only twice in the Qurʾān. The first occasion is 19:56–58:

---

b. Adam. She bore him Noah, the prophet – may God pray for him and give him peace!' (tr. Rosenthal). Ginzberg, *Legends of the Jews*, i, 159, notes a tradition that Noah's wife was Naʿamah the daughter of Enosh (Bat Enosh), but the basis of this assertion is unclear. Edna, of course, occurs as the name of Raguel's wife in Tob. 7:15–16 and 8:12.

[20] See the commentary on 1 Chronicles by a pupil of Saadya's edited by R. Kirchheim, *Peyrush ʿal Divrey ha-Yamim meyuḥas le-ʾeḥad mi-talmidei Saʿadyah ha-Gaʾon*, Frankfurt a. M. 1874, 36. That some of the so-called minor midrashim or even the Sefer Yosippon were influenced by some form of Jubilees should not be ruled out.

[21] See L. T. Stuckenbruck, *The Book of Giants from Qumran*, Tübingen 1997.

[22] J. T. Milik, *The Books of Enoch*, Oxford 1976, 128–35.

> And mention in the Book Idrīs. He was a true man (*ṣiddīq*), a prophet. And we raised him to a high place (*wa-rafaʿnāhu makānan ʿaliyyan*). Those were of the prophets on whom God bestowed His grace, of the posterity of Adam, and of those whom We carried with Noah, and of the posterity of Abraham and Israel, of those whom We guided and chose.[23]

The second is 21:85–86:

> And [mention] Ismāʿīl, Idrīs and Dhū ʾl-Kifl – each was of the patient (*ṣābirīn*). And We admitted them into Our mercy; they were of the righteous.

Now it seems abundantly clear that although the identification of Idrīs with Enoch is standard in the Tafsīr literature (we find it also, for example, in Bayḍāwī and Ibn Kathīr), the Qurʾān was not, in fact, referring to Enoch. The name Idrīs is nothing like the name Enoch, and no convincing link between the two has ever been suggested. Various proposals have been made as to whom the Qurʾān actually meant. The most plausible is C. C. Torrey's suggestion that Idrīs is in fact a variation of the name Esdras, a Greek form of the biblical name Ezra.[24] Ezra is certainly known in the Qurʾān. He is mentioned several times under the Hebrew-derived form of his name ʿUzayr. Certainly Ezra, both in biblical and in post-biblical Jewish tradition could be said to be a 'righteous man' (*ṣiddīq*), and post-biblical tradition would amply justify calling him a prophet, since he was depicted as receiving revelations from God.[25] In fact, already within the Bible, he is portrayed as a second Moses (cf. Nehemiah 8). The statement 'we raised him to a high place' might refer to the fact that Ezra was appointed a high official at the Persian court (which turned out, under providence, to be beneficial for the Jews), or if, as later tradition interpreters thought, the phrase refers to an ascension to heaven, then it might allude to a post-biblical tradition about an ascent of Ezra to receive revelations from God. It is unclear why in Sūra 21:85 Ezra should be said to exemplify patience (*ṣabr*), but the term is sufficiently imprecise to cause no specific problem for the identification.

The identification of Idrīs with Enoch has come about through a clever secondary exegesis of the Qurʾān, which is strongly reminiscent of the way in which Jewish commentators exploited the ambiguities of the text of Genesis in order to read into it traditions about Enoch which were decidedly not there. The nub of the identification must be the phrase 'and we raised him to a high place' (*wa-rafaʿnāhu makānan ʿaliyyan*). This was taken as a reference to an ascent to heaven. As I have already noted it does not for certain mean this: *rafaʿa* can mean 'exalt, honour', as well as physically 'lift up to a height'. And too much stress should probably not be placed

[23] Tr. A. J. Arberry, *The Koran Interpreted*, London 1955.

[24] *The Jewish Foundation of Islam*, (repr.) New York 1967, 72.

[25] For a useful survey of Ezra traditions see T. A. Bergren, "Ezra and Nehemiah Square off the Apocrypha and Pseudepigrapha", in Bergren and Stone, *Biblical Figures*, 340–66.

on *ʿaliyyan*. Bell argues that it is secondary.[26] However, the verb *rafaʿa* is used elsewhere in the Qurʾān of Jesus,[27] and in these contexts it was widely understood as referring to Jesus' bodily transfer up to heaven; so some probably took it in the same sense when applied to Idrīs. That the reference here is to Enoch is further supported by the mention in the context of Noah, since Enoch lived in the time of Noah. It is all very ingenious, but, I would repeat, very secondary, and its purpose was to help domesticate a body of alien tradition within Islam.

The Harranians and Enoch/Hermes

Ṭabarī did not invent the identification of Idrīs with Enoch. It seems to have been already old in his day. As I have just argued, the equation of Enoch with Idrīs turns on understanding the phrase *wa-rafaʿnāhu makānan ʿaliyyan* in the Qurʾān in the sense of 'we took him up to heaven'. But Ṭabarī in fact, like the classic rabbinic commentators, does not believe that Enoch was taken up into heaven. He says that he died in the normal way.[28] It follows, therefore, that he is using an identification which was already widespread, the textual basis of which he either did not know or had forgotten. Who then did invent the identification? I would like here to make a proposal which, though speculative, is not without merit and which, if correct, throws considerable light on how these traditions developed. I would suggest that the identification of Enoch with Idrīs in the Qurʾān first emerged not among Muslim scholars but among the so-called Sabians of Harran. Let me try and spell out my reasons. The Sabians of Harran are a curious group. They were devotees of a very ancient local cult of the moon at Harran who managed to preserve their worship more or less intact, despite the coming of the Greeks and the rise of Christianity and of Islam. They identified themselves with the Sabians mentioned in the Qurʾān.[29] There are good reasons for thinking that they are not, in fact, the Sabians of the Qurʾān but that they arrogated the title to themselves, so that they could claim the status of 'people of the book' (*ahl al-kitāb*), and avoid the threat of forced conversion. The

---

[26] Richard Bell, *A Commentary on the Qur'an*, Manchester 1991, i, 511: 'In v. 58 we have the double rhyme, so that *ʿaliyyan* is probably an addition; the grammar is smoother without it.' But this is not entirely convincing since *makānan* seems weak on its own.

[27] Sūra 3:55, 'Behold God said: "Jesus, I will take you and raise you (*wa-rāfiʿuka*) to myself"'; Sūra 4:157–58, 'for of a surety they did not kill him. Rather God raised him up (*rafaʿahu*) unto himself'.

[28] See i, 176. In i, 177 the 'raising up' of Enoch/Idrīs mentioned in the Qurʾān seems to be interpreted as a reference to his death. In exactly the same way Bereshit Rabba 25:1 (quoted above) interprets 'for God took him' in Genesis 5:24 not as indicating translation to heaven but rather natural death.

[29] On the problem of the historical identity of the Qurʾānic Sabians and their relationship to the Harranians see Tamara M. Green, *The City of the Moon God*, Leiden 1992, 94–123; Şinasi Gündüz, *The Knowledge of Life: The Origins and Early History of the Mandaeans and their Relationship to the Sabians of the Qur'an and to the Harranians* (JSSS, 3), Oxford 1994. D. Chwolson's monumental and pioneering study, *Die Ssabier und der Ssabismus*, 2 vols, St Petersburg 1856, remains of fundamental importance.

threat was real, as the story told by al-Nadīm of a visit to Harran by the Caliph al-Ma'mūn (*c*. 830) suggests.[30]

At some point in late antiquity local intellectuals in Harran attempted to create a theology for this old Semitic local moon-cult that would universalize it and draw it into the mainstream of Hellenistic religious thought. To achieve this they used Hermetic theology. They claimed that one of the founders of their cult was Thrice Great Hermes (Hermes Trismegistus), to whom a whole body of quasi-mystical literature and theology had been attributed – the so-called Hermetic literature.[31] This abstruse doctrine cannot have meant much to the average Harranian devotee of the moon, or to the average Harranian priest. It would have appealed exclusively to elitist intellectuals. But it served a useful political purpose in giving the cult intellectual credibility in the Graeco-Roman world, and it helped to buttress its independence when it was faced with the great ideological juggernauts, first of Christianity and possibly Zoroastrianism in the pre-Islamic period, and subsequently of Islam itself. A rather similar process seems to have taken place within late antique paganism when it was challenged by the radical criticism of an increasingly confident and successful Christianity. Attempts were made by Iamblichus and his followers in the fourth century to develop a reformed paganism intellectually underpinned by Neoplatonism and Neo-pythagoreanism, in which Pythagoras was promoted as a sage and prophet to rival Jesus. This reformed paganism may ultimately have won the support of the Emperor Julian and been incorporated into his abortive attempt to re-establish the supremacy of paganism. The Harranians after the triumph of Christianity may have stressed for political ends the equation of Hermes Trismegistus with Enoch. They may not have invented this identification but simply taken it over from earlier Hermeticism. It is certainly attested in the Mesopotamian region in late antiquity in the magical bowls.[32] There was an obvious convergence of characteristics: Hermes, like Enoch, was a bringer of culture, an inventor of writing and the founder of the sciences. And there is evidence that the Books of Enoch were known to some of the authors of the Hermetic literature.[33] Just as claiming that Hermes was one of their teachers placed the Harranian cult on the Hellenistic intellectual map, so identifying Hermes with Enoch placed it on the Christian map and gained for it respectability and antiquity. I would suggest that the Harranians played the same card a third time when

---

30 See al-Nadīm, *The Fihrist*, ch. 9. The story does not have to be literally true to contain historical truth. There may well have been serious consequences for the Harranians under Islam if they were classified as pagans and they may well have identified themselves as the Sabians of the Qur'ān to avoid those consequences.

31 Green, *City of the Moon God*, 85–93.

32 See Milik, *The Books of Enoch*, 132–5.

33 See Alexander, "From Son of Adam to Second God", 115–16. Further, M. Philonenko, "Une allusion de l'Asclépius au livre d'Henoch" in J. Neusner (ed.), *Christianity, Judaism and other Greco-Roman Cults*, Leiden 1975, ii, 161–3. As we noted above (note 21), the Manichaeans knew the Enochic Book of Giants. There is evidence for a Manichaean presence in Harran: see Green, *City of the Moon God*, 80.

Islam became the dominant religion of the region. They identified themselves with the Sabians of the Qur'ān and equated their great teacher with the mysterious Idrīs of the Qur'ān.[34] But in the process of identifying Hermes with Idrīs they automatically identified Enoch with Idrīs: Hermes = Enoch; Hermes = Idrīs; *ergo* Enoch = Idrīs.[35] In fact Enoch may have been the key to the identification. Certain things said about Idrīs in the Qur'ān allowed him to be identified with Enoch. But Enoch, on the grounds of quite different characteristics, had already been identified with Hermes Trismegistus, and this formed the basis for linking Hermes and Idrīs. In other words historically speaking the syllogism may actually have been: Enoch = Hermes; Enoch = Idrīs; *ergo* Idrīs = Hermes.

That these Harranian ideas could have got out into general circulation is easily imagined. Harran was a considerable centre of learning in the late antique and early Islamic periods, and the Abrahamic connections of the city would have drawn the attention of Muslims. It is surely not too rash to suppose that Harranian scholars made a contribution to the general intellectual life of their day. Here the case of Thābit b. Qurra is instructive.[36] He was born in Harran in 826 into a prominent and learned family. He appears to have translated some Hermetic writings into Syriac. Significantly, he seems to have got into trouble with the local religious authorities and to have had to withdraw from the city. He was then appointed court astronomer in Baghdad, where he spent the latter part of his life, and where he acted as a friend at court for his co-religionists. He died in 901. He apparently remained a pagan to the end and stoutly defended his beliefs. It was probably men like Thābit who exploited Hermeticism in order to provide an intellectual underpinning for the moon-cult at Harran, who identified the Harranians with the Sabians of the Qur'ān, and who equated Hermes with Idrīs. Through his wide circle of contacts among the intellectuals of Baghdad, he could easily have popularized these Harranian ideas.[37]

There were clear advantages to Muslims in accepting this identification. The commentators on the Qur'ān probably had little idea who Idrīs was. This identification solved that problem at a stroke and was in itself unobjectionable. But it served a more important cultural function as well. The Qur'ān must have seemed a very strange document indeed when it was first encountered by intellectuals in the great centres of culture in the Middle East. It touched their mental map only tangentially. It was necessary to tie it into general near eastern knowledge, history and culture. The Bible

---

[34] The major texts are collected by Chwolson in *Ssabier und der Ssabismus*.

[35] The fact that Enoch was supposedly a great writer of books was also helpful in establishing the Harranians' claim to be 'a people of the book'.

[36] See J. Ruska, 'Thabit bin Kurra', *EI1*, viii, 733. The article on Thābit in *EI2*, x, 428–9 by R. Rashed and R. Morelon concentrates on his mathematical achievements.

[37] It is an intriguing fact that Thābit (826–901) and Ṭabarī (839–923) were in Baghdad at the same time. Saadya (882–942) came a little later. It is possible he could have met Ṭabarī, but surely not Thābit.

was one of the universal cultural 'maps' of late antiquity, and relating the Qur'ān to it was a way to dispel its strangeness and domesticate it within middle eastern tradition. A major aim of early Tafsīr was precisely to link the Qur'ān to the Bible's grand narrative, and it helped immensely that the Qur'ān already contained significant allusions to the biblical story. As knowledge of the Qur'ān deepened and the Middle East became more Islamic, this need diminished. The Qur'ān moved centre stage and achieved cultural primacy. Alien traditions now had to be tied somehow to *it*. The early attempts to dovetail the Qur'ān and the Bible remained, however, as the extensive body of Isrā'īliyyāt. A well-established historical pattern is involved here. When Jews and Greeks came first into contact a mutual comparison of their cultural maps took place and an attempt was made to overlap one with the other. And a similar phenomenon occurred when Christianity spread out from its Jewish homeland into the wider Graeco-Roman world. This is all well documented; so it should cause no surprise that the pattern was repeated when Islam burst upon the middle eastern scene.

Ṭabarī paints a sober picture of Enoch/Idrīs. The more daring ideas about Enoch which we found in the Jewish tradition are totally absent from his writings. They would probably have offended him for the same reasons as they offended the rabbis. However, it is worth noting in passing that Idrīs was taken up into Islamic folklore, becoming the subject of many folktales, and that in certain branches of the Shī'a and in Sufism he undergoes a dramatic transformation which parallels the transformation of Enoch in Jewish tradition. He plays, for example, a significant role in the writings of the great mystic Ibn al-'Arabī (1165–1240), who was born in Spain but spent the latter part of his life in Damascus. Ibn al-'Arabī, in his *Risālat al-Anwār*, uses the old Jewish apocalyptic motif of the ascent through the heavens to the throne of God to set out symbolically the stages through which the mystic must pass on his journey to sainthood. When the mystic reaches the fourth heaven, the heart of the planetary spheres, he encounters Idrīs, who imparts to him certain esoteric knowledge. Ibn al-'Arabī designates Idrīs 'the Pole' (*al-Quṭb*), that is to say, he regards him as the heavenly exemplar of the perfect man.[38] All this bears more than a passing similarity to Heikhalot and Qabbalistic traditions about Enoch/Metatron and suggests that there must have been ongoing cross-fertilization between the two traditions.

[38] Idrīs also plays a significant role in Ibn al-'Arabī's *al-Futūḥāt al-Makiyya* ch. 367 and in his *Fuṣūṣ al-Ḥikam* chs 4 and 22 (tr. R. W. J. Austin, *The Bezels of Wisdom*, London 1980, 82–9, 228–35). Ibn 'Arabī seems to vacillate as to whether Idrīs is to be identified with the biblical Enoch or with Elijah (Ilyās). The motif of the ascent to heaven was, of course, popularized in Islam by the story of the Prophet's ascent (the *mi'rāj*). See also Ibn al-'Arabī's *Kitāb al-Isrā' ilā 'l-maqām al-Asrā*: Michel Chodkiewicz, *Seal of the Saints: Prophethood and Sainthood in the Doctrine of Ibn 'Arabi*, Cambridge 1993, esp. 147–82, offers a useful analysis of this material. Ibn al-'Arabī may have had some influence on later Ismā'īlī and Nuṣayrī developments of the figure of Idrīs. On the concept of 'the Pole', see F. de Jong, 'al-Kutb' in *EI2*, v, 543–46.

Concluding Theses on Jewish Tradition in Early Islam

Our brief analysis of one tradition clearly does not entitle us to formulate any general theory of the Isrāʾīliyyāt. However, it throws up a number of theses which deserve to be tested further.

(1) It suggests that the Isrāʾīliyyāt provide a suitable case for the application of the tradition-historical methods that have long been applied in the analysis of tradition in the Bible, in early Judaism and in early Christianity. The discussion of the Isrāʾīliyyāt has tended to concentrate on identifying individual Jewish sources and has worked with rather simple models of borrowing. Many major studies consist of little more than the juxtaposition of texts and references and betray the classic symptoms of parallelomania. It is necessary to consider the Islamic materials in the context of a comprehensive tradition-history in which the dynamics of the tradition are fully explored, and to clarify the antecedent Jewish and Christian trends and developments *before* tackling the Islamic texts.

(2) As a corollary of the foregoing, we should not treat the boundary between Judaism and early Islam as marking a radical break in the tradition, any more than we would now be inclined to recognize as a radical break the boundary between Judaism and early Christianity. The principles which govern the evolution of the tradition on the Islamic side of the religious divide are exactly the same as those which operate *within* Judaism. Ṭabarī's use of Jewish sources is really no different from rabbinic use of earlier Jewish material. From the tradition-historical perspective we are dealing with *one* tradition.

(3) As a further corollary, we should eschew all accusations of plagiarism. This charge, explicit in early research on the Isrāʾīliyyāt, still seems implied by some more recent work, which seems to insinuate that Islam is derivative in some faintly pejorative sense from Judaism or Christianity. In general the Isrāʾīliyyāt impress me with the creative way in which the Muslim writers have made use of Jewish tradition. Ṭabarī makes the Jewish tradition just as much his own as does the most original of the Jewish *darshanim*.

(4) In the analysis specifically of the Enoch/Idrīs traditions within Islam, I am struck by the discontinuity between the early Tafsīr and the Qurʾān. Early Tafsīr seems to be fundamentally a process of indigenizing or domesticating within central near eastern culture a text, the Qurʾān, which had originated on the cultural periphery in the Ḥijāz and was seen as rather puzzling and alien. There are, of course, Jewish traditions in the Qurʾān itself, but for the most part they may reflect the views of the small Jewish community in the Ḥijāz, which lived on the margins of the Jewish world, and which, cut off from the great centres of Jewish intellectual and religious life in Palestine and Iraq, was probably never thoroughly rabbinized. This may be why so

often the Qur'ān's Jewish material seems slightly strange. Similar reasons can probably be invoked to explain the oddities of the Christian material in the Qur'ān.

(5) The discontinuity between Qur'ān and Tafsīr seems to point to a rather traditional view of the origins of the Qur'ān. Our brilliant and much missed colleague Norman Calder argued that Tafsīr and Qur'ān actually developed side by side. While acknowledging that I cannot begin to match Norman Calder's profound knowledge of the Islamic sources, I must nevertheless state that I find this view problematic. Certainly in the case of many of Isrā'īliyyāt which I have investigated, I detect a fundamental discontinuity between Qur'ān and Tafsīr. That discontinuity makes no sense to me if the two bodies of literature were developing side by side in a constant dialectic.

(6) Finally, and here again I would take issue with Norman Calder, many of the post-Qur'ānic Isrā'īliyyāt suggest to me that the contacts between Muslims and Jews which ensured the transmission of traditions from Judaism to Islam were basically at a scholarly level. The transfer took place across the restricted front of scholarly dialogue, and may well have been based to some extent on written sources. Norman Calder argued that the transfer was largely through popular story-telling and folklore. I do not see it that way – at least with regard to post-Qur'ānic developments. Most of the traditions which I have studied are deeply learned and the dynamic which drives the tradition forward is not folklore but theological and textual hermeneutics. The traditions' dominant characteristics, therefore, indicate that they have been passed on through scholarly interchange.

Al-Muʿtaṣim's 'bridge of toil' and Abū Tammām's Amorium *qaṣīda**

Julia Bray (University of St Andrews)

I

'Actions speak louder than words' is a message which should have appealed to the caliph al-Muʿtaṣim (r. 218–227/833–842), who excelled as a doer rather than a thinker in both ʿAbbasid and modern estimates.[1] Yet after a campaign against the Byzantines which culminated in the sack of Amorium (223/838), his response to Abū Tammām's victory poem *as-sayfu aṣdaqu anbā'an mina 'l-kutubi*,[2] which carries this very message, is reported to have been grudging. Abū Tammām had to recite his masterpiece three days running in order to attract the caliph's attention sufficiently to get himself paid. This story is told by a seventh/thirteenth-century source, Ibn Khallikān. Another anecdote, closer in time to Abū Tammām, is told by al-Ṣūlī (d. towards the mid-fourth/tenth century). Set in al-Muʿtaṣim's new capital, Sāmarrā, after his return from Amorium, it revolves around an unspecified *qaṣīda* in honour of the victory, and describes the caliph's reluctance to listen to the young Syrian poet's hoarse voice (remembered from a previous occasion in al-Maṣṣīṣa), and his lack of comment once the poem had been recited by a more pleasing substitute. The modern scholar Najīb al-Bahbītī argues that the poem the caliph heard at al-Maṣṣīṣa and had so little recollection of may have been none other than the Amorium *qaṣīda*.[3] Predicated on the stereotype

---

* This piece has a little to do with theology, but nothing at all to do with *fiqh*. I dedicate it to Norman with love and gratitude, because we also talked about literature.
Preliminary versions of this paper were given to the American Oriental Society and to the Mediaeval History Research Seminar, University of St Andrews, in 1998. I should like to thank Michael Cook and Hugh Kennedy for helpful remarks on those occasions.

[1] E.g. Hugh Kennedy, *The Prophet and the Age of the Caliphates: The Islamic Near East from the Sixth to Eleventh Century*, 7th impression, London–New York 1996, 158–68. Some ten years younger than his brother al-Ma'mūn, al-Muʿtaṣim, who had been a soldier all his life, succeeded him at the age of about thirty-eight.

[2] Abū Tammām Ḥabīb b. ʿAws al-Ṭā'ī, (*c.* 189–*c.* 232/*c.* 805–*c.* 845), *Dīwān Abī Tammām bi-sharḥ al-Khaṭīb al-Tibrīzī* (henceforth *Dīwān AT/T*), ed. Muḥammad ʿAbduh ʿAzzām, 3rd edn, Cairo 1972, i, no. 3, 40–74; *Sharḥ al-Ṣūlī li-Dīwān Abī Tammām* (henceforth *Dīwān AT/Ṣ*), ed. Khalaf Rashīd Nuʿmān, Baghdad 1977, i, no. 3, 189–207.

[3] Aḥmad b. Muḥammad Ibn Khallikān (650–708/1252–1308), *Wafayāt al-Aʿyān* (ed. Iḥsān ʿAbbās), Beirut n. d. [1968–71], ii, 23, no.147; Abū Bakr Muḥammad b. Yaḥyā al-Ṣūlī (d. *c.* 335/946), *Akhbār Abī Tammām* (ed. Muḥammad ʿAbduh ʿAzzām, Khalīl Maḥmūd ʿAsākir and Naẓīr al-Islām al-Hindī), Beirut 1400/1980, 143–4. The anecdote is said to have been told by Abū Tammām himself to his host Muḥammad b. Rawḥ al-Kilābī, who told it to Aḥmad b. Ibrāhīm [al-Qaysī or al-Ghanawī], who told it to al-Ṣūlī (the middle links in this *isnād* are unidentified): 'He told me that he wrote a praise poem for al-Muʿtaṣim at Sāmarrā after the victory of Amorium. Ibn Abī Du'ād informed the caliph, who said to him: "Isn't he the one who recited us a poem at al-Maṣṣīṣa – the one with the hoarse voice?" He replied: "Commander of the Faithful, he has a *rāwī*, who recites beautifully." Al-Muʿtaṣim gave permission for Abū Tammām's *rāwī* to recite his poem in praise of him. He passed no comment on it, but ordered him to be paid a large sum of silver drawn on Isḥāq b. Ibrāhīm al-Muṣʿabī. Abū Tammām said: "I went to him with the note of hand and recited a poem in his honour, which he

of al-Muʿtaṣim as a bluff soldier, these anecdotes epitomise a paradox of literary history: the greatest military and the greatest poetic genius of the age were tied together by court protocol, but had nothing to communicate to each other.[4]

The topos, however, is not free-floating; it is fixed at a particular point in time. After taking Amorium, the mother city of the reigning Byzantine dynasty, al-Muʿtaṣim had had to break off further campaigning to deal with a plot by disaffected generals to murder him and put his nephew on the throne. The excuse for the plot was that he was a usurper (the 'military power ... coupled with [the] forceful and determined personality ... [of his brother, having] induced al-Maʾmūn to set aside the claims of his own son [al-ʿAbbās]'); the real reason seems to have been that in his five years in power he had ridden roughshod over vested interests, displacing not only his nephew but also generals who had been favourites under al-Maʾmūn. The conspiracy involved 'a number of eastern Iranian officers, some of them from very prominent families'. According to al-Ṭabarī, the secret of the conspiracy was let slip as a result of squabbles between officers during the taking of Amorium; the plotters were unmasked and covertly put to death one by one during the march home. Al-ʿAbbās b. al-Maʾmūn, who had died of torture, was publicly cursed when al-Muʿtaṣim arrived in Sāmarrā and his siblings put away.[5] At this juncture, the caliph had other things on his mind than listening to poetry.

But even in more favourable circumstances, al-Muʿtaṣim's intimates do not seem to have expected much from him by way of reaction to Abū Tammām's often taxing performances in support of the regime. According to al-Ṣūlī, al-Ḥasan b. Wahb (assistant to al-Muʿtaṣim's vizier Ibn al-Zayyāt, and, like the vizier, himself a poet and one of Abū Tammām's dedicatees) once asked Abū Tammām: 'Did al-Muʿtaṣim ever understand a word of your poetry?' and may have been rather surprised at the reply: 'He once asked me to repeat three times the line: *wa-inna asmaja man tashkū ilayhi hawan * man kāna aḥsana shay'in ʿindahu l-ʿadhalu*, "The most horrid person to confide in about the pains of love * Is someone who thinks nothing nicer than

---

liked so much that he gave me only slightly less than al-Muʿtaṣim had paid me, swearing that if the Commander of the Faithful had ordered me to be paid in gold instead of silver coin, he would have done the same."' Najīb al-Bahbītī's views on whether the Amorium poem was recited in al-Maṣṣīṣa or in Sāmarrā are undecided, see *Abū Tammām al-Ṭāʾī, ḥayātuh wa-shiʿruh*, [Cairo, repr. from 1st edn, 1945] n. d., 137, 141.

[4] *Taʾrīkh Baghdād* however asserts that Abū Tammām was al-Muʿtaṣim's favourite poet, al-Khaṭīb al-Baghdādī, Abū Bakr Aḥmad b. ʿAlī (392–463/1002–1071), *Taʾrīkh Baghdād aw Madīnat al-Salām*, Cairo 1349/1931; repr. Beirut [1967], viii, 248 no. 4352 (Ḥabīb b. Aws, Abū Tammām); but neither in this entry nor in that on al-Muʿtaṣim himself is the Amorium *qaṣīda* mentioned.

[5] Kennedy, *The Prophet and the Age of the Caliphates*, 159, 167; al-Ṭabarī, *Taʾrīkh al-rusul waʾl-mulūk* (eds S. Guyard and M.J. de Goeje), Leiden 1881, iii, 1249–50, 1256–8, 1265, 1268; (tr. C. E. Bosworth), *The History of al-Ṭabarī*, xxxiii: *Storm and Stress along the Northern Frontiers of the ʿAbbāsid Caliphate*, Albany 1991 (henceforth *SS*), 112–3, 121–3, 130, 134.

nagging".[6] He said he liked it, and then told Ibn Abī Du'ād: "Abū Tammām is more like a Baṣran poet than a Syrian one"'.[7] The comment is not insensitive, and may be humorous, as S. P. Stetkevych says. But I do not think that the *badīʿ* of the antithesis 'horrid/nice' will bear the weight of her suggestion that the caliph, whom she believes to have been pro-Muʿtazilī, may have seen and approved it, and Abū Tammām's poetry generally, as a reflection of 'Baṣran', i.e. Muʿtazilī, creative logic.[8] More probably, the story is a comment on al-Muʿtaṣim's taste and implies how little patience he had with the poetry Abū Tammām wrote for state occasions. On the strength of one mercifully uncomplicated line in a 47-line panegyric, he is shown as identifying Abū Tammām not with classicizing poetry, of which he was the leading exponent, but with the diction and sentiment of the *style galant* of the day (of which Abū Tammām was also a master in his love poetry). This was what the caliph felt at home with, according not only to *Kitāb al-Aghānī*, which is of course slanted towards lyrical verse, but also to al-Ṭabarī. For all his fierce temper and regal presence, he liked simple, sentimental poetry, and was particularly fond of the love songs of Ibn Jāmiʿ and the light verse of the (Baṣran) poet al-Ḥusayn b. al-Ḍaḥḥāk[9] – the kind of verse in which, for the wealthy social consumer, a bland version of *badīʿ* served as a substitute for thought, not as a tool of enquiry.

Abū Tammām wrote a number of state poems for al-Muʿtaṣim who, on the above evidence, could be expected to endure rather than enjoy them, and is unlikely to have been their prime literary target. Yet he recognized that he must follow custom and support high poetic art; he paid Abū Tammām well for his Amorium *qaṣīda*, according

6 *Dīwān AT/T* (ed. ʿAzzām), 2nd edn, Cairo 1970, iii, no. 111, l.2 (poem in praise of al-Muʿtaṣim).

7 al-Ṣūlī, *Akhbār Abī Tammām*, 267.

8 S. P. Stetkevych, *Abū Tammām and the Poetics of the ʿAbbāsid Age*, Leiden 1991 (henceforth *Stetk/AT*), 15–6.

9 On al-Ḥusayn b. al-Ḍaḥḥāk, see Julie Scott Meisami and Paul Starkey (eds), *Encyclopedia of Arabic Literature*, London–New York 1998 (henceforth *EAL*), i, 297–8, s.v. 'al-Ḥusayn ibn al-Ḍaḥḥāk' (P. F. Kennedy). On al-Muʿtaṣim's literary tastes, see Abū ʾl-Faraj ʿAlī b. al-Ḥusayn al-Iṣfahānī (284–*c*. 363/897–*c*. 972), *Kitāb al-Aghānī* (Būlāq 1285–6/1868–70), v, 28, 57: [as a youth, in the reign of his father, Hārūn al-Rashīd] al-Muʿtaṣim admires Ibn Jāmiʿ above all other singers (cf. *EI2* s.v. 'Ibn Djāmiʿ' [A. Shiloah], 74: 'With his tender, sensitive, stirring and expressive character, possessing a voice vibrant with emotion, [he] embodied the typical image of a romantic musician of the period. The flautist Barṣawma said: ... [he] is like a pot of honey all of which is delicious.'); *Aghānī*, v, 68–9: the poet-musician Isḥāq al-Mawṣilī recites al-Muʿtaṣim a simple accession poem, for which he rewards him more than all the other poets and orators; he recites him another simple poem 'on the day he returned from waging holy war'; al-Muʿtaṣim asks him to set both poems to music; *ibid*., 74–5: al-Muʿtaṣim's pleasure in simple love songs; he rewards Isḥāq al-Mawṣilī with 2,000 gold pieces for a song the musician does not think worth two copper coins; *Aghānī*, v, 88: he prefers love songs to hunting songs; *Aghānī*, vi, 174–5: al-Ḥusayn b. al-Ḍaḥḥāk, disgraced by al-Maʾmūn, is sent for by al-Muʿtaṣim when he becomes caliph; he recites a simple accession poem for which he receives a huge reward; *ibid*., 181: he wins over an angry Muʿtaṣim with simple verses begging forgiveness after writing a poem in praise of the former heir apparent, al-ʿAbbās b. al-Maʾmūn; *Aghānī*, vi, 31: al-Muʿtaṣim obliges the singer Mutayyam al-Hāshimiyya to move to Sāmarrā and lodges her in the Jawsaq palace, although this means she must leave her child in Baghdad; *Aghānī*, v, 115: he recites a simple, 7-line poem by the early Islamic poet Abū Khirāsh al-Hudhalī (*Dīwān al-Hudhaliyyīn*, Cairo 1385/1965, ii, 157–9) and makes a childish mistake; *Aghānī*, xiv, 99: his fondness for the poetry of Labīd, also early Islamic (the examples given are of simple, gnomic verse); he recites a passage from Labīd, to the admiration of his drinking companions; al-Ṭabarī, *Taʾrīkh*, iii, 1323, 1329; *SS*, 208, 215: in his last illness, he weeps as he sails on the Tigris listening to his flautist play him the melody of some sad love verses; he admires a singing-girl and the word-picture Isḥāq al-Mawṣilī paints of her.

to Ibn Khallikān, and for the unspecified victory poem, according to al-Ṣūlī, having only recently paid him for a poem to his general al-Afshīn (see note 11). Given his own indifference, who, at al-Muʿtaṣim's court, was this sort of poem really aimed at?

As a preliminary, let us look more closely at the people mentioned in al-Ṣūlī's two anecdotes (the first is given in full in note 3), which are among the comparatively few in early sources that relate to the reception of Abū Tammām's poems by their dedicatees and are the only ones involving al-Muʿtaṣim. In the course of his eight-year reign, al-Muʿtaṣim did not, in fact, have to listen to more than six or seven *qaṣīda*s addressed to him personally by Abū Tammām,[10] although he would also have had to listen to poems addressed to his victorious generals, etc.[11] Though there had been others since, notably the poem on the execution of Bābak (*Dīwān AT/T*, iii, no.130), the only one of which the first Ṣūlī anecdote shows him having a dim recollection was the poem recited by Abū Tammām 'to us at al-Maṣṣīṣa ... with a hoarse voice'. If this poem is not, as al-Bahbītī argues, identical with the Amorium *qaṣīda*, and if it has survived in Abū Tammām's *dīwān* – and it seems unlikely that it would not have done, since he had gained a footing as a court poet in the previous reign[12] and his earlier, politically unimportant juvenilia have been preserved – this may have been the *qaṣīda* addressed to al-Muʿtaṣim's brother al-Maʾmūn after one of three campaigns against the Byzantines during the years 215–217/830–832 in which al-Muʿtaṣim also took part (*Dīwān AT/T*, iii, no. 133, see note 11),[13] or else one composed for al-Muʿtaṣim himself on his journey home to Baghdad after al-Maʾmūn's death at al-Bud(h)andūn/Podandos during his last campaign of 218/833. (The route has not been

[10] *Dīwān AT/T*, i, no. 3 (metre *basīṭ*, rhyme *ubi/abi*, 71 lines – the Amorium *qaṣīda*); ii, no. 71 (metre *kāmil*, rhyme *aru*, 32 lines): this is the famous 'Spring' *qaṣīda*, possibly addressed to al-Maʾmūn (tr. Julia Ashtiany [Bray], "Abū Tammām's 'Spring' *Qaṣīda*: *raqqat ḥawāshī ʾl-dahri*", *JAL*, 25 (1994), 217–9); but as Abdul Haq points out, the reference to 'nineteen years' in line 8 could support the alternative accession date for al-Muʿtaṣim of 219 cited by al-Masʿūdī, *Murūj al-dhahab wa-maʿādin al-jawhar* (tr. C. Barbier de Meynard); rev. Charles Pellat, *Les prairies d'or*, Paris 1962–97 (henceforth *Prairies*), iv, para. 2786; equally, the poem could mark a 'royal reception' given in the year following al-Muʿtasim's accession, Abdul Haq, "Historical Poems in the Diwān of Abū Tammām", *Islamic Culture*, 14 (1940), 18. Since al-Muʿtaṣim was the eighth ʿAbbāsid caliph, the positioning of this reference in line 8 may support Haq's suggestions; no. 72 (metre *kāmil*, rhyme *āri*, 61 lines; the poem celebrates al-Muʿtaṣim's destruction of his former ally and general al-Afshīn, 226/841, and praises the crown prince Hārūn al-Wāthiq as a worthy heir to his father); iii, no. 111 (metre *basīṭ*, rhyme *ilu/alu*, 47 lines; possibly an accession poem, see lines 14–16); no. 112 (metre *ṭawīl*, rhyme *āXilu*, 42 lines; possibly an accession poem, see lines 19–25); no. 126 (metre *ṭawīl*, rhyme *āXili*, 32 lines; dates from before the disgrace of al-Afshīn and celebrates him and the caliph jointly); no. 130 (metre *kāmil*, rhyme *ali*, 88 lines; celebrates the spectacular execution of the rebel Bābak the Khurramī in 223/838, shortly before the Amorium campaign, tr. *Stetk/AT*, 156–65).

[11] See al-Ṭabarī, *Taʾrīkh*, iii, 11233; *SS*, 92: '[After the death of Bābak] Al-Muʿtaṣim ... had poets brought in to praise [al-Afshīn, who had defeated him] and ordered presents for them. This was on Thursday, the thirteenth of Rabīʿ II (14 March 838). Among the poetry eulogizing [al-Afshīn] were the words of Abū Tammām al-Ṭāʾī: The stout warriors subdued (*badhdha*) al-Badhdh [...]', *Dīwān AT/T*, iii, no. 166, 1.1, metre *kāmil*, rhyme *īnu*, 36 lines.

[12] Poems to al-Maʾmūn: *Dīwān AT/T*, ii, no. 48 (*madīḥ*, metre *mutadārik*, rhyme *adi/idi*, 46 lines; perhaps Abū Tammām's first poem to the caliph, see lines 43–4); possibly no. 71 (*madīḥ*, the 'Spring' *qaṣīda*, see note 10 above); no. 77 (*madīḥ*, metre *basīṭ*, rhyme *aru*, 4 lines); iii, no. 133 (on an unspecified victory over the Byzantines, metre *kāmil*, rhyme *āmu*, 54 lines).

[13] Tr. *Stetk/AT*, 110–120. She dates the poem to 215/830–1, *ibid.*, 121, but it could equally refer to the campaign of 216/832 on which al-Muʿtaṣim accompanied al-Maʾmūn, see *EI2*, s.v. 'al-Maʾmūn' (M. Rekaya), 338.

described by historians but would have passed through al-Maṣṣīṣa.)[14] Either of nos 111 and 112 in the *Dīwān* might qualify; both could be accession poems (see note 10), and line 2 of no. 111 is the 'Basran' line quoted above, which al-Muʿtaṣim liked.

As interesting as al-Muʿtaṣim, with his preference for simplicity, is the cluster of lesser patrons who appear in the two anecdotes. The stories are exemplary and may be entirely symbolic, but if so they were fabricated by someone who understood the terms of Abū Tammām's career under al-Muʿtaṣim (something of which, in its overall structure, al-Ṣūlī's *Akhbār Abī Tammām*, the source of both stories, gives only a loose idea).[15] Both episodes turn equally on al-Muʿtaṣim and on his entourage. In the first, at Sāmarrā, after the taking of Amorium, Aḥmad b. Abī Duʾād (the chief *qāḍī*, the caliph's chief councillor, a poet and a patron of letters), introduces Abū Tammām and his victory poem to the reluctant caliph who, after hearing it, gives the poet a note of hand for a substantial payment to be collected from Isḥāq b. Ibrāhim al-Muṣʿabī, who was the long-serving *ṣāḥib al-shurṭa* (chief of police/military governor of Baghdad), and also the caliph's spymaster.[16] Abū Tammām has a praise poem ready for Ibn Muṣʿab, with which he nearly doubles his takings. This much more appreciative addressee would have been happy to pay the poet in gold coin what the caliph paid him in silver. In the second anecdote, Abū Tammām reviews his career under al-Muʿtaṣim (from the mildly irreverent tone of the story, we may assume that by this time the caliph was dead) at the prompting of al-Ḥasan b. Wahb (literary expert and long-serving official). He recalls a scene between himself, the caliph and Aḥmad b. Abī Duʾād, who here plays the part of the caliph's literary confidant, just as, in the first anecdote, it was he who coaxed him to listen to Abū Tammām's *qaṣīda*.

The roles of the *qāḍī*, the soldier-policeman and the *kātib* are not explained; but they are not ornamental, and can be deduced from other sources. Al-Ḥasan b. Wahb belonged to a family which had served in the caliphal bureaucracy since late Umayyad times[17] and was to maintain a steady presence in ʿAbbasid administrations, rising ultimately to the vizierate. He himself, as noted, was the vizier Ibn al-Zayyāt's right-hand man and one of the new generation of *kātib*s who were acknowledged men of letters as well as patrons.[18] As importantly, he was a great enthusiast of Abū

---

[14] See Guy Le Strange, *The Lands of the Eastern Caliphate*, Cambridge 1905, map facing 127 and 133–4; *SS*, 127 n. 350.

[15] Though it is the earliest source for Abū Tammām's life other than his own poetry, it was composed well after the poet's death, and together with its prefatory epistle is less a biography than a theoretical and thematic apology for his poetic style.

[16] Appointed under al-Maʾmūn, he held this post for twenty-eight years, deputising in Iraq for caliphs absent on campaign and dying in the reign of al-Mutawakkil in 235/849; see Dominique Sourdel, *L'état impérial des califes abbassides, viiie–xe siècle*, Paris n. d. [1999], 101–2, 134.

[17] Muḥammad b. Isḥāq Ibn al-Nadīm (d. between 380 and 388/990 and 998), *al-Fihrist*: (ed. and tr. Bayard Dodge), *The Fihrist of al-Nadīm: A Tenth-Century Survey of Muslim Culture*, New York 1970 (henceforth *Dodge/Nadīm*), i, 267; Dominique Sourdel, *Le vizirat ʿabbāside de 749 à 936 (132 à 324 de l'Hégire)*, Damascus 1959–60, i, 312.

[18] *Dodge/Nadīm*, i, 268, 367; Sourdel, *Vizirat*, i, 256, 263; ii, 733.

Tammām's poetry. In support of his claim that for sustained inventiveness he far surpassed the Ancients, he is said to have quoted the following lines from the Amorium *qaṣīda* as an unbroken sequence, declaring them flawless: lines 12, 13–6, 18, 17 (*sic*), 21–2, 25–9, 32–5, 37, 39, 40, 50, 55, 68–70.[19] Abū Tammām dedicated some thirteen poems to him. Many of them are occasional pieces which indicate a footing of some intimacy.[20] His master the vizier Muḥammad b. ʿAbd al-Malik al-Zayyāt does not appear in either anecdote, but received seven poems from Abū Tammām, the same number as the caliph, though some are less weighty compositions.[21] 'Not the major force in the formation of government policy ... [Ibn al-Zayyāt was nevertheless] in undisputed control of financial business' (Kennedy), and, as Sourdel points out, he was a political henchman,[22] together with the chief *qāḍī* Aḥmad b. Abī Duʾād, who figures in both anecdotes, and Isḥāq b. Ibrāhīm al-Muṣʿabī, who appears in the first. A bully and a torturer, Ibn al-Zayyāt was also a poet, specializing in the miniature panegyrics which seem to have been a feature of Samarran ceremonial and were perhaps devised to avoid overstraining al-Muʿtaṣim's attention.[23] He composed a pretty couplet describing the painted elephant which was to bear the rebel Bābak, like some honoured grandee, through Sāmarrā to his mutilation and disembowelment, just before the Amorium campaign (early in 223/838).[24] The same combination of visual irony and sadistic sarcasm is found, with more sophistication, in Abū Tammām's Amorium poem (lines 24, 32–5, 58–9, 63–6).

When, less than two years after the triumph of Amorium, in which he had played a major part, the general al-Afshīn was accused by the caliph of treason, it was Ibn al-Zayyāt, Ibn Abī Duʾād and Ibn Muṣʿab who presided over the show trial. The chief *qāḍī* and the chief of police were old hands; it was they who had been the enforcers in Iraq of the inquisition which al-Maʾmūn set on foot in the last months of

---

19 al-Ṣūlī, *Akhbār Abī Tammām*, 109–14.

20 *Dīwān AT/T*, i, no. 6 (occasional, thanks for a robe of honour, metre irregular, rhyme *ābih*, 8 lines); no. 9 (*madīḥ*/occasional, thanks for the gift of a boy slave, metre *kāmil*, rhyme *abu*, 28 lines); ii, no. 52 (occasional, request for a gift of wine, metre *wāfir*, rhyme *ādi*, 7 lines); no. 79 (*madīḥ*, metre irregular, rhyme *su*, 34 lines); no. 103 (*madīḥ*/occasional, on the gift of a horse, metre *kāmil*, rhyme *aqi*/*uqi*, 40 lines); no. 104 (*madīḥ*, metre *wāfir*, rhyme *āqi*, 20 lines); iii, no. 114 (*madīḥ*, metre *kāmil*, rhyme *ili*/*ali*, 49 lines); no. 121 (occasional, a verse letter asking for news of him, metre *kāmil*, rhyme *ālī*, 13 lines); no. 161 (to the brothers al-Ḥasan and Sulaymān b. Wahb, *madīḥ*, metre *ṭawīl*, rhyme *ānihi*, 13 lines); no. 169 (occasional, postscript to no. 168, plea for Sulaymān b. Wahb to help a relative of the poet Diʿbil, metre *basīṭ*, rhyme *āni*, 6 lines); no. 175 (*madīḥ*, metre *wāfir*, rhyme *iyyi*, 47 lines); iv, no. 437 (occasional, erotic, metre *basīṭ*, rhyme *iXari*/*aXari*, 9 lines); no. 449 (*iʿtāb*, metre *basīṭ*, rhyme *aXamu*/*iXamu*, etc., 14 lines); no. 475 (occasional, description of a drinking party, metre *ṭawīl*, rhyme *ni*, 14 lines).

21 *Dīwān AT/T*, i, no. 18 (*madīḥ*, metre *basīṭ*, rhyme *abu*, 60 lines); no. 19 (*madīḥ*, metre *kāmil*, rhyme *ibi*, 14 lines); no. 24 (occasional, wishing him recovery from an illness, metre *basīṭ*, rhyme *abu*, 3 lines); no. 25 (occasional, *ditto*, metre *basīṭ*, rhyme *ab*, 3 lines); ii, no. 99 (*madīḥ*, metre *kāmil*, rhyme *afi*, 33 lines); iii, no. 128 (*madīḥ*/*iʿtāb*, metre *ṭawīl*, rhyme *alā*/*ilā*, 52 lines); no. 129 (*madīḥ*, metre *ṭawīl*, rhyme *āXilu*, 60 lines).

22 Kennedy, *The Prophet and the Age of the Caliphates*, 163; Sourdel, *Le vizirat ʿabbāside*, 256–8.

23 See *EAL*, ii, 544, s.v. 'Muhammad ibn ʿAbd al-Malik, known as Ibn al-Zayyāt' (E. K. Rowson); Yūnus Aḥmad al-Sāmarrāʾī, *Sāmarrā fī adab al-qarn al-thālith*, Baghdad 1968, 147–8.

24 al-Ṭabarī, *Taʾrīkh*, iii, 1230, 1303; *SS*, 87, 179–80.

his life.[25] Ibn Muṣʿab was a versatile servant. He was a successful and bloody general; Abū Tammām wrote him a poem celebrating an ambush of Bābak's followers in which he slaughtered 30,000 of them and sent their severed ears to al-Muʿtaṣim (*Dīwān AT/T*, iii, no. 162). He and his brother Muḥammad, another general, were cousins of the Ṭāhirids, who had been the regime's most trusted lieutenants since throwing their military support behind al-Maʾmūn in his long struggle to seize the caliphate and control an empire beset by rebellion and civil war. The clan was not only powerful and loyal, but also cultured. Arabs only by courtesy, they were prominent patrons who helped to harness new fashions in Arabic literature to the needs of the empire's developing court cultures and service aristocracies of bureaucrats, provincial as well as metropolitan.[26] These were, in fact, their own needs, for the Ṭāhirids–Muṣʿabids consolidated their position by becoming servants of the caliph to the extent of proclaiming dependence on him and accepting a variety of functions from him across the empire. (In this they differed from the military as a professional body – a recent creation of al-Muʿtaṣim's own – which had only a fighting function and no recognized cultural bases or attributes.)[27]

In some ways, Ibn Abī Duʾād's situation was analogous, as a man whose first concern was to uphold the authority of the caliph and whose own position was voluntarily dependent upon him, in contrast to the religious-minded in general, who were largely independent of authority and had less predictable loyalties or potential disloyalties than administrators or soldiers, and who could be divided, at least as far as al-Maʾmūn and al-Muʿtaṣim saw it, into those who would and those who would not acknowledge the sovereign's control. Hence al-Maʾmūn's inquisition, continued briefly by al-Muʿtaṣim when he became caliph,[28] and the willing help given to it by a state servant such as Ibn Muṣʿab, who had no religious training or standing.

Abū Tammām dedicated some eight poems to Ibn Muṣʿab,[29] and thirteen to Ibn Abī Duʾād.[30] Of the pair, and perhaps of anyone at al-Muʿtaṣim's court, only Ibn Abī

[25] See notes 28, 32 below. Al-Muʿtaṣim had been in charge of organizing the inquisition in Egypt and Syria, *SS*, xvi.

[26] On the Ṭāhirids as patrons and poets, see C. E. Bosworth, "The Ṭāhirids and Arabic Culture", *JSS*, 14 (1969), 45–79. On the careers of Isḥāq b. Ibrāhim al-Muṣʿabī and his brother Muḥammad under al-Muʿtaṣim, and al-Muʿtaṣim's esteem for them as mainstays of his brother's regime, see *SS*, 98 n. 282, 149, 214 (Muḥammad), xv, 3–4, 7, 88–9, 179–80, 186, 212–5 (Isḥāq).

[27] Kennedy, *The Prophet and the Age of the Caliphates*, 158–61.

[28] *SS*, xvi; *EI2*, s.v. 'Miḥna' (M. Hinds).

[29] *Dīwān AT/T*, i, no. 17 (*madīḥ*, metre *basīṭ*, rhyme *abā*, 16 lines); no. 33 (*madīḥ*, prelude to iii, no. 135, metre *wāfir*, ryhme *īḥā*, 4 lines); ii, no. 76 (authenticity questioned by ʿAzzām; *madīḥ*, metre *wāfir*, rhyme *ārā* 14 lines); iii, no. 135 (*madīḥ*, metre *basīṭ*, rhyme *amā*, 53 lines); no. 150 (*madīḥ*, metre *kāmil*, rhyme *ūmi*, 53 lines); no. 162 (*madīḥ*, metre *wāfir*, rhyme *ayni*, 37 lines); iv, no. 395 (*iʿtāb*, metre *kāmil*, rhyme *ūʿā*, 8 lines); no. 429 (*iʿtāb*, adapted from i, no. 17, lines 1, 7, 8, 11, 14, 15, 16, metre *basīṭ*, rhyme *abā*, 8 lines).

[30] *Dīwān AT/T*, i, no. 34 [misnumbered] (*madīḥ*, metre *khafīf*, rhyme *ādi*, 34 lines); no. 35 (*madīḥ/iʿtidhār*, metre *wāfir*, rhyme *ādi*, 51 lines); no. 36 (occasional, metre *wāfir*, rhyme *ādi*, 2 lines); no. 37 (*madīḥ/iʿtidhār*, metre *kāmil*, rhyme *ūdi*, 56 lines); no. 38 (occasional: postscript to no. 37, metre *ṭawīl*, rhyme *īdu*, 4 lines); ii, no. 75 (*madīḥ*, metre *ṭawīl*, rhyme *īru*, 7 lines); no. 88 (*madīḥ*, metre *kāmil*, rhyme *iḍā/aḍā*, 25 lines); no. 89 (*madīḥ*, metre *khafīf*, rhyme *āḍi*, 28 lines); iii, no. 117 (occasional, metre *basīṭ*, rhyme *alu/ilu*, 10 lines); no. 136 (*madīḥ*, metre *ṭawīl*, rhyme *āXimu*, 35

Du'ād could be seen as an intellectual of Abū Tammām's own calibre; and given his unchallenged position in the caliph's esteem and the overriding influence he was said to exert, it is easy to see him as the real target of performances directed at al-Muʿtaṣim. Certainly *Ta'rīkh Baghdād*, in the entry on Ibn Abī Du'ād, makes much of Abū Tammām's attempts to woo him, and says that he was a good enough poet himself to have been included in Diʿbil's *Kitāb al-Shuʿarā'*.[31] Unfortunately Ibn Abī Du'ād is, at least during this period, very much a cipher; his function, and the nature of his thought and of his influence on the caliph, are hard to pinpoint, in spite of the fact that he led al-Ma'mūn's 'Muʿtazilī' inquisition and al-Muʿtaṣim made him chief *qāḍī* immediately on becoming caliph. But Martin Hinds has argued that it is a misnomer to call al-Ma'mūn's inquisition (or his belief in a created Qur'ān, the test question in the inquisition) Muʿtazilī, and that both may rather have been Ḥanafī in origin. He points out that al-Ma'mūn was said to be an expert in Ḥanafī *fiqh*, that the createdness of the Qur'ān (used to validate an approach to legislative authority that draws on first principles as well as on explicit Qur'ānic prescriptions and Prophetic precedent) was a tenet held by some Ḥanafīs, and that despite similarities between Ḥanafī and Muʿtazilī thinking on this point 'this is not to say that the *miḥna* necessarily came from the Muʿtazilīs or that its initial purpose was the imposition of Muʿtazilī doctrine'.[32] Its purpose seems rather to have been to curb the rabble-rousing behaviour of those who saw themselves as the guardians of literalist Islam and of the Prophet's *sunna*. There is circumstantial evidence for Ḥanafī involvement in caliphal politics from an early date; al-Ma'mūn's father Hārūn al-Rashīd appointed, as the first *qāḍī 'l-quḍāt*, Abū Yūsuf, the close follower of Abū Ḥanīfa (and perhaps the source of al-Ma'mūn's knowledge of Ḥanafī *fiqh*?). As for the unintellectual al-Muʿtaṣim, Hinds concludes that inheriting the inquisition from his brother was something that he merely 'had to cope with'.[33] Al-Muʿtaṣim in any case halted the inquisition when he removed his court and army to Sāmarrā in 221/836 and the 'dumb insolence' (Hinds) of the populace of Baghdad in defence of their beliefs receded as an irritant. The *miḥna* was resumed only during his final illness, though throughout his reign Ibn Abī Du'ād remained, as al-Ma'mūn had directed, his closest councillor. However, it was not until some years after al-Muʿtaṣim's death that al-Jāḥiẓ began to address to Ibn Abī Du'ād (still in office at Sāmarrā) epistles 'in which he dwelt

lines); no. 165 (occasional, metre *munsariḥ*, rhyme *ani/uni*, 6 lines); iv, no. 435 (*iʿtāb*, metre *ṭawīl*, rhyme *āruhā*, 8 lines); no. 448 (*iʿtāb*, metre *kāmil*, ryhme *ami/imi*, 4 lines).

31 al-Khaṭīb al-Baghdādī, *Ta'rīkh Baghdad*, iv, no. 1825 (Aḥmad b. Abī Du'ād), 144–7, 143.

32 *EI2*, s.v. 'Miḥna' (Hinds), 5–6. See also note 40 below and *SS*, 96, n. 271 on Ḥanafī involvement in al-Ma'mūn's *miḥna*. Josef van Ess points out that the image of Ibn Abī Du'ād handed down by ʿAbbasid historians and littérateurs is untrustworthy, and that 'Die Häresiographen nehmen von Ibn Abī Duwād kaum Notiz. Als Theologe ist er nicht hervorgetreten. ‹Philosophie› im Sinne des Naẓẓām war ihm offenbar direkt unsympatisch ... es scheint, daß man [i.e. the literary and historical sources] seinen Standort bewußt verwischt oder schon bald nicht mehr erkannt hat. Denn er war vermutlich gar kein Muʿtazilit', *Theologie und Gesellschaft im 2. und 3. Jahrhundert Hidschra: Eine Geschichte des religiösen Denkens im frühen Islam*, Berlin–New York 1991–7, iii, 481.

33 *EI2*, s.v. 'Miḥna' (Hinds), 3; see also *SS*, xvii.

at length on the details of Muʿtazilite doctrine, and furnished [him] with arguments'.[34] Ibn Abī Du'ād published no arguments of his own.[35] Significantly for Hinds' analysis of the probable nature of the inquisition, Sourdel seems to suggest that 'caliphal' Muʿtazilism developed under al-Muʿtaṣim's son al-Wāthiq;[36] and even this may have been an uneven process, for 'the most distinguished of [Ibn Abī Du'ād's sons] Abū al-Walīd' (who became his adjutant and was also a recipient of al-Jāḥiẓ's *risālas*) 'wrote a number of books about the law, agreeing in point of view with Abū Ḥanīfah'.[37]

Perhaps the most important thing about Ibn Abī Du'ād, for most of al-Muʿtaṣim's reign and from al-Muʿtaṣim's perspective, is that he was an unfailingly wise, kindly and disinterested helper,[38] and that, above all, unlike his state bureaucrats or indeed many of his generals, he appears to have come to him as a new man, of imprecise origins and free from the demands of a family network and the freemasonry of a service ethic. As *Ta'rīkh Baghdād* points out, his personal sway over al-Muʿtaṣim was identical to that held over al-Ma'mūn for many years by his chief *qāḍī* Yaḥyā b. Aktham al-Tamīmī, a similarly 'new' man but a firm believer in the uncreatedness of the Qur'ān;[39] he was supplanted at the end of al-Ma'mūn's life by Ibn Abī Du'ād, whom he bequeathed to al-Muʿtaṣim on his deathbed with the admonition, according to al-Ṭabarī, to 'take no *vizier* [my emphasis] who is not above reproach', but rely on Ibn Abī Du'ād in all things, 'for you know what I suffered from Yaḥyā b. Aktham's dealings and from his scandalous propensities'. According to al-Ṭabarī, al-Ma'mūn made no mention of either man's beliefs, and claimed to have dismissed Ibn Aktham for peculation and immorality. Emile Tyan notes in general terms that 'sous les Abbassides, un kāḍi al-kuḍāt qui se faisait particulièrement apprécier par son souverain devenait *naturellement* [my emphasis] son conseiller habituel et, en fait son premier ministre'. This was not a matter of chance; the progression was 'natural' insofar as the office of chief *qāḍī* as conceived by Harūn al-Rashīd and his sons seems to have been an appointment to the palace and to the personal service of the sovereign.[40]

---

[34] *EI2*, s.v. 'Aḥmad b. Abī Du'ād' (K. V. Zetterstéen/Ch. Pellat), i, 271; s.v. 'al-Djāḥiẓ' (Ch. Pellat), ii, 85. Pellat dates the epistles to Ibn Abī Du'ād (d. 240/854) and his son (d. 239/853) to after the fall of Ibn al-Zayyāt (d. 233/847).

[35] *Dodge/Nadīm*, i, 409–10: 'no book of his is recorded ... no compositions or books of his are known'. See also note 32 above.

[36] Sourdel, *L'état impérial*, 150–1.

[37] *Dodge/Nadīm*, 410.

[38] al-Khaṭīb al-Baghdādī, *Ta'rīkh Baghdād*, iv, 149–50.

[39] al-Khaṭīb al-Baghdādī, *Ta'rīkh Baghdād*, xiv, no. 7489, 191–204.

[40] Émile Tyan, *Histoire de l'organisation judiciaire en pays d'Islam*, 2nd edn, Leiden 1960, 348. Norman Calder, summarizing the anecdotal material, says of the first chief *qāḍī*: 'Abū Yūsuf rose to high rank, showing himself a willing and capable servant of the state, a courteous and wily courtier ... the Ḥanafīs had in him a model of honourable and cunning service to the government', *Studies in Early Muslim Jurisprudence*, Oxford 1993, 105–6. (On Abū Yūsuf's own role, and on his conception of the caliph's role, cf. also Patricia Crone, *Slaves on Horses: The Evolution of the Islamic Polity*, Cambridge 1980, 71 and 253 n. 536.) According to Bosworth's reading of al-Ṭabarī, just as Ibn Abī Du'ād seems to have accompanied al-Muʿtaṣim's army (see *Chronology*, **18**, below), so Ibn Aktham may also occasionally have acted the part of a soldier, al-Ṭabarī, *Ta'rīkh*, iii, 1105; (tr. C. E. Bosworth), *The History of al-Ṭabarī*, xxxii: *The Reunification of the ʿAbbāsid Caliphate*, Albany

On such evidence, Muʿtazilism in an intellectually serious and coherent form is unlikely to have been, as Stetkevych argues, the dominant 'cultural context' of al-Muʿtaṣim's court and of the poetry Abū Tammām produced for it.[41] Abū Tammām's poems to the supposed founders of caliphal Muʿtazilism, al-Maʾmūn and al-Muʿtaṣim, have still been only sketchily studied, as have those to al-Wāthiq, who may well have been its real promoter; so they cannot yet be used as internal evidence to the contrary. The poems to Ibn Abī Duʾād also await detailed study. On the general stylistic level, *badīʿ*, self-consciously 'modern', rhetoricized poetic expression, seems to have arisen, a good generation before Abū Tammām, from a confluence of feelings of cultural and intellectual malaise which cannot all be traced to a single intellectual impulse or milieu; it rapidly became the language of fashion, its subversive origins forgotten, although its creative potential was far from played out. Abū Tammām has come to be seen as setting the definitive stamp on *al-madhhab al-kalāmī*, the 'dialectical' style, which Stetkevych sees as a totalizing poetic vision and identifies as the direct product of Muʿtazilī-inspired ways of conceptualizing, though without giving much information about Muʿtazilī thought itself. Here again, there is room for debate; and I shall argue that the Amorium poem demonstrates Abū Tammām's capacity to mould his vision to a particular situation.

Meanwhile, al-Muʿtaṣim's Sāmarrā – a combination of cantonment and palace complex, with a wholly imported population of soldiers, bureaucrats and providers of supporting services – was not the centre of experiment and enquiry that al-Maʾmūn's Baghdad had been. Literary culture, though, was well represented on various levels, and acted as a softer connecting tissue to the framework of brute power: a poet such as Abū Tammām, who chose his patrons well, could move between the caliph's bureaucrats, his strong men and his most trusted confidant, picking up political clues as he went. Some courtiers, like Ibn Abī Duʾād, Ibn Muṣʿab (in Baghdad) or al-Ḥasan b. Wahb, were appreciative of the demands made by Abū Tammām's poetic style; others, like Ibn al-Zayyāt, perhaps, or like the caliph himself, preferred the facile or the familiar. The poetry that Abū Tammām wrote for al-Muʿtaṣim probably circulated outside the court soon after being performed there; but whatever the reception it may have had from

1987, 180, though the phrase referring to the sacking and burning of Byzantine fortresses may in fact apply to Abū Isḥāq [al-Muʿtaṣim]. The account of al-Maʾmūn's deathbed words to his brother, a piece of oratory apparently designed to portray his complexities and contradictions, is at al-Ṭabarī, *Taʾrīkh*, iii, 1139. Ibn Aktham himself may have introduced his supplanter to court, *Dodge/Nadīm*, i, 410; *EI2*, s.v. 'Aḥmad b. Abī Duʾād', i, 271. Much later, Ibn Abī Duʾād was in turn supplanted by Ibn Aktham when the caliph al-Mutawakkil turned against the doctrine of the created Qurʾān. A further parallel to Ibn Abī Duʾād's role, and comment on his Muʿtazilism, can be found in section two of the sixth chapter of the *Fihrist*, which deals with Ḥanafī scholars, where Ibn al-Nadīm remarks of Abū Bakr Aḥmad b. ʿUmar al-Khaṣṣāf that 'he was such a favourite of the caliph al-Muhtadī (r. 255–6/869–70) that people declared: "He's reviving the *dawla* of Ibn Abī Duʾād and promoting *jahmiyya*!"' (*Fihrist* [ed. Riḍā Tajaddud], n. p. [Tehran], n. d. [1st edn, *c*. 1971], 259). See *EI2*, s.v. 'Djahmiyya' (W. Montgomery Watt) for the connection with Ḥanafism. Most of the above parallels are evident analytical *topoi*.

41 *Stetk/AT*, 8, 15, 200.

discriminating sensibilities elsewhere, it is important to bear in mind that it was designed in the first instance for a new community in a new setting, where public spectacles of bloody punishment had already become an institution.

II

The Amorium *qaṣīda* has a complicated and intriguing chronological scheme, which will be outlined in detail in part III, where a translation of the poem is also given. The main narrative of the siege of Amorium itself is interrupted by references to earlier incidents of the campaign (lines 21, 49, 50–8). The same events are approached from different angles (e.g. there is chronological overlap between lines 23–9, 30–5: the taking of the city, and lines 30–5, 63–6: the raping of the city's women), and there are anticipations (lines 10–14, 20 summarize the events that will be chronicled in lines 21–35, 41–5, 49–59, 60–6), flashbacks (e.g. the *casus belli*, the Byzantine attack on Zibaṭra, is not referred to until line 46), and even combined flashbacks (e.g. line 46 flashes back to the *casus belli*, lines 50–7 back to the routing of the emperor at Anzen, before the siege of Amorium; line 58 then flashes forward to the burning of Amorium and line 59 to the city's total defeat. This is expanded in lines 60–1; line 62 is another flashback, to the storming of the city walls, and is followed chronologically by the rape of the women in lines 63–6). The poem's 'historical' prelude, lines 1–10 and more especially lines 3–9, is particularly complex in terms of chronology and will be discussed at length both in the *Chronology* in part III and in the analysis of the poem in part IV.

The reason for this choice of structure I think lies outside the poem itself. The crushing of Bābak's long rebellion, which al-Muʿtaṣim had waited for before setting out for Amorium, had been a straightforward if not a conclusive triumph. But the Amorium campaign was marred by treachery in the Muslim ranks. The panegyrist had the task of resolving the contradiction of a brilliant victory followed immediately by a spate of executions as the caliph reasserted his authority. This Abū Tammām tried to do by, among other things, resorting at key points to simple diction, so as to smooth over the ugly aftermath of the campaign and maintain an unwavering heroic impetus. Coupled with this, the sequence of events is broken up and regrouped by theme around a series of abstract triumphalist slogans which are illustrated, as we shall see, by reference to recognizably true incidents. These serve to carry the half-truth of the poem's last line: 'the Arabs are exalted'. So al-Muʿtaṣim's Arabs (and some of his Turks) were – but only as a result of the uncovering of the treason of many of the eastern generals, the traditional props of the ʿAbbasid regime and more especially of al-Maʾmūn's, which crystallised, ironically, at the moment the walls of Amorium were breached.[42]

In most analyses of the poem, the events leading up to the expedition – the Byzantine attacks on Muslim frontier towns which spurred al-Muʿtaṣim to retaliation – have been discussed to the exclusion of those following it. But uppermost in the minds of the court and the army, when the caliph returned to Sāmarrā, would have been the depleted ranks of his officers, some seventy of whom were tortured to death on the march home,[43] and the public cursing of his murdered nephew for treason, which spelled out that the old ʿAbbasid order had passed, and, in some quarters, meant the shelving of plans to welcome a new caliph who might have prolonged the old confederacies of self-interest.

Vague schemes to unseat al-Muʿtaṣim may have been hatched as soon as the expedition was planned, on the evidence supplied by the poem, for which there is no direct support in the surviving histories closest to it in date. Al-Ṣūlī's and al-Khaṭīb al-Tibrīzī's commentaries throw little light on the predictions derided in the opening nine lines of the poem. Al-Ṣūlī's gloss on line 1 reads: 'they [unspecified] said the city could not be taken in that season' (*Dīwān AT/Ṣ*, [i], 189); al-Tibrīzī's gloss combines Muslim and Byzantine predictions: 'the astrologers predicted that al-Muʿtaṣim would not take Amorium, and the Byzantines wrote to him saying: "Our city can be captured only when the fig and the grape are ripe"' (*Dīwān AT/T*, i, 40).[44] In the glosses on lines 8–9, there are remarks on the technicalities of astrology but little on their application, although the allusions here seem to be to Muslim predictions. Al-Tibrīzī's gloss on the comet of line 7, a sign commonly associated with the death of princes, says only: 'they had predicted that the appearance of the aforementioned star would mean great civil strife (*fitnatan ʿaẓīmatan*) and some change in the dispositions of rule (*taghayyura amrin fī ʾl-wilāyāti*)', and al-Ṣūlī, though much closer to events, is silent; but in his biographical entry on Abū Tammām, Ibn Khallikān, from the vantage of the seventh/thirteenth century, states baldly: 'When al-Muʿtaṣim went to fight the Byzantines, the astrologers predicted that he would not return'.[45] It was an ominous fact that both the caliph's predecessors, his father Hārūn al-Rashīd and his brother al-

---

[42] See note 4 above and *SS*, 112, n. 314 for chronology. The treason was plotted during the early stages of the campaign and uncovered on the march home according to the account al-Ṭabarī appends to his main narrative of the campaign, *SS*, 120–3, 123–34.

[43] *SS*, 133, n. 371.

[44] Specifically Byzantine predictions are clarified in the two commentators' glosses on line 59 and in al-Ṣūlī's *Akhbār Abī Tammām*, 30–2, in which both lines 1 and 59 are taken to refer to Byzantine predictions. This seems to be the correct interpretation, see part IV below.

[45] Ibn Khallikān, *Wafayāt*, ii, 23; so too Jalāl al-Dīn ʿAbd al-Raḥmān b. Abī Bakr al-Suyūṭī (849–911/1445–1505), *Taʾrīkh al-Khulafāʾ* (ed. M. Muḥyī al-Dīn ʿAbd al-Ḥamīd), [repr.] Beirut–Sidon 1989/1402, 382; (tr. H. S. Jarrett), *History of the Caliphs*, Calcutta 1881, lxxxvii; repr. Amsterdam 1970, 350.

Ma'mūn, had died on campaign;[46] and it would not have been hard for anyone at his court to guess that al-Muʿtaṣim's first expedition away from home as caliph might provide the opportunity for supporters of his dispossessed nephew to strike. The poem tacitly admits this unwelcome fact into the fabric of its argument (indeed, one-tenth of it is devoted to pouring scorn on the astrologers), and addresses itself not only to celebrating victory, but also to forging renewed confidence among the loyal and not so loyal. On this occasion, the task of affirming to those courtiers who had not accompanied the army, and to the people of Sāmarrā and Baghdad, that the caliph was secure on his throne may have fallen chiefly to the poets, for although there were a large number of important Christian captives to display, it seems that there were no traitors left alive to be made an example of by the time the caliph reached home.[47] (The execution of the heresiarch Bābak had provided an unprecedented spectacle for Sāmarrā and that of his brother for Baghdād, and his head was afterwards sent to Baghdad as a trophy and around the provinces as a warning.)[48] As I shall argue in part V, even if he received no encouragement from al-Muʿtaṣim, Abū Tammām seems to have conceived his poem as a piece which could serve to proclaim the caliph's total victory over all his enemies to the public at large.

It is interesting to note, though, that where Ibn Khallikān pays tribute to the poem's subsequent standing with the *topos* of al-Muʿtaṣim's eventually paying 1,000 *dirhams* per line for it,[49] al-Ṭabarī, rounding off his main account of the Amorium expedition, does not even mention it, but instead quotes lines by one of al-Muʿtaṣim's favourites, al-Ḥusayn b. al-Ḍaḥḥāk, which honour not the caliph but al-Afshīn and couple his victory over the emperor just before the taking of Amorium (see below, *Chronology*, 5) with his recent triumph over Bābak.[50] Perhaps the reason al-Ṭabarī chose an excerpt from this poem, rather than Abū Tammām's more famous and accomplished *qaṣīda*,[51] was to show events pointing both backwards and forwards. The crushing of Bābak had left unfinished business, and according to al-Ṭabarī, Bābak, cornered by al-Afshīn's troops, wrote to the emperor Theophilus urging him to mount a diversionary attack on the Muslims. This led to the Byzantine sacking of Zibaṭra, in which followers of Bābak took part, and so gave al-Muʿtaṣim the idea of resuming his

---

46 The penultimate paragraph of al-Masʿūdī's account of al-Ma'mūn concludes with a couplet by Abū Saʿd al-Makhzūmī, a poet who lived into the reign of al-Muʿtaṣim, which says that the stars (*al-nujūm*) abandoned al-Ma'mūn at Ṭarsūs as they abandoned Hārūn at Ṭūs, *Prairies*, iv, para. 2784.

47 See *SS*, 119, n. 331 on prisoners and note 99 below on the gibbeting of the body of the commander of Amorium. *Ta'rīkh Baghdād* claims that al-Muʿtaṣim captured 60 patricians, but does not say what became of them, and continues: 'He also brought the gate [of Amorium] to Iraq, where it still frames one of the doorways of the Dār al-Khilāfa, the one next to the Friday Mosque in the *qaṣr*', iii, no.1451 (Muḥammad amīr al-mu'minīn al-Muʿtaṣim billāh), 344.

48 al-Ṭabarī, *Ta'rīkh*, iii, 1231, more fully, *Prairies*, iv, para. 2812.

49 Ibn Khallikān, *Wafayāt*, ii, 23.

50 al-Ṭabarī, *Ta'rīkh*, iii, 1256; *SS*, 120–1.

51 Bosworth draws attention to the omission: *SS*, 121 n. 339.

father's and brother's operations against the Byzantines.[52] Al-Afshīn, instrumental in both campaigns, remained loyal at Amorium when other easterners were plotting the caliph's murder, and was appointed the executioner of their 'candidate' al-ʿAbbās b. al-Ma'mūn.[53] Al-Ḥusayn b. al-Ḍaḥḥāk's verses, by making al-Afshīn, not the caliph, the hero of the day, may serve, for the purposes of al-Ṭabarī's *History*, to foreshadow the suspicion that was shortly to fall on him of having independent ambitions. (Al-Masʿūdī, however, quotes from two pieces which al-Ḥusayn b. al-Ḍaḥḥāk recited on the occasion, one in honour of al-Afshīn, the other addressed to the caliph.)[54] Al-Ḥusayn b. al-Ḍaḥḥāk's poem to al-Afshīn is adequate as a piece of instant propaganda; but Abū Tammām's is more daring and more far-sighted, suggesting that he had access to better intelligence – for al-Afshīn is purged from his *qaṣīda*, in which al-Muʿtaṣim stands alone as the instrument of victory;[55] and Abū Tammām links his triumph not to recent successes over rebel heretics of no scriptural standing, but to a far stronger legitimating proof, the cosmic mission of Islam against Christianity and the caliph's part in bringing it to fulfilment (see part V).

III

Like A. J. Arberry's and S. P. Stetkevych's translations,[56] my English rendering of Abū Tammām's Amorium *qaṣīda* is able to suggest only some aspects of the poem. It misses the depth of the more complex lines, and tries instead, unlike Arberry and Stetkevych's, to convey the directness of the simpler ones, emphasizing what I take to be leading themes of argument. (But even the simpler lines have elements of deliberate ambivalence; those which are factually relevant are discussed in footnotes to the translation and in part IV.) As I have not been able to reproduce the stylistic contrast between difficult and easily accessible lines, I have emboldened those which are fairly, or very, straightforward in vocabulary and in construction, either in themselves or once their terms of reference are known (these form a high proportion of the poem, cf. al-Ḥasan b. Wahb's appreciation of it, part I above). I have also italicized the lines or part-lines which carry the organizing slogans referred to in part II above. In the right margin of the poem are numbers referring to the real, or linear, chronology of the *casus belli*,

52 Bosworth doubts that this version of events is chronologically feasible 'even though it is possible that [Bābak] ... did send a general appeal to the emperor', *SS*, 94–5 n. 266. On the followers of Bābak who had previously enlisted with the Byzantines, see *ibid*., 95, nn. 268, 269.

53 al-Ṭabarī, *Ta'rīkh*, iii, 1265; *SS*, 130.

54 al-Masʿūdī, *Kitāb al-Tanbīh wa'l-Ishrāf* (ed. M. J. de Goeje), Leiden 1894, 169–70; (tr. B. Carra de Vaux), *Le livre de l'avertissement et de la révision*, Paris 1897, 230–2.

55 *Ta'rīkh Baghdād* reflects the picture of a single-handed victory, claiming that al-Muʿtaṣim *fataḥa ʿAmmūriyyata bi-nafsihi*, iii, no. 1451, 343. In all, Abū Tammām wrote only one poem to al-Afshīn, the one celebrating the execution of Bābak, *Dīwān AT/T*, iii, no. 166 (see note 11 above), and one poem addressed to him and al-Muʿtaṣim jointly, celebrating victory over Bābak, *Dīwān AT/T*, iii, no. 126 (see note 10 above).

56 A. J. Arberry, *Arabic Poetry: A Primer for Students*, Cambridge 1965, 50–62; *Stetk/AT*, 187–97.

the campaign and the events of the march back to Sāmarrā, which I give below. This is based mainly on the fullest Arabic account, that of al-Ṭabarī. Like Stetkevych, I have divided the poem into sections; I have also added headings to signpost what I see as the scheme of the poem, or rather one layer of it.

The translation serves to show my general interpretation of the poem; but, in my analysis in part IV, I sometimes revert to word-for-word rendering instead of quoting my verse translation.

Chronology[57]

I, II, etc., in the *Chronology* = points omitted by Abū Tammām, or contradicted by him, or which cannot be identified with certainty in the poem.
0 in the margin of the poem = points not explained in Arabic sources.

1 Early in 223/838 according to al-Ṭabarī (837 according to Bury, *History*, 260), the emperor Theophilus invades the Upper Euphrates and burns the fortress of Zibaṭra, slaughtering the men and enslaving the women and children; he then threatens Malaṭya. 'It was reported that the refugees [from Zibaṭra] came as far as Sāmarrā' (tr. C. E. Bosworth, *Storm and Stress* [henceforth *SS*], 95).

2 According to al-Ṭabarī (*SS*), 'al-Muʿtaṣim regarded this event as a great catastrophe, and ... when news of it finally reached him, he raised a call to arms in his palace'. According to al-Masʿūdī, the poet-prince Ibrāhīm b. al-Mahdī (al-Muʿtaṣim's uncle) recites to him 'a long poem detailing the woes' of Zibaṭra and Malaṭya, urging him to Holy War (*jihād*) and calling upon [him as] the righteous wrath of God (*yā ghayrata llāh*); al-Muʿtaṣim immediately sets out on campaign in the dress of a *ghāzī*.[58] According to al-Ṣūlī, *Dīwān AT/Ṣ*, and al-Tibrīzī, *Dīwān AT/T*, gloss on line 46, a captive Zibaṭran woman calls on al-Muʿtasim for aid (or vengeance). On being informed, he instantly sets forth (al-Ṣūlī)/he puts aside his wine goblet, ordering it to be kept, and finishes drinking from it only on his return from Amorium (al-Tibrīzī). According to al-Ṭabarī, lengthy military preparations ensue; first, though, in a symbolic gesture, al-Muʿtaṣim 'mounted his horse and attached behind his saddle shackles, an iron plowshare, and a provision bag ... [and] held a meeting in the Public Audience Chamber [of Sāmarrā], having summoned thither from [Baghdad]' the two *qāḍī*s of Baghdad and al-Ruṣāfa and 328 legal witnesses to his testamentary provisions (*SS*, 95–6). But not until the rebel Bābak, who is still active in the eastern provinces, has been

---

[57] Based on Bosworth, footnotes to *SS*, 93–121, which (a) summarize and discuss the relevant points in J. B. Bury, *A History of the Eastern Roman Empire from the Fall of Irene to the Accession of Basil I (A.D. 802–867)*, London 1912; A. A. Vasiliev, *Byzance et les Arabes*, I: *La Dynastie d'Amorium* (ed. and tr. Henri Grégoire and Marius Canard), Brussels 1935, (b) note points in the Arabic historians not investigated in Vasiliev, and (c) review recent scholarship not cited by Stetkevych, *Stetk/AT*, 187–211.

[58] *Prairies*, iv, para. 2816.

defeated, does he decide on Amorium, which the Byzantines are believed to hold especially dear, as his target (*SS*, 97).

3 At some unspecified point not noted by the historians, either during the preparations for the expedition or those for the siege itself, but more likely the former, 'the astrologers predicted that al-Muʿtaṣim would not take Amorium' (al-Tibrīzī, *Dīwān AT/T*, gloss on line 1); 'when al-Muʿtaṣim went to fight the Byzantines, the astrologers predicted that he would not return' (Ibn Khallikān, *Wafayāt*, ii, 23).[59] 'Marvels' are predicted to take place from which Fate itself will shy in terror 'in (*fī*) fateful Ṣafar (*Ṣafar al-Aṣfār*) or in Rajab' (Amorium *qaṣīda*, line 6, not explained by al-Ṣūlī and al-Tibrīzī). Given the length of al-Muʿtaṣim's preparations, it seems likely that the astrologers had to hedge their bets about when doom would fall.[60]

4 Al-Ṭabarī lays particular stress on the fact that al-Muʿtaṣim 'equipped himself in a manner that no previous caliph had ever done in regard to weapons ... leather water troughs for the animals ... beasts of burden for carrying water, goatskins for water' (*SS*, 97–8). Nevertheless, during the first leg of the campaign '[his] army was reduced to extreme distress because of lack of water and fodder' (*SS*, 103).

5 As part of a carefully planned series of preliminary operations, al-Afshīn routs the emperor at Anzen (*SS*, 105 n. 305).

6 Al-Afshīn attacks Ankara, whose inhabitants flee, leaving the city empty when the emperor sends troops to relieve it. The emperor orders his deputy to proceed to Amorium instead (*SS*, 107).

7 A captive leads the thirsty Muslim troops 'to a river valley with abundant herbage' (*SS*, 104).

8 The emperor sends an envoy to negotiate a peace, but al-Muʿtaṣim refuses to see him and meets with him only after Amorium is taken (*SS*, 107 n. 308, 117–8).

9 Al-Muʿtaṣim and al-Afshīn effect a junction at Ankara and plan their attack on Amorium (*SS*, 108).

I Al-Muʿtaṣim orders all the villages between Ankara and Amorium to be burnt and their inhabitants taken captive (*SS*, 107–8).

10 The first body of Muslim troops arrives outside Amorium and encamps 'two miles away at a place that had water and herbage' (*SS*, 108). During the siege, 'a watering place three miles' from the city is used (*SS*, 117).

11 'The Commander of the Faithful divided the city between his commanders as they were circling around it. He allotted to each one of them a certain number of the city's defensive towers' (*SS*, 108).

---

59 See above, part II and note 45.

60 Going against her own translation, Stetkevych, in her analysis, reads this as a metaphor, not as part of the prediction: 'the very days flee for refuge *to* [my emphasis] the pre-Islamic sacred months of Ṣafar and Rajab during which fighting was taboo', *Stetk/AT*, 188, 201.

12 'Meanwhile, the inhabitants ... had entrenched themselves behind their fortifications and had prepared for a siege' (*SS*, 108).

13 The siege begins in Ramaḍān (*SS*, 119, Ibn Khallikān, *Wafayāt*, ii, 23).

14 The Byzantines send word to al-Muʿtaṣim (*rāsalathu al-Rūm*, according to al-Tibrīzī's gloss on line 1, *Dīwān AT/T*) that the city can be taken only when the figs and grapes ripen: 'We find it written in our books/prophetic scriptures (*najidu fī kutubinā*) that ...'. Further on in the same gloss, a variant on the prediction is attributed to 'the monks (*ruhbān*) of Amorium'. In al-Ṣūlī, *Dīwān AT/Ṣ*, gloss on line 59 and *Akhbār Abī Tammām*, 31, al-Muʿtaṣim learns during the siege that the Byzantines have a saying to this effect: 'It is a tradition among us (*la-narwī*) that ...'. (It is the veteran's account retailed in *Akhbār Abī Tammām, loc. cit.*, that fixes the prediction at the time of the siege.) Not mentioned by Muslim or, apparently, Byzantine historians.[61]

II In addition, the Byzantines say that the city can be taken only by 'whoresons' (*awlād al-zinā*) (al-Ṣūlī, *Dīwān AT/Ṣ*, gloss on line 59, *Akhbār Abī Tammām*, 31; al-Tibrīzī, *Dīwān AT/T*, gloss on line 59). Al-Muʿtaṣim remarks that he would rather not wait for the ripening of the figs and grapes but that his army has sufficient whoresons in it.[62]

III Amorium is betrayed. A renegade Muslim married to an Amorian woman tells al-Muʿtaṣim where the wall is weakest (*SS*, 108–9), and the messengers sent by the commander Yāṭis/Aetius to inform the emperor of his plans to attempt a sortie are captured and suborned and paraded before the city to demoralize the defenders (*SS*, 109–10).

15 Al-Muʿtaṣim 'set up mangonels [at the weak spot in the defences] (**IV**) ... and the wall was breached in that spot' (*SS*, 109, see also 110).

V It is rivalries over the fighting in the breach that bring to a head the plot to murder the caliph and set al-ʿAbbās b. al-Maʾmūn on the throne (*SS*, 112–3).

16 The battles in the breach are hard-fought: 'The next day, the Muslims fought them in the breach ... but it was narrow and impossible to fight in. Al-Muʿtaṣim therefore sent for the great catapults ... and ordered them to fire on the place. Al-Afshīn and his troops were the combatants [that day]; they fought well and advanced ... On the

---

61 In the more usual context of *dalāʾil al-nubuwwa*, 'proofs of [Muḥammad's] prophethood', the phrase 'we find it written in our *kutub*' [or synonyms]is traditionally ascribed to Jews, Christians and others whose scriptures or other books contain prophecies of Muḥammad's advent, cf. the formulation in Abū ʿUthmān ʿAmr b. Baṣr al-Jāḥiẓ (*c.* 160–255/*c.* 776–860 or 9), *Kitāb al-Ḥayawān* (ed. ʿAbd al-Salām Muḥammad Harūn), Cairo 1356–64/1938–45, iv, 202.

62 Interestingly, the loyal and treacherous generals insult each other as *awlād al-zinā* in al-Ṭabarī's account of the rivalries that break out at this point of the siege, al-Ṭabarī, *Taʾrīkh*, iii, 1249; *SS*, 112; Bosworth emphasizes the term. In *Taʾrīkh Baghdād*, the prophecy is set 'during the march towards Byzantine territory', and like al-Ṣūlī's is an eye-witness account, though from a different source (in both *Dīwān AT/Ṣ* and *Akhbār Abī Tammām*, 'the father of ʿAwn b. Muḥammad al-Kindī'; in *Taʾrīkh Baghdād*, iii, no. 1451, 344, 'the father of ʿAbd al-ʿAzīz b. Sulaymān b. Yaḥyā b. Muʿādh'). A monk emerges from his cell, and in answer to the Muslims' questions tells them that Amorium can be taken only by 'a king most of whose company are whoresons'. On hearing this, al-Muʿtaṣim declares this is what most of his troops are, since they are Turks and *aʿājim*.

third day, the troops of the Commander of the Faithful bore the brunt of the battle ... they fought well and widened the breach' (al-Ṭabarī, *Ta'rīkh* [iii], 1248, 1250, cf. *SS*, 111, 113).

17 The end of the siege. 'A detachment [of Byzantines] went along to a big church situated in one corner of ʿAmmūriyyah and fought there fiercely, but the Muslim troops burned the church over them (**VI**); they were burned to death to the last man' (*ibid.*, 115). This is followed by the surrender of the commander, Yāṭis (*SS*, 115–6). Bosworth follows al-Yaʿqūbī's dating of the fall of Amorium to 17 Ramaḍān 223/12 August 838, and thinks that, although 'the Christian sources are imprecise', the whole siege may have lasted no more than twelve or fifteen days (*SS*, 116 n. 321). Al-Masʿūdī says that al-Muʿtaṣim occupied and burned the city for four days, *Prairies* (tr. Barbier de Meynard/Pellat), iv, para. 2818.

18 A great number of captives are taken; it takes five days to sell them. Al-Muʿtaṣim appoints 'a man from Aḥmad b. Abī Duwād's staff to keep an account of the gains that [each] commander made. What proved saleable was sold, and he ordered that the remainder should be thrown on the fire' (**VII**) (*SS*, 116–7).

VIII The march home. Soldiers and prisoners are tormented by thirst; prisoners who cannot keep up are killed piecemeal; there is a mass slaughter of 6,000 men. Al-Muʿtaṣim saves his troops by erecting leather water troughs (*SS*, 118–9).

IX The march home. The execution of the traitors, 'the greater part of those [officers] participating in the ʿAmmūriyyah camapaign, by various methods, beheading, strangling, gibbeting on a wooden beam, etc.' (*SS*, 133 n. 371), and also by jolting on unsaddled pack-mules, burying alive, feeding while withholding water (*SS*, 128–33); this is how al-ʿAbbās b. al-Ma'mūn dies, at Manbij (*SS*, 130).

X In the purged army that arrives back in Sāmarrā, free commanders will in future form a minority, with officers and troops recruited 'from the fringes of empire' and an increasing proportion of slave-soldiers.[63]

Translation

The following conventions apply: **bold** = lines of which the diction is relatively simple in the original Arabic; *italics* = 'organizing slogans' (see Part II above); numerals in right-hand margin (see *Chronology* above) = points on which the historians and Abū Tammām agree; Roman numerals = points mentioned by historians but omitted by Abū Tammām; 0 = points mentioned by Abū Tammām but omitted by historians.

[63] Kennedy, *The Prophet and the Age of the Caliphates*, 160; *SS*, 133–4 n. 371.

Signs

1. ***The sword gives truer tidings than do scriptures*;**[64] **14**
its edge is what tells *zeal* from *vanity*;[65]
2. **White blades, not the black letters on the page – these**
reveal misguided doubts for what they are;
3. **And knowledge flashes from the starry spears**
when armies meet, not from the Pleiades. **3**

4. **Where now the oracle, where now the stars** **14, 3**
invoked to trump up fallacy and *lies* –
5. A slanderous tissue of apocrypha
that's fit for nothing when all's said and done.
6. **Such marvels as they claimed! saying Fate itself**
in that doomed month (which one?) would bolt from them,[66]
7. **Scaremongers who declared the western comet**
would usher in a dark catastrophe,
8. Who said stability and revolution
are ordered by the zodiacal spheres,
9. ***Indifferent* as they are, fixed or revolving;**
yet from them they determine destiny!

10. ***The idols and the cross and what befell them,*** **VI, 17**
***if stars predict, this could not have been hid*;**

64 This line is multi-layered. On the conventional level, it is informed by the banal antithesis 'sword/[pen]', which it inverts. On a topical level, the *prima facie* meaning of *kutub* may be the letter(s), *risāla*(s), written by the Byzantines to al-Muʿtaṣim, see above *Chronology*, **14**. However, the *message*(s) sent by the Byzantines concern their *books* [of prophecy] (*ibid.*: *najidu fī kutubinā*; see also note 61 above). This sense of *kutub* establishes a more forceful antithesis with 'the sword'. Moreover, in routine acceptance the words *kutub*, l.1, *ṣaḥā'if*, l.2, *riwāya*, l.4 and *aḥādīth*, l.5, translated here as 'scriptures', 'page', 'oracle' and 'apocrypha', recall the positive meanings of '[true] scriptures' and '[Muslim] traditions', while *anbā'*, 'tidings', l.1, has strong Qurʾānic connotations; I do not believe that these can be deleted by the conventional/topical discourse of the poem so early in its development. In addition, the line is cast as a *ḥikma*, aphorism, and should therefore express a general truth as well as a particular one. Line 1 is thus a riddle for the listener: should it be read only in the topical or conventional senses, or in the general sense? If the latter, is the sword/scripture antithesis blasphemous? The rest of the poem will, progressively, provide the answer.

65 In the Qurʾān, the root *l-ʿ-b*, translated here as 'vanity', is associated with the word *khawḍ* and with those who deny the truth of God's Book, or who 'enter into false or vain discourse ... respecting [O]ur signs', E. W. Lane, *An Arabic–English Lexicon*, London 1863–93, s.v. *khawḍ*. It has eschatological connotations, see especially Qurʾān, 52 (al-Ṭūr): 11–12: *fa-waylun yawma'idhin liʾl-mukadhdhibīna ʾlladhīna hum fī khawḍin yalʿabūna*, 'Woe on that day to those who call [Our signs/words] lies and who now wallow in vanity'.

The next line is sometimes read: 'White blades are not [the same as] the black lines on the page, for it is in their edges that lies the clarification of doubt'.

66 See note 60 above.

11. **A victory of victories, so sublime**[67]
prose cannot speak nor verse can utter it;
12. **A victory at which Heaven threw wide its gates,** **0, VIII**
which Earth put on new dress to celebrate:[68]
13. **O battle of Amorium, from which**
our hopes returned engorged[69] **with milk and honey,**
14. ***The Muslims hast thou fixed in the ascendant,***
pagans and pagandom fixed in decline!

The city in her pride

15. **This was their dear mother city; mothers**
and fathers all they would have given for her;
16. **Too bold she was for Chosroes to tame her,**
and Abū Karib, King of Yemen,[70] **she shunned;**
17. **A virgin undeflowered by misfortune,**
whom mishap never ventured to approach
18. **Since before Alexander; and thus Time**
grew white-haired; but not so Amorium.
19. ***So God with jealous parsimony churned***
***the years*, and she the cream of aeons was,**
20. **Till, dazzled, black disaster came upon them**
whose city had been called Deliverer.[71]

---

[67] al-Ṣūlī adopts the reading *al-muʿallā an*, al-Tibrīzī the reading *taʿālā an*, echoing the phrase routinely applied to God, of which Ibn al-Mustawfī, cited in ʿAzzām's footnote, points out the blasphemous impropriety.

[68] This implies rain and flowers; but the campaign took place during July and August, see *SS*, 119 and *Chronology*, **13** above; and, as noted in the *Chronology*, the Muslims were plagued throughout by drought. Perhaps the allusion is to the ending of Ramaḍān, the month in which Amorium was besieged. The same image was used by Abū Tammām in a poem to al-Muʿtaṣim and al-Afshīn on a victory over Bābak which may also have taken place in Ramaḍān, *Dīwān AT/T*, iii, no. 126, l. 27, cf. *EI2*, s.v. 'Bābak' (D. Sourdel).

[69] Like the udders of a milch-camel, an age-old Arab term of reference. So too are the references to the casting of lots and to infectious mange in ll.21, 22.

[70] By contrast, here the reference to an Arab hero of pre-Islamic antiquity is fanciful and hyperbolic.

[71] al-Ḥasan b. Bishr al-Āmidī, who died some forty years after al-Ṣūlī in 371/987 and lived most of his life under Buyid rule, produces an astonishingly loyalist interpretation of this line. Reading *kāribatan minhā* ('approaching her') instead of *sādiratan minhā* ('dazzling her'), he interprets *al-kurbatu ʾl-sawdāʾu*, 'black disaster', as an allusion to the 'black banners' [of the ʿAbbasids], and the *-hā* of *kāna smuhā farrājata ʾl-kurabi* as referring not to Amorium but to these banners ('their name was Deliverer'), which saved [the Muslims] from the Umayyads [i. e. those very banners which delivered the Muslims bring disaster to the Christians], *al-Muwāzana* (eds Aḥmad Ṣaqr and ʿAbdallāh Ḥamd Muṣārib), Cairo 1392–1410/1972–90), iii (i), 349. Here, though, in contrast to line 1, the *prima facie* reading is the stronger one: [as their birthplace] Amorium was the deliverer/protectress [of the imperial family/empire] – but no longer.

The city warned and destroyed

21. ***Amorium drew an unlucky lot***
***at Ankara*, her courts left desolate,** **5, 6**
22. **And when she saw her sister now in ruins,**
the rot spread to her faster than the mange. **9**

23. **Within the city's battlements, how many**
brave horsemen, red-locked with hot-flowing blood!
24. **The sword prescribed that their own blood should be**
their dye, not henna as Islam prescribes.
25. **Commander of the Faithful, there you gave**
defeated stone and wood up to *the flames;* **17, VII**
26. **You left there *darkest night as broadest daylight*,**
driven from the city's heart by a dawn of fire,
27. **As if the cloak of darkness had forsworn**
its colour, and the sun had never set;
28. **Brightness of burning in the clinging gloom,**
and murk of smoke amid a sickly daylight,
29. **Here the sun rises after it has set;**
there the sun sinks away before its setting.[72]

The city in Muslim hands (i)

30. Clear as if clouds had parted over it,
Fate shows the battle both pure and uncleansed:
31. For on that day the sun did rise upon
no man but chaste, nor set upon a virgin.[73] **13, II**

32. **The city in her ruins looked as lovely**

---

[72] al-Āmidī notes that this passage echoes the day/night inversion coined by the pre-Islamic poet al-Nābigha, *Muwāzana*, iii (i), 349; *Dīwān al-Nābigha al-Dhubyānī* (ed. M. A. F. Ibrāhīm), 2nd edn, Cairo [1985], 83.

[73] Literally 'no husband/bridegroom ... no unmarried man'; *ʿazab*, 'celibate', can however apply to women (the raped Byzantine women) as well as to men (their Muslim ravishers). The line can be read on three levels: (i) as an inclusive phrase applying wholly to the Byzantines: 'no [Byzantine] male survived the day'; (ii) as an antithesis between Byzantines and Muslims: all the Byzantine men were killed, and the Muslims ravished their women, either or both losing their 'celibacy/viriginity' (cf. *Stetk/AT*, 205); (iii) as an antithesis applying wholly to the Muslims, in allusion to the fact that the siege took place during Ramaḍān. From sunrise to sunset, the Muslim soldiers were required to remain chaste; after sunset, they raped their captives, thus becoming ritually (not morally) unclean (l.30: 'both pure and uncleansed'). In this reading, the continence of the troops parallels the elective chastity of al-Muʿtaṣim in lines 46–7, see note 79 below.

as Mayy's haunts in their heyday to Ghaylān,[74]
33. **Her cheek, though streaked with grime, appeared as tempting**
as cheeks aflush with maiden modesty.
34. **Gazing on her disfigurement, no need**
had we of beauty or of pleasant sights,
35. **Seeing so smiling a reverse of fortune**
follow upon such foul adversity.

Destiny and history

36. ***Had it but known it, heathendom's deserts***
lay in wait down the ages in our weapons:
37. ***Such was God's supplicant's, His devotee's,***
His champion's, al-Muʿtaṣim's, grand design.

38. **With victory his daily bread,** his spearheads,
undulled, beg audience of no shielded soul;
39. **Wherever he campaigns, in holy warfare,**
a host of terrors is his harbinger;[75]
40. **Were he not leader of a mighty squadron,**
he alone would stand legion in the field.

41. **God flung thee at the city's towers and razed her –** **11, 15**
none but God casts with such unerring aim;[76]
42. With bristling garrison, in her they trusted, **12**
but God unlocks the best-manned citadel. **III**
43. 'They'll find no pasture for their beasts', their captain
declared, 'nor water to sustain their siege'[77] – **0**
44. Fond hopes of which our swords' edges despoiled them,
our spoiling lances made them all in vain,
45. **For steel and javelins are twofold vessels,**

---

[74] I.e. the Umayyad poet Dhūʾ l-Rumma; he and Mayya were a proverbial pair of romantic lovers. Stetkevych points out the implied pun and antithesis between 'the inhabited/flourishing (*maʿmūran*) abode of Mayya' and the desolate condition of Amorium, the Arabicized form of which, ʿAmmūriyya, 'the All-Flourishing', is an intensive pattern of the same root, *Stetk/AT*, 205.

[75] Here M. M. Bahjat cites the *ḥadīth nabawī*: *nuṣirtu bi ʾl-ruʿbi masīrata shahrin, al-Tayyār al-Islāmī fī Shiʿr al-ʿAṣr al-ʿAbbāsī al-Awwal*, (Silsilat al-kutub al-ḥadītha no.18), Baghdad 1402/1982, 666.

[76] Stetkevych points out that this is an allusion to Qurʾān 8 (al-Anfāl):17, which refers to the battle of Badr and paves the way for line 70, *Stetk/AT*, 206. In his earlier poem to al-Muʿtaṣim on the crushing of Bābak, Abū Tammām applied the same image to the caliph: 'He flung al-Afshīn at [Bābak]', *Dīwān AT/T*, iii, no. 130, l.21.

[77] The Arabic historians do not record the Byzantines taunting the besiegers in these terms.

of death, and of the wells and herbs of life.[78] **4, 7, 10**

46. ***Summoned***[79] ***by the Zibaṭran woman's cry,***
you poured away the wine of sleep and love; **2**
47. In hot pursuit, cool lips, refreshing kisses,
spurned, in the teeth of your realm's frontier's wrongs, **1**
48. **Your answer, with drawn sword and battle-cry –**
only the sword can answer such a summons –
49. **To fell the mainstay of the pagan tent,**
not swerving to undo its pegs and guys.[80] **I**

50. **Now when Theophilus had looked on war,** **5**
which signifies wrath and expenditure,
51. **With moneys he attempts to turn its course,** **8**
but cannot stem the ocean's heaving billows.
52. **Rather, *the very earth beneath his feet***
***quaked* at no plunderer's onslaught, but *a Reckoner's*,**[81] **1, 2**
53. **Who not for lack of golden coin had lavished**
a store of gold beyond all measuring:
54. **The lions, yea, the lions of the thicket**
spoil for the kill alone, not for its spoils.[82]

55. **The emperor fled.** The spears had tied his tongue;
beneath his speechlessness his guts were clamouring;
56. He left his retinue to die, urged on

---

78 Another multi-layered line with three levels of reference: topical, intertextual and aphoristic. For the pre-Islamic, intertextual resonances of the image of the spear as a well-rope/rope and bucket, drawing up virtuous deeds from 'a people's ... conceptual "bank"/[cistern] of inherited virtue', see Nadia Jamil, "Ethical Values and Poetic Expression in Early Arabic Poetry" (unpublished DPhil. thesis, University of Oxford 1999), 28–9.

79 *Labbayta*, like a pilgrim in a state of *iḥrām*; hence, in the second hemistich, al-Muʿtaṣim renounces women, and real wine is transformed into metaphorical wine. The renunciation however is voluntary and sealed by an uncanonical sacrifice; literally: 'you poured away/offered up to [the cry] (*haraqta lahu*) the wine-cup of sleep and the saliva of beloved women'. This is a pre-Islamic Arab ethical concept: 'a man commits a sin, subject to divine sanction, if he drinks wine when, prior to fulfilling a purificatory duty of compact, he is unclean', Jamil, *Ethical Values*, 109. At the same time, the wine-cup is an ancient near eastern symbol of kingship. In putting it aside, al-Muʿtaṣim is thus vowing to win renewed divine legitimation for his rule.

80 For *munʿafiran*: '[you left the mainstay of pagandom] *smeared with dust/rolled in the dust*', al-Tibrīzī cites the variant *munʿaqiran*, which echoes Qurʾān 54 (al-Qamar): 20: [God chastises the wicked people of ʿĀd by loosing against them a wind which leaves them] 'like trunks of *uprooted* palms'. I have followed the variant.

81 Like line 31, this can be read on three overlapping levels: al-Muʿtaṣim is settling scores with the emperor; in so doing he is dealing out God's reckoning; and he is anticipating his own reward on the Day of Reckoning, *Stetk/AT*, 194, 208.

82 According to al-Maṣūdī, this line of the *qaṣīda* at least did make an impression on al-Muʿtaṣim, since two years later he used it to taunt the rebel al-Māzyār Muḥammad b. Qārin when he tried to bargain for his life, *Prairies*, iv, para. 2820.

his fastest steed of cowardly desertion,
57. Seeking the trusty vantage of the hills 5
with fearful not with joyous nimbleness.[83]

58. **Though he runs like an ostrich from the heat,**
the *hellish flames* you set spread with much kindling:
59. **The ninety thousands like the fabled lions,**[84]
whose lifespan '*ripened ere the fig and grape*'.[85] 14

The city in Muslim hands (ii)

60. The Romans' root has been plucked out, and ah!
how sweet to Muslim souls no musk could sweeten,
61. Their anger dead, and by the sword restored
to lively satisfaction, the foe slain.
62. Our war stands firm, and holds the narrow pass **III, IV, 15, V, 16**
which brings all else who stand there to their knees.[86]

63. How many dazzling beauties in its glare,
embraces in its scowling gloom were taken; **18, VIII**
64. How many neck-cords there slit open, that
the gently-nurtured virgin might be had;
65. How many a shapely form with quivering flanks
won by the quivering rapiers ready drawn,
66. White arms that, bared from out their sheaths, proved fitter
fellows to white-armed maidens than their veils!

---

[83] Cf. *SS*, 105–7 nn. 305–8.

[84] Literally 'the lions of al-Sharā', a proverbial place in Arabia once known for its many lions. The origins of the expression are obscure.

[85] It is reasonable to suppose that *al-ʿinabi*, 'the grape', provided the rhyme of the poem and that Abū Tammām took the false Byzantine prophecy, which according to the veteran's account in al-Ṣūlī, *Akhbār Abī Tammām*, 31, did the rounds of the Muslim camp, as the basis for the *qaṣīda*. Some critics saw the phrase as unpoetic; al-Ṣūlī defends it on the grounds that it is a historical quotation.

[86] There are no helpful commentaries, medieval or modern, on this line, which makes sense only if 'war' is made to side with the Muslims in specific reference to the fighting in the breach. (At this point it may be noted that all the weaponry referred to in the poem is conventional/heroic; but as it happens, the modern machines on which al-Muʿtaṣim had spent so much time and money, 'the siege towers, mangonels, scaling ladders and such remained ineffective', especially during the fighting in the breach, 'and in the end were [broken up and] burned', al-Ṭabarī, *Taʾrīkh*, iii; *SS*, 111.) The topical reference to the narrowness of the breach is extended metaphorically ('those standing in it kneel in humiliation', *tajthūʾl-qiyāmu bihī ṣughran ʿalā ʾl-rukabi*) in an allusion to a Qurʾānic use of the root *ṣ-gh-r* so apposite as itself to be near-topical, see Qurʾān 9 (al-Tawba): 29: [the Muslims are exhorted to fight unbelieving and wrongdoing People of the Book] 'until they pay tribute (*jizya*) ... and are humiliated (*wa-hum ṣāghirūna*)'.

The true meaning of events

67. **Caliph of God! may God reward your labours**
for faith's true stock, for Islam and renown;
68. ***You looked upon the Peace of God and saw that***
to reach it you must cross a bridge of toil.

69. **If it be that the haps of time bear kinship**
in an unbroken line, or stand allied,
70. ***Then surely this your triumph that God gave you***
is of the noble lineage of Badr;[87]
71. **Whereby** ***the Paleface, yellow as his name,***[88]
is downcast**, and the Arabs are exalted!** **IX, X**

IV

The fullest discussion to date of the poem in English is that of S. P. Stetkevych; her reading picks up points made by Andras Hamori and M. M. Badawi,[89] and subordinates them to a controlling concept, that of metaphor, which she states as follows:

> Relying neither on traditional *qaṣīdah* structure[90] nor on the chronology of the historical event to determine the form of the poem, [Abū Tammām] instead forges a unique literary construct based on two poetic principles: (1) metaphor, that is, the interpretation of the current political event in terms of the Jāhilī concept of *tha'r* [blood vengeance]; this in turn establishes the major themes of the poetic imagery – the personification of the conquered city as a woman and the conquering armies as her ravishers. This metaphor then is the basis for the second principle (2) antithesis, that is, the dialectical progression of images derived from the masculine heroic motifs of the *madīḥ* and the lyrical feminine motifs of the *nasīb*. Within this antithetical framework a series of oppositions take their place: passivity (the astrologers and their books) *versus* action (the Caliph and his sword); light *versus* darkness; purity *versus* pollution; al-

[87] In the poem to al-Muʿtaṣim on the crushing of Bābak, Abū Tammām drew the same parallel: 'The angels of heaven came down upon the Muslims', *Dīwān AT/T*, no. 130, l.49. The parallel established here would seem to be not just between al-Muʿtaṣim/the Prophet, who defeated the pagan Meccans with God and His angels on his side, but also, as a forthcoming article by Hugh Kennedy will argue, between the first warriors of Islam, who forged the Muslim *umma*, and the troops of al-Muʿtaṣim's new, professional army.

[88] See note 107 below.

[89] Andras Hamori, *On the Art of Medieval Arabic Literature*, Princeton 1974, 125–34; M. M. Badawi, "The Function of Rhetoric in Medieval Arabic Poetry: Abū Tammām's Ode on Amorium", *JAL*, 9 (1978), 43–56.

[90] For the purposes of Stetkevych's argument, 'traditional' *qaṣīda* structure can be taken as: prelude (*nasīb*): reflections on transience, usually in connection with love; transition: re-engagement with the business of life, usually through the metaphor of a journey to the patron; praise of the patron (*madīḥ*). Quite often, though, an aphoristic prelude is substituted for the *nasīb*. In the Amorium *qaṣīda*, an aphoristic opening merges into a long historical prelude. Abū Tammām had already used historical preludes, e.g. in the poem to al-Afshīn, 'The stout warriors subdued al-Badhdh', *Dīwān AT/T*, iii, no. 166, which was written during the preparations for the Amorium campaign, see note 11 above and *Chronology*, **2**.

> Muʿtaṣim *versus* Theophilus; and ultimately Islam *versus* Infidelity. Military conquest is perceived as an enactment of the sacrificial pattern of the [pre-Islamic and Arab] blood-vengeance ritual, the Muslims' killing and raping of the Byzantines effects the revitalisation of the [Islamic] Ummah and the devitalization of the Infidel...

This scheme is conceived within:

> the Muʿtazilite cultural context ... as a comment on that fiercest of battles among the Mutakallimūn, that between ... the proponents of ... free-will and predestinarianism. Not unexpectedly ... Abū Tammām promotes free-will, that tenet without which ... [Muʿtazilism] could not stand.[91]

Persuasive as it is, this reading is nevertheless in a sense a *lecture à rebours*, shaped in part by Stetkevych's belief that the survival of the *qaṣīda* as a poetic form must ultimately be explained in terms of pre-Islamic archetypes and in part by her identification of dialectical poetry, *al-madhhab al-kalāmī*, with her rather unspecific conception of Muʿtazilism.[92] In the light of these generalities, her interpretation breaks up the poem's structure (which rather than 'not relying' on conventional *qaṣīda* structure, or even accepted modifications of it, deviates strikingly from it), and restates it in terms of an abstract process, 'the dialectical progression of images'. This has the effect of stereotyping the relationships between the ideas that the poem develops; Stetkevych largely overlooks their interplay and the fact that, as the poem progresses, its images start to work simultaneously on more than one level. If instead the poem's themes are taken in sequence, and it is recognized as reshaping, but by no means ignoring the real chronology of events, its structure can be given due prominence, and the ways in which arguments and images are marshalled can be seen in concrete terms.

In outline and in some aspects of its general expository technique, the poem is reminiscent of a Qur'ānic warning story. It opens with an obscurely minatory passage full of coded and incomplete allusions to narratives outside itself; it then describes the city of Amorium in its heedless pride, thinking itself inviolable, only for God to smite it unawares; it gloats over the ironies of its destruction and the ineluctability of God's purpose; it is punctuated by simple, rhythmic passages rallying the faithful, repeatedly juxtaposes their righteous satisfaction with the abasement of the Byzantines, as the Qur'ān does the fates of the saved and the damned, and expresses itself in antitheses.

---

[91] *Stetk/AT*, 233, 200.

[92] Cf. *Stetk/AT*, xiv: 'Part II [of the book] ... demonstrates first the new ritual role of the ʿAbbasid courtly *qaṣīdah*: that of validating, through the merging of the Jāhilī and Islamic traditions, the ʿAbbasid hegemony. Second, it demonstrates how, through the manipulation of the ritual substructure of the classical *qasidah*-form, Abū Tammām ... [reintegrated] the tribal ritual of pre-Islamic poetry into the larger paradigm of ancient Middle Eastern rituals of sacred kingship'; *ibid.*, 37: '*al-madhhab al-kalāmī* should be taken to mean the conceptualizing mentality of the *mutakallimūn*'. Earlier on the same page she defines *al-madhhab al-kalāmī* by reference to 'the effects of *kalām* – speculative theology in particular, but in more general terms the spirit of logical disputation and rational investigation that affected every aspect of the arts and sciences in the "Muʿtazilite Era"'.

This familiar, though non-poetic pattern becomes apparent as the *qaṣīda* unfolds, and the following passages all explicitly spell it out: lines 10–14 ('The idols and the cross and what befell them ... A victory at which Heaven threw wide its gates ... The Muslims hast thou fixed in the ascendant ...'), 36–7 ('Had it but known it, heathendom's deserts * Lay in wait down the ages in our weapons: Such was God's ... champion's, al-Muʿtaṣim's, grand design'), 41–2 ('God flung thee at the city's towers and razed her ... God unlocks the best-manned citadel'), 46–9 (al-Muʿtaṣim consecrates himself to laying low heathendom), line 52(ii) (he is a Reckoner), line 70 (his triumph is God-given, like the Prophet's at Badr), lines 25–9, 58 (the burning of the city), 52(i) (the quaking of the earth beneath the emperor's feet), and 68 (the caliph crosses a bridge of toil to his reward) – line 52(ii) and the last three passages being prefigurations of the Last Judgement.

Yet despite its simplicity of outline, this is not a simple poem. Hamori discusses it, or rather its use of *tajnīs* (paronomasia), under the heading of 'Ambiguities',[93] which is appropriate, for the poem is built on them. The first two lines launch the Qurʾānic pattern just described, although this is not immediately evident, for line 1 is compounded not of direct antitheses but of oblique contradictions. The first lies in the contrast between its bold diction and its disorientating message. Books/scriptures, understood as God's 'tidings', his *anbāʾ* – a root heavily used in the Qurʾān – are generally accepted as the highest bearers of truth and the sword as its enforcer. What books then are these; why are sword and scripture set in opposition? The second imbalance is lexical. The *ṭibāq* does not quite form a natural metonymic pair, as would the words 'sword/pen'. There is also a logical imbalance in the abstract pair *jidd/laʿib* in the second hemistich. *Jidd*, the positive term, must apply to the caliph; but to whom does *laʿib* apply, and in what sense? Stetkevych takes 'books' to mean 'astrological charts', indifferently those of the Muslims and the Byzantines,[94] and reads lines 1–10 as a block informed by a single antithesis, that between the caliph's freewill (*jidd*) and the fatalism (*laʿib*) of all astrologers, Muslim and Christian. But if instead line 1(i) is seen as echoing the prophecy of the monks of Amorium: 'we find it written in our books ...' (see *Chronology*, **14**, and notes 44, 61, 85 above), and the contrast in line 1(ii) is understood as being between the zeal inspired by true faith and the complacency which their false scriptures, or false understanding, inspire in the Christians, the two images yield a balanced, and non-metaphorical, antithesis between historical adversaries of comparable stature and significance (see part V below). In this passage, Abū Tammām seems to be building on the ambivalence felt towards the Christian scriptures in Muslim polemic. The usual polemical theme, derived from the Qurʾān, is the accusation that the Christians distort or misread their scriptures, which are actually true and foretell the

[93] Hamori, *On the Art of Medieval Arabic Literature*, *loc. cit.*
[94] *Stetk/AT*, 200.

coming of Muḥammad. Here Abū Tammām seems to be accusing the Christians of being unable to distinguish between divine and human writings. Line 2 amplifies the opening antithesis, using the words *shakk* and *riyab*, 'doubts', which recall Qur'ānic passages in which the peoples whom God is about to punish misread the scriptures he has sent them, such as Qur'ān 11 (Hūd): 110: 'And We gave Moses the Book ... and they are in doubt of it disquieting (*innahum la-fī shakkin minhu murībin*)'.[95] This underpinning allows the lines also to be read as an uncomplicated triumphalist slogan: the Muslims wage war in earnest with right on their side; the Christians in their vanity play at war; the outcome is not in doubt.

It seems equally unlikely that Abū Tammām's audience would have disregarded either obtrusively sacred vocabulary or reference to the 'books' of the Amorian monks, invoked during the siege from which many of them had just returned. Again in lines 46 ('a Zibaṭran cry'), 59 ('whose lifespan 'ripened ere the fig and grape' ') and 62 ('[Our] war stands firm and holds the narrow pass'), Abū Tammām draws allusively on such shared memories of the high points of the campaign; the purpose of this will be discussed shortly.

Meanwhile, his opening proclamation is not, despite its lapidary formulation, a summation nor even an exposition, but the starting point of an argument, whose progression will owe more to imaginative association than to strict logic. In line 3, Abū Tammām begins to interweave the earlier predictions of al-Muʿtaṣim's astrologers with the Byzantine prophecies circulated during the siege ('Knowledge flashes from the ... spears ... not from the Pleiades': *ʿilm*, true knowledge, that is, true religion, is placed in double contrast with the errors of the Christians in the preceding line and those of the astrologers in the line following). He conflates the two sets of predictions in line 4(i), 'Where is the *riwāya*' (cf. al-Ṣūlī's gloss on line 59: [the Byzantines said] '*la-narwī*', see above *Chronology*, **14**) 'and where the stars?'. Only in line 4(ii) does he finally supply the word *kadhib*, 'lie', which is the expected and implied second member of the antithesis established in line 1(i) with 'truer tidings' as its first member, and which therefore, I think, can be taken, like the fully stated sword/scriptures antithesis, as a premise of the poem. It will, however, be some time before its full meaning is developed; for the root *k-dh-b* means not only 'to tell lies (knowingly)', or 'to state a falsehood (mistakenly believing it to be true)', like the astrologers and the monks, but also, of men in battle, to fail to live up to appearances;[96] and this is exactly what the Byzantines do, in the persons of their taunting captain (lines 43–5) and their cowardly emperor (lines 50–8). The city herself belies her name of ʿAmmūriyya, 'All-Prosperous' (line 32, see note 74) and her title of Deliverer (i.e. protectress of the Amorian

---

[95] A. J. Arberry (tr.), *The Koran Interpreted*, London 1964, 224.

[96] *Wörterbuch der Klassischen Arabischen Sprache* 2 (ed. Helmut Gätje with Anton Spitaler and Jörg Kraemer), Wiesbaden 1960, 92, s.v. *k-dh-b*.

emperors), (line 20), and yields up her children to rape and death. This mocking of Amorium as virgin mother and protectress could be seen as another twist to the usual terms of anti-Christian polemic.[97] It leads into the irony of line 24(ii): '[their locks flowing] with henna of their own blood, thanks to the *sunna* of the sword, not the *sunna* of religion and Islam'. (A similar visual pun, and the same spiteful glee at the joke of mock conversion, are displayed in an earlier poem praising al-Maʾmūn after one of his Byzantine forays: 'Their [slashed] garments dropping from [their wounded bodies] like leaves, as if they had converted to Islam and found themselves suddenly reduced to pilgrims' garb', *Dīwān AT/T*, no. 133, l.46.) The bundle of anti-Christian themes in lines 1–2, 20, 24 (together with the associated themes of lines 10, 14, 21, 36) is tied together in the last line of the poem by another visual pun, as the Palefaces blench under a humiliation for which God has predestined them since mankind split into races following the Flood. (They are pale-skinned, *aṣfar*, because they are the children of Japhet, son of Noah, by descent from their eponym al-Aṣfar, see note 107.)

Appearances are doubly deceptive, in that they may be true as well as false, as the counterbalanced first and last lines of the poem demonstrate; and it is on this corollary that Abū Tammām builds what Stetkevych takes to be a Muʿtazilī opposition between free will (al-Muʿtaṣim's energy and his dismissal of signs) and predestinarianism (the fatalism of the astrologers). In fact, there is no opposition. Abū Tammām argues first against appearances, and then from them. The signs adduced by the astrologers are false: the comet of line 7 does not presage misfortune for al-Muʿtaṣim, for God has made the stars indifferent to human fate (line 9). God himself, on the other hand, uses signs to dazzle and mislead the unbelievers (lines 19–20: Amorium's pride comes before her fall).[98] He condenses sign and signified, and makes events into true signifiers of their own meaning – one might say *āyāt* (the battle of Amorium, lines 10–4, 36–7, 70, the unlocking and razing of the citadel, lines 42, 41); and He reveals the meaning of history by showing it as a foretaste of the Last Things (the flames that seem to overturn the natural order, lines 25–9, and which prefigure hell, line 58; the 'bridge of toil' crossed by al-Muʿtaṣim, which prefigures the bridge of judgment, line 68). With grim Qurʾānic irony, He even uses signs that astrologers and other diviners would recognize, and these can be clearly read by the Muslims, although the Christians at first seem blind to them (line 14: 'The Muslims has thou fixed in the ascendant'; line 21: 'Amorium drew an unlucky lot'; line 59: 'The ninety thousands ...

97 It also shows the development of Abū Tammām's vocabulary of metaphors. In the poem to al-Muʿtaṣim on the execution of Bābak written shortly before the Amorium *qaṣīda, Dīwān AT/T*, iii, no. 130 (see notes 10, 76 above), ll. 35–6, he had used the simpler image of the enemy's city as a nursing mother torn from her unweaned child. Line 41 of the Amorium *qaṣīda* is calqued on the same poem (see note 76 above) and displays a similar heightening.

98 Cf. the Qurʾānic theme of the unbelievers lulled into false security by God, root *d-r-j*, Qurʾān 7 (al-Aʿrāf): 182; 68 (al-Nabāʾ): 44, and root *m-k-r*, Qurʾān 3 (Āl ʿImrān): 54; 7: 99; 8 (al-Anfāl): 30; 10 (Yūnus): 21; 13 (al-Raʿd): 33, 42; 14 (Ibrāhīm): 46; 27 (al-Naml): 50; 71 (Nūḥ): 22.

whose lifespan "ripened ere the fig and grape"'; line 71: the Sallowfaces, sickly as their ancestral name (*banī ʾl-aṣfari ʾl-mimrāḍi ka-ʾsmihim*) are left yellow-faced, *ṣufra ʾl-wujūhi*). On the side of action and free will, it is true that al-Muʿtaṣim has displayed zeal (*jidd*, line 1), foresight (*tadbīr*, line 37: 'such was ... al-Muʿtaṣim's grand design'), disinterestedness in pursuit of holy war (lines 52–4) and energy (line 67: 'your labours'; line 68: 'You looked upon the Peace of God and saw that * to reach it you must cross a bridge of toil'). But he first enters the scene in person only in line 25, by which time God has amply prepared the fate of Amorium. Like the Prophet before him, and like good Muslims since, he embraces the role that God has assigned to him (line 41: 'God flung thee ... none but God casts with such unerring aim', see note 76; line 49: 'You answered (*labbayta*) a Zibaṭran cry', see note 79). This is certainly a form of free will. It is, however, a unifying concept of human choice, and one that all Muslims, not just Muʿtazilīs, would subscribe to. Similarly, submitting to astrologers (predestinarianism in Stetkevych's interpretation) would have incurred condemnation from all theological camps, whatever its wisdom as a political course. In fact, caliph, Muslims/Arabs and Christians alike are all predestined, the former to be 'exalted', the latter to be 'downcast' (line 71). In counterpart to the Byzantines' inescapable heritage of 'yellowness', the battle of Badr (line 70) supplies the genealogical link which reflects God's will concerning the Muslims (see part V).

What could, on the other hand, be read if not as a Muʿtazilī message, then as a message of blunt absolutism, is the opening declaration that the [caliph's] sword resolves doubts concerning 'scripture'. If this contains a veiled reference to the inquisition, then it is hyperbolical (for the *miḥna* stopped short of executing non-jurors), and could be taken as a threat of future action. However, the application of this is then shown to be non-Muslim; the *sunna* of the sword is coupled ironically with that of Islam (line 24), and at the end the caliph and his troops are represented as following in the footsteps of the Prophet and his community at Badr (line 70). A shock statement which asserts caliphal supremacy is followed by populist rallying-cries, a tactic which makes it relevant once again to consider the poem as a performance designed for the new culture of Sāmarrā and produced just after (or even during) a severe political crisis.

As suggested in part II, poetry may have had a more than usually important public part to play after the Amorium campaign, to compensate for the chilling circumstances of the caliph's homecoming, and perhaps – arguing from the reticence of the historical sources – for the lack of trophies and public executions it provided for the people of Sāmarrā. (Only al-Masʿūdī mentions that the body of Yāṭis/Aetius, the commander of Amorium, was put on display there, and then only in passing as a gloss on a line by Abū Tammām on the three gibbets that bore the bodies of Bābak, Yāṭis and the most recently executed rebel, al-Māzyār.)[99] There are no accounts of the death of Yāṭis. This may be a reason for the full-bloodedness of the poem's evocations of rape (lines 30–5, 63–6, prepared in lines 15–20), which modern scholars have been reluctant to acknowledge, and to which Stetkevych rightly draws attention.[100] Scholars including Stetkevych have been equally embarrassed to account for the genuinely startling effect of the poem's opening lines and for their function in the poem. Hamori and to a lesser extent Badawi discuss the Amorium *qaṣīda* almost as a non-programmatic musical composition; Stetkevych sees it as appealing to extremes of high culture, antiquarian Arab and modernist theological, and her analysis suggests that these strands are thematically juxtaposed, and are drawn together only by the intellectual effort required to apprehend them. However, the 'Arab' literary touches that she believes to underpin the restatement of a pre-Islamic ritual of vengeance are in fact, except for the fanciful reference to Abū Karib in line 16, not pre-Islamic: Mayy's devoted lover, Ghaylān/Dhū ʾl-Rumma, line 32, was Umayyad; and the mechanical vocabulary of female desirability, lines 63–6, echoing lines 46(ii) and 47(i), is a feature of 'modern' poetry.[101] Mass rape and enslavement are similarly 'modern' methods of revenge: the due reward of holy war (as we shall see in part V), they were made possible only by the large-scale Muslim armies which superseded pre-Islamic tribal bands. The poem's opening statement and its repeated insistence on the rape of the Christians are thus of a piece. For the participants in the Amorium campaign, there was nothing 'metaphorical', as Stetkevych puts it, in an 'interpretation of the current political event' as a just war against a traditional religious opponent on whom they had the right to wreak punishment. On this level there is nothing metaphorical either in the statement that 'the sword gives truer tidings than do scriptures'; events had proved it to be literally true, by extension in respect of al-Muʿtaṣim's would-be assassins as well as of the Byzantines. The literalness would have been still more compelling if, as al-Bahbītī suggests, the poem was recited not at Sāmarrā, when the plotters were safely dead, but at al-Maṣṣīṣa, on the march home, as they were being picked off one by one, and while memories of rape and dominance were still fresh in the minds of the now thirsty, frightened and demoralized soldiers (cf. *Chronology*, **VIII, IX** above).

---

[99] *Prairies*, iv, para. 2821; *Dīwān AT/T*, ii, no. 72, l. 46. See also note 47 above. Other court poets also accumulated references to al-Muʿtaṣim's past victories, see Bahjat, *al-Tayyār al-Islāmī*, 407–8. Yāqūt (575–626/1179–1229) retails a tall story told by the *nadīm* Ḥamdūn b. Ismāʿīl of how al-Muʿtaṣim deflowered the daughters of Bābak, al-Māzyār and 'the patrician of Amorium' on the same day, between draughts of wine, '*wa-hādhā nihāyatu ʾl-mulki yā Ḥamdūn*', remarks the caliph after the deed, 'this is the height of kingliness', *Muʿjam al-udabāʾ* (ed. Iḥsān ʿAbbās), Beirut 1993, i, no. 46 (Aḥmad b. Ibrāhīm ... Ibn Ḥamdūn), 168.

[100] *Stetk/AT*, 201–5, 207, 209–10.

[101] The reinforcing function of pre-Islamic verbal and ethical echoes in the poem is neverless considerable, see notes 69, 72, 78, 79 above. There are no doubt more than I have been able to detect. The same goes for the Qurʾānic echoes. All of those identified in notes 64, 65, 76, 86 above not only enrich the texture of the poem, also a function of the pre-Islamic echoes, but are structurally functional. (It should be pointed out that Qurʾān 30 (al-Rūm) does not supply points of reference for the poem since its treatment of the Byzantines [verses 1–6] is positive.)

Slaughter, rape and destruction form nine-tenths of the poem's subject-matter, and are stated as facts, which copious use of *tajnīs* (paronomasia) and *ṭibāq* (antithesis) serves to fix and glorify, not to transmute or render aesthetically acceptable. What is particularly to be noted is that the ubiquity of these figures forms part of a rhetorical strategy which encompasses the whole of the poem: that of establishing the objectivity of the poet's utterances and consequently their inevitability. Pun and antithesis in combination form tightly bound self-verifying statements. The polyvalence of the 'signs' constituted by a *tajnīs* is restricted by the bipolarity of the terms of a *ṭibāq*; conversely, the fact that only the, often paradoxically, yoked terms of a *ṭibāq* can fix the meaning of the terms of a *tajnīs* proves the paradox to be true. Lines 1–2 are the most prominent and complex example of this self-glossing: '(1) The sword is more truthful in its tidings than the books/scriptures (*kutub*); * in its blade/edge (*ḥadd*) lies the limit/edge between/true definition (*ḥadd*) of what constitutes seriousness/endeavour/zeal as against levity/idleness/vanity. (2) The white broad-bladed [swords] (*ṣafā'iḥ*), not the black books/writings (*ṣaḥā'if*) – it is in * their edges (*mutūn*) [implied: and not the texts (*mutūn*) of the latter] that lies the unveiling (*jilā'*) of doubt and disquiet'. *Tajnīs-ṭibāq* combinations of this degree of concentration recur periodically, for example in line 66 ('White [swords] which, when they are unsheathed from their protective coverings/veils/scabbards turn out to be * more truly entitled to act as companions to white [maidens] than their veils'), a riddle, like line 2 and line 38 ('his spearheads have never been kept from the presence of any soul that is secluded from the public gaze/has a protective covering'), which it echoes. Elsewhere, the force with which the formula is established at the beginning of the *qaṣīda* lends the same exegetical authority to the less fully developed examples which occur throughout the poem, e.g. line 50: 'When Theophilus beheld war (*ḥarb*) with his own eyes – * the meaning of war (*ḥarb*) deriving etymologically from wrath/loss of wealth (*ḥarab*)'. Once again, the last line of the poem ties up a a bundle of ideas launched in its opening two lines, this time by means of a double visual pun echoing line 2: '[Your battle] has left the Children of the Yellow One, who are as sickly as their name, * yellow-faced, and has made glorious the faces of the Arabs'. *Jallat*, 'has made glorious', comes from the root *j-l-l*, but echoes the root *j-l-w*, 'to reveal', used in line 2. (It may also suggest that the glory is divine, since *jalla* is routinely applied to God.)

This general procedure is extended to longer rhetorical, or rather oratorical, units, where it operates less intensively and in several different ways. Thus lines 3–10 (whose technical jargon was probably without much mystery to an audience familiar with astrology) adopt a stance not only of derision but, as importantly, of common sense. In the ensuing sections of the poem, historical narrative or allusion always immediately follows or precedes a generalization which proves it to be true on a supra-historical scale, again smoothing the effort of comprehension by appealing to the listeners' sense of divinely dictated cause and effect.

In this way, the poem is able to give the appearance of working spontaneously on the raw material of the battle. Positioned to lead from one such sequence of proof and confirmation to the next, the cries of victory have the same ring of inevitability as the puns and antitheses out of which they are constructed, and seem to be forced out of the poet involuntarily (lines 11–4, 20, 37, 41, 42(ii), 54, 59, 67, 68, 71). Their quality of simple, visceral truth is one that they share with Abū Tammām's love poetry and mourning poetry, and helps to explain why the poet-*kātib* ʿAbdallāh b. al-Ḥusayn b. Saʿd (d. 292/905) claimed that he was a genuinely popular poet – however restricted the bearing of the term *al-ʿāmma* in the mouth of a courtier.[102]

Another aspect of these procedures of objectivization is that nowhere does Abū Tammām use the conventional poetic 'I' or self-apostrophe; instead, he makes himself the impersonal mouthpiece of events, and it is in this capacity that he apostrophizes the caliph (lines 25–6, 41, 46–9, 58, 67–71) and, before him, the battle itself (lines 13–4). Once only, Abū Tammām steps outside the third and second persons and uses 'we' (line 34: 'Gazing on her disfigurement, no need * had we of beauty or of pleasant sights'); and once, in a passage which on silent reading appears gauche and redundant except as an intertextual echo (see note 72), he makes dramatic use of verbless present-tense description and of the active participle (line 28: 'Brightness of burning ...'; line 29: 'Here the sun rises [*faʾl-shamsu ṭāliʿatun min dhā*]... there the sun sinks away [*waʾl-shamsu wājibatun min dhā*] ...'). These last devices recreate the shared excitement of battle as experienced by the rank and file; and the two rape passages (lines 30–5, 63–6), which they precede, are also written from the viewpoint (though not in the language) of the ordinary soldier. The otherwise obscure line 62 similarly speaks for the unity through shared experience of Muslim brothers-in-arms, eliding the quarrels between their captains: it is a condensed evocation of the fighting in the breach, which brought the Byzantines 'to their knees' only after three days, and in which the main Muslim contingents took their turn one after the other, humiliating the modern Christians as Muḥammad had humiliated the People of the Book of his day.[103]

The impersonal forces of nature are harnessed, similarly, to provide both proof and drama. There is one instance of a conventional panegyric use of the pathetic fallacy, in line 12: 'A victory at which Heaven threw wide its gates, * which Earth put on new dress to celebrate'. For the rest, Abū Tammām's resources are pictorial and dramatic: he

[102] *Prairies*, iv, para. 2841: 'les vers devenus classiques [*mā yutamaththalu bihi*] et cités non seulement par les gens lettrés [*wa-yujrā ʿalā alsunati ʾl-khāṣṣa*], mais même par le peuple [*wa-kathīrin mina ʾl-ʿāmma*], s'élevaient à cent cinquante; je ne connais pas de poète du paganisme ou de l'Islam dont on cite dans la conversation un pareil nombre de vers'. On this Ibn Saʿd, see al-Masʿūdī, *Murūj* (Arabic text) (ed. C. Barbier de Meynard and Pavet de Courteille); rev. Charles Pellat, Beirut 1966–79, vii, Index, 470.

[103] See note 86 above. Note that the original reads *al-ḥarb*, 'War'; 'our' is supplied in the translation.

mounts a visual display in which light and fire, darkness, smoke and dust, hold the eye. Once more, the device is established at the beginning of the poem, in line 2 with the word *jilā'*, which means 'bringing to light', mentally or physically, and then more strongly in line 3, where the precedence of mental and physical significances of light is reversed: 'True knowledge flashes from the sparkling [blades of the] spears ... not from the seven sparkling planets'. Physical pictures dominate in lines 25–9, a tableau of the burning city, though these are images of an apocalyptic reality to come as well as of present reality. A system of visual echoes is built up, based on broad impressions of light, dark, and occasionally colour (line 23: 'red-locked with hot-flowing blood'; line 33: 'cheeks in which bashfulness has caused the blood to flow'). It includes shifts between close and distant focus. Thus the two rape passages, lines 30–5 and 63–6 are two views of the same situation, the first contemplative, the second a re-enactment. Within the first passage, there are further shifts. In lines 32–4, the purpose of modulated focus can be taken as purely literary on one level, sensual on another (line 32, distant focus, literary echoes of Umayyad poetry of frustrated love: 'The city in her ruins looked as lovely * as Mayy's haunts to [the poet Dhū ʾl-Rumma]'; line 33, close focus, literary echoes of ʿAbbasid erotic poetry of soon-to-be-fulfilled lust: 'Her cheek, though streaked with grime, appeared as tempting * as cheeks aflush with maiden modesty'; line 34, shift back to distant focus: 'Gazing on her disfigurement, no need * had we of beauty or of pleasant sights', implying that the pleasures of reality outdo those of fancy). But this passage is framed by two others in which distancing is used as an interpretative device. Line 30 ('Clear as if clouds had parted over it * Fate shows the battle ...') effects a link between the quasi-apocalyptic chastisement of the Byzantines, expressed in the tableau of lines 25–9, and the carnal rewards of the holy warriors, a symmetrical prefiguration of heavenly rewards to come. Line 35 shows the same events as the product of the cycle of earthly fortune (*ḥusnu munqalabin ... su'i munqalabi*, good and bad luck). This is an ironic affirmation through *tajnīs* of what was stated in the form of a denial in line 8, where the movements of the stars through the houses of the zodiac, *munqalib* or *ghayr munqalib*, were said to be heedless of human affairs. There is nothing for nature's sympathy here: this is what Fate (*al-dahr*, line 30) and fortune have decreed. A possibly more ambivalent series of moral perspectives seems to unfold in lines 55–7, 58–9. As Theophilus scurries into the distance, his heaving sides receding from view, the results of his cowardice are revealed on the horizons of vision, first with contempt (lines 56–8(i): 'He left his retinue to die ... he runs like an ostrich from the heat'), then with righteous gloating (line 58[ii]: 'the hellish flames you set spread with much kindling'), perhaps finally with some admiration and pity for the victims (line 59; 'The ninety thousands like the fabled lions * whose lifespan "ripened ere the fig and grape"').

V

Presented to the caliph immediately after the campaign, the poem uses a high proportion of non-poetic imaginative categories designed to appeal to the instincts of a wider audience; and if we go back to the accounts of how the campaign began, we can see where the inspiration for appealing to such an audience came from (see *Chronology*, **2**). Al-Ṭabarī's account shows al-Muʿtaṣim, before embarking on his lengthy preparations, indeed before even deciding on Amorium as his objective, making two seemingly spontaneous, symbolic public gestures aimed at the people of Sāmarrā and Baghdad respectively: raising a call to arms in his palace, he mounts his horse, as if ready to set off at once and punish the Byzantines; and he sends for the judges of Baghdad and over three hundred witnesses to his readiness to die in the cause. In al-Tibrīzī's gloss on line 46, the caliph's gesture has only a courtly audience: he sets aside his wine-cup (an ancient near eastern symbol of kingship), from which he will not drink again until he has done his duty as a Muslim ruler.[104] Al-Masʿūdī's dramatically condensed account conflates court and popular audiences: the caliph, roused to his duty by a court poet, at once dons the dress of a *ghāzī* and sets off on campaign, the people flocking to his colours.[105]

Al-Maʾmūn and Hārūn al-Rashīd before him had repeatedly waged holy war against the Byzantines; but these narratives are unique to al-Muʿtaṣim's Amorium campaign. They seem to reflect a considerable degree of stage management, perhaps by parties at court rather than by the caliph himself. Whichever narrative is followed, the aim seems to have been to establish al-Muʿtaṣim in the public eye as an exemplary holy warrior; but the call to holy war may not have emanated from or been designed to profit al-Muʿtaṣim himself. Al-Ṭabarī notes that 'it was reported that the fleeing refugees [from Zibaṭra] came as far as Sāmarrā' (*SS*, 95). This gives some credibility to al-Masʿūdī's account of the caliph's poet uncle Ibrāhīm b. al-Mahdī calling him to avenge them in the name of the 'righteous wrath of God', supposedly the first time such words had been used to a caliph (*Prairies*, iv, para. 2816); yet some ten years before, Ibrāhīm b. al-Mahdī had briefly usurped the throne from al-Maʾmūn. Which court or army interest was he acting for in urging al-Muʿtaṣim to take the field in person and expose himself to the risks of death on campaign or disorder at home? In al-Ṭabarī's account, a motive can be guessed. The conspirators press al-ʿAbbās b. al-Maʾmūn to strike down al-Muʿtaṣim during the height of operations; but he refuses to 'spoil' the campaign (*ghazāh*).[106] This

[104] See note 79 above. Stetkevych does not point this out as a ready-made instance of the integration of 'ancient Middle Eastern rituals of sacred kingship' with Islam, see note 92 above and *Stetk/AT*, 193, 207.

[105] *Prairies*, iv, para. 2817: 'les enseignes furent déployées ... et la levée en masse fut proclamée ... De tous les points de l'empire musulman accoururent les troupes régulières et les volontaires'.

[106] al-Ṭabarī, *Taʾrīkh*, iii, 1257–8; *SS*, 122–3.

suggests that al-ʿAbbās, if he had not changed his mind about letting himself be made caliph, wished to make capital out of the war. Apart from the astrologers, who advised al-Muʿtaṣim to stay safely at home, and who one might guess spoke for the higher bureaucracy against the growing strength of the military, several parties, taking a chance on the opportunities the caliph's absence might offer, may have wished to encourage him to make the preparations for war as solemn and irreversible as possible. Like the key passages in Abū Tammām's poem (italicized in the translation), the gestures designed to secure this end spoke a natural and immediately intelligible language, that of holy war as conceived in the popular imagination.

Futūḥ literature had been well established since at least the time of Hārūn al-Rashīd, and the style of the examples that have come down to us suggests that they were based on many previous tellings. Prose narratives of the Islamic conquests of the first caliphs, they show the divine mission of the Prophet's Islam carried forward into history, transferred to his community and confirmed by success in battle. In the wars with the empires, the Persians count for little; it is the Byzantines who are the arch-enemy, stereotyped as sallow, *aṣfar* – a sign both of their descent[107] and of their decadence. They are boastful and 'lying' in the sense of 'failing to live up to appearances in battle'. (Lines 70–71 of Abū Tammām's poem provide a rapid synopsis of this scenario.) Zestful expression is given to Muslim heroism in the *Futūḥ al-Shām* of al-Azdī, writing probably late in the reign of Hārūn al-Rashīd at around the time when he began to 'emphasize [his] role as leader of the Muslims against the traditional enemy'.[108] Historical *futūḥ* narratives such as al-Azdī's have underlying themes in common with popular apocalyptic; but in the latter the battles between Muslims and Byzantines are projected into the future; the soldiers' rewards of rape and pillage are dwelt upon, as they are not in historical *futūḥ*; and apocalyptic traditions condemn the present and reject history. When at last the Muslims overcome the Byzantines, the End of Time will follow, and this is the goal of the *ghāzī*.[109] The Amorium *qaṣīda* is notable for taking the apocalyptic themes of rape and cataclysm and marrying them to historical events which justify the present. The only future projected by the *qaṣīda* is al-Muʿtaṣim's own, in which he can be sure that, thanks to his efforts, he will partake of the peace of God, *al-rāḥa al-kubrā* (line 68).

Between them, apocalyptic traditions and historical *futūḥ* cover a wide range of attitudes towards the times in which they circulated. In counterpart to al-Azdī, though dating from only a little later, probably to the reign of al-Maʾmūn, the *Kitāb al-Futūḥ* of

---

107 See al-Masʿūdī, *Murūj* (Arabic text), vi, Index s.v. 'Rūm', 340: lineages attributed to the Byzantines' descent from al-Aṣfar 'the sallow'.

108 Kennedy, *The Prophet and the Age of the Caliphates*, 145. On Abū Ismāʿīl Muḥammad b. ʿAbdallāh al-Azdī, *fl. c.* 190/805, see *EAL*, s.v. 'al-Azdī' (L. I. Conrad), i, 117–8.

109 For a survey of typical themes, see David Cook, "Muslim Apocalyptic and *Jihād*", *Jerusalem Studies in Arabic and Islam*, 20 (1996), 83–93.

Ibn Aʿtham al-Kūfī[110] is in many ways a poetic and allegorical account of the divine historical mission of Islam, seen from the viewpoint of a Zaydī Shīʿī for whom ʿAbbasid rule had no divine mandate. Ibn Aʿtham shows the seeds of corruption in the primitive, heroic *umma*, pointing forward to the day 'when ... your men of religion shall tell your leaders only what they wish to hear ... and when you shall seek counsel of your slaves and eunuchs',[111] words directed at ʿAbbāsid developments and placed in the mouth of a Christian monk, whose foreknowledge, like that of some other Byzantine Christians, is true and inspired.[112] For Ibn Aʿtham, the modern *umma* lacks a righteous ruler to lead it to complete its divine destiny; how it will be realised remains an unanswered question. His is a troubled as well as heroic vision. Nevertheless, like those of al-Azdī and of the apocalyptic traditionists, it is expressed in graphic gestures, striking visual tableaux, and often in bold, populist slogans.

Both Abū Tammām's poem and the court propaganda set on foot before the campaign, on which the poem draws, are attempts to make the language of Islamic nostalgia, springing for the most part from disillusionment, speak not only to eschatological but to present fulfilment. Hence the elision by which the 'Arabs' of the poem's last line are equated with the Muslim community, with unity and success, as in a mythical early Islam when all Muslims were Arabs, the paramount enemy was the Christian outsider, and there were no divisions within the ranks of the *umma*. Hence too – though this is never mentioned in connection with his function as a court poet – Abū Tammām's aptness as a spokesman if, as was alleged, he was a Christian renegade.

VI

One last aspect of Abū Tammām's poem deserves to be discussed at greater length than there is space to do here. Kennedy brackets the poem and al-Ṭabarī's narrative together as '[reflections of] the public relations side of the exercise';[113] but some distinction needs to be made. It is clear that the poem speaks the language of holy war in the belief that, since this was how the campaign was launched, this was what the caliph would still wish to hear, though it seems that Abū Tammām may have miscalculated. Nevertheless, the poem is an immediate and functional response to the campaign itself, or to battlefield reports of it, and also to the propaganda campaign that preceded it. In this sense, it is a first-hand historical source, at least for the circumstances of its own

110 See *EAL*, i, 314, s.v. 'Ibn Aʿtham al-Kūfī' (L. I. Conrad).
111 Ibn Aʿtham al-Kūfī, *Kitāb al-Futūḥ* (ed. Muḥammad ʿAbd al-Muʿīd Khān), Hyderabad 1388–95/1968–75, i, 283.
112 See Julia Ashtiany Bray, "Jabala and the Historians", in Lawrence I. Conrad (ed.), *History and Historiography in Early Islamic Times: Studies and Perspectives*, Princeton forthcoming.
113 Kennedy, *The Prophet and the Age of the Caliphates*, 166.

genesis. Al-Ṭabarī's two-part narrative is more problematic. (The second part, dealing in detail with the attempted coup and execution of the generals, forms a separate section after the main account of the campaign.) Both parts are visibly composite, but lack *isnāds* to suggest any dating of their components; we do not know whether it was al-Ṭabarī himself, writing a generation later (he was born in or around the year of Amorium), or someone closer to events who put them together or shaped their general outline; and they are differently constructed and sometimes at variance in their interpretation of events.

Despite these differences, or indeed because of them, it would be relevant to compare Abū Tammām's management of narrative perspective both with *futūḥ* narratives (with which the poem has many themes in common, al-Ṭabarī's narrative none, except for the tableaux of the caliph's symbolic gestures) and with al-Ṭabarī's narrative (there are many overlaps between his and Abū Tammām's accounts of the campaign), and to consider the ways in which Abū Tammām combines poetic narrative with the non-narrative perspectives available to poetry and to the Qur'ān but not to the historian. Here there is space only to consider, and attempt to situate, some of the poetic perspectives, and to attempt a brief comparison with al-Ṭabarī.

Abū Tammām assigns different topics and points of vantage to the chronicler (as in his descriptions of Theophilus' attempts to negotiate and his flight, lines 50–1, 55–7), to the panegyrist (lines 37, 38–40, 46–9, 67–71), to the interpreter of events (lines 1–2, etc.) and to the companion in imagination of the rank-and-file soldier. His diction, themes and degree of detailed historicity vary to some degree, though not consistently, according to these viewpoints. However, there are also recurrent and interwoven themes (weaponry; signs; modulations of the notions of whiteness/light/flames, blackness/catastrophe/smoke, reward/punishment, beauty/ugliness, etc.), and above all an overall similarity of texture achieved by the unremitting use of coupled *tajnīs* and *ṭibāq*. Nearly every instance of *tajnīs* with *ṭibāq* refers backwards and forwards to those around it and to reiterated themes. This technique by contrast is so consistent that there is scarcely an image or figure that serves only for a single line or passage and lacks a foregrounded lexical and visual connection to the rest of the poem – perhaps only lines 19(ii) (which however recalls the 'milk and honey' of line 13[ii]), line 49 (though in most readings the image of the tent with its mainstay 'smeared with dirt' is subliminally connected with the 'grime-streaked cheeks' of Amorium in line 33), lines 55–7 (but here again, in line 57[ii], the *tajnīs tāmm* which carries the visual joke 'with the nimbleness of fear, not the nimbleness of joy' echoes that of line 24[ii]: 'by the *sunna* of the sword, not the *sunna* of religion and Islam'), and lines 60–61 (though the 'white swords' of line 61 connect the paired lines to two of the poem's dominant themes).

The effect is one of synaesthesia: what is suggested acoustically is also demonstrated visually, and is simultaneously confirmed by being translated into the language of cause and effect. *Tajnīs* – more accurately rendered in this context as 'cognation' or even 'cognition' than as pun or word-play – is the operative element, revealing a genuine kinship behind verbal affinities. Not for nothing does Abū Tammām use the phrase 'Now when Theophilus had looked on war (*ḥarb*) * which signifies wrath (*ḥarab*)' (line 50) to introduce the dénouement of the central historical narrative.

Though the poem's vocabulary is that of war, such techniques of circular argumentation are in fact ones associated above all with 'modern' love poems, which like the Amorium poem are built on saturated cross-reference, generating their own logical premises and terms of argument. The application of the technique to a long *qaṣīda*, and to narrative schemes and motifs which do not fall within the normal conventions of the *qaṣīda*, is a remarkable achievement, but is not a conceit altogether unique to Abū Tammām. Though usually executed on a much smaller scale, it is a typically 'modern' way of bringing new subjects into the poetic repertory. Its main point of interest in the present context, though, is that it is a means of unifying the picture set before the listener and directing response down familiar channels.

Al-Ṭabarī's two narratives combine details which must derive from differently placed informants at court, in al-Muʿtaṣim and al-Afshīn's armies and in the entourages of other generals. The first narrative is more complex than the second; but both are quasi-novelistic. In both, the blending of sequences of events and viewpoints is controlled by an author, who does not use stylistic differentiation to mark transitions between narratives of different provenance and type (e.g. dramatic, as in the case of al-Muʿtaṣim's symbolic gestures; descriptive/analytical, as in the case of his siege strategies). Moments of psychological truth are marked by the use of dialogue; but again, the transition between indirect and direct style is unmarked. As well as obvious differences, there are technical parallels here with the unifying viewpoint that Abū Tammām develops in the Amorium *qaṣīda*. At a basic level, al-Ṭabarī, or an earlier chronicler or chroniclers, and Abū Tammām, whether or not he witnessed any of the fighting himself, must have proceeded in similar fashion, picking out reports from different parts of the palace and the battlefield and blending them in a single viewpoint.

It must be stressed, though, that, in terms of stylistic and thematic conventions, no two pieces of writing could be more unalike than al-Ṭabarī's narratives and Abū Tammām's *qaṣīda*. Although their main accounts of the campaign are constructed on broadly similar principles and out of similar reports, Abū Tammām leads his listener through a series of increasingly simple resolutions, while al-Ṭabarī subjects his readers to a sequence of disillusionments. His narrative framework establishes a contrast between the noble simplicity of the campaign's inception, the near-disaster of the waterless march home in the first narrative, and the closing catalogue of sadistic executions in the second. Where Abū Tammām uses a combination of anticipation and flashback to show all events converging on the same triumphant outcome, al-Ṭabarī fills in his antithetical frame by combining narrative threads in such a way as gradually to disclose the formidable accumulation of odds that al-Muʿtaṣim had to contend with. He then shows in detail the grimness of their resolution, which is brought about by a mixture of chance (discord and unpreparedness in both the Christian ranks and those of the plotters) and of al-Muʿtaṣim's own iron nerve, ruthlessness, planning, and ability to improvise. The first narrative ends with a brief chronology, al-Ḥusayn b. al-Ḍaḥḥāk's verses in praise of al-Afshīn, and the terse mention that 'in [this] year, al-Muʿtaṣim imprisoned al-ʿAbbās b. al-Maʾmūn and ordered him to be publicly cursed' (*SS*, 119–21). The second concludes, with equal dispassion: 'The remainder of the commanders, comprising Turks ... and others, none of whose names have been preserved, were killed in their entirety. Al-Muʿtaṣim reached Sāmarrā safely and in the best of circumstances. On that day al-ʿAbbās [whose death was described three pages before] was publicly called "The Accursed One" [and his siblings consigned to custody, where they died]' (*SS*, 133–4, 130).

What this reflects overall, in terms of al-Muʿtaṣim's public relations, is a quite different aspect from that elaborated by Abū Tammām: the politics of terror instead of the rhetoric of *jihād* and unity. Only the passages which show the caliph's eagerness to become a *ghāzī*, and the passage in which he restores order among his troops and prevents them dying of thirst (*Taʾrīkh* [iii], 1255; *SS*, 119), can be identified with the message of the *qaṣīda*.

The fact remains that there is a substantial degree of factual agreement between al-Ṭabarī's Amorium chronicle and Abū Tammām's *qaṣīda* – the latter, as an undoubtedly contemporary source, serving to confirm the former, rather than *vice versa*. (No other early accounts of the campaign are so detailed, have so many points in common, or show anything like the same degree of interpretative coherence.) Both are also practised pieces of writing which assume a practised audience. Their overlaps provide a useful basis for considering some of the technical, rather than thematic, assumptions that underlie the management of historical narrative. A parallel between poetry and historiography is neither forced nor anachronistic. Whoever read history also read poetry; whoever composed poetry, especially political poetry, was necessarily familiar with historical *akhbār*. To this extent, the historian and the poet were each conscious of what could be accomplished by the other. The reason for hesitating to bracket them on a functional level is that the historian worked at a remove from his subject-matter and usually from his audience as well. The court poet was under the immediate eye of his political master, which made the terms of his task very different, even though he might use the same *akhbār* as the historian, capturing them at source where the historian had access to them only through a chain of intermediaries.

VII

Within the Arabic cultural complex, poetry, not unlike jurisprudence as Norman Calder has characterized it, was pulled between 'transmission and creativity', and as with *fiqh*, on occasion 'normative and virtuoso patterning' could seemingly 'become ends in themselves ... primary generators of change and development' in the formation of a body of thought.[114] How far the reiteration of poetic themes and structures is normative and how far creative has recently been discussed extensively, with reference to points on the time-scale ranging from the pre-Islamic *qaṣīda* and Umayyad panegyric to ʿAbbasid ceremonial poetry and early twentieth-century Egyptian *rithāʾ*.[115] One conclusion to emerge is that stereotyping could be used to harness poetry to new functions, by giving a pedigree, 'classical' depth and a familiar framework of meaning to new ideas. It should be added, though, that ʿAbbasid poetry, for all its reliance on intertextual reference, was not self-contained, but, on the market level, was written to serve social needs and ideological interests. One reason for thematic and stylistic stereotyping was that poetry would have lost its prestige had it simply followed demand without imposing its own norms. Thus it not only absorbed surrounding thought, but shaped it to its own conventions. This in turn allowed virtuoso poets to dictate to the market and broaden the range and social reach of poetic discourse, whether innovative or banal. The circle of reactions thus established was elastic and far from wholly predictable. This is especially true of the third century AH, a period of simultaneous diversification and intense stereotyping. The well-attested interdependence of ʿAbbasid love poetry and occasional poetry and of romantic anecdotes, social codes of sentiment, etiquette and material artefacts is one example of such reciprocity, of which prose was the major beneficiary. A less foreseeable but no less momentous transaction was the transformation of logical and theological categories of argument into systems of imaginative association and reasoning in poetry (*badīʿ*, and ultimately *al-madhhab al-kalāmī*, of which Abū Tammām was the exemplar). As medieval scholars observed, the poets of this period also made a practice of transposing *maʿānī*, poetic themes, from one poetic genre into another. Abū Tammām's Amorium poem goes further, and

---

114 Calder, *Studies in Early Muslim Jurisprudence*, 192, 199.

115 See e.g. J. E. Montgomery, *The Vagaries of the Qaṣīda: The Tradition and Practice of Early Arabic Poetry*, n. p. [Aris and Phillips for] E. J. W. Gibb Memorial Trust 1997; Suzanne Pinckney Stetkevych, "ʿUmayyad Panegyric and the Poetics of Islamic Hegemony: al-Akhṭal's *Khaffa al-Qaṭīnu* ('Those that dwelt with you have left in haste')", *JAL*, 28 (1997), 89–122; Andras Hamori, *The Composition of Mutanabbī's Panegyrics to Sayf al-Dawla*, Leiden 1992; Yaseen Nourani, "A Nation Born in Mourning: The Neoclassical Funeral Elegy in Egypt", *JAL*, 28 (1997), 38–67.

transposes generic techniques, under cover of which it also succeeds in absorbing well-established *prose* topoi (and indeed sacred ones) into its scheme.

Within this nexus of interactions, the use (in the slightly later sources cited here) of anecdote to give a context to poetry, and especially of poetry to illustrate historical accounts, should not be dismissed as trivial. On the one hand, panegyric poets lived by political guesswork; the dedications of their poems can show what sources of power they had access to, and the structure of an anecdote may be a starting point for trying to retrace the configurations of influence in which they were involved. On the other, their poetry registers responses to ephemeral political factors that retrospective prose accounts regularize or omit. ʿAbbasid historians seem to have acknowledged as much by selecting poetic sources with as much care as narrative ones; al-Ṭabarī's and al-Masʿūdī's choices of verse connected with the Amorium campaign are evidence of this (see Part II above, last paragraph). Poems may similarly be looked to as an immediate embodiment of ʿAbbasid thought, rather than merely as supporting evidence for its reconstruction. Thus the Amorium *qaṣīda* not merely supports the thesis that al-Muʿtaṣim's court was not Muʿtazilī; it also gives some indication of the flavour of the ideas circulating there, and again, no doubt – and no less importantly – of their ephemerality, exploited to serve a particular occasion and then abandoned.

To be read fully, ʿAbbasid poetry should therefore certainly be read in context; the problem, as with *fiqh*, is to pin down the context and see what aspects of a poem are genuinely likely to have been determined by it. Leaving aside the question of the many shorter pieces that are variously attributed and undatable, biographical information on even major poets such as Abū Tammām is sketchy, and their intellectual terms of reference must be deduced chiefly from the design of their poems. The fact of a poem's having been composed for a particular person or occasion does not mean that the dedicatee approved its programme, still less that he dictated it, since poems were written on spec, remained the property of their authors, and might be recycled (and even re-dedicated).

Abū Tammām's poem celebrating the caliph al-Muʿtaṣim's capture of the Byzantine fortress of Amorium in 223/838 has as clear a context as one could hope for, yet it is sparsely documented in the surviving sources closest to the event. Though it soon became a favourite, and is famous to the point of being over-familiar, there is no evidence that it was a success with the caliph. It was, typically, a speculative venture, and can only be approached speculatively by modern critics. In many ways it remains problematic on the level of basic understanding. The most comprehensive English discussion of it has been that of Suzanne Pinckney Stetkevych. Her arguments are of particular value for being set within a framework of enquiry which, for the first time in English, tries to show an ʿAbbasid poet's general involvement in the ideas and ideologies of his time. Nevertheless, her discussion of the poem seems to me too abstract, in terms of the poem's function, and even in terms of Abū Tammām's own poetic ideas and techniques, leaving aside the question of how accurate and apposite her conception of the Muʿtazilism of this period may be and the fact that she does not examine the theological options with which she contrasts it.[116]

Quite different approaches to the poem and to the circumstances that gave rise to it are possible, and in my own analysis, I have tried to show that it is topical in specific senses, and that there is evidence that makes it possible to speculate about its purpose, and the way in which Abū Tammām designed it to be received, in reasonably concrete (even if sometimes negative) terms. This analysis rests on the principle of not deleting topical or routine conceptual connotations that are felt by some modern readers to be inappropriate to what they see as the generic conventions of ʿAbbasid panegyric and its limited effectual range,[117] and I have assumed that a *qaṣīda* is capable of sustaining the construction of thought as well as the deployment of 'poetic principles'. The Amorium *qaṣīda*, to use a phrase of Stetkevych's own, 'interprets history', but it does so actively and not as a ritual gesture, for it is intimately engaged in a dangerous and crucial series of happenings. Thus I have tried to show that, despite Abū Tammām's reputation for logic-chopping and philosophizing, learned theology does not seem, historically or on the internal literary evidence of the poem, to be a relevant point of reference. On the other hand, popular, or populist, religious ideas do; and although they are recast in *badīʿ* terms, at key points in the poem they echo the rousing simplicity of their *futūḥ* prototypes. The result is a poem which combines narrative excitement with densely plotted orchestration[118] and near-flawless psychological coherence; the poem is neither banal in terms of its expressivity (this is especially true of its handling of visual experience) nor lacking in intellectual sinew. (It is both hard-hitting and persuasively devious, so much so that its version of events has barely been challenged even by modern critics unhappy with its violence, even though they have sought to privilege its aesthetic harmony over its message.) Abū Tammām's versatility across a range of poetic genres is itself good grounds for being prepared to accept that his *madhhab kalāmī* might be capable of absorbing more than one current of ideas. In this instance, he shaped it to what he calculated to be the prevailing populist mood.

---

116 Her earlier analysis of the poem gave greater emphasis to 'Islamic' thought, without trying to link it to Muʿtazilism, but already considered Jāhilī concepts to provide not only 'the language and imagery by which the city and its conquest are described' but also the poem's 'inner structure', "The ʿAbbāsid Poet Interprets History: Three Qaṣīdahs by Abū Tammām", *JAL*, 10 (1979), 64.

117 The seminal examples of a more circumstantial approach to ʿAbbasid panegyric are J. D. Latham, "Towards a Better Understanding of al-Mutanabbī's Poem on the Battle of al-Ḥadath", *JAL*, 10 (1979), 1–22, and Hamori, *The Composition of Mutanabbī's Panegyrics*.

118 To borrow a musical metaphor from Hamori, who has also analysed the poetic management of visual perspectives and their functions in detail with reference to al-Mutanabbī, see *The Composition of Mutanabbī's Panegyrics*, *passim*.

A propos du *Kitāb al-radd ʿalā al-Shāfiʿī* attribué à Abū Bakr Muḥammad Ibn al-Labbād al-Qayrawānī (m. 333/944) et des réfutations de Shāfiʿī dans le mālikisme ancien[*]

Éric Chaumont (CNRS, Aix-en-Provence)

Le livre de la réfutation de Shāfiʿī (*K. al-radd ʿalā al-Shāfiʿī*) attribué à Abū Bakr Muḥammad Ibn al-Labbād al-Qayrawānī (m. 333/944) est l'un des derniers maillons d'une longue tradition mālikite de controverse directement dirigée contre la pensée ou la personne de Shāfiʿī (m. 204/820). C'est aussi le seul témoin de cette tradition qui soit parvenu jusqu'à nous en son intégralité grâce à un *unicum* de la bibliothèque de Kairouan,[1] où sont également conservés quelques fragments plus anciens de *La preuve en matière de réfutation de l'Imām al-Shāfiʿī* (*al-ḥujja fī al-radd ʿalā al-Imām al-Shāfiʿī*) de Yaḥyā b. ʿUmar (m. 289/902).

On s'explique facilement l'existence, chez les mālikites, d'une tradition anti-shāfiʿienne, visant les enseignements de Shāfiʿī en personne. Mālik b. Anas (m. 179/795) fut le principal maître de Shāfiʿī; durant une petite dizaine d'années, à Médine, il fréquenta assidûment son cercle. Après plusieurs années de pérégrinations dans l'Empire musulman,[2] Shāfiʿī s'installe vers 198/813 à Fusṭāṭ en Égypte où il est fort bien accueilli par la grande famille mālikite des Banū ʿAbd al-Ḥakam qui le considérait probablement comme l'un des leurs. Muḥammad b. ʿAbdallāh b. ʿAbd al-Ḥakam (m. 268/882), sur le conseil de son père, devint son disciple. Plus tard, il écrira une réfutation de Shāfiʿī sur laquelle nous reviendrons parce qu'elle est, je pense, au principe du livre attribué à Ibn al-Labbād le Kairouanais.

Les rapports entre Shāfiʿī et les mālikites égyptiens se dégradèrent rapidement et gravement. La raison principale en est qu'à Fusṭāṭ, Shāfiʿī rédigea un traité très critique à l'endroit de la pensée légale de Mālik, traité connu sous le titre de *Kitāb ikhtilāf Mālik wa'l-Shāfiʿī* (*Le livre de la divergence entre Mālik et Shāfiʿī*). Ce livre fut justement considéré par les mālikites comme une 'réfutation' de Mālik (Ibn al-Labbād l'appelle le *Kitāb al-radd ʿalā Mālik*,[3] *Le livre de la réfutation de Mālik*). Par ailleurs, bien des

---

* Ce texte reprend, sous une forme très remaniée, une communication orale faite lors du colloque *al-Qayrawān markaz ʿilmī mālikī bayna al-Mashriq wa'l-Maghrib ḥattā al-qarn al-khāmis* li'l-ḥijra, Kairouan en avril 1994. Je remercie mon collègue et ami Mounir Arbach pour sa relecture de mon texte.

1 Abū Bakr Muḥammad b. al-Labbād al-Qayrawānī, *Kitāb al-radd ʿalā al-Shāfiʿī* (éd. Dr ʿAbd al-Majīd b. Ḥamduh), Tunis 1986 (désormais *Radd* dans les notes).

1 Abū Bakr Muḥammad b. al-Labbād al-Qayrawānī, *Kitāb al-radd ʿalā al-Shāfiʿī* (éd. Dr ʿAbd al-Majīd b. Ḥamduh), Tunis 1986 (désormais *Radd* dans les notes).

2 Pour plus de détails sur la biographie de Shāfiʿī, v. É. Chaumont dans *EI2*, ix, 187–91.

3 V., par exemple, *Radd*, 72.

passages de la seconde version de la *Risāla*, également rédigée par Shāfiʿī en Égypte, pouvaient être lus comme des critiques s'adressant aussi, et parfois en priorité, à la pensée légale de Mālik ou, plus précisément, au manque de fondements théoriques (*uṣūl*) de sa doctrine et des principes censés l'établir. L'indépendance affichée de Shāfiʿī vis-à-vis de toutes les autorités de son temps (qui n'est que la traduction pratique de la critique radicale du 'conformisme' [*taqlīd*] exposée dans la *Risāla*) lui attira naturellement la rancœur de ceux qui se réclamaient de l'une ou l'autre de ces autorités. Si cette inimitié prit un tour aussi violent du côté des mālikites,[4] c'est que ceux-ci voyaient la critique shāfiʿienne de Mālik comme une forfaiture et ils la vivaient comme une désillusion; Shāfiʿī était un disciple – et pas n'importe lequel: le plus brillant de sa génération – qui avait trahi le Maître. Telle est l'origine du phénomène des réfutations de Shāfiʿī au sein du mālikisme ancien: il s'agit de la riposte mālikite au *Kitāb ikhtilāf Mālik wa'l-Shāfiʿī* de Shāfiʿī.

Dans les pages qui suivent, j'aimerais tenter d'éclaircir une question que soulève *Le livre de la réfutation de Shāfiʿī* d'Abū Bakr b. al-Labbād. Elle est relative au statut de cet ouvrage en tant qu' 'écrit' par rapport à la tradition, foncièrement orale, dont il est issu. Je tâcherai de montrer pourquoi et comment il faut considérer cet ouvrage comme la dernière version d'une série de feuillets dont l'origine remonte à Muḥammad b. ʿAbdallāh b. ʿAbd al-Ḥakam: problématique qui concerne la transmission du savoir dans le contexte de l' 'ordre légal' (*al-sharʿiyyāt*) durant la période cruciale où il passe de l'oralité à l'écriture et se métamorphose en conséquence.

Le Kitāb al-radd ʿalā al-Shāfiʿī *d'Abū Bakr b. al-Labbād: un 'écrit' issu de la tradition orale ?*

En partant de la plus ancienne, la liste des réfutations mālikites de Shāfiʿī antérieures à celle d'Ibn al-Labbād est la suivante:

1) Muḥammad b. Saḥnūn (m. 256/870, d'origine syrienne, installé à Kairouan): *Kitāb al-radd ʿalā al-Shāfiʿī wa-ʿalā ahl al-ʿIrāq* 'en cinq livres (*kutub*)';[5]

2) Ḥammād b. Isḥāq (m. 267/880 en Irak; le frère d'Ismāʿīl b. Isḥāq al-Qāḍī): *Kitāb al-radd ʿalā al-Shāfiʿī;*[6]

3) Muḥammad b. ʿAbdallāh b. ʿAbd al-Ḥakam (m. 268/882 en Égypte): *Kitāb al-radd ʿalā al-Shāfiʿī fīmā khālafa fīhi al-Kitāb wa'l-Sunna;*[7]

---

4 Rappelons que selon certaines sources, Shāfiʿī mourut des suites d'une blessure que lui avait infligée un mālikite fanatisé.

5 *ʿIyāḍ* (= al-Qāḍī ʿIyāḍ, *Tartīb al-madārik wa-taqrīb al-masālik li-maʿrifat aʿlām madhhab Mālik*, i–vii [éd. royale marocaine], Rabat 1982), iv, 207; *Ibn Farḥūn* (= Ibn Farḥūn al-Mālikī, *Al-Dībāj al-mudhahhab fī maʿrifat aʿyān ʿulamāʾ al-madhhab* [éd. Abū an-Nūr], i-ii, Le Caire s. d.) ii, 169–73.

6 *ʿIyāḍ*, ii, 181–2; *Ibn Farḥūn*, i, 341.

7 *ʿIyāḍ*, iv, 160; *Ibn Farḥūn*, ii, 163–5; Tāj al-Dīn al-Subkī, *Ṭabaqāt al-shāfʿiyya al-kubrā*, i–x (éd. al-Ṭanāḥī et al-Ḥulw), Le Caire 1964–7, ii, 67–71.

4) ʿAbdallāh b. Ṭālib al-Qāḍī Abū al-ʿAbbās (m. 275/888–9) a écrit un ouvrage de réfutation de Shāfiʿī;[8]

5) Ismāʿīl b. Isḥāq al-Qāḍī (m. 282/895 en Irak): *Kitāb al-radd ʿalā al-Shāfiʿī;*[9]

6) Yūsuf Abū ʿUmar al-Maghāmī (m. 288/901 à Kairouan) a écrit un ouvrage 'virulent' en dix parties (*ajzāʾ*) contre Shāfiʿī;[10]

7) Yaḥyā b. ʿUmar b. Yūsuf b. ʿĀmir (m. 289/902 à Sousse): *Kitāb al-ḥujja fī al-radd ʿalā al-Shāfiʿī;*[11]

8) Aḥmad b. Marwān b. Muḥammad (Abū Bakr al-Mālikī al-Miṣrī, m. 298/910 en Égypte): *Kitāb al-radd ʿalā al-Shāfiʿī;*[12]

9) Abū ʿUthmān Saʿīd b. Muḥammad b. al-Ḥaddād (m. 302/914): *Kitāb al-Radd ʿalā al-Shāfiʿī.*[13]

De cette 'littérature', nous ne sommes ici directement concernés que par les *kutub* attribués à Muḥammad b. ʿAbd al-Ḥakam, ʿAbdallāh b. Ṭālib al-Qāḍī, Yūsuf Abū ʿUmar al-Maghāmī, Yaḥyā b. ʿUmar et à Abū Bakr b. al-Labbād (j'ai signalé déjà que seuls quelques fragments du texte de Yaḥyā b. ʿUmar ont été conservés ainsi que le texte d'Ibn al-Labbād). Pour ce qui est du *Kitāb* de Yaḥyā, son titre complet est très vraisemblablement: *Kitāb al-ḥujja fī al-radd ʿalā al-Shāfiʿī fīmā [khālafa fīhi] Kitāb Allāh – tabāraka wa-taʿāla! – wa-sunnat nabiyih Muḥammad – ṣlʿm! –.*[14] Quant au texte d'Ibn al-Labbād, qui fut élève de Yaḥyā b. ʿUmar,[15] son titre complet est le suivant: *Kitāb fīhi radd ʿalā Muḥammad b. Idrīs al-Shāfiʿī fī munāqaḍa qawlih wa fīmā qāla bihi min al-taḥdīd fī masāʾil khālafa fīhā al-Kitāb waʾl-sunna.* L'un et l'autre de ces deux titres rappellent (le second sous une forme allongée) celui de l'ouvrage, perdu, qui est attribué à Muḥammad b. ʿAbdallāh b. ʿAbd al-Ḥakam (*Kitāb al-radd ʿalā al-Shāfiʿī fīmā khālafa fīh al-Kitāb waʾl-sunna*).

Mon hypothèse est que l'archétype du *Kitāb fīhi radd ʿalā Muḥammad b. Idrīs al-Shāfiʿī fī munāqaḍa qawlihi wa-fīmā qāla bihi min al-taḥdīd fī masāʾil khālafa*

---

[8] *ʿIyāḍ*, iv, 310.
[9] *Ibn Farḥūn*, i, 282–90.
[10] *Ibn Farḥūn*, ii, 366; *Shīrāzī* (=Abū Isḥāq al-Shīrāzī al-Shāfiʿī, *Ṭabaqāt al-fuqahāʾ* [éd. Iḥsān ʿAbbās], Beyrouth 1981), 163.
[11] *Ibn Farḥūn*, ii, 354–7.
[12] D'origine irakienne, Abū Bakr al-Mālikī eut Ismāʿīl al-Qāḍī pour maître. Traditionniste, peu fiable selon Dāraquṭnī, il s'installa et finit sa vie en Égypte. Outre une réfutation de Shāfiʿī, on lui attribue un *K. fī faḍāʾil Mālik* et un *K. al-mujālasa*; v. *Ibn Farḥūn*, i, 152–3.
[13] Abū al-ʿArab Muḥammad b. Aḥmad b. Tamīm al-Qayrawānī, *Classe des savants de l'Ifrīqīya* (trad. M. Ben Cheneb, Argel 1920), 234–6. Bakr b. al-ʿAlāʾ al-Qushayrī (m. 344/955), Muḥammad Abū Bakr al-Abharī (m. 395/1005) et Aḥmad b. Abī Yaʿlā (m. 400/1009) réfutèrent également Shāfiʿī (ou Muzanī dans le cas du deuxième) dans l'un ou l'autre de leurs écrits, v. *Ibn Farḥūn* i, 313–5; ii, 206–10 et i, 173. Deux autres mālikites irakiens ont réfuté Shāfiʿī: Aḥmad b. Abī Yaʿlā (*K. al-radd ʿalā al-Shāfiʿī*) et Aḥmad b. Muḥammad b. ʿUmar al-Dahhān (*K. fī naqḍ kitāb al-Shāfiʿī*) mais Ibn Farḥūn ne précise pas les dates de ces légistes, v. *Ibn Farḥūn* i, 173.
[14] Dr Muḥammad Abū al-Ajfān, "Yaḥyā b. ʿUmar min khilāl kitābihi *Al-ḥujja fī al-radd ʿala al-Imām al-Shāfiʿī*" (dans *Majalla maʿhad al–makhṭūṭāt al ʿarabiyya*, xxix/2 [1405–6/1985), 713–47 [désormais *Yaḥyā b. ʿUmar* dans les notes]), 732 où Abū al-Ajfān signale que le titre du traité est: *Kitāb al-ḥujja fī al-radd ʿalā al-Shāfiʿī*, suivi de deux mots 'illisibles', suivi de *min Kitāb Allāh tabāraka wa-taʿālā wa-sunnat nabiyih Muḥammad ṣlʿm.*
[15] *Ibn Farḥūn*, ii, 354.

fīhā al-Kitāb wa'l-sunna justement attribué à Abū Bakr b. al-Labbād est le texte de Muḥammad b. ʿAbdallāh b. ʿAbd al-Ḥakam, ou, plus précisément, que les *dires* consignés de ce dernier (par lui-même ou par l'un de ses disciples immédiats) sont à l'origine du texte d'Ibn al-Labbād, que cet écrit ne contient probablement rien d'original mais qu'en revanche il reflète directement, avec un degré de fidélité difficile à déterminer précisément, les controverses ayant opposé Shāfiʿī et Muḥammad b. ʿAbdallāh b. ʿAbd al-Ḥakam.

Muḥammad b. ʿAbd al-Ḥakam[16] (182–268/799–882) suivit l'enseignement de Shāfiʿī et, selon le shāfiʿite Abū Isḥāq al-Shīrāzī (qui ne lui attribue aucune réfutation de Shāfiʿī), il resta son disciple jusquà la fin de sa vie de sorte que dans son *Répertoire des légistes*, il le compte pleinement parmi les shāfiʿites.[17] La grande majorité des biographes le rangent pourtant parmi les mālikites tout en signalant qu'il fut pour un temps proche de Shāfiʿī avant de se rétracter (*rujūʿ*) et de réintégrer les rangs du mālikisme de ses pères. Telle est sans doute la relation la plus exacte des faits. Ghazālī,[18] qui admet la rétractation de Muḥammad b. ʿAbd al-Ḥakam, l'explique par des raisons personnelles peu avantageuses (une banale affaire de jalousie entre disciples 'préférés' du Maître) et laisse ainsi entendre que sa rétractation ainsi que son *kitāb* anti-shāfiʿien ne doivent guère être pris au sérieux. Le son de cloche est évidemment bien différent chez les biographes mālikites. C'est au terme d'un examen critique de la doctrine shāfiʿienne aux résultats négatifs que Muḥammad cessa d'y adhérer. On croira plus pertinemment, à mon sens, qu'en se mettant à l'écoute de Shāfiʿī, Muḥammad était en réalité convaincu qu'il restait dans le sillage de Mālik et qu'il se rendit compte de sa méprise lorsque son nouveau maître se montra trop critique et trop indépendant vis-à-vis de Mālik dans son *Kitāb ikhtilāf Mālik wa'l-Shāfiʿī*. Ayant rompu avec Shāfiʿī, il rédigea alors son *Kitāb al-radd ʿalā al-Shāfiʿī fīmā khālafa fīhi al-kitāb wa'l-sunna*. Cet écrit est perdu, nous n'en avons aucune description et pourtant nous en conservons probablement la substance.

ʿAbdallāh b. Ṭālib al-Qāḍī[19] (227–275/841/2–888/9) fut cadi de Kairouan à deux reprises. Parmi ses maîtres, l'on compte Saḥnūn à Kairouan et Muḥammad b. ʿAbd al-Ḥakam en Égypte. Plus réputé comme orateur que comme écrivain, il écrivit néanmoins 'pour réfuter les contradicteurs de Mālik', notamment Shāfiʿī. Ibn al-Labbād suivit son enseignement et le tenait en très haute estime.[20]

Yūsuf Abū ʿUmar al-Maghāmī[21] (m. 288/901 à Kairouan) grandit et reçut sa première formation à Cordoue auprès notamment de Yaḥyā b. Yaḥyā. Il s'installa un temps en Égypte, voyagea dans le Ḥijāz et au Yémen avant de s'installer définitivement à

16 *ʿIyāḍ*, iv, 157–65.
17 *Shīrāzī*, 99.
18 D'après *ʿIyāḍ*, iv, 160 qui conteste cette version des faits.
19 *ʿIyāḍ*, iv, 308–31; *Ibn Farḥūn*, i, 421–3.
20 *ʿIyāḍ*,v, 286.
21 *Ibn Farḥūn*, ii, 365–6.

Kairouan où Ibn al-Labbād suivit son enseignement (*akhadha ʿan*).[22] 'Il était virulent à l'encontre de Shāfiʿī et rédigea (*waḍaʿa*) [un texte] en dix parties à fin de la réfuter'.[23]

Yaḥyā b. ʿUmar[24] (213/828 à Cordoue–289/902 à Sousse) exerça son activité de légiste principalement à Kairouan. Ce fut également un grand voyageur; sa *riḥla* le mena jusqu'au Ḥijāz en passant par l'Égypte où il fréquenta la plupart des maîtres mālikites. Le Cadi ʿIyāḍ ne signale pas Muḥammad b. ʿAbd al-Ḥakam parmi les gens qu'il fréquenta en Égypte. Mais, à en croire l'un des fragments conservés de sa réfutation de Shāfiʿī , c'est bel et bien directement d'après Muḥammad b. ʿAbd al-Ḥakam qu'il transmit une partie de la substance de ce *kitāb* (en d'autres occurrences, Yaḥyā b. ʿUmar se réfère à la doctrine de Shāfiʿī *via* le *Mukhtaṣar* de Muzanī).[25] On lui attribue une œuvre écrite considérable. Yaḥyā b. ʿUmar fut l'un des maîtres d'Ibn al-Labbād, apparemment le plus important puisqu'on le range parmi ses 'disciples' (*min aṣḥāb Yaḥyā b. ʿUmar*).[26]

A l'inverse de ses trois maîtres kairouanais et de tant de ses contemporains, Abū Bakr b. al-Labbād[27] fut un sédentaire invétéré: il n'accomplit ni *riḥla* ni même le pèlerinage. Toute sa science fut acquise à Kairouan où trois de ses maîtres sont réputés avoir écrit une réfutation de Shāfiʿī. C'est donc très certainement là qu'il faut chercher les sources immédiates du *K. al-radd ʿalā al-Shāfiʿī*, et, par l'intermédiaire de ces sources, la réfutation d'Ibn al-Labbād se trouve ainsi reliée à celle de Muḥammad b. ʿAbd al-Ḥakam.[28]

L'attribution du *K. al-radd ʿalā al-Shāfiʿī* à Ibn al-Labbād pose pourtant le problème suivant: aucun biographe ne le cite dans la bibliographie d'Ibn al-Labbād. C'est étonnant dans la mesure où Ibn al-Labbād était fort loin d'être une personnalité peu connue et qu'une œuvre faite de textes précisément déterminés lui est attribuée.[29] On reviendra sur ce silence des biographes. Qu'il s'agisse pourtant bien d'un texte, ou d'une 'transmission' (*riwāya*), d'Ibn al-Labbād (ou, plus précisément, d'un texte directement transmis d'après Ibn al-Labbād par son élève Abū ʿAbdallāh Muḥammad b. Ḥārith al-Khushanī) paraît hors de doute; son éditeur, ʿAbd al-Majīd b. Ḥamduh, en a fait la démonstration irréfutable.[30]

On peut ainsi tracer le tableau généalogique du *K. al-radd* d'Ibn al-Labbad:

22 *ʿIyāḍ*, v, 286.
23 Shīrāzī cité en *Ibn Farḥūn*, ii, 266.
24 *ʿIyāḍ*, iv, 357–64.
25 *Yaḥyā b. ʿUmar*, 734.
26 *ʿIyāḍ*,v, 286.
27 *ʿIyāḍ*, v, 286–95.
28 Ibn Ṭālib fréquenta Muḥammad b. ʿAbd al-Ḥakam lors de son séjour en Égypte (v. *ʿIyāḍ*, iv, 308) de même, très probablement, que Yaḥyā b. ʿUmar le rencontra également.
29 Le Cadi ʿIyāḍ lui attribue les ouvrages suivants: *K. al-ṭahāra*, *K. ʿiṣma al-nabiyīn (= K. ithbāt al-ḥujja fī bayān al-ʿiṣma)*, *K. faḍāʾil Mālik b. Anas* et le *K. al-āthār waʾl-fawāʾid* 'en dix parties', v. *ʿIyāḍ*, v, 288.
30 *Radd*, 33–5.

K. fīhi radd ʿalā Muḥammad b. Idrīs al-Shāfiʿī fī munāqaḍa qawlihi wa-fīmā qāla bihi min al-taḥḍīd fī masāʾil qālahā (sic) *khālafa fīhā al-kitāb waʾl-sunna* (Abū Bakr Ibn al-Labbād, m. 333/944, Kairouan)

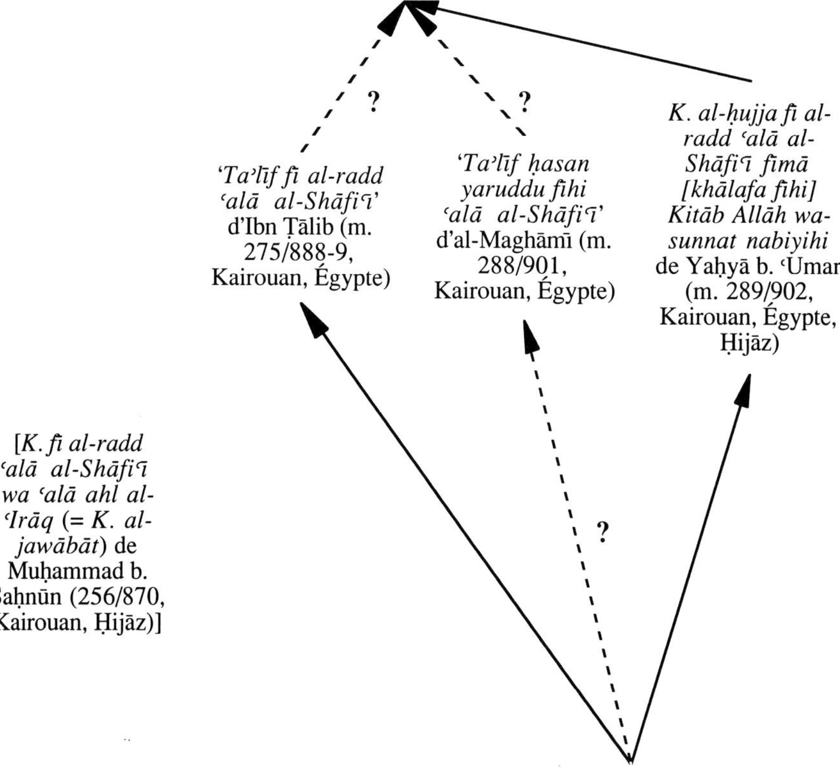

K. al-radd ʿalā al-Shāfiʿī fīmā khālafa fīhi al-Kitāb waʾl-sunna de Muḥammad b. ʿAbdallāh b. ʿAbd al-Ḥakam (m. 268/882, Égypte)

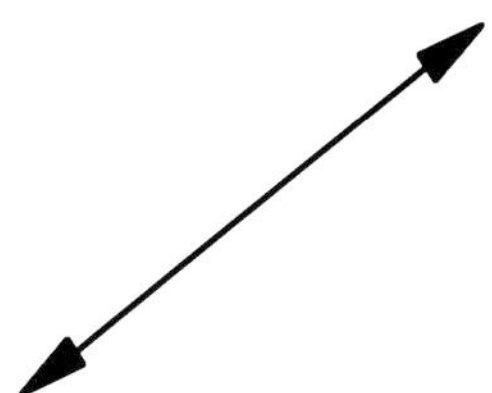

[*K. ikhtilāf Mālik waʾl-Shāfiʿī* (=*K. al-radd ʿalā Mālik* mentionné par Ibn al-Labbād) de Muḥammad b. Idrīs al-Shāfiʿī (m. 204/820)]

Le *K. al-radd ʿalā al-Shāfiʿī* d'Ibn al-Labbād n'est pas un livre 'homogène'. Entrant immédiatement dans le vif du sujet, sans du tout l'introduire, l'auteur y aborde 36 questions controversées entre Mālik et Shāfiʿī, questions relèvant autant des *ʿibādāt* que des *muʿāmalāt*.

La première question est introduite de la sorte: *Bāb mā qāla al-Shāfiʿī fī al-taḥdīd fī masāʾil shattā bi-raʾyihi. Abū ʿAbdallāh qāla qāla lanā Abū Bakr b. Muḥammad qāla Muḥammad b. Idrīs al-Shāfiʿī* ... Titre qui laisse entendre que nous avons là un premier chapitre (*bāb*) de l'ouvrage, qui sera suivi d'autres chapitres pareillement signalés. Il n'en est rien; le livre s'achève apparemment sur ce premier, dernier et seul chapitre. Pourtant, une division bipartite du livre s'impose immédiatement dès sa première lecture.

En faisant abstraction des deux premières questions,[31] incomplètement éditées en raison de la mauvaise condition du premier folio du manuscrit, les questions 3 à 15[32] sont toutes présentées de la même manière, sur le canevas suivant: 'Abū Bakr a dit: On a dit à Shāfiʿī: Qui de vous deux suit de plus près le dire du Messager de Dieu, Mālik lorsque ... ou toi lorsque ...?' (*wa ayyukumā atbaʿ/ashadd iʿẓāman li-ḥadīth Rasūl Allāh/limā ruwiya ʿan Rasūl Allāh Mālik ḥīna ... am anta ḥīna ...?*). Le contenu de ce premier ensemble est également homogène. Pour chacune des questions débattues, il est question de la supériorité de Mālik sur Shāfiʿī en ce qui regarde l'usage de 'ce que l'on rapporte d'après le Messager de Dieu'. Seule la *sunna* est ici concernée: alors que Mālik est un exemple de fidélité au modèle prophétique tel que transmis dans le *ḥadīth*, Shāfiʿī est accusé, parfois peu courtoisement,[33] de manipuler, ou d'ignorer, le *ḥadīth* en s'appuyant sur son propre *raʾy*,[34] c'est-à-dire, en langage de l'époque (et conformément à la critique shāfiʿienne du *raʾy* présente dans la *Risāla*), de manière arbitraire, sans preuve (*dalīl*) à l'appui.

Le discours est toujours sur le mode direct. Shāfiʿī y est pris comme interlocuteur immédiat, comme si l'écrit reproduisait mot-à-mot ce qui avait été dit lors d'une séance de *disputatio* (*jadal*). C'est sans doute le cas. Concernant cette première partie de l'ouvrage, on remarquera encore, *primo*, l'absence totale de mention de légiste faisant autorité antérieur à Ibn al-Labbād (il en va comme si celui-ci s'adressait à Shāfiʿī en personne), et, *secundo*, qu'il est souvent fait référence à la doctrine de Shāfiʿī telle qu'exposée dans '[son] (dans le texte: 'ton')' ou '[ses] ('tes') livre(s)'.[35]

La seconde partie de l'ouvrage diffère considérablement de la première. La présentation des débats se fait sur un modèle différent, plus 'classique' ('Shāfiʿī a dit ... On

---

31 *Radd*, 47–9.

32 *Radd*, 49–75.

33 *Radd*, 51: 'Tu dis que Mālik – Dieu soit satisfait de lui! – parle en fonction du comble de l'ignorance (*qāla bi-ghāya al-jahl*) alors que l'ignorance est plus proche de toi!'

34 Par exemple: *Radd*, 66 (*Innamā takallamta fī dhālika bi-raʾyik*).

35 *Radd*, 54 et 58 par exemple.

lui dira/Nous lui disons ...' (*wa-qāla al-Shāfiʿī ... fa-yuqāl lahu/fa-qulnā lahu ...*) et il est appliqué de façon moins systématique. La matière est plus vaste en ce sens que les questions abordées n'ont pas toutes le *ḥadīth* comme fondement: Shāfiʿī s'y voit aussi reprocher des interprétations erronées du Coran,[36] d'enfreindre l'Accord unanime (*al-ijmāʿ*)[37] et des raisonnements (*qiyās*) fautifs.[38]

Alors que l'homogénéité formelle et matérielle de la première partie du *K. al-radd* lui procure une réelle unité, on a plutôt affaire ici à un assemblage disparate de questions dont le seul point commun est la critique de Shāfiʿī. Chacun des chapitres abordés se présente d'ailleurs comme une unité autonome par l'usage répété d'une courte formule pieuse de clôture (le plus souvent: *wa-billāh al-tawfīq*).

Mais c'est surtout en ce qui regarde les *isnād*s que les choses changent spectaculairement: ils abondent alors qu'ils étaient inexistants auparavant. Chacune, ou presque, des questions abordées s'accompagne de la citation d'un ou de plusieurs *ḥadīth*s qu'Abū Bakr b. al-Labbād tient invariablement de Yaḥyā b. ʿUmar (d'après, le plus souvent Yaḥyā b. ʿAbdallāh b. Bukayr,[39] mais aussi d'après Saḥnūn b. Saʿīd,[40] Abū al-Ṭāhir[41] et d'autres). Est-ce l'indice que l'ensemble de cette seconde partie de l'ouvrage reproduit sous une forme peut-être remaniée le *Kitāb al-ḥujja fī al-radd ʿalā al-Shāfiʿī fīmā [khālafa fīhi] kitāb Allāh wa-sunnat nabiyihi Muḥammad* de Yaḥyā b. ʿUmar? Ce que l'on sait de ce dernier ouvrage d'après ses fragments conservés ne permet pas de l'affirmer de manière péremptoire mais l'hypothèse s'impose.

Deux sections intercalées dans cette seconde partie de l'ouvrage se singularisent. A propos de la question d'*al-yamīn maʿa al-shāhid*,[42] Ibn al-Labbād cite *in extenso* un argument (*ḥujja*) dirigé contre Shāfiʿī qu'il met dans la bouche (*fa-akhbaranī*) d'Ibn Ṭālib. Celui-ci le tenait de Saḥnūn et l'aurait exposé à Muḥammad b. ʿAbd al-Ḥakam qui l'aurait fait sien. La question suivante (*al-tazwīj bi-sūra min al-Qurʾān*) est introduite par un simple *Muḥammad b. ʿAbdallāh b. ʿAbd al-Ḥakam a dit ... (qāla Muḥammad ...)* et l'auteur, en l'occurrence simple transmetteur, n'ajoute rien aux dires de ce dernier ni ne les commente.

Un indice extérieur vient confirmer l'hypothèse selon laquelle la matière du *K. al-radd ʿalā al-Shāfiʿī* d'Ibn al-Labbād n'est pas originale et que ce livre fait écho, certes sous la plume d'Ibn al-Labbād, à des débats plus anciens. Dans la seizième question de l'ouvrage,[43] Ibn al-Labbād s'en prend à Shāfiʿī pour avoir accusé Mālik d'avoir 'falsifié' (*ṣaḥḥafa*) les noms de certains transmetteurs (*ruwāt*) de traditions (en l'occurrence:

[36] *Radd*, 81–3.
[37] *Radd*, 101–5.
[38] *Radd*, 86–7.
[39] Traditionniste égyptien mort en 231/846.
[40] La plus grande autorité du mālikisme kairouanais, auteur de la *Mudawwana*, mort en 240/854.
[41] Abū al-Ṭāhir Aḥmad b. ʿAmr: traditionniste égyptien mort en 250/864.
[42] *Radd*, 78–9.
[43] *Radd*, 75–7.

ʿUmar b. ʿUthmān pour ʿAmr b. Uthmān et ʿAbd al-Malik b. Qurayb pour ʿAbd al-ʿAzīz b. Qurayb). Outré que l'on puisse s'en prendre aussi légèrement à Mālik en matière de *ḥadīth*, Ibn al-Labbād affirme que ces falsifications bien réelles doivent être imputées à des personnes plus tardives ayant transmis du *ḥadīth* d'après Mālik, et non à Mālik lui-même. Cet argument se trouve déjà réfuté chez un auteur shāfiʿite, Ibn Abī Ḥātim al-Rāzī (m. 327/939, soit cinq ans avant Ibn al-Labbād), qui montre que, comme le disait Shāfiʿī, ces erreurs doivent bel et bien être imputées à Mālik lui-même.[44] On peut aussi comparer les développements consacrés à la question d'*al-yamīn maʿa al-shāhid* dans l'un et l'autre livres[45] pour conclure qu'en partie tout au moins, le contenu du *K. al-radd ʿalā al-Shāfiʿī* appartient au fond commun de la polémique mālikite anti-shāfiʿienne dont les origines sont probablement très anciennes, contemporaines de Shāfiʿī et de Muḥammad b. ʿAbdallāh b. ʿAbd al-Ḥakam.

Le *K. al-radd ʿalā al-Shāfiʿī* d'Ibn al-Labbād appartient à la littérature juridique musulmane ancienne à laquelle N. Calder s'était intéressé dans ses *Studies in Early Muslim Jurisprudence* (Oxford 1993). L'étude de ce corpus l'avait amené à reconsidérer la datation de plusieurs de ses textes importants, moins anciens selon lui que ne le veut la tradition musulmane.

Le cas du *K. al-radd ʿalā al-Shāfiʿī* d'Ibn al-Labbād est différent. Rien ne permet de douter de l'attribution, ni de la datation de cet écrit; il s'agit bien, comme l'a établi son éditeur, d'un texte d'Ibn al-Labbād le Kairouanais. Il ne s'agit pas pour autant d'un 'livre', au sens moderne du terme, ayant pour 'auteur' une personne déterminée.

Il apparaît évident que l'écrit d'Ibn al-Labbād amalgame deux textes antérieurs différents. Rien ne permet de déterminer l'origine précise du premier de ces deux textes et il n'est pas exclu que sa forme particulière (*Ayyukumā aṭbaʿ li-ḥadīth Rasūl Allāh ...*) soit du cru d'Ibn al-Labbād. Qu'aucun biographe n'attribue de *K. al-radd ʿalā al-Shāfiʿī* à Ibn al-Labbād amène néanmoins à en douter. Le second texte est plus que vraisemblablement celui, attesté par les biographes, de Yaḥyā b. ʿUmar.

L' 'écrivain' est ici celui 'qui dit' (*qāla*) et dont le dire est consigné. C'est plus précisément celui qui 'transmet' (*rawā*) du savoir (*ʿilm* ou, en l'occurrence, *fiqh*), comme l'on transmet des informations traditionnelles. Le transmetteur rapporte un savoir antérieurement acquis, qui n'est donc pas 'sien' à l'origine, et il se l'approprie en le transmettant à son tour. Lorsque cette transmission se fait par l'écrit, le transmetteur devient écrivain mais il n'est pas l' 'auteur' au sens moderne de cet écrit. Une conception hautement 'dépersonnalisée', ou plus naturellement impersonnelle, de l'ordre du savoir est sous-jacente à cette appropriation en forme de transmission de la science. Cette conception impersonnelle du savoir paraît caractériser l'ordre légal musulman ancien et

44 Abū Muḥammad ʿAbd al-Raḥmān b. Abī Ḥātim al-Rāzī, *Ādāb al-Shāfiʿī wa-manāqibuh* (éd. ʿAbd al-Khāliq), Alep s. d. (désormais *Ādāb*), 224ff.

45 *Radd*, 78–9 et *Ādāb*, 167–9 où Ibn Abī Ḥātim rapporte la controverse en question d'après Muḥammad b. ʿAbdallāh b. ʿAbd al-Ḥakam.

c'est pourquoi la question de l'authenticité des textes légaux musulmans anciens (souvent impossible à résoudre, et pour cause ...) n'est en réalité guère pertinente.

L'une des caractéristiques de l'ordre légal musulman classique, par rapport à l'ancien, est précisément la diminution progressive du caractère impersonnel de la conception du savoir légal (même si l'on y trouve encore quelques exemples flagrants d'appropriation du savoir par transmission).[46] Cette évolution s'explique en partie par la place de mieux en mieux assurée à l'écriture au sein de cet ordre, mouvement progressif qui a métamorphosé l'écriture qui, d'instrument de transmission, à l'instar de la parole, est devenu l'instrument privilégié d'*élaboration* du *fiqh*. C'est seulement à partir de ce moment, me semble-t-il, que pouvait naître une littérature légale musulmane faite de 'livres' ayant un auteur personnel clairement identifiable. Elle croîtra très rapidement en engendrant la monumentale bibliothèque que l'on sait.

[46] En voici deux: le volumineux *Kitāb al-Tamhīd fī uṣūl al-fiqh* du ḥanbalite Kalwadhānī (m. 510/1116) reproduit presque à l'identique la *ʿUdda fī uṣūl al-fiqh* de son maître, le Qāḍī Abū Yaʿlā (m. 458/1066), v. ma recension des éditions de ces deux ouvrages dans *Bulletin Critique des Annales Islamologiques*, 10 (1993), 43–9. De même, le *Kitāb al-lumaʿ fī uṣūl al-fiqh* du shāfiʿite Shīrāzī (m. 476/1083) est textuellement inséré dans le *Kitāb al-faqīh waʾl-mutafaqqih* de son ami traditionniste al-Khaṭīb al-Baghdādī (m. 463/1071). Ni dans un cas, ni dans l'autre, il ne convient de parler de plagiat.

The Khārijites and the caliphal title

Patricia Crone (Institute for Advanced Study, Princeton)

How long did the Khārijites continue to call their imams *khalīfa* and *amīr al-mu'minīn*? According to E. A. Salem, they abandoned both titles at some point, apparently after they had begun to establish local dynasties: 'The title of "Commander of the Believers" is of early usage, at a time when the Khawārij were vigorously undertaking the conversion of the Muslim empire into a model Khāriji state. Since then the title of "Imam" has been more consistently adhered to, while "khalifa" was completely forsaken.'[1] On the basis of Salem, Crone and Hinds conjectured that the Khārijites rejected the caliphal title because it was generally taken to stand for *khalīfat allāh*, 'deputy of God', which did not seem an appropriate title for a Khārijite ruler.[2] But in fact neither Salem's claim nor Crone and Hinds' conjecture is correct. With the exception of the Ibāḍīs of Arabia, all the Khārijites who established local dynasties are on record as having applied the title of *khalīfa* and/or *amīr al-mu'minīn* to their imams; and though the Arabian Ibāḍīs did deem it wrong for a local imam to style himself *amīr al-mu'minīn* (and thus, presumably, also *khalīfa*), this was not because they disapproved of the title 'deputy of God'. In what follows I shall substantiate these points in reverse order.

Khalīfat allāh

Like other early Muslims, the Khārijites, or at least the Ibāḍīs, held righteous rulers to be deputies of God. Thus Wā'il b. Ayyūb al-Ḥaḍramī leader of the Ibāḍīs in Basra from *c.* 170/786 onwards, speaks of the Prophet's *sīra* 'which the imams of justice followed after his death ... and which is practised by God's deputies on earth' (*sāra bihā a'immat al-'adl ba'dahu ... ya'malu bihā khulafā' allāh fī arḍihi*).[3] Abū 'l-Mu'thir, a third/ninth century Omani, specifies that 'the imams are God's trustees and deputies on earth (*umanā' allāh wa-khulafā' allāh fī 'l-arḍ*) as long as they adhere to God's justice and fulfil the compact'.[4] The much later North African Muḥammad b. Zakariyyā' b. Mūsā al-Bārūnī (writing *c.* 970/1562–3) cites a poem by his uncle

[1] E. A. Salem, *Political Theory and Institutions of the Khawārij*, Baltimore 1956, 53.
[2] P. Crone and M. Hinds, *God's Caliph*, Cambridge 1986, 12 n. 16; cf. also 57.
[3] In S. I. Kāshif (ed.), *al-Siyar wa'l-jawabāt*, Cairo (Salṭanat 'Umān, Wizārat al-turāth al-qawmī wa'l-thaqāfa) 1986, ii, 57.9. On him, see P. Crone and F. Zimmermann, *The Epistle of Sālim b. Dhakwān*, forthcoming Oxford 2000, Appendix 1, no. 4.
[4] In Kāshif, *Siyar*, i, 157.8. On him, see Crone and Zimmermann, *Epistle*, Bibliography, section A, s.v.

lamenting 'the Persian deputies of our Lord on earth who rose in our land' (*khalāʾifa rabbina fī arḍihi ʿan al-fursi najamū bi-arḍinā*), with reference to the Rustumids.[5] When, back in the second/eighth century, the Ibāḍī Abū Ḥamza and the presumably Ṣufrī ʿAbd al-Sallām al-Yashkurī comment sarcastically on the behaviour of people who claim to be deputies of God (the Umayyads and al-Mahdī respectively), there is accordingly no reason to assume that their sarcasm extends to the title.[6]

Since the Khārijites are unlikely to have accepted an Umayyad innovation, this adds yet another nail, if further nails be needed, to the coffin of the idea that it was the Umayyads who created the title *khalīfat allāh* in preference to the more modest *khalīfat rasūl allāh.* The supposedly Umayyad version of the title is pan-Islamic. (The Zaydīs, for whom Crone and Hinds declared themselves unable to come up with an attestation, have since been found by Cook also to endorse the title in its supposedly Umayyad form.[7]) Al-Azmeh is probably wrong when he claims that *khalīfat allāh* is attested on an Arab-Sasanian coin struck in the time of ʿUmar,[8] but he is certainly right that the title must be very early. Everything suggests that it is the form in which the caliphal title was actually born.[9]

The Ibāḍīs and amīr al-muʾminīn

The Ibāḍī discussion of the imam's titulature came up in the context of the problem posed by the coexistence of two imamates. (The title discussed is always *amīr al-muʾminīn*, not *khalīfa*; but since one could not address a man as the former without acknowledging him as the latter, the titles were presumably synonymous, cf. the list below, nos 4–7, 11.) There had briefly been two imams in the 740s, one in Arabia and another in North Africa, and there were soon to be two on a long-term basis, for in 161/778 the Ibāḍīs of North Africa established the Rustumid imamate, which lasted down to 296/909, and in 177/794 another imamate was founded in Oman, where it survived down to 280/893.[10] In principle, there could only be one imam: how then was one to cope with two, what was the relationship between them, were both to be addressed as *amīr al-muʾminīn*? Such questions were submitted to the Omani judge

---

[5] At the end of al-Shammākhī, *Kitāb al-Siyar* (ed. A. al-Sayābī), n. p. [Salṭanat ʿUmān, Wizārat al-turāth al-qawmī waʾl-thaqāfa], 2nd printing, 1992, ii, 223.

[6] Cf. Crone and Hinds, *God's Caliph*, 12, 18, who were not sure.

[7] Crone and Hinds, *God's Caliph*, 18; Michael Cook, private communication referring to al-Hādī ilā ʾl-Ḥaqq (d. 298/911), *Aḥkām*, ms. Vienna, Glaser 63, fol. 202a; and Ibn al-Wazīr (d. 914/1508f.), *Hidāyat al-afkār*, ms. British Library, Or. 3792, fol. 217b.

[8] A. Al-Azmeh, *Muslim Kingship*, London 1997, 74f. The reference is deficient and the coin is unknown to the numismatists I have been able to consult.

[9] Al-Azmeh strangely balks at this conclusion, insisting that *khalīfat allāh* came to supplement an earlier title expressing succession to the Prophet. But it is only from the ʿAbbāsid period onwards that *khalīfàt allāh* and *khalīfat rasūl allāh* are found together. It hardly seems likely that *khalīfat rasūl allāh* should have been used for two years under Abū Bakr and then disappeared for some hundred and twenty years to reappear under the ʿAbbāsids.

[10] For the Omani dates, see Crone and Zimmermann, *Epistle*, Appendix 2.

Muḥammad b. Maḥbūb (d. 260/873),[11] who explained that the coexistence of two imams was not against the rules as long as their domains were not contiguous; each imam was autonomous within his own jurisdiction, but neither was to be addressed as *amīr al-mu'minīn*; 'Abdallāh b. Yaḥyā (the imam in the Arabian revolt of the 740s) had not been known by this title, he said, 'for the Commander of the Faithful is someone who is in command of (all of) them like Abū Bakr and 'Umar, who ruled the *ahl al-qibla* (in their entirety)';[12] an imam in a single *miṣr* 'may not style himself *amīr al-mu'minīn*, for that is a title uniting the believers in all the *amṣār*'. This, he said, was the ruling laid down by his father, the Basran leader Maḥbūb b. al-Raḥīl (d. *c*. 210/825).[13]

Contrary to what Ibn Maḥbūb claims, 'Abdallāh b. Yaḥyā does seem to have borne the titles of *khalīfa* and *amīr al-mu'minīn* (cf. the list below, no. 5). But then the intention had been to enthrone him over the entire Muslim world, not just to make him a local imam, and once the Ibāḍīs of Arabia had settled for a local imamate in Oman (occasionally one in Oman and another in Ḥaḍramawt), they do seem to have left the caliphal titles alone. No imam of theirs is known to have styled himself *khalīfa* or *amīr al-mu'minīn* and al-Ka'bī (d. 319/931) explicitly observes that the Ibāḍīs do not call their imams *amīr al-mu'minīn*.[14] He must be basing himself on eastern informants here, for the Maghribī Ibāḍīs freely applied the caliphal titles to the Rustumid imams, at least down to reign of al-Aflaḥ (208–258/824–872) (cf. nos 6–9). Intriguingly, it was to North Africans that Ibn Maḥbūb explained his views on the impropriety of calling a local imam *amīr al-mu'minīn*, in a letter answering questions on this and many other things submitted by them,[15] presumably in the reign of al-Aflaḥ, with whom Ibn Maḥbūb was contemporary, though the last imam they mention is his predecessor 'Abd al-Wahhāb (d. 208/824).[16] Practically all their questions are concerned with government abuses. It is impossible not to wonder whether this has anything to do with the apparent disappearance of the title from Ibāḍī North Africa after al-Aflaḥ, but this may be going too far, especially as the disappearance may be more apparent than real.

[11] Muḥammad b. Maḥbūb in Kāshif, *Siyar*, ii, 265ff. For the author, see Crone and Zimmermann, *Epistle*, Appendix 1, no. 5 (iii). The gist of his response is quoted by Abū 'l-Mu'thir in Kāshif, *Siyar*, ii, 186.

[12] Kāshif, *Siyar*, ii, 267.5.

[13] Kāshif, *Siyar*, ii, 268.7, where his father's ruling is triggered by the coexistence of imams in Oman and Ḥaḍramawt, not in Oman and North Africa. On Maḥbūb, see Crone and Zimmermann, *Epistle*, Appendix 1, no. 5.

[14] al-Shahrastānī *al-Milal wa'l-nihal*, ed. W. Cureton, London 1846, i, 100; ed. M. S. Kaylānī, Cairo 1961, i, 134. For al-Ka'bī, i.e. the Mu'tazilite Abū 'l-Qāsim al-Balkhī, see *GAS*, i, 622f.

[15] His epistle is addressed *ilā jamā'a man kataba ilayhi min al-muslimīn min ahl al-maghrib* (Kāshif, *Siyar*, ii, 223).

[16] Kāshif, *Siyar*, ii, 266.1.

List of attestations

I here list all the attestations known to me of Khārijites known by the titles of caliph and/or commander of the faithful, sorted by sub-sect and geographical provenance. It is unlikely to be complete. Even so, however, it is noteworthy that the Azāriqa seem to be the first to have called their leaders *khalīfa* and *amīr al-mu'minīn* (nos. 1–4), and that of all the Khārijite rebels active in the second civil war they were apparently the only ones to do so. If Ibn Abī 'l-Ḥadīd is to be trusted, the Jazīran Shabīb rapidly followed suit (no. 11), but it is not until the 740s that we get a veritable spate of Khārijite caliphs, in Arabia, North Africa and Khurāsān (nos. 5, 12–14, 16). The Arabian caliph remained unique, and the attestations rapidly peter out again among the Ṣufrīs in North Africa. But in Ibāḍī North Africa they continue down to al-Aflaḥ, as mentioned already (and further attestations may well turn up). In Sīstān they continue into the tenth century (no. 19).

Azāriqa

1) The Azāriqa called Ibn al-Azraq *amīr al-mu'minīn*.[17]

2) Ibn al-Māḥūz, who took over when Nāfiʿ b. al-Azraq was killed at Dūlāb, was addressed as caliph (*yukhāṭabu bi'l-khilāfa*).[18]

3) When the Azāriqa split up, one party joined the *mawlā* ʿAbd Rabbih al-Kabīr 'and gave him allegiance as caliph (*fa-bāyaʿūhu bi'l-khilāfa*)'.[19]

4) The other party joined Qaṭarī b. Fujā'a. He too was saluted as caliph (*sullima ʿalayhi bi'l-khilāfa*),[20] i.e. he would be greeted in the form *salām ʿalayka yā amīr al-mu'minīn*.[21] He is addressed as *amīr al-mu'minīn* with some frequency in the sources,[22] and appears as such on coins as well.[23]

Ibāḍīs

Arabia

5) Abū Ḥamza swore allegiance to ʿAbdallāh b. Yaḥyā Ṭālib al-Ḥaqq, as caliph (*bāyaʿahu bi'l-khilāfa*) in 128/745–6 or 129/746–7 according to a number of sources (none Khārijite);[24] he was addressed as commander of the faithful (*khūṭiba bi-amīr al-mu'minīn*), as al-Masʿūdī puts it.[25]

---

[17] Ibn Aʿtham, *Kitāb al-Futūḥ*, Hyderabad 1968–75, vi, 3.

[18] Ibn Abī 'l-Ḥadīd, *Sharḥ Nahj al-balāgha* (ed. M. A.-F. Ibrāhīm), Cairo 1965–7, iv, 144.–5; cf. 141 for his identity.

[19] Ibn Aʿtham, *Futūḥ*, vii, 63.

[20] al-Dhahabī, *Siyar aʿlām al-nubalā'*, iv (ed. Sh. al-Arna'ūṭ and M. al-Ṣāghirjī), Beirut 1981, 152.

[21] For this explanation, see E. W. Lane, *An Arabic–English Lexicon*, London 1863–93, s.v. 'sallama'.

[22] al-Balādhurī, *Ansāb al-ashrāf*, ms. Süleymaniye Kütüphanesi (Reisülküttap Mustafa Efendi), no. 598, p. 63, ult.; Ibn Aʿtham, *Futūḥ*, vii, 55, 57.

[23] J. Walker, *A Catalogue of Arab-Sassanian Coins*, London 1941, 112f.

[24] al-Ṭabarī, *Ta'rīkh al-rusul wa'l-mulūk* (ed. M. J. de Goeje *et al.*), Leiden 1879–1901, ii, 1943.1 (year 128); al-Azdī, *Ta'rīkh al-Mawṣil* (ed. ʿA. Ḥabība), Cairo 1967, 77 (year 129); Abū 'l-Faraj al-

North Africa

6) The Ibāḍīs paid allegiance to ʿAbd al-Raḥmān b. Rustum *biʾl-khilāfa* according to Ibn Khaldūn.[26] He was addressed as *amīr al-muʾminīn* by his advisers according to the Ibāḍī Abū Zakariyyāʾ.[27]

7) Of the second Rustumid imam, ʿAbd al-Wahhāb b. ʿAbd al-Raḥmān, we are told by the Ibāḍī al-Shammākhī that he wanted to go on pilgrimage when he had secured the caliphate (*lamma tamakkana min al-khilāfa*).[28] Abū Zakariyyāʾ depicts ʿAbd al-Wahhāb's subjects as referring to him as *amīr al-muʾminīn*,[29] and al-Shammākhī later refers to his grandson as Yaʿqūb b. Aflaḥ *al-imām* ibn ʿAbd al-Wahhāb *amīr al-muʾminīn*.[30]

8) When ʿAbd al-Wahhāb died, the *khilāfa* passed to Aflaḥ, according to the non-Ibāḍī Ibn Ṣaghīr.[31]

9) Of Aflaḥ b. ʿAbd al-Wahhāb the non-Ibāḍī Ibn al-Faqīh observed that he was of Persian descent and saluted as caliph (*yusallamu ʿalayhi biʾl-khilāfa*), a point also made by Ibn Khurdādhbih.[32] The latter calls him Maymūn, confusing him with another son of ʿAbd al-Wahhāb who had been killed by the Nukkār in ʿAbd al-Wahhāb's lifetime. Other non-Ibāḍī authors also call him Maymūn, claiming that he was head of the Ibāḍiyya, Ṣufriyya and and Wāṣiliyya (i.e. the Muʿtazilite Zanāta) and that he was saluted as caliph.[33] The first half of this claim is implausible, but it is difficult to agree with Masqueray when he objects to the second half that the real Maymūn would only have been known as imam, not as caliph, if he had lived to become head of state.[34]

Iṣbahānī, *Kitāb al-Aghānī*, Cairo 1927–74, xxiii, 227, ult.; Ibn al-Athīr, *al-Kāmil fī ʾl-taʾrīkh*, ed. C. J. Tornberg, Leiden 1851–76, v, 267; ed. Beirut 1965–67, v, 351 (year 128).

25 al-Masʿūdī, *Murūj al-dhahab* (ed. C. Pellat), Beirut 1966–79, iv, §2290 (ed. Paris 1861–77, vi, 66).

26 *Taʾrīkh*, vi, Beirut 1971, 121.18 = *Histoire des Berbères*, tr. [M.] de Slane, i, Paris 1925, 243.

27 Abū Zakariyyāʾ, *Kitāb Siyar al-aʾimma wa-akhbārihim* (ed. I. al-ʿArabī), Algiers 1979, 54.-11 = *Chronique d'Abou Zakaria*, tr. E. Masqueray, Algiers 1878, 53.

28 al-Shammākhī, *Kitāb al-Siyar*, Cairo 1301, 158; ed. A. al-Sayābī, Oman (Wizārat al-turāth al-qawmī waʾl-thaqāfa), 2nd printing 1992, i, 140; ed. M. Ḥasan (North African part only), Tunis 1995, 66.-4. The account comes from Abū Zakariyyāʾ, *Siyar*, 76, where this formulation is not however used.

29 Abū Zakariyyāʾ, *Siyar*, 79.-2, 80.5.

30 al-Shammākhī, *Siyar*, ed. Sayābī, ii, 47; ed. Ḥasan, 333.

31 A. de C. Motylinski (ed. and tr.), "Chronique d'Ibn Ṣaghīr sur les imams rostemides de Tahert", *Actes du XIVe Congrès International des Orientalistes, Alger 1905*, Paris 1908, 23 = 81.

32 Ibn al-Faqīh, *Kitāb al-Buldān* (ed. M. J. de Goeje), Leiden 1885, 79.13; Ibn Khurdādhbih, *Kitāb al-Masālik waʾl-mamālik* (ed. M. J. de Goeje), Leiden 1889, 87, ult.

33 al-Bakrī, *al-Mughrib fī dhikr Ifrīqiya waʾl-Maghrib* (ed. and tr. M. de Slane), 2nd edn, Paris 1965, 67 = 139 (160 of the first edition); Ibn Khaldūn, *Taʾrīkh*, vi, 121.-2 = 243. See the discussion in U. Rebstock, *Die Ibāḍiten im Maġrib (2./8.–4./10. Jh.)*, Berlin 1983, 172 n. 2, 192.

34 In his note to *Chronique d'Abou Zakaria*, 76. His claim is odd given that Abū Zakariyyāʾ himself describes the Ibāḍīs as addressing their Rustumid imam as *amīr al-muʾminīn* (above, notes 27, 29).

Ṣufrīs[35]

Jazīra

11) Shabīb b. Yazīd al-Shaybānī (active in the time of al-Ḥajjāj, from 76/695 to 78/697–8 at the latest) received allegiance *bi'l-khilāfa*; everyone would salute him *bi-imrat al-mu'minīn* and then pay him allegiance.[36]

12) Al-Ḍaḥḥāk b. Qays al-Shaybānī received allegiance from 120,000 soldiers *'alā madhhab al-ṣufriyya*. When he took Kufa (in 127/745), a number of Qurashīs paid allegiance to him as caliph and saluted him as such (*bāya'ahu bi'l-khilāfa wa-sallama 'alayhi bihā*).[37]

North Africa

13) Maysara al-Matjarī received allegiance as caliph.[38]

14) When Maysara was killed in 124/741–2, a section of the Ṣufrīs accepted Khālid b. Ḥumayd as their leader. One of Khālid's generals by the name of 'Abd al-Wāḥid b. Yazīd al-Hawwārī later had himself proclaimed caliph in defiance of Khālid, but fell in battle soon thereafter.[39]

15) In 153/770 the Muhallabid governor of North Africa, 'Umar b. Ḥafs, was killed by a coalition of Khārijite Berbers. By then the Ṣufrī Abū Qurra al-Ifranī had been saluted as caliph for forty days[40] or, according to some sources, forty years.[41] According to Ibn Khaldūn, it was in 148/765–6 that he had received allegiance as caliph.[42]

Khārijites of Khurāsān and Sīstān

16) Of Shaybān b. Salama al-Ḥarūrī, whose sectarian sub-affiliation is unknown, we are told that he was saluted as caliph (*yusallamu 'alayhi yawma'idh bi'l-khilāfa*) in Khurāsān in 130/747–8.[43]

---

[35] For the problematic nature of the classification, see K. Lewinstein, "Making and Unmaking a Sect: The Heresiographers and the Ṣufriyya", *Studia Islamica*, 76 (1992).

[36] Ibn Abī 'l-Ḥadīd, *Sharh*, iv, 252.ult., 253.2; cf. *EI2*, s.v. 'Shabīb b. Yazīd'.

[37] Ibn Ḥazm, *Jamharat ansāb al-'arab* (ed. 'A.-S. M. Hārūn), Cairo 1962, 322.10. In general, see *EI2*, s.v. 'al-Ḍaḥḥāk b. Ḳays al-Shaybānī'.

[38] Ibn 'Abd al-Ḥakam, *Futūḥ Miṣr* (ed. C. C. Torrey), New Haven 1922, 218.2; al-Raqīq, *Ta'rīkh Ifrīqiya wa'l-Maghrib*, ed. M. al-Ka'bī, Tunis 1968, 110; ed. 'A. 'A. al-Zaydān and 'I.-D. 'U. Mūsā, Beirut 1990, 74; Ibn 'Idhārī, *al-Bayān al-mughrib* (ed. G. S. Colin and E. Levi-Provençal), i, Leiden 1948, 53.-3, citing al-Raqīq; Ibn Khaldūn, *Ta'rīkh*, vi, 110.-5 = i, 217; cf. Rebstock, *Ibāḍiten*, 36f.

[39] Khalīfa b. Khayyāṭ, *Ta'rīkh* (ed. S. Zakkār), Damascus 1967f., 529.3, 530.5, 531.3 (cf. Rebstock, *Ibāḍiten*, 38, who appears to misunderstand it).

[40] al-Ṭabarī, iii, 371.2; Ibn 'Idhārī, *Bayān*, i, 77.-4 (without indication of period).

[41] al-Azdī, *Mawṣil*, 216.8, wisely adding *fīmā qīla*; Ibn al-Athīr, *Kāmil*, v, 457; ed. Beirut, v, 599 (year 151). Similarly one Ṭabarī ms. (cf. Tab. iii, 371, note d).

[42] *Ta'rīkh*, vi, 112.18 = i, 221; followed by Rebstock, *Ibāḍiten*, 101.

[43] al-Ṭabarī, ii, 1993.3.

17) Ḥamza al-Khārijī the famous Sīstānī rebel whose affiliation has turned out to be Shuʿaybī was called *amīr al-muʾminīn* by his followers when he took to fighting Bayhasī Khārijites and killed a large number of them.[44]

18) In 259/872–3 Yaʿqūb the Coppersmith displayed in Nishapur the severed head of a Khārijite by the name of ʿAbd al-Raḥmān who had called himself caliph for thirty years in Herāt, or so according to al-Ṭabarī. The *Tārīkh-i Sīstān* agrees that the Khārijite, here called ʿAbd al-Raḥīm, had taken the caliphal title and adds that he had adopted the regnal name of al-Mutawakkil ʿalā Allāh, but according to this source he was killed by fellow-Khārijites, not by Yaʿqūb, with whom he had come to an understanding when the latter invaded Herāt. The Khārijites replaced him with one Ibrāhīm b. Akhḍar, who was also on excellent terms with Yaʿqūb. The latter sent ʿAbd al-Raḥīm's head to the caliph al-Muʿtamid.[45]

19) A Muʿtazilite by the name of Abū ʾl-Ḥusayn ʿAlī b. Laṭīf told al-Tanūkhī (d. 384/994) that he once crossed the Quzdār area in the Sīstān-Makrān region where the caliph of the Khārijites (*al-khalīfa min al-khawārij*) resided, it being their land and residence. The story illustrates that there was no theft or cheating among them, but has no further information on the caliph.[46]

---

44 al-Baghdādī, *al-Farq bayna ʾl-firaq* (ed. M. Badr), Cairo 1910, 77.-4, -2, with a poetic attestation; cf. Crone and Zimmermann, *Epistle*, ch. 8, for his affiliation.

45 al-Ṭabarī, iii, 1882; *Tārīkh-i Sīstān* (ed. M. Bahār), Tehran 1314, 217–9, 225; tr. M. Gold, Rome 1976, 172f., 178.

46 al-Tanūkhī, *Nishwār al-muḥāḍara wa-akhbār al-mudhākara* (ed. ʿA. al-Shaljī), Beirut 1971–2, iii, 88 (no. 60) = D. S. Margoliouth, *The Table-Talks of a Mesopotamian Judge, Parts II & VIII*, Hyderabad n. d., 166 (reprinted from *Islamic Culture* iii–v). The story is also cited in Yāqūt, *Muʿjam al-buldān* (ed. F. Wüstenfeld), Leipzig 1866–73, iv, 86f., s.v. 'Quzdār'.

Narrative and doctrine in the first story of Rūmī's *Mathnawī*

Dick Davis (Ohio State University, Columbus)

I first read medieval Persian in Tehran, in the early 1970s, under the tutelage of my friend, later my PhD adviser, Norman Calder. We began, hubristically enough, with the first book of Jalāl al-Dīn Rūmī's (d. 1273) Mathnawī, *which Norman guided me through with exemplary kindness, patience, enthusiasm and erudition. Now, almost thirty years later, I look back with deep nostalgia and pleasure on those afternoons we spent together in Tehran, parsing Rūmī and talking about poetry both Persian and Western. As I certainly owe my subsequent professional involvement with Persian to Norman's initial guidance, I gratefully offer this essay on those same opening pages of the* Mathnawī *to his memory.*

I

Rūmī is explicit in acknowledging his debts to his predecessors in the genre of the mystical mathnawī, Ḥakīm Sanā'ī (d. *c.* 1130) and Farīd al-Dīn ʿAṭṭār (d. *c.* 1220), and his own mathnawī is clearly written within the tradition that they had established and developed. The couplet form is used to string together anecdotes interspersed with mystically oriented homily; the anecdotes refer to people in many walks of life (kings, merchants, servants, peasants, etc.), so that the audience/reader both has a sense that all human life contributes to the vision adumbrated, and that the vision is in turn applicable to individuals at all levels of human society. The anecdotes refer to the famous and the anonymous, to figures of religious significance and to secular princes, to historical personages and to mythological ones, so that the human panorama not only permeates all social levels but all imaginative levels as well. And within these all-inclusive concerns, one can detect in the work of all three authors a particular affection for the poor, the humble and the anonymous as they figure in the stories. These characteristics of the mystical mathnawī as a genre, laid down by Sanā'ī and elaborated by ʿAṭṭār, are shared by Rūmī's work.

But, despite this acceptance of the overall features of the genre as laid down by his predecessors, Rūmī's *Mathnawī-yi Maʿnawī* begins, when compared with the mathnawīs of Sanā'ī and ʿAṭṭār, in a very peculiar way. The first significant mystical mathnawī in Persian is Sanā'ī's *Ḥadīqat al-Ḥaqīqat*, and Rūmī's mathnawī is in many ways closer to Sanā'ī's pioneering work than it is to the intervening and apparently more sophisticated examples of the genre created by ʿAṭṭār. His poem, like Sanāʾī's, lacks a frame narrative (a device ʿAṭṭār particularly favoured); like Sanāʾī's it tends not to separate homily and anecdote into the aesthetic compartments habitually set up by ʿAṭṭār, but to mingle them apparently promiscuously; and there is frequently a kind of impatient or blunt roughness to the diction of Rūmī's *Mathnawī* which looks like a deliberate harking back to the relative asperity, jaggedness even, of Sanāʾī's verse, rather than to the more mellifluous and poetically beguiling work of ʿAṭṭār. But Rūmī does not follow Sanāʾī's example when it comes to the exordium to his work.

The *Ḥadīqat al-Ḥaqīqat* begins with a direct address to God (*ay darūn parwar birūn ārā-ī*) and this leads into an introduction, of approximately one hundred and sixty lines, devoted to God's praise. This introduction is divided into five sections; the first is on God's unity (*tawḥīd*), the second on the knowledge (*maʿrifat*) of God, the third is again on his unity (*waḥdat*) and glory (*ʿaẓmat*), the fourth on his transcendence (*tanzīh*), and the last on the necessity for purity (*ṣafā*) on the part of those who would approach and know God. The rhetoric is overwhelmingly directed towards establishing the majesty and omnipotence of God, and the inviolable certainty of God's inexpressible but insistently invoked attributes. Only after this rhetoric, centred almost exclusively on the divine, does Sanāʾī turn to the first story of his poem, that of the blind men of Ghūr who attempted to describe a visiting king's elephant. In so far as the human has entered the poem before this story it is as a foil to the divine, as ignorant and weak, and unable to comprehend or approach the nature of God (an insight forcibly underlined by the first story).

Let us now look for a moment at how a number of the mathnawīs by his other predecessor, ʿAṭṭār, begin. In the exordia to his *Musībatnāmah*, *Ilāhīnāmah*, *Asrārnāmah* and *Manṭiq al-Ṭayr*, ʿAṭṭār starts with the invocation of God as the omnipotent creator (*ḥamd-i pāk az jān-i pāk ān pāk-rā* [*Musībatnāmah*]; *bih nām-i kardagār-i haft aflāk* [*Ilāhīnāmah*]; *bih nām-i ānkih jān-rā nūr-i dīn dād* [*Asrārnāmah*]; *āfarīn jān āfarīn-i pāk-rā* [*Manṭiq al-Ṭayr*]). In the first lines of ʿAṭṭār's mathnawīs God is, as in Sanāʾī's poem, invoked by epithets that focus attention either on his capacity as creator, or on his purity and transcendence, or on both, and the subsequent lines elaborate the same *topoi*. ʿAṭṭār's normal practice is to provide a link between this praise of the divine and the fallen world of quotidian humanity by passages in praise of religious leaders, especially though not exclusively the Prophet Muḥammad. Only after some hundreds of lines of such praise (over 550 in the case of the *Manṭiq al-Ṭayr*, smaller but still substantial numbers in the case of his other mathnawīs) does ʿAṭṭār move to his poems' narrative anecdotes and the world of human life unilluminated by divine revelation.

About the only thing that the opening of Rūmī's *Mathnawī* shares with these exordia is that, like Sanāʾī's *Ḥadīqat al-Ḥaqīqat*, it opens in the second person, with a direct address (*Bishnaw az nay chūn ḥikāyat mīkunad*).[1] It is far shorter than its predecessors (thirty-five lines, as against over one hundred, and over five hundred in the case of the *Manṭiq al-Ṭayr*) and, most significantly of all, it ignores the subject matter of all previous mathnawī introductions. This is clear as soon as we look at the opening address, which is not to God, or to a prophet illumined by God, but to the poem's audience/reader; i.e. to fallen humanity.

It is difficult to overestimate the effect of these simple but transfiguring innovations. The first line is spoken by an unmediated authorial voice (i.e. by 'Rūmī'), but with the second line we move to a poetic persona, that of the reed, who speaks of the pain of separation from its reed-bed, and which we immediately allegorize as the pain of the soul's separation from the divine. With line 9 Rūmī himself again speaks, and at line 27 he compares himself putatively to the reed. The two speakers, 'Rūmī' and the reed, are thus conflated as mouthpieces of the soul's longing for the divine. The divine is invoked obliquely, as an absence; this is wholly different from the exordia of Sanāʾī's and ʿAṭṭār's mathnawīs, in which the divine is invoked explicitly, as an overwhelming, omnipotent presence. The focus of Rūmī's exordium is the turbulent emotional state of the human soul when divided from the divine: the focal points of the exordia to ʿAṭṭār's and Sanāʾī's mathnawīs are not the human soul but God, not turbulence but the certainty of theological truth, and not the specifics of emotional longing but the order of God's creation. In ʿAṭṭār's and Sanāʾī's poems there is a wide gap between the subject matter of the exordia and the poems' audiences, and this gap itself, in the emphasis placed on God's transcendence, functions partly as a confirmation of that subject matter. In Rūmī's poem, the subject of the exordium, the confused and unhappy human soul, is also the addressee of the exordium. The genre has been brought from the heavenly, the divine, and the eternal, to the earthly, the human, and the quotidian. Above all it has been brought from the unknowable to the known, and from transcendent truth to immediate experience. The trope by which Rūmī effects this transition is in itself significant. In ʿAṭṭār's exordia the intermediary between the world of secular humanity and the divine is the existence of the prophets: in Rūmī's poem we do not move up the scale from unillumined humanity in order to find a mouthpiece for truth, but down from it, to the vegetable world, to the reed, and it is less a clear, divine, eternal truth that is invoked than a confused, human, experiential one. We descend into the mud of the reed-bed. (It is perhaps worth remarking here that our own romanticization of the reed, partly because of this very passage, and also because of the association of the reed-flute's tones with *samāʿ* [musical audition], would have been largely irrelevant in Rūmī's time. The reed was a folk instrument, played by the

[1] Jalāl al-Dīn Rūmī, *Mathnawī-yi Maʿnawī* (ed. R.A. Nicholson), Leiden 1925–33, reprinted Tehran 1350/1971–2, i, 1. (All quotations from the *Mathnawī* are from this edition, and they are referred to by volume and verse number.)

uneducated, and gathered and fashioned in the wilderness, and largely retaining its association with rural life. It was an emblem of a hard and often subsistence pastoral existence, i.e. of human life at its most recalcitrant and unregenerate. The reed metaphor at the opening of the *Mathnawī* needs to be stripped of some of the mystical and transcendent patina that has subsequently accrued to it, in order for us to feel how forcefully Rūmī locates the opening of his poem in the dirt – in 'the foul rag and bone shop of the heart', to quote a poet from another tradition[2] – instead of locating it, as his predecessors had located theirs, in the divine.)

In so far as Sanāʾī and ʿAṭṭār draw attention to themselves in their introductions, it is as generic poets or generic Moslems: Rūmī's insinuation of himself into his poem is less emblematic and more personal. His reference to his own love-longing is of course to be read as a longing for the divine, but also, specifically and notoriously, for the divine as mediated by Shams-i Tabrīzī; this is hinted at in the exordium and made explicit in the poem's first tale. We see him locating his poem in the human, the autobiographical and microcosmic, rather than in the divine and universal. It is this personal concern that propels the poem so quickly into its first narrative: if we may use an architectural metaphor, Sanāʾī's and ʿAṭṭār's mathnawīs are preceded by elaborate facades that are, or at least certainly appear to be, radically different in kind from the buildings to which they provide entrance. Rūmī's entrance is relatively homely and abrupt, and of a piece with the building as a whole: one is no sooner on the threshold than in the body of the house as it were.

When ʿAṭṭār and Sanāʾī embark on the anecdotal portions of their mathnawīs, they too turn from assurance to longing, and from omnipotence to weakness, but these all too human states literally follow on from, and are thus to be read in the light of, the massive unchanging certainties of the poems' openings. Rūmī begins not with the certainties of theology, but with the fallibility of the human, and not with the dignified invocations of eternal truth, but with an *in medias res* emotional turmoil associated generically with the ghazal rather than with the mathnawī, and with fiction rather than doctrine. He abandons the certainty of structure (and, without being too cute about it, we can also say he abandons the structure of certainty) evoked and elaborated by Sanāʾī and ʿAṭṭār. The *Mathnawī-yi Maʿnawī* is a mystical mathnawī that begins by flouting the conventions of mystical mathnawīs, and by drawing on apparently extraneous traditions to make its very striking rhetorical point (so striking that it's probably safe to say that its opening lines are among the three or four best-known pieces of Persian verse ever written).

[2] W. B. Yeats, *Collected Poems*, London 1958, 392.

II

When we turn to the first narrative of Rūmī's *Mathnawī* we see that, as with his treatment of the conventional prologue, he has quite radically recast the way in which his poem's opening narrative is presented. Again a comparison with the work of Sanā'ī and ʿAṭṭār makes this plain.

Sanā'ī's story of the blind men of Ghūr (a tale Rūmī himself was later to use) is presented in a very simple, straightforward manner. The tale is told as a brief uninterrupted narrative, and it is concluded by three lines of general commentary (summed up by the line *az khudā-i khalāyiq āgāh nīst / ʿaqlā-rā dar īn sukhan rāh nīst*: 'Men have no understanding of God / In this discourse reason can make no headway'). A separate section of eleven lines, with its own heading, then follows, explaining the meaning of the tale and its application to man's search for religious truth. The first narrative within the overall frame tale of ʿAṭṭār's *Manṭiq al-Ṭayr* is again a relatively brief story: it is told by the hoopoe to the nightingale, and is an allegory of the nature of false love. The hoopoe, (who stands in for ʿAṭṭār in the poem) presents the tale without any exegetical commentary. The stories are short (much shorter than the exordia they follow on from), and are presented to the audience's understanding as either unequivocal in meaning or unmediated by authorial commentary. Sanā'ī explicitly tells us what his story means; ʿAṭṭār, by not including any exegesis, implies either that the story's meaning is obvious, or that he intends it to work in the recipient's mind unencumbered by commentary or other kinds of extraneous material.

The most striking way that the first narrative of the *Mathnawī-yi Maʿnawī* differs from the opening narratives of these two poems is in its relative length: it is much longer than the exordium it follows on from, so reversing the relationship set up by Rūmī's predecessors. One reason for this length is that, unlike the opening tales by Sanā'ī and ʿAṭṭār, it is filled with extraneous material. Neither Sanā'ī nor ʿAṭṭār leave their tales while they are in progress;[3] Rūmī does so frequently, and at one point (i. 143) he has to admonish himself to return to the story he is ostensibly telling but has apparently forgotten about. Because of the fluid nature of his narrative technique, it is sometimes difficult to say exactly where narrative ends and commentary begins,[4] but

[3] By 'their tales' I mean here the opening tales of the *Ḥadīqat al-Ḥaqīqat* and the *Manṭiq al-Ṭayr*. It is true that both poets do interpolate commentary into some other stories in their mathnawīs, but they do so relatively sparingly and virtually never to the extent, or in the multiform ways, that Rūmī does in the *Mathnawī*'s opening narrative. Sanā'ī's technique is often one of didactic homily illustrated by very brief anecdotes (i.e. the extended narratives are relatively few), rather than of narratives to which are added homilies as introductions and/or addenda (ʿAṭṭār's most frequent way of proceeding).

[4] This is particularly the case when Rūmī resorts, as he frequently does, to passages of extended illustrative imagery, which tend to move from fictional verisimilitude to commentary/explication and back again within a few lines. For instance, the images of a thorn in someone's foot and another thorn placed under a donkey's tail (i. 150–56) are there at first sight as veridical detail, but it is clear that their main function is to provide illustrative commentary.

my rough estimate is that of the 210 lines devoted to the story, approximately 90 (i.e. more than 40 per cent) can be considered as commentary.[5]

The word 'commentary', although the obvious one to use for non-narrative additions to an avowedly mystical and didactic text, hardly does justice to the nature of Rūmī's interpolations. There are two extended passages that can be seen as commentary of the expected exegetical kind: these are the brief excursus on *adab* (ii. 79–85), and the closing presentation of the story's moral import, in the manner of Sanā'ī. A third passage, which looks at first as if it will be of this kind, is the long interpolation on the nature of love, which begins at i. 109 and continues to i. 144. This passage is noticeable because of its highly personal character, in that it inserts Rūmī himself into the text, and it also introduces there two other historical individuals, Shams-i Tabrīzī and Rūmī's amanuensis, Husām al-Dīn Chalabī. Shams-i Tabrīzī is invoked as a beloved absence, and Chalabī, who was in a sense Shams's successor, is there as a necessary but provoking presence in that, in his role as amanuensis, he is the tale's transmitter, but one with whom the dictating poet has a fairly severe altercation. As well as literally being the tale's first audience, Chalabī here also seems to be a surrogate for the poem's putative future audiences, in that he appears to raise precisely the objections that 'we', the tale's subsequent readers, feel as the tale goes forward.

The frequency of the interruptions to the narrative flow, and their often personal nature, together produce a quite complex aesthetic effect. On the one hand, the tale's status as an edifying narrative is insisted upon, and the constant interruptions prevent our maintaining any Coleridgean 'willing suspension of disbelief' in the story as such. In fact we could say, staying with the same poet's explorations of the relationship between belief and fiction, that Rūmī functions as his own 'person from Porlock', in that as soon as the narrative flow has been established he interrupts it. This means that the reader is frequently diverted away from the story *as* a story, in order to be reminded of its existence as an illustrative moral anecdote: the story is lifted away from its status as narrative and placed in an interpretive, didactic context in which what finally matters is moral meaning, *natījah*.[6] But, at the same time as this insistent abstraction of spiritual meaning is going on, the highly personal, unresolved emotionalism of the text, centred on three historical individuals (Rūmī, Shams, Chalabī – two of whom we see playing out a fraught, even angry, relationship before our eyes), regrounds the text in the specifics of particular human lives. The interpolations both cut through the fictional

[5] This is taking i. 36–246 as constituting the text of the tale. If we consider the concluding lines of commentary as a separate section (analogous to the commentary under a separate heading that follows on from Sanā'ī's first tale), we are left with *c*. 66 lines of commentary out of 186 lines of text. This is still over a third of the total.

[6] The effect is not dissimilar from that which the twentieth-century German poet and playwright Brecht strove to achieve, in that he deliberately incorporated such distancing devices into his narratives, in order that the audience would not sink into the story as such but be forced to view it from a didactic/ideological perspective.

narrative in the interests of abstract interpretation, and at the same time subvert the abstract by insisting on an immediate and experiential 'historical' narrative (the circumstances of the tale's dictation). This is noticeably unlike the effects of both Sanāʾī and ʿAṭṭār, which tend to be altogether simpler. Sanāʾī has little interest in the experiential as such, and virtually always foregrounds the *natījah* of his tales. ʿAṭṭār is of course also concerned with *natījah*, but while he is narrating a story (especially a love story) he rarely interrupts it and appears concerned to maintain narrative continuity, and hence a 'willing suspension of disbelief'. During the process of narration the aesthetics of the fictional narrative tend to be primary for ʿAṭṭār, so that the reader is invited to enter into the fictional world virtually for its own sake, and the tale's didactic import is only insisted upon after the story is over.[7] And in so far as Sanāʾī and ʿAṭṭār introduce themselves into their mathnawīs, they present themselves as accomplished poets and knowledgeable mystics (i.e. as poets who ask for our attention precisely to the extent that they have risen above human imperfection). They do not present themselves – as Rūmī does – as individuals still caught within the experiential mire of quotidian human life. Both ʿAṭṭār and Sanāʾī do this in their ghazals, where it is generically appropriate, of course, but it is one of the innovative characteristics of Rūmī's *Mathnawī* that he imports this *topos* (of a speaker caught within the toils of all-too-human need) and its attendant aesthetic, from the ghazal to a didactic work (in which the expectation is that the narrator's persona, in so far as it is present, is of one who has reached a stage beyond such spiritual and emotional bewilderment, and is thereby able to help others transcend them).

III

The ambiguous effect of the interpolations in the narrative is further complicated by another characteristic of Rūmī's tale which becomes very distinct when we compare it with those of his predecessors, and this is its detailed verisimilitude. The clearest instance of this is the scene when the visiting physician questions the girl as to her sickness. The way that his gentleness is insisted upon, the detail of his taking her pulse and noting her reaction to different names,[8] the apparently gratuitous location of the love affair in specific places (Samarqand, Sar-i pul, Ghātafar) make the scene, in its plenitude of particulars and in its humane psychology, like something one would expect to find in a nineteenth-century European novel. The plethora and specificity of human detail here seem to resist any attempts to schematize what is presented as (mere)

[7] A good example of this occurs in ʿAṭṭār's presentation of the tale of the Princess and the Slave (*op. cit.*, 463–71, ll. 3794–870) in which the interests of telling a beguiling story almost obliterate the tale's ostensible didactic import.

[8] Interestingly enough this precise vignette reappears, a hundred or so years later, in the *Decameron* of Boccaccio, an author who is often seen as the 'father' of the modern European novel (see the eighth Story of the second Day).

allegory. This location of the tale's details in the recalcitrantly quotidian is also clear in Rūmī's wonderfully exuberant and inventive imagery. Annemarie Schimmel,[9] and more recently Fatemeh Keshavarz,[10] have both drawn attention to the fecundity and inventiveness of Rūmī's original imagery (which is rivalled, and apparently valued, by few if any other medieval Persian poets), and such images play a large part in establishing the story's atmosphere of insistent realism.

As is usual with Rūmī, the imagery is frequently present as a brief moment of illustrative commentary, which both draws the reader away from the tale being told, but by its informality and immediacy resists any impulse toward interpretative abstraction. In this way it is similar to those interpolations in which Rūmī introduces himself, Shams-i Tabrīzī and Husām al-Dīn Chalabī, in that we leave the tale not in order to move toward abstract speculation but to insist on an experiential, physical, context or parallel. The images can have the pithy force of folk aphorisms (i. 107, *bū-yi har hīzum padīd āyad zi dūd*, 'the scent of each wood is apparent from its smoke'; or i. 215, *īn jahān kūhast u fiʿl-i mā nadā / sū-yi mā āyad nadāhā-rā ṣadā*, 'this world is a mountain and our actions a call / the echo of our calls comes back to us'); they can insist with some violence on a homely analogy for the inexpressible (i. 114, *chūn qalam andar niwishtan mīshitāft / chūn bi-ʿishq āmad qalam bar khud shikāft*, 'as the writing pen was scurrying forward, it came to love and split open'); or they can refer to the ineffable with a kind of sly erotic humor (i. 138, *mī nakhusbam bā ṣanam bā pīrhan*, 'I don't sleep with my lover in my shirt'). They can also be very tender, as when the physician says to the sick girl, at line 172, *ān kunam bar tu kih bārān bā chaman* ('I will do to you as the rain does to the meadows'). Certainly the most extraordinary cluster of images in the story concerns the thorn located first in a person's foot, when we are given what seems like a moment of *ekphrasis* that describes a Hellenistic statue with the sufferer propping his foot on his knee and probing for the thorn with a needle.[11] And then we have another of Rūmī's images involving violence, in that the thorn is thrust under a donkey's tail, and the animal's distracted pain is offered as a metaphor for the pains of love in general, and for the girl's secret agony in particular. What is especially noticeable here is the way that the metaphor almost brutally implies that the girl's love is a false physical (*mujāzī*) love. If the donkey here stands in for the girl, as it clearly does, *zīr-i dum* (under the tail) can be taken as meaning 'in the vulva', so categorizing the girl's love-longing as simply a gross and painful genital irritation.

[9] Annemarie Schimmel, *The Triumphal Sun: A Study of the Works of Jalaloddin Rumi*, London–The Hague 1978, 59–222.

[10] Fatemeh Keshavarz, *Reading Mystical Lyric: The Case of Jalal al-Din Rumi*, Columbia, SC 1997, *passim*, but see especially 31–48 and 72–99. Dr. Keshavarz is mainly concerned with the *Dīwān-i Shams-i Tabrīzī*, but her illuminating remarks on imagery are in general equally applicable to the *Mathnawī-yi Maʿnawī*.

[11] The subject is part of the repertory of Hellenistic statuary, and a particularly fine example exists of a shepherd boy, in exactly the pose conjured up by Rūmī's description.

The cumulative effect of the imagery in the story, which is less conventional (and more frequent, vivid, and occasionally violent than the relatively traditional tropes favoured by Sanāʾī and ʿAṭṭār), is to give the narrative a context that is folksy, homiletic and humanly recognizable (the man probing for the thorn with a needle), but also strongly and even aggressively reductionist (love is at basis a sexual wound) in its insistent physicality.

IV

How then is one to interpret the story, and the extraneous matter with which Rūmī loads it? Clearly to take the narrative at face value is to set oneself up for a severe disappointment; Rūmī himself acknowledges this in his admonitions to Chalabī during its course, and to the reader after it is over. He does not expect his audience to like his tale. We disapprove, but he says, we are like Moses reproaching Khiḍr in the eighteenth *sūra* of the Qurʾān, in that we have leapt to judgement because we don't understand what is going on.

The tale begins as a love story, of a traditional recognizable kind, but it soon betrays the expectations set up by such a story. As Margaret Mills has pointed out,[12] the tale 'can be regarded as an antiromance or antifolktale' in that it deploys motifs common to such tales and then subverts them. The type of tale in question involves 'beautiful young people [who] conceive an idealized love for each other ... [who are then] separated by another male, superior in strength and usually in age and status to the male lover'. In the normal development of such a tale 'after some time and considerable struggle, the senior male adversary is neutralized or killed and the young couple are united', and it is this dénouement which is of course reversed in Rūmī's version. One may also remark that the tale bears a close resemblance to another folk type too, the Cinderella story, in which a poor girl is chosen as his beloved/bride by a prince and after some tribulations the two are united. Here the difference in Rūmī's version lies not in the dénouement, but in the nature of the obstacles to love between the rich suitor and the poor girl, which are not external (the families of the lovers) but internal (the girl's previous commitment to another lover, a topos that subverts yet another folk motif – that first love is true love).

Familiarity with the didactic mathnawī tradition dictates that we read the story as allegory. But this by no means clears up a reader's difficulties. The usual expectation in allegory is that motifs and characters once assigned a symbolic meaning keep that meaning for the duration of the tale. This is as true of Western allegories (e.g Spenser's

12 Margaret Mills, "Folk Tradition in the Mathnawī and the Mathnawī in Folk Tradition", in Amin Banani, Richard Houannisian and Georges Sabagh (eds), *Poetry and Mysticism in Islam: The Heritage of Rumi*, Cambridge 1994, 145.

Faerie Queene) as it is of Persian mathnawīs. For example, in the tale of the blind villagers arguing about the nature of the elephant, in Sanā'ī's *Ḥadīqat al-Ḥaqīqat*,[13] both the villagers and the elephant retain their symbolic meanings (fallible 'blind' humanity, the nature of divine truth, respectively) throughout the tale. Similarly, in the story of the king who drives away an ungrateful dog but allows him to keep his jewelled collar as a reminder of his origin, in ʿAṭṭār's *Manṭiq al-Ṭayr*,[14] both the king and the dog retain their symbolic meanings (God, fallen humanity, respectively) while the tale continues. But if we consider the characters in Rūmī's tale, we see that matters are clearly much more complex and unpredictable. In overall terms it seems plain enough that the king in the story represents God, the girl the human soul, and the goldsmith the meretricious attractions of the physical world. As Abdolhossein Zarrinkub has put it, 'until the soul is able to escape from its connections to the world of glittering appearances, which the goldsmith of Samarqand ... represents ... it will not find its way to the love that leads to truth/God (*ḥaqq*), represented by the king', and 'The story of the servant girl and the king ... demonstrates that until the soul frees itself from its attachments to the physical world it cannot be united with the king, who represents God, and this represents the stage of detachment from the world (*tabattul*), i.e. freedom from the self'.[15] The problem is not simply that the tale tends to run away with the allegory (so that we feel sympathy for the lovers, much as the reader of Dante's *Inferno* feels sympathy for the explicitly condemned Paolo and Francesca), a fact that Rūmī exasperatedly comments on, but that this overall allegorical meaning is not sustained in the story's details. For example, if we follow the most famous premodern commentary on the *Mathnawī*, that of Anqarawī,[16] we find that during the meeting of the king and the visiting physician the king is to be taken as a *murīd* and the physician as his *murshid*.[17] Similarly, when the king mounts his horse, Anqarawī reads this as an allegorical representation of setting out on the sufi path,[18] so that the king is here, it would seem, to be taken as representative of the sufi aspirant. Common sense would suggest that a character cannot simultaneously represent an omnipotent God, a sufi aspirant, and a *murshid*'s *murīd*, or if he does we are not dealing with a 'stable' allegory in the manner of Sanā'ī or Spenser. And in the same way, in Rūmī's text, that one character can represent a multiplicity of concepts, so one concept can be represented by a plurality of characters: during the king's courtship of the girl, for example, it would appear that both in some sense represent the human soul, he in his need and she in her error. This shifting of allegorical referents, so that the reader must remain constantly

[13] *Ḥadīqat al-Ḥaqīqat wa Sharīʿat al-Ṭarīqat* (ed. Modarres Razavi), Tehran n. d. (3rd printing), 69–70.
[14] Farīd al-Dīn ʿAṭṭār, *Manṭiq al-Ṭayr* (ed. Ahmad Ranjbar), Tehran 1366/1987–8, 272–3, ll. 2183–94.
[15] Abdolhossein Zarrinkub, *Palah Palah tā Mulāqat-i Khudā*, Tehran 1371/1992–3, 260 and 266.
[16] *Sharḥ-i Kabīr-i Anqarawī bar Mathnawī-yi Mawlawī* (tr. Akbar Behruz), Tehran 1348/1969–70.
[17] *Ibid.*, i, 127.
[18] *Ibid.*, i, 101. Anqarawī gives a similar interpretation to the physician's journey (123–4).

alert for new meanings, is not entirely without precedent in some of the more complex tales told by ʿAṭṭār,[19] but neither ʿAṭṭār nor Sanāʾī ever challenge the reader's attention with such a kaleidoscopically unstable set of referents within the one tale.

The multiplication of meanings and referents does not end here. At times motifs function with a simultaneous plurality of meanings (in contrast to the serial meanings located in, for example, the figure of the king), and this is most obviously the case in Rūmī's introduction of Shams in his discourse on love. The way that *shams* is used to indicate three different overlapping and mutually dependent referents (the historical individual Shams-i Tabrīzī, the sun, the 'sun of the soul' [*khurshīd-i jān*]) is well explicated in the contemporary commentary by Muḥammad Taqī Jaʿfarī.[20] The ramifications of polysemy set out in Jaʿfarī's commentary remind one at first sight of Dante's apparently similar explanation of the various layers of meaning to be found in the language of his *Commedia*,[21] with the difference that Dante's meanings are considerably more stable, and as it were answerable to exegesis, than Rūmī's, which seem designed precisely to evade or at least complicate fixed interpretation.

Given this bewildering plethora of allegorical meanings present in Rūmī's text, it might be thought that the only way to proceed is to read the text with minute allegorical spectacles, explicating everything in sight. And indeed the monumental, multi-volume commentaries on the *Mathnawī* by Anqarawī, Jaʿfari, and others, indicate that there have been those more than ready to take up this challenge. But I referred above to the insistent specificity and physicality of Rūmī's narrative style, and one of the characteristics of such a style is that it recalcitrantly resists such treatment. When it comes to the location of the girl's beloved for example, Anqarawī is able to explicate parts of his address (*Samarqand, sar-i pul*) in ways that one might expect: Samarqand is explicated as 'the natural world' (*shahr-i ṭabīʿiyyat*), and *sar-i pul* is glossed entirely predictably (a bridge is not a place of rest, and in the same way the world is not a place of rest but of passing over), but he is stumped by other parts. Ghātafar is explicated as simply 'the name of a place in Samarqand'.[22] This inability to provide an allegorical meaning for Ghātafar might be thought a minor matter, but in reality it seriously

---

19 E.g in the last story of the *Manṭiq al-Ṭayr* the king and the boy at different points in the tale each appear to represent both God and the human soul. I have discussed this story and its allegorical technique in "The Journey as Paradigm in ʿAṭṭār's Manteq al-Tayr", *Edebiyyat*, 4 (New Series), 173–83.

20 Muḥammad Taqī Jaʿfarī, *Tafsīr wa Naqd wa Tahlīl-i Mathnawī*, Tehran 1366/1987–8 (11th printing), i, 111–5.

21 Dante, letter to Can Grande. The Latin text of the relevant portion of the letter (which interestingly enough includes the Greek borrowing 'polysemos' to describe the phenomenon), together with an English translation, may be found in William Anderson's *Dante the Maker*, New York 1982, 333–4. Dante distinguishes four possible meanings to be found simultaneously in his text; the literal, the allegorical, the moral, and the anagogical (although the last three may be subsumed under the general heading 'allegorical').

22 *Op. cit.*,153. Jaʿfarī, *op. cit.*, 117, repeats word for word Anqarawī's description ('the name of a place in Samarqand'), and Karīm Zamānī in his commentary, *Sharḥ-i Jāmiʿ-i Mathnawī-yi Maʿnawī*, Tehran 1374/1995–6, i, 103, has an almost identical phrase. None of these commentators assign an allegorical meaning to Ghātafar.

undermines the whole edifice of explication. Because Ghātafar cannot be assigned an allegorical meaning it drags Samarqand back from being 'the natural world' to being simply Samarqand, a specific central Asian city. Another place at which the commentary falters is in describing the death of the goldsmith; the goldsmith's dying curse seems incapable of being given an edifying mystical explication (especially as, given the story's apparent allegorical scheme, it is God whom he is cursing). Like Ghātafar, it appears to be there simply as veridical detail. This is not at all of course to claim that the practice of allegorical explanation, of which Anqarawī's and Jaʿfarī's commentaries are respectively among the most prized traditional and modern representatives, is in any sense mistaken. Clearly the poem calls out for allegorical explication, but equally clearly the tale's allegory is shifting, open and unstable; and at times it breaks down altogether into specific *verismo* detail that resists interpretation as anything but itself (Ghātafar is simply Ghātafar). The narrative refuses to be shifted wholesale into the realm of the spiritual, and this insistence on the quotidian, experiential and physical is further confirmed by the always homely and familiar, and often deliberately bestial and gross, imagery that Rūmī employs. In a sense Rūmī himself, within his tale, sets out these contradictory parameters, by including the little excursus recommending *adab* (ii. 79–85), which is set within a tale which is consistently, as it were, *bī-adab*, in that it adumbrates, and even appears to celebrate, conventions that it then cheerfully breaks. What one is left with is a text which simultaneously demands and resists interpretation, which points to meanings that are no sooner summoned than they are subverted, and which remains stubbornly rooted in the vulgar complexities of untranscended human experience.

Two classical Shīʿī theories of *qaḍāʾ**

Robert Gleave (University of Bristol)

Introduction

> If Shīʿī *fuqahāʾ* took up judicial posts with *de facto* governments, this was a concession to the exigencies of political life not a recognition of legitimacy.[1]

This was Norman Calder's conclusion concerning Imāmī juristic attitudes towards the legitimacy of government during the *ghayba*. Though a scholar may work for a particular government as a judge (*qāḍī*), this did not imply that he considered that government to be legitimate. Rather, the only legitimate government was that of the Imam, and when the Imam is in hiding, all governments share a *de jure* illegitimacy. This, Calder argued, was the mainstream Imāmī position, as found in their works of positive law (*furūʿ al-fiqh*) until the twentieth century. Shīʿī scholars may have written works in praise of a Shah (one thinks of the Mirrors written during the Ṣafavid period), but in their academic works of law, in which they attempted to describe God's intended rule for humanity (the *sharīʿa*), they consistently viewed any government in the absence of the Imam as *jāʾir* and *ẓālim* (illegitimate and oppressive). Scholars could take up posts as judges, but this was due to the fact of the Imam's *ex ante* delegation, not official appointment.

If Calder was correct in this assessment, then the Imāmī view differs markedly from Sunnī accounts of judicial authority, where the *qāḍī*, generally speaking, only gains authority through appointment by the *de facto* ruler. On the whole, the rules concerning judicial procedure (*qaḍāʾ*) are remarkably similar within the Sunnī and Imāmī juristic tradition; but this is undoubtedly one area of difference.[2] In this essay, I examine Imāmī thought on two issues: the conception of an appointing authority and the imagined structure of the judiciary. These two areas are undoubtedly linked in that the

---

* An earlier version of this paper was delivered at the 2nd Joseph Schacht Conference on Theory and Practice in Islamic Law, 15–20 December 1997, Granada, Spain. Norman Calder was to have delivered a paper at the conference, but his illness prevented him from attending. He was, however, able to make some comments on the ideas contained within this essay. As usual, his comments clarified my own thoughts in a number of important ways.

[1] N. Calder, "The Structure of Authority in Imāmī Shīʿī Jurisprudence", unpublished PhD thesis, University of London 1979, 90.

[2] Another area of difference, perhaps linked to the legitimacy question, concerns *kitāb al-qāḍī ilā ʾl-qāḍī*. An examination of the reasoning behind this difference awaits further research. Calder also argues that the judiciary is conceived of as diffuse and non-hierarchical in Imāmī *fiqh*, whilst in Sunnī *fiqh* the judiciary is considered structured and centrally organized. See Calder, "The Structure of Authority", 70–85.

internal structure of the judiciary can be determined by the appointing authority (signified by the terms *sulṭān* or *imām* in Sunnī *fiqh*) through decree or bureaucratic organisation. In Shīʿī *furūʿ*, these issues are generally kept separate.

The office of *qāḍī* is held in low prestige by most Shīʿī authors, as exemplified by the following famous *ḥadīth*:

> From Abū ʿAbdallāh [Imām al-Ṣādiq]: There are four [types] of *qāḍī*. Three are in hell and one in heaven. A man who judges unjustly (*biʾl-jawr*) and knows it, is in hell. The one who judges unjustly and does not know it, is in hell. The one who judges justly, but does not know it, is in hell. The one who judges justly and knows it, he is in heaven.[3]

In order to illustrate the distinctive Shīʿī discussions in this area, I have selected two works of *furūʿ al-fiqh*: *Kifāyat al-aḥkām* of Muḥammad Bāqir al-Sabzawārī (d. 1090/1679)[4] and *Mafātīḥ al-sharāʾiʿ* of Muḥsin Fayḍ al-Kāshānī (d. 1091/1680).[5] I have chosen these authors for their (supposed) school loyalties: Sabzawārī is described as a *mujtahid* and hence an Uṣūlī and Kāshānī is usually described as an Akhbārī, though later (Uṣūlī-written) accounts attempt to play down this allegiance.[6]

The Akhbārī–Uṣūlī conflict remains under-researched. The works of Kohlberg, Modarressi and Newman have contributed greatly to the development of knowledge in this field, but their depictions of the character of the Akhbārī challenge to Uṣūlī *fiqh* do not resound with unanimity.[7] The fundamental distinction between Akhbārīs and Uṣūlīs concerned the legitimacy of the juristic practice of *ijtihād*. The Akhbārī denial of the necessity and legitimacy of *ijtihād* had its most obvious consequence in the doubt cast over the status of the *mujtahid* class. Newman and others have argued that with the denial of *ijtihād*, the authority of the scholarly class as a whole (*ʿulamāʾ*) was undermined, and that the Akhbārīs denied a role to the *ʿulamāʾ* in a whole range of

---

[3] Muḥammad b. Yaʿqūb al-Kulaynī (d. 328/940–41), *al-Kāfī*, Tehran 1388, vii, 407; Shaykh al-Ṣadūq Ibn Babūya (d. 381/991), *Man lā yaḥḍuruhu al-faqīh*, Qum 1404, iii, 4; Shaykh al-Ṭāʾifa Muḥammad b. Ḥasan al-Ṭūsī (d. 460/1067), *Tahdhīb al-aḥkām*, Tehran 1390, vi, 218.

[4] Muḥammad Bāqir al-Sabzawārī, *Kifāyat al-aḥkām*, Lith., Tehran 1269/1852–3.

[5] Muḥsin Fayḍ Muḥammad b. Murtaḍā, *Mafātīḥ al-sharāʾiʿ*, Qum 1401/1981.

[6] For biographies of Sabzawārī see Muḥammad al-Ḥurr al-ʿĀmilī (d. 1104/1693), *Amāl al-āmil*, Qum 1362, ii, 250; Mīrzā ʿAbd Allāh al-Iṣbahānī Afandī (d. *c.*1130/1718), *Riyāḍ al-ʿulamāʾ*, Qum 1401, v, 44; Muḥammad Bāqir al-Khwānsārī (d. 1313/1895), *Rawḍāt al-jannāt*, Beirut 1411/1991, ii, 67–72; Muḥammad b. Sulaymān al-Tunukābunī (d. 1302/1884–5), *Qiṣaṣ al-ʿulamāʾ*, Tehran, n. d., 386–7; Mīrzā Muḥammad ʿAlī Mudarris, *Rayḥānat al-adab*, Tehran, 1374), v, 242. For Kāshānī see al-Ḥurr al-ʿĀmilī, *Amāl*, ii, 305; Afandī, *Riyāḍ*, v, 170; Yūsuf b. Aḥmad al-Baḥrānī (d. 1186/1772), *Luʾluʾat al-baḥrayn*, 1306/1987, 121–31; Khwānsārī. *Rawḍāt*, vi, 793–7; Tunukābunī *Qiṣaṣ*, 322–33; Mudarris, *Rayḥāna*, iv, 369–84.

[7] E. Kohlberg, "Aspects of Akhbari Thought in the Seventeenth and Eighteenth Centuries", in J. O. Voll and N. Levtzion (eds), *Eighteenth Century Renewal and Reform in Islam*, Syracuse 1987, 133–60, and his 'Akbārīya', *Encyclopaedia Iranica*, Leiden 1985, i, 718; H. Modarresi Tabataba'i, "Rationalism and Traditionalism in Shīʿī Jurisprudence", *Studia Islamica*, 59 (1984), 141–58; A. Newman, "The Development and Political Significance of the Rationalist (Uṣūlī) and the Traditionalist (Akhbārī) schools in Imāmī Shīʿī History from the Third/Ninth to the Tenth/Sixteenth Century", unpublished PhD thesis, University of California, Los Angeles 1986; and his "The Nature of the Akhbārī/Uṣūlī Dispute in Late Safawid Iran: Part 1, ʿAbdallāh al-Samāhijī's *Munyat al-Mumārisīn*", *BSOAS*, 55 (1992), 22–51, "Part 2, The Conflict Re-assessed", *BSOAS*, 55 (1992), 250–61.

community functions (the collection and distribution of community taxes, the leadership of Friday prayer and most importantly for my discussion here, the execution of judicial functions). Newman further argues that this rejection was in some way linked to a rejection of the legitimacy of any government in the absence of the Imam.[8]

If this bundle of ideas (no *ijtihād*, no interpretation of revelation, no need for a scholarly elite, no accommodation with the existing government) is an accurate description of the dominant themes within Akhbārism, then one would expect Akhbārīs to have a distinctive theory of *qaḍāʾ*, if they had a theory at all. It is an examination of this question with which I am concerned in this paper.

The authors

According to the biographical tradition, Muḥammad Bāqir al-Sabzawārī and Muḥsin Fayḍ al-Kāshānī were both associated with the Ṣafavid Iranian court during the reign of Shāh ʿAbbās II (r. 1642–66) and Shāh Sulaymān (r. 1666–94). Sabzawārī, born in Sabzawār, received a religious education from his father until the latter's death. He then studied in Iraq, before settling in the Ṣafavid capital of Isfahan. He rose to high office in the city, becoming *imām al-jumʿa waʾl-jamāʿa* and *shaykh al-islām*. He enjoyed a close relationship with the Shah's ministers and became a figure of considerable influence in the city. Khwānsārī, the nineteenth-century biographer, records that members of Sabzawārī's family held the post of *shaykh al-islām* continuously until the nineteenth century.[9]

Whilst in Isfahan, Sabzawārī met and became friends with Kāshānī.[10] Kāshānī holds an ambivalent position in the biographical literature. At times he is accused of being influenced by Ibn al-ʿArabī (and hence is condemned by the anti-Ṣūfī biographers); other writers play down this issue, praising his work in *furūʿ al-fiqh* and *akhbār* (his most famous work is probably *al-Wāfī*, a collection of the sayings and actions of the Imams). He is also famous as a poet of some distinction, particularly for his *Dīvān*. Kāshānī was born in Qum in 1008 and went first to Shiraz where he studied *fiqh* and philosophy (the latter with Mullā Sadrā, whose daughter he later married). The possibly fanciful anecdotes of Tanukābunī portray Kāshānī as having a particularly close relationship with the courts of both Shahs ʿAbbās II and Sulaymān. In one tale,

[8] Newman's argument is slightly more sophisticated in that he claims that the text by Samāhijī (d. 1135/1723) indicates that there was a range of scholarly opinion on the Akhbārī–Uṣūlī dispute, signified by a number of titles given to scholars: *mujtahid*, *mujtahid-muḥaddith*, *muḥaddith*, Akhbārī. There may be a range of titles used, which may correspond to a range of views on the question of the adoption of the Imam's role during the *ghayba*. However, I have seen no evidence (Samāhijī's text included) which indicates that the conferment of the title Akhbārī on a scholar was occasioned by anything other than a rejection of *ijtihād*.

[9] Khwānsārī, *Rawḍāt*, ii, 67.

[10] Khwānsārī adds that they agreed on many matters of law (though clearly not all, since Khwānsārī later mentions a dispute between them), *ibid*.

relevant to our discussion here, Kāshānī is asked by Shāh ʿAbbās to account for an earthquake in Shīrwān. Kāshānī answers that it was a punishment for the veniality of the Shāh's judges who gave invalid rulings in return for bribes. Kāshānī's advice is to appoint Sabzawārī as *qāḍī* of Isfahan. The Shah agrees, but expresses doubts that Sabzawārī will accept the position. 'You must force him to accept', replied Kāshānī *(vajib ast kih ʾūrā jabr kunī bar qabūl kardan)*.[11] The appointment was never made as the Shah died before returning to Isfahan (though Sabzawārī did, later it seems, become *shaykh al-islām* of Isfahan). Some subsequent biographical accounts refer to Kāshānī as an Akhbārī, though others label him with the less loaded term *muḥaddith*. Such a judgement depends upon what one means by an Akhbārī; certainly Kāshānī's system of legal theory, described in his work *Safīnat al-Najāt* owes much to the Akhbārī ideas of the so-called founder of the school, Muḥammad Amīn al-Astarābādī (d. 1030/1640).[12]

Legitimacy

The first topic I have selected for examination is the legitimacy of the *qāḍī*-appointing authority. As in most works of Sunnī *furūʿ*, in Shīʿī *fiqh*, a *qāḍī* should be appointed by a legitimate authority (*sulṭān, imām*). In Shīʿī *fiqh* the right to appoint *qāḍī*s belongs to *al-imām al-ʿādil*. This phrase undoubtedly refers to one of the twelve Imams in Ithnā-ʿasharī Shīʿism. Many *akhbār* warn believers from turning to a *qāḍī* appointed by an illegitimate authority (i.e. an appointment made by a Sunnī leader), even if the *qāḍī* happens to make the right judgement.[13] The *qāḍī* derives his legitimacy from the appointing authority, and if the authority is illegitimate *(jāʾir)*, the *qāḍī*'s judgement is invalid. In twelver Shīʿism, the occultation (*ghayba*) of the twelfth Imam effectively removes the presence of a legitimate appointing body.[14]

To avoid a crisis of legitimacy, Shīʿī jurists developed a sophisticated theory of delegation, whereby the Imam delegated a class of society to perform the functions of *qaḍāʾ* in the absence of the Imam. *Akhbār* (particularly the *maqbūla* of Ibn Ḥanẓala and the *khabar* of Abū Khadīja) were interpreted as favouring such a delegation and are cited in nearly all Shīʿī works of *furūʿ*.[15] The delegation (*niyāba*) of the *ʿulamāʾ* was not a concept unique to *qaḍāʾ*; other activities which had been considered the exclusive

[11] Tunukābunī, *Qiṣaṣ*, 328–9.
[12] See the account by Kohlberg, "Aspects", 136–46.
[13] See for example the *akhbār* translated in the appendix.
[14] Literature on the legitimacy of government during the *ghayba* is ever expanding. For the variety of western scholarly opinion, see W. Madelung, "A Treatise of Sharīf al-Murtaḍā on the Legality of Working for the Government", *BSOAS*, 43 (1980), 18–31; Calder, "The Structure of Authority", *passim* (on *qāḍī*s see 70–107); A. Lambton, *State and Government in Medieval Islam*, London 1981, 219–88; H. Enayat, *Modern Islamic Political Thought*, London 1982, 167–75; S. A. Arjomand, *The Shadow of God and the Hidden Imam*, Chicago 1984 (on *qāḍī*s see 71); A. K. Moussavi, *Religious Authority in Shiʿite Islam*, Kuala Lumpur 1986, *passim* (and on *qāḍī*s , see 64–73).
[15] I have translated these two reports as an appendix to this article.

right of the Imam (and hence lapsed – *sāqiṭ* – during the *ghayba*) were recovered, and the *ʿulamāʾ* were appointed as the deputies of the Imam in his absence.[16] Whether such theories increased the power of the scholarly elite, or merely justified their already-established power base is, as yet, unclear. By the time of Kāshānī and Sabzawārī, the theory of *niyāba* had become central to the activation of most areas of the Sharīʿa in the absence of the Imam, *qaḍāʾ* included. Such a position was reflected in works of *furūʿ al-fiqh*.

On the matter of gaining the permission of the Imam to perform *qaḍāʾ*, one can compare the following two passages from the relevant chapters (*kitāb al-qaḍāʾ*) in the works of Sabzawārī and Kāshānī:

Sabzawārī	Kāshānī
The permission of the Imam, when he is present, be it specific or general (*khuṣūṣan aw ʿumūman*), is a precondition for establishing the authority of a judge. There is no difference of opinion amongst us on this; even if the *ahl al-balad* seek judgement from a *qāḍī* whose authority has not been proven.	There is no escaping [the necessity of] the permission of the *imām al-aṣl* (upon whom be peace): from [Imam] Ṣādiq [it is related]: 'Be wary of government (*al-ḥukūma*), for government only belongs to the *imām* who is knowledgeable about *qaḍāʾ* and enacts justice amongst the Muslims, like a prophet, or a prophet's deputy.' When he is present and in power, his designation must be specific.
As for when he [the Imam] is not present, the judgement of *al-faqīh al-jāmiʿ li-sharāʾiṭ al-fatwā* becomes effective. He has permission from the Imam. It is well known amongst the *aṣḥāb* that such a ruling is permitted.[17]	When he is absent or not in power, the ruling of *al-faqīh al-jāmiʿ lil-sharāʾiṭ* is effective. He has the permission from Ṣādiq generally (*ʿumūman*), according to the two famous and established [*khabar*s].[18]

For both scholars, there are two types of delegation, specific and general. Specific delegation indicates that the Imam has delegated a person, or a certain type of person, to perform a specific task; this type of delegation ended with the *ghayba*. General delegation refers to the Imam appointing a person, or a specific type of person to represent the Imam across a number of functions. It is considered by most authors that a general delegation continues after the Imam's disappearance.

Kāshānī and Sabzawārī agree on the fact that the Imam has designated the *faqīh* as the one with authority (*wilāya*) to perform *qaḍāʾ* during the *ghayba*. For both, the

[16] See N. Calder, "*Zakāt* in Imāmī Shīʿī Jurisprudence, from the Tenth to the Sixteenth Century A.D.", *BSOAS*, 44 (1981), 468–80 and also his "*Khums* in Imāmī Shīʿī Jurisprudence, from the Tenth to the Sixteenth Century A.D.", *BSOAS*, 45 (1982), 39–47; Moussavi, *Religious Authority*, 147–224; A. Sachedina in his *The Just Ruler (al-sulṭān al-ʿādil) in Shīʿite Islam, passim* (on *qāḍī* see chapter 4, 119–72).
[17] Sabzawārī, *Kifāya*, 262.
[18] Kāshānī, *Mafātīḥ*, iii, 247.

evidence for this delegation lies in the two famous delegation traditions of ʿUmar b. Ḥanẓala (the *maqbūla*) and Abū Khadīja. The importance of the term *al-faqīh al-jāmiʿ lil-sharāʾiṭ (*or *li-sharāʾiṭ al-fatwā* in Sabzawārī*)* is discussed below. At this point I wish to concentrate on the two different manners in which history is divided by the two authors. Sabzawārī divides history into periods when the Imam is present and periods when he is absent. Kāshānī, on the other hand, sees history as divided into periods when the Imam is present *and* in power, and periods when he is absent or present *and not* in power.[19]

This distinction does not make a difference to the delegation during the *ghayba*. For both writers this is general in nature. The distinction is only relevant to our discussion here given the emphasis each author places on different facts: for Kāshānī the type of delegation is dependent upon the legitimacy of the government; for Sabzawārī, it is dependent upon the presence of the Imam. This signifies a difference in emphasis between the two writers, where the Akhbārī considers an empowered Imam to be the critical prerequisite for the full functioning of the Sharīʿa. It is also important to note that this does not affect the authority of the jurist, who assumes the duties of the Imam during the *ghayba* when the Imam is both absent and not in power.
What then is the status of the courts appointed by an illegitimate power (*sulṭān al-jawr*)? Sabzawārī states:

> It can be gained from the *khabar* of ʿUmar b. Ḥanẓala, and Abū Khadīja, and others, that it is not permitted to refer to the *qāḍī*s of illegitimacy, be they Muslims or not. It is clear from the two *khabar*s that it is not permitted to take notice of their *ḥukm*, even if it is a correct one.[20]

From this it would seem that the whole judicial system of the illegitimate ruler (i.e. the non-Imamic *sulṭān*) is to be avoided. However, Sabzawārī follows this with a quotation from the author of *Masālik al-Afhām* (al-Shahīd al-Thānī Zayn al-Dīn al-ʿĀmilī [d. 960/1559]) to which he raises no objection:

> He makes an exception in taking a case to the *ahl al-jawr*, 'If obtaining the truth of [the case] is dependent upon it [i.e. taking the case to *ahl al-jawr*] then it is permitted ... The prohibition in these *akhbār*, and in others also, is interpreted as meaning "referring to them by choice (*ikhtiyāran*) when there is a possibility that one can achieve the same aim through the *ahl al-ḥaqq*".'[21]

---

[19] It is possible to argue that Kāshānī's distinction between when the Imam is present and in power and all other periods is attributable to his Akhbārī position. According to Kohlberg one of the central tenets of Akhbārism is that there is no difference between the *ghayba* and post-*ghayba* period (see Kohlberg, "Aspects", 135). I am not convinced that this was a central tenet since Akhbārī writers (Kāshānī included) do distinguish between when the Imam is present and when he is absent, at least in their works of *furūʿ al-fiqh* (see R. Gleave, "Akhbārī Shīʿī Jurisprudence in the Writings of Yūsuf b. Aḥmad al-Baḥrānī [d. 1186/1772]", unpublished PhD Dissertation, University of Manchester, 1996, 142–90).
[20] Sabzawārī, *Kifāya*, 262.
[21] *Ibid.*

Furthermore, in the section on illegitimate trades in the *kitāb al-tijāra*, Sabzawārī states:

> Helping the *ẓālim* in what is forbidden [is an illegitimate trade]. As for that which is not forbidden, like tailoring and other things, then these are clearly permitted, though the most cautious course of action is to avoid them because some of the *akhbār* say they are forbidden.[22]

This is followed by a citation from the Qurʾān (Q11:113) and a quotation from Ṭabrisī's *tafsīr Majmaʿ al-Bayān* in which Ṭabrisī (al-Faḍl Ibn al-Ḥasan [d. 548/1153]) allows social intercourse, trade and mixing with the *ẓālim*, but not any activity which will aid the *ẓālim's* oppression.[23]

It appears that the community is to utilize the courts of the *ahl al-jawr*, but unwillingly, and because they have no other choice. The *qāḍī* can work for the *ẓālim*, but his legitimacy derives from his delegation by the hidden Imam, not from the illegitimate governor. The *qāḍī* can even receive payment for his work:

> If [the *qāḍī*] is appointed by the Imam... then it is not permitted for him to take wages for [the work]. This is the *mashhūr* position. If he is not appointed [by the Imam], then the most popular opinion is that if he becomes rich from [the *qāḍī*-ship], then it is not permitted; and if he does not, then it is permitted.[24]
>
> The purpose of the *bayt al-māl* [public treasury] is the good of the Muslims, and amongst these is the *qāḍī*, for his upholding of beneficial matters in this type of system, like protecting the oppressed and *al-amr biʾl-maʿrūf waʾl-nahy ʿan al-munkar*. It is permitted for him [the *qāḍī*] to make his living from [the *bayt al-māl*] ... more than one of the *aṣḥāb* have stated that it is reprehensible for him to take [the wages] if he already has sufficient.[25]

The composite picture gathered from these statements is that the court system of any ruler other than the Imam is inherently illegitimate. However, if a *qāḍī* considers that the most effective way of 'enjoining the good and prohibiting the evil' is to accept an appointment from the illegitimate *sulṭān*, then he can do so. He may even receive wages for this activity (though he may not become rich from this work), but he must not forget that his legitimacy derives not from the *sulṭān*, but from the Imam (from whom he has received a general delegation to perform *qaḍāʾ*). The people in such circumstances may, because of the lack of availability of another court system, turn to the *sulṭān's* court system for redress, though they too should remember the enduring illegitimacy of the system.

The following citations from Kāshānī demonstrate that his position is not so different:

---

22 *Ibid.*, 86.

23 *Ibid.*; Abū ʿAlī al-Faḍl al-Ṭabrisī, *Majmaʿ al-bayān*, Tehran 1406/1987, v, 304–9 (the passage cited by Sabzawārī is at 307).

24 Sabzawārī, *Kifāya*, 88.

25 *Ibid.*, 262.

> If the performance [of the *qāḍī*'s duties] is dependent upon accepting the wages of the *jā'ir*, then it is permitted, rather perhaps it is obligatory.[26]
>
> Just as co-operating in the action of a *jā'ir* is forbidden, so it is forbidden to help them, and write the name [of the Imam] in their *dīwān*; as has been derived from the many, clear texts on this matter ... Our *aṣḥāb* say: except when it is possible to perform *al-amr bi'l-ma'rūf wa'l-nahy 'an al-munkar*, or when one is compelled through fear for [the security of] oneself, property, people or some of the Muslims. In these circumstances it is permitted to co-operate with what is ordered, except with regard to *al-dimā'* [an opaque phrase meaning 'the shedding of blood']. It is possible that the proof of this position is [found] in some of [the texts], and in the necessity of relieving the suffering of the poor of the Muslims, and eliminating their hardship ... As for taking the wages [of the *jā'ir*], it is permitted without disagreement, just as buying and selling and other contracts [are permitted].[27]

Kāshānī is keen to allow the possibility of a *qāḍī* working for an illegitimate *sulṭān*, if a *qāḍī* is forced to accept the appointment, or as long as it is recognized that the state court system is only a means whereby *al-amr bi'l-ma'rūf wa'l-nahy 'an al-munkar* can be achieved. The *qāḍī*, like others who deal with the state, is permitted to accept wages for his work.

The exception to this is that the *qāḍī* is not to co-operate with the system if it involves *al-dimā'*. Sabzawārī, in his *Kitāb al-amr bi'l-ma'rūf wa'l-nahy 'an al-munkar*, has a long discussion on the meaning of this term. In his section on 'enjoining the good and forbidding the evil, when there has been no explicit designation from the Imam to do so' he cites a number of opinions relating to *al-dimā'*.[28] Al-Shaykh al-Ṭūsī and the author of the *Masālik al-Afhām* maintain the term applies both to homicide cases (*qatl*) and to cases of injury (*jarḥ*). Shahīd I (Ibn al-Makkī al-'Āmilī [d. 786/1384]) in his *al-Lum'a al-Dimashqiyya* considers only *qatl* to be included; a judge can give a ruling concerning *jarḥ* cases. The reason for this is mentioned by his commentator, Shahīd II:

> *Al-jarḥ* is included in the category of the permitted because the text says that there is [only] no *taqiyya* in killing (*qatl al-nufūs*).[29]

This comment highlights a factor underlying the discussions of both Sabzawārī and Kāshānī: the *qāḍī* who takes a post in government, and receives wages for his work, does so from pious dissimulation (*taqiyya*); that is, it is permitted for a *qāḍī* to accept a post when he, or the community, might be endangered by his refusal. The danger may come from direct oppression by the *jā'ir*, or it may come from neglect of *al-amr bi'l-ma'rūf wa'l-nahy 'an al-munkar*.

The conclusion of this analysis is that, at least with respect to the system of *qaḍā'*, there is little discernible difference between these two writers. Both consider the

---

26 Kāshānī, *Mafātīḥ*, iii, 247.
27 *Ibid.*, iii, 9–10.
28 Sabzawārī, *Kifāya*, 81–3.
29 *Ibid.*, 83.

state illegitimate, but accept that its use by the Shīʿī community may be necessary. This is perhaps the reason for Kāshānī's advice to the Shāh that if Sabzawārī refused the judgeship in Isfahan, the Shāh must force him to accept it. For Sabzawārī should, as a good jurist, refuse to be a *qāḍī* of the *jāʾir* unless he is compelled to do so. This analysis also acts as a warning that merely because a Shīʿī jurist worked with a particular ruler, it does not necessarily follow that he considered that ruler legitimate in his legal writings, whatever he may have written outside of the legal genre of *furūʿ al-fiqh*.[30]

Prerequisites for a judge

Both Kāshānī and Sabzawārī begin their chapters on *qaḍāʾ* with a list of the prerequisite qualities of a judge:

Sabzawārī	Kāshānī
Concerning the *qāḍī*, it is prerequisite that he is mature, of sound intelligence and faith. There is no debate or doubt about this. It is also clear that there is no debate on the condition of legitimate birth and being male. The agreement of the *aṣḥāb* on the applicability of these conditions can be derived from their writings. Knowledge (*ʿilm*) is also included in this.[31]	It is prerequisite for a *qāḍī* that he be mature, of sound intelligence, of faith, just, of legitimate birth, male and have insight. There is no dispute on any one of these amongst us ... as for insight it is [included] because it is forbidden to speak of God without knowledge (*ʿilm*).[32]

Both writers clearly consider the condition of 'insight' or 'knowledge' as in some way problematic; both cite *akhbār* immediately after the above passages which are intended to convince the reader of the validity of this prerequisite. Sabzawārī quotes the *khabar* about three out of four judges being in hell. Kāshānī cites the *maqbūla*. Since Kāshānī clarifies the meaning of 'insight' (*fiqh*) as meaning 'knowledge' (*ʿilm*), one can take his and Sabzawārī's condition of *ʿilm* as the same.

The only difference between these early items on the list of prerequisites is Kāshānī's inclusion of justice (*ʿadāla*). This may imply that Kāshānī is advocating a stricter set of prerequisites for a *qāḍī* than does Sabzawārī.

Sabzawārī adds a further condition:

---

[30] See Enayat, *Modern Islamic Political Thought*, 162–3; N. Calder, "Legitimacy and Accommodation in Ṣafavid Iran: The Juristic Theory of Muḥammad Bāqir al-Sabzavārī", *Iran*, 25 (1987), 91–105.

[31] Sabzawārī, *Kifāya*, 261.

[32] Kāshānī, *Mafātīḥ*, iii, 246.

> There is no dispute amongst the *aṣḥāb* that he [the *qāḍī*] should be a *faqīh jāmiʿ li-sharāʾiṭ al-iftāʾ*. The agreement on this is transmitted in their writings and is [also] proven by the *maqbūla* of Ibn Ḥanẓala.[33]

Kāshānī also includes this condition in the passage cited earlier, though he uses the locution *faqīh jāmiʿ lil-sharāʾiṭ*. It is possible that the omission of *al-iftāʾ* is not a significant difference. Kāshānī's phrase may be an abbreviation of that used by Sabzawārī.[34] Alternatively, it is also possible that one has here a significant difference between the two writers. 'The jurist in whom the prerequisites of giving legal opinions (*fatāwā*) are present/ and 'the jurist in whom the prerequisites are present' may signify two separate sets of conditions, the former being more demanding. The conditions to which Kāshānī is alluding could be the conditions which he has already outlined (mature, of sound intelligence, etc.). The condition of a *faqīh jāmiʿ lil-sharāʾiṭ* merely adds the condition that the person be a jurist (*faqīh*).

That Sabzawārī has an elitist view of *qāḍī*-ship is confirmed by his next condition, which is absent from Kāshānī's account:

> The well-known opinion is that he [the *qāḍī*] should be a *mujtahid muṭlaq*. In the *Masālik [al-afhām]* it is stated: 'His *ijtihād* in some *aḥkām* and not in others is not sufficient'. He does not mention any difference of opinion on this matter. This statement is clear.[35]
>
> *Ijtihād* is a condition for a *qāḍī* in all times and circumstances, and this is a point of agreement.[36]

Now it is possible that Sabzawārī's condition that the *qāḍī* be a *mujtahid muṭlaq* is not as elitist as it first appears. It is possible that his qualifications for *ijtihād* are not so stringent. However, it is clear that he views the *qaḍāʾ* delegation of the Imam as applying to a section of the *fuqahāʾ* (the upper echelons) whereas Kāshānī allows a greater number of jurists to qualify for *qāḍī*-ship. The difference between the Akhbārī and the Uṣūlī writers on this point is not *whether* there is permission to perform *qaḍāʾ* in the absence of the Imam, but the *extent* of the delegation. The Uṣūlī envisages a hierarchical scholarly elite in which only those with the greatest learning can qualify for *qāḍī*-ship. The Akhbārī envisages a greater number of scholars for whom the adoption of judicial functions is a legitimate possibility. The question of whether the *fuqahāʾ* are delegated does not arise.

Explanations for the omission of the prerequisite of *ijtihād* in Kāshānī's account must be traced to his Akhbārī allegiance. *Ijtihād* could not be a prerequisite for a *qāḍī* because, as far as he was concerned, *ijtihād* was not a legitimate exegetical process.

---

33 Sabzawārī, *Kifāya*, 261.

34 In the chapter on Friday Prayer, Kāshānī uses the locution *al-faqīh al-jāmiʿ li-sharāʾiṭ al-fatwā* (see Kāshānī, *Mafātīḥ*, i, 18) and concerning the distribution of taxes, he uses *faqīh* on its own (see *ibid*., i, 229).

35 Sabzawārī, *Kifāya*, 261.

36 *Ibid*., 262.

For him, the *mujtahid* did not occupy a more elevated position than an ordinary *faqīh*; indeed there is a levelling of the scholarly elite, in which the *ʿulamāʾ* are treated as a unified group (who receive delegations *en masse*) rather than a hierarchically stratified social class. To say that Akhbārī legal theory undermined the authority of the clerical elite is inaccurate. Akhbarism may have undermined the authority of the *mujtahid* section of the *fuqahāʾ*, but, at least in Kāshānī's version of it, the scholarly elite remain the representatives of the Imam during the *ghayba*, and are portrayed as the class to whom the population should be loyal.

The relationship between judges

Consider the following passages from Sabzawārī and Kāshānī:

Sabzawārī	Kāshānī
When a full *mujtahid* can be consulted [as *qāḍī* in a case], a partial one is insufficient.[37]	There are two positions concerning the permissibility of a less worthy person as judge when a more worthy person can be found [i.e. that it is not permitted and that it is permitted]. They are based upon the specification to follow (*taqlīd*) the most learned, or the ability to choose [respectively]. In the secure [*khabar*, i.e. the *maqbūla*] it states: 'The true ruling is the ruling of the most just, the most truthful in the [transmission] of *ḥadīth* and the most pious. One should not incline towards what the other rules.' Whenever it is impossible to go to the most worthy, it is certain that the duty to respect his decision is lapsed.[38]

In line with his elitism, described above, Sabzawārī states that it is not permitted to turn to a partial *mujtahid*, when a full *mujtahid* is present. The implication here (though Sabzawārī does not state it explicitly) is that if a full *mujtahid* cannot be found, a partial *mujtahid* will suffice.

Kāshānī's position, that a less worthy person (*mafḍūl*) cannot be a judge when a more worthy person (*al-afḍal*) can be found, makes his system elitist, to a certain degree also. Only the most worthy person in an area can act as a judge. If, however, consulting him is impossible (Kāshānī does not describe the circumstances in which this might occur), then a less worthy person can be consulted.[39]

---

[37] *Ibid.*, 261.

[38] Kāshānī, *Mafātīḥ*, iii, 247.

[39] It is possible to make a connection in Kāshānī's use of *afḍal* here with Shīʿī *kalām*: one of the qualities of the Imam is that he must be *afḍal al-nās* (sometimes termed *afḍal min ghayrihi* or *afḍal*

For Sabzawārī, the pool of possible judges is restricted to the full *mujtahids* in an area. If an area is devoid of full *mujtahids*, a partial *mujtahid* will suffice. For Kāshānī, the pool of possible judges is not limited to *mujtahids*; the judge can be drawn from any member of the *fuqahā'*. However, the selected person must be the most worthy person (*al-afḍal*) in the area; to settle for less than this (*al-mafḍūl*) is not permitted if *al-afḍal* is available. If, for some reason, it is impossible to use *al-afḍal*, then it is permitted to use *al-mafḍūl*. Kāshānī does not state whether this *mafḍūl* must be the most worthy from the remaining *fuqahā'*, but his reasoning would seem to force him to such a conclusion.

From this it can be seen that though, at first sight, Kāshānī seems less hierarchical in his conception of the qualities which make a *faqīh* eligible for *qāḍī*-ship, he is actually stricter in his requirements for it is only the most worthy *faqīh* who may be a legitimate judge. The means whereby a candidate's worthiness is measured are presumably by the criteria set out in the *khabar* (justice, reliability in transmission of *ḥadīth* and piety).

A judge's decision is normally depicted as final in Islamic law, with no recourse to an appeal. There are, however, exceptions.[40] Kāshānī envisages a situation where a *qāḍī* can overrule the decisions of a previous incumbent if he considers them manifestly unsound:

> If the first *qāḍī* makes a ruling, it is not obligatory for a later *qāḍī* to discuss it. It is permitted for him merely to enforce it. But, if he does consider it, and it becomes clear to him that it was a mistaken judgement, it is obligatory to overturn it. If the defendant has been imprisoned, and the punishment has not yet been discharged, then [the second *qāḍī*] must look at the ruling of the first judge, just as when a convicted person claims that the first judge ruled in an unjust manner (*bi'l-jawr*), because it is a claim that must be heard and the matter cannot be brought to a close except in this manner.[41]

The judge is not obliged to review cases, but if he does, he must rectify any mistakes he notices. He must always reconsider a case in which a convicted person claims to have been treated unjustly.

Sabzawārī does not tackle this question as explicitly as Kāshānī, though he clearly envisages only one judge operating in any particular area. When a *qāḍī* arrives in an area, Sabzawārī explains the correct procedure:

> He should ask, before entering [the area], or when he has just entered it, for one of the *'ulamā'* or the notaries, so that he might know who he can rely on and trust ... he should set himself up in the centre of the area, so that he might be fair

---

min al-ra'īya) – meaning 'more worthy, or the most worthy of the people'. If this connection is intended by Kāshānī, the role of the judge as a substitute Imam would be enhanced. See Muḥammad b. Ḥasan al-Ṭūsī, *Kitāb tamhīd al-uṣūl*, Tehran n. d., 261–362; al-'Allāma al-Ḥillī, *al-Bāb al-ḥadī 'ashr*, Mashhad 1372, 44; al-'Allāma al-Ḥillī, *Kashf al-murād fī sharḥ tajrīd al-i'tiqād*, Qum 1415, 366. I thank Professor Ulrich Rebstock for making this point.

40 J. Schacht, *An Introduction to Islamic Law*, Oxford 1964, 189.

41 Kāshānī, *Mafātīḥ*, iii, 250–51.

> to all the people of the area, as much as is possible. He should sit for court in a prominent place, like a central square or an open space so that people can reach him easily if they wish ... He should receive the *dīwān al-ḥukm*. This is what the previous judge had, containing the cases, the court records, the affairs of orphans and those who are absent, the endowments, the evidence of the deposits made by the people [mentioned] in the *dīwān*. This is so that he can know the details of the people's situation and know their rights and needs.[42]

All of this presumes the existence of only one judge in a particular area.[43]

As for cases where a *qāḍī* can overturn the ruling of a previous judge, Sabzawārī does mention that the new incumbent should review some previous cases, particularly those involving imprisonment or property.[44] In relation to the former, the *qāḍī* should review the cases of prisoners and set free those he considers deserving. This refers to those prisoners who have debts, and does not necessarily constitute an overturning of a previous judge's ruling, merely a recognition that the debt has been paid, or the prisoner is declared bankrupt. In cases of property, Sabzawārī does envisage a member of the scholarly elite (*ahl al-ʿilm waʾl-ijtihād*) bringing to the *qāḍī*'s attention a mistake by the previous *qāḍī*. If this proves to be the case, then the person who gains property from the mistaken ruling should give it back. 'If it is not possible [because the property has been sold or spent] then the *bayt māl al-muslimīn* should pay', the reason being (presumably) that the state is responsible for employing the *qāḍī*, and hence is responsible for compensating his mistakes.[45] As with Kāshānī's analysis, the overturning of a decision happens only in the context of a new judge in an area reviewing the cases of a previous judge. Unlike Kāshānī, Sabzawārī considers it normal practice (*adab*) for a judge to follow these review procedures when taking up a new post.

Conclusion

I have set out here the answers to the questions of legitimacy and judicial structure as described in the works of an Akhbārī and an Uṣūlī jurist. On the question of legitimacy, both consider the Imam as the only legitimate appointing authority of judges. This does not exclude the possibility that a judge may work for, and accept payment from, an illegitimate *sulṭān al-jawr*, but the *qāḍī* in such a position is, in truth, appointed by the Imam, and works for the illegitimate power either because he is forced to do so (through threat to his life, property or the Muslims in general) or because there is the

---

42 Sabzawārī, *Kifāya*, 262.

43 The terminology used for the geography of the area under the *qāḍī's* jurisdiction is instructive. *Balad* is the standard name given to an area under a single *qāḍī*, though Kāshānī permits a *balad* to be divided into *aṭrāf*, each under a particular judge. There is no recognition of non-Shīʿī judges operating in a particular area (a possibly significant factor considering Ṣafavid policy on their Sunnī Muslim minorities).

44 *Ibid.*, 263.

45 *Ibid.*

possibility of *al-amr bi'l-ma'rūf wa'l-nahy 'an al-munkar*. It is only the *fuqahā'* who are delegated with the responsibility of executing justice in the absence of the Imam, not the government of the day. There is a difference between Kāshānī and Sabzawārī concerning the division of history (periods of Imam in power/the remainder vs. periods of Imam's presence/periods of absence respectively), and it is possible that this difference can be traced to their Akhbārī and Uṣūlī persuasions (though it is not obvious how). It is important to remember that this distinction does not affect the role ascribed to the *fuqahā'* during the *ghayba*.

On the matter of the structure of the judiciary, both writers place the *fuqahā'* in a position of authority over the people; an authority they derive from the general delegation of the Imam. Though one might expect an Akhbārī to undermine the authority of the *fuqahā'* in this function (due to their denial of *ijtihād*), one actually finds that the Akhbārī (Kāshānī) has a more elitist view of who is eligible for *qāḍī*-ship than the Uṣūlī (Sabzawārī), accepting only the most worthy (*al-afḍal*) as permitted to take the role of judge in a particular area. Sabzawārī stipulates that the *qāḍī* need only be a *mujtahid muṭlaq* (of which there may be a number in the area). Both writers envisage a scholarly elite which is hierarchically structured, the only difference being that the Uṣūlī sees *ijtihād* as the basis for this structure, whereas the Akhbārī relies on the (less tangible?) qualities of piety and reliability in *ḥadīth* transmission. The issue under debate is not whether the scholarly elite should assume the governmental functions of the Imam, but how to decide which members of the scholarly elite should assume this task. The omission of *ijtihād* in Kāshānī's section on *qaḍā'* can clearly be traced to his Akhbārī allegiance, but dropping this prerequisite does not prevent him from constructing a theory of *qaḍā'* in which the *fuqahā'* play the crucial mediating role between the Sharī'a and judicial cases.

Such an analysis demonstrates that conceptions of Akhbārism which describe the movement as anti-clerical and anti-hierarchical are in need of some revision, and that Akhbārīs and Uṣūlīs, at least in their works of *fiqh*, do not have widely varying views on the legitimacy of government during the absence of the Imam, or the authority of the scholarly elite in the *ghayba*. The differences that do exist between Akhbārī and Uṣūlī writers in their theory of *qaḍā'* are part of the *ikhtilāf* of texts within the Shī'ī juristic tradition and cannot obviously be attributed to their loyalty to a particular school of *uṣūl al-fiqh*.

Appendix

Shīʿī Delegation akhbār

1. From Aḥmad b. ʿĀʾid b. al-Ḥusayn from Abū Khadīja Sālim b. Mukarram al-Jummāl. He said: Abū ʿAbdallāh Jaʿfar b. Muḥammad al-Ṣādiq [...] said,
'Let not one of you call another for judgement before the *ahl al-jawr*. Instead look towards one who knows you and who knows something of our judgements and make him [a judge] between you, for I have made him a judge. Seek judgement from him.'[46]

2. The *maqbūla* of ʿUmar b. Ḥanẓala. He said:
I asked Abū ʿAbdallāh about two of our companions between whom there was a dispute over debt or inheritance. They took their case to the *sulṭān* and *qāḍīs*. 'Is this permitted?'

He [...] said, 'Whoever seeks judgement from them, whether [he is] in the right or in the wrong, has only sought judgement from *ṭāghūt*. Whatever decision is made for him is abomination, even if his claim is valid, because he has accepted the judgement of *ṭāghūt*. God ordered that he be considered an unbeliever. God says, "They wish to take their disputes to *ṭāghūt*, yet they have been commanded to disbelieve in him"[Q4:60].'

So I said, 'What are they to do?'

He said, 'They should look to one who has related our *ḥadīth*, observes our *ḥalāl* and our *ḥarām* and knows our *aḥkām*. You should accept his judgement, for I have made him an arbiter between you. Whenever he gives a ruling, according to our rules, and the litigant does not accept it, then he has scorned God's judgement and rejected us. The one who rejects us, rejects God and it [the rejection] is equivalent to associating [something other than God] with God (*al-shirk billāh*).'

I said, 'What if each one of them chooses a man and each [of the two men] differ over [the implications of] our *ḥadīth*?'

He said, 'Whatever the more just, more knowledgeable, more truthful in relating our *ḥadīth* and more pious decides is [accepted as] the ruling. He should not turn towards what the other one rules.'

I said, 'They are both just and accepted by our companions. One is not seen as better than the other.'

He said, 'Whatever they related on the matter [from the Imams], on which their judgement is based, should be compared with [the ruling] which is decided by *ijmāʿ* *(al-mujmaʿ ʿalayhi)*. This would be accepted [as] our ruling and the isolated one, which is not well-known amongst our companions, rejected. The thing agreed by *ijmāʿ* is without doubt. Matters are of three types: things whose guidance is clear, they should be followed; things whose error is clear, they should be avoided; and unclear things whose rulings should be referred to God and the Prophet. The Prophet himself said:

The permitted is clear; the forbidden is clear; between them are unclear things. Whoever avoids the unclear things saves himself from unlawful things. Whoever adopts unclear things, adopts the unlawful and perishes because he does not know [what is lawful and unlawful].'

I said, 'What if the two *khabar*s from you are well-known, both having been related by trustworthy men from you?'

He said, 'They should be examined and whatever agrees with the Book, the *sunna* and opposes the Sunnīs should be taken. Whatever opposes the Book, the *sunna* and agrees with the Sunnīs should be abandoned.'

I said, 'Make me your sacrifice. What if the two *muftī*s [*faqīh*s in some versions] base their knowledge upon the rulings of the Book, the *sunna* and we find two *khabars*, one which agrees with the Sunnīs and the other not. Which should be taken?'

He said, 'That which opposes the Sunnīs, for there is [true] guidance in it.'

I said, 'Make me your sacrifice. If they both agree with the Sunnīs?'

---

[46] Variants: Kulaynī, *al-Kāfī*, vii, 412; Ibn Bābūya, *Man lā*, iii, 3 [this version]; al-Shaykh, *Tahdhīb*, vi, 219.

He said, 'Look at what their [the Sunnīs'] *ḥukkām* and their *qāḍīs* say and ignore it. The other should be taken.'

I said, 'If their *ḥukkām* agree on the two *khabars* together?'

He said, 'When this happens, put off judgement until you meet your Imam. Hesitating on doubtful things is better than rushing into oblivion.'[47]

[47] Variants: Kulaynī, *al-Kāfī*, i, 113–15 (this version); Ibn Bābūya, *Man lā*, iii, 8–11 (abbreviated); al-Shaykh, *Tahdhīb*, vi, 303.

Discussion in Islamic law of being prevented from completing a pilgrimage (*iḥṣār*)

G.R. Hawting (School of Oriental and African Studies)

An issue which is the subject of relatively extensive discussion in works of *fiqh* concerns the circumstances which may cause, and the consequences which flow from, an inability to complete a pilgrimage. If one has stated the intention to perform *ḥajj* or *ʿumra* (or both) and entered the sacral state of *iḥrām* in order to fulfil the intention, but then something happens to prevent its completion, how can the state of *iḥrām* be ended and what, if any, obligations remain?

The issue is usually discussed under the heading *iḥṣār* (sometimes *ḥaṣr*), understood to mean 'being held back or prevented (*scil.* from completing *ḥajj* or *ʿumra*)', and the discussions involve frequent reference to Qurʾān 2:196. That verse begins: *wa-atimmū ʾl-ḥajja waʾl-ʿumrata lillāhi fa-in uḥṣirtum fa-mā ʾstaysara min al-hadyi wa-lā taḥliqū ruʾūsakum ḥattā yablugha ʾl-hadyu maḥillahu*... (Fulfil the *ḥajj* and the *ʿumra* for God, and if you are held back then [you should make] an [animal] offering within your means. And do not desacralize [literally 'do not shave your heads'] until the offering reaches its place of slaughter...).

Discussions of the issue also often refer to the traditional reports about the Prophet's unsuccessful attempt to perform an *ʿumra* in the year just before his conquest of Mecca and the Kaʿba from his Meccan opponents. According to those reports, in 6/628 he and some of his companions decided to try to go to Mecca from Medina in order to make an *ʿumra*. They took with them a number of animal offerings intended for slaughter at the conclusion of the *ʿumra* rituals. They were unable to reach Mecca, however, being stopped by the Meccans at the place called al-Ḥudaybiyya. There the Prophet made an agreement with his opponents, which, among other things, gave him the opportunity of going to Mecca to perform the *ʿumra* in the following year. After concluding the agreement the Prophet ordered his companions to slaughter their offerings there at al-Ḥudaybiyya, to desacralize (to come out of *iḥrām*), and to return to Medina. In the following year he and some companions went to Mecca and performed an *ʿumra*, most commonly known in the tradition as *ʿumrat al-qaḍāʾ* or *ʿumrat al-qaḍiyya*, the 'Umra of Completion'.[1]

In his *The Origins of Islamic Law: The Qurʾān, the Muwaṭṭaʾ and Madinan ʿamal*, Yasin Dutton discusses the differences between the Mālikī, Ḥanafī and Shāfiʿī

[1] E.g., Ibn Hishām, *Sīra* (ed. Muṣṭafā al-Saqqā, *et al.*), Cairo 1955, ii, 308–22; al-Wāqidī, *Maghāzī* (ed. Marsden Jones), Oxford 1966, ii, 571–633; in general see *EI2*, s.v. 'al-Ḥudaybiyya'.

madhhabs on the issue of *iḥṣār* and seeks to explain them.[2] He summarizes the main points upon which these Sunnī legal schools differ concerning the nature of *iḥṣār* and how a *muḥṣar* (someone prevented from completing a pilgrimage) may be released from the state of *iḥrām*; and he offers an account of the reasons why the different schools reached their conclusions.

Dutton's explanations of the Shāfiʿī and Ḥanafī stances are based on works of *fiqh* in which the scholars themselves explicitly set out the reasoning which they say lies behind the positions they have adopted. For the Mālikīs, however, he relies mainly on the *Muwaṭṭaʾ*. That text is generally not so explicit or so detailed about the reasons for the positions it takes, and the explanations provided by Dutton seem relatively more subjective.

For the Shāfiʿīs he accepts the claim made in the *Umm* that al-Shāfiʿī's position was conditioned by the generally agreed fact that Q2:196 was revealed at the time of the Ḥudaybiyya incident. The verse has to be understood, therefore, in the light of the Prophet's behaviour at al-Ḥudaybiyya when he was held back by his Qurashī enemies from finishing his *ʿumra*. Although the command to 'fulfil the *ḥajj* and the *ʿumra* for God' is to be understood generally, the subsequent reference to what someone should do if held back (*in uḥṣirtum*) must be understood as specifically concerned with the conditions faced by the Prophet at al-Hudaybiyya. It is not to be applied to all cases where the pilgrim is 'held back'.

For that reason, claim the Shāfiʿīs, a distinction has to be made between being held back by an enemy (*iḥṣār bi-ʿaduww*) and being held back by other causes such as sickness (*iḥṣār bi-ʾl-maraḍ*). For the former, the words *mā ʾstaysara min al-hady* ('a animal offering within your means') provide a way of ending the pilgrimage and abandoning the *iḥrām*; while someone who has been held back by any other cause has to obey the injunction to 'fulfil' or 'complete' (*atimmū*) the pilgrimage. In other words, the Shāfiʿī position seems to be that the verse contains some material of general validity and some applicable only to situations which parallel that of the Prophet at al-Ḥudaybiyya.[3]

Abū Ḥanīfa, on the other hand, according to Dutton, applied 'primarily linguistic considerations' to the verse. He thus saw no need to distinguish between being held back by an enemy and being so by any other reason. Although the Ḥanafīs too accept the Ḥudaybiyya incident as the occasion of revelation for the verse, they nevertheless

---

[2] Richmond, 1999, 92–6.

[3] al-Shāfiʿī, *Kitāb al-Umm* (ed. M. Maṭarjī), Beirut 1993, ii, 236ff. (in the *Kitāb al-Ḥajj*). At 245 Shāfiʿī repeats that he knows nobody who denies that the verse was revealed in connection with al-Ḥudaybiyya, which was a case of *iḥṣār bi- ʿaduww*. The verse's *in uḥṣirtum*, therefore, refers to that sort of situation, and what to do in such a situation was made clear by the Prophet's behaviour. But the initial command to 'fulfil the *ḥajj* and the *ʿumra* for God' is a general one, binding on every pilgrim, apart from the exception made by God and the *sunna* established by His Prophet regarding *al-ḥaṣr biʾl-ʿaduww*.

hold that there is only one way to come out of *iḥrām* in a case of *iḥṣār* and that must apply to all causes – sickness, an enemy, and anything else.[4]

As for Mālik, Dutton's analysis is that the weight the Medinese Imam accorded to *ʿamal* (the practice of Medina) led him to distinguish, like al-Shāfiʿī, between the *iḥṣār* which resulted from an enemy and that resulting from anything else. In the latter case the rulings contained in Q2:196 apply. *Iḥṣār* caused by an enemy, however, is understood as a special case where the Medinese local practice prevails. That *ʿamal* was based on what the Prophet had done at al-Ḥudaybiyya and the behaviour subsequently of companions of the Prophet who followed his example.

Although the Mālikīs and Shāfiʿīs both distinguish between the *muḥṣar bi-ʿaduww* and the pilgrim who is prevented from finishing by any other cause, Dutton sees their reasoning, which leads to that distinction being made, as different. It is the importance accorded to *ʿamal* by Mālik, Dutton argues, which leads, in the case where someone is held back by an enemy, to at least three exceptions being made to the provisions set out in the Qurʾānic verse. In other words, for the Mālikīs, the rulings contained in Q2:196 were not considered to apply to a case where completion of the intended pilgrimage is prevented by an enemy, or to other cases of a similar nature: the rulings apply to cases of *iḥṣār* where no enemy is involved.[5]

Dutton deduces that the *ikhtilāf* between the schools on the question of *iḥṣār* 'centred around the interpretation of Q2:196'. Abū Ḥanīfa, Mālik and al-Shāfiʿī each approached and understood the verse with differing presuppositions and hermeneutic principles, and each, therefore, understood it in a different way and reached different conclusions about *iḥṣār*. Dutton's analysis focuses on the reasoning of the three imams and seems to accept that that reasoning does indeed account for the positions they take. He is not concerned with possible historical developments in the discussions of *iḥṣār*, or with whether the reasoning which each school claims lies behind its position is really the cause of it.

Nevertheless, it is evident that the links between Q2:196 and the different positions of the three *madhhab*s are quite complex and difficult to follow. That is plain from the summaries already given and it becomes even more so when one attempts to understand each of the specific differences between the schools in the light of the reasoning claimed for them. Furthermore, it is obvious that in the *fiqh* works much of the argumentation is defensive in nature – justifying the conclusions of one's own school against the criticisms of another and seeking to undermine the views of

---

4 E.g., al-Kāsānī, *Badāʾiʿ al-ṣanāʾiʿ* (ed. Zakariyā ʿAlī Yūsuf), Cairo n. d. iii, 1207: 'We hold to the general sense of God's words, and *al-iḥṣār* is *al-manʿ* like that which comes from an enemy, a sickness, or anything else. We go by the general sense of the words and not by the particular cause. The ruling depends on the words not the cause (of the words).'

5 Dutton, *Origins*, 94–6. See especially p. 95: 'It is thus clear that the first scenario [i.e., *iḥṣār* resulting from an enemy] although it derives from the same historical incident that occasioned the revelation of the verse, diverges from the verse's overt meaning in three respects.'

opponents. The ingenuity of the scholars in doing that is, indeed, one of the most interesting features of their discussions of *iḥṣār*. In those discussions the scholars naturally often present their conclusions as arising from, or being in accordance with, the Qur'ān and based on reason, but the complexity of some of the arguments, as well the fact that diametrically opposed views are each claimed to be in accordance with the Book, make that questionable. It seems likely that already established positions, the causes of which are not immediately evident, are being justified by using texts rather than arising out of them. While it is true that in most of the works of *fiqh* (one notable exception is the *Muwaṭṭa'*) the arguments 'centre around' the interpretation of Q2:196, that does not necessarily mean that they arose primarily out of different understandings of the verse.

The main specific differences concerning *iḥṣār* between the three *madhhab*s discussed by Dutton are the following.

The Ḥanafīs make no distinction between causes of *iḥṣār*. Anyone who is held back from completing a pilgrimage (although some deny that there can be *iḥṣār* regarding *'umra* since there is no time limit for the 'minor pilgrimage'), by whatever cause, may only come out of *iḥrām* by having an animal offering (*hady*) slaughtered in the *ḥaram*. The *muḥṣar*, therefore, has a choice. He may wait until the cause of the *iḥṣār* has disappeared and he is free to continue and complete the intended pilgrimage; or he may send a *hady* (or money to purchase one) ahead, agreeing with his companions on the time when it will be slaughtered, and ending his *iḥrām* at that time. If he chooses the latter course, he must still fulfil the aborted pilgrimage – just as the Prophet had fulfilled his aborted *'umra* by making the *'umrat al-qaḍā'* in the year following al-Ḥudaybiyya.

The Shāfi'īs and Mālikīs, on the other hand, regard the pilgrim who has been prevented from completing his *ḥajj* or *'umra* by the action of, or fear of, an enemy as a special case. They allow the *muḥṣar bi-'aduww* (to which are sometimes assimilated a slave 'held back' by his master and a woman by her husband) to desacralize at the place where the *iḥṣār* has occurred and to return home thence with no further obligation (unless the pilgrimage intended had been the once in a lifetime obligatory *ḥajj*, in which case that must still be performed at some time in the future). Although the Prophet had made the *'umrat al-qaḍā'* in the year after al-Ḥudaybiyya, the Mālikīs and Shāfi'īs do not understood that as a precedent binding on others subject to *iḥṣār bi-'aduww*.

There is some disagreement between the Mālikīs and Shāfi'īs on whether a *hady* must be offered to complete the desacralization of a pilgrim held back by an enemy. The Mālikīs say that one must be slaughtered only if the pilgrim has one with him, while the

Shāfiʿīs seem to insist more on the obligation of offering an animal in order to complete the desacralization.[6]

As for the *muḥṣar* by other causes, both Mālikīs and Shāfiʿīs say that he can only desacralize by coming to Mecca and in effect performing the rites of *ʿumra* (*ṭawāf* of the *bayt* and *saʿy* [also called *ṭawāf*] between al-Ṣafā and al-Marwa). They are not very different from the Hanafis in this respect although they express themselves differently: they put emphasis on the *ʿumra* rituals as achieving desacralization whereas the Ḥanafīs put it on the slaughter of the *hady*. If the intention had been to perform *ḥajj*, they all agree that the pilgrim must await the next *ḥajj* and fulfil the original intention then.

Discussion of *iḥṣār* occurs also in texts produced outside the three *madhhabs* treated by Dutton, and it may be useful here to note the views of the Imāmīs and of Ibn Ḥazm.

The Imāmīs apparently share the Mālikī and Shāfiʿī position to the extent that al-Kulaynī has two separate terms: *maḥṣūr* for someone held back by illness and suchlike, *maṣdūd* for someone held back by an enemy.[7]

Ibn Ḥazm's Ẓāhirī position is an unusual amalgamation. Like the Ḥanafīs he makes no distinction between causes of *iḥṣār*: a *muḥṣar* is someone who is unable to complete his started pilgrimage for whatever reason. But, for him, any such person may desacralize at the place where he has been 'held back' and he has no duty to fulfil the intended pilgrimage (unless he had never made *ḥajj* and *ʿumra* previously, in which case the once in a life time obligation has to be fulfilled). This latter position is reminiscent of that of the Mālikīs and Shāfiʿīs regarding the *muḥṣar bi-ʿaduww*, but it goes against them insofar as the *muḥṣar bi-ghayri ʿaduww* is concerned and it is entirely opposed to the Ḥanafī doctrine for the *muḥṣar* by whatever cause.

---

[6] Dutton, *Origins*, 92, penultimate paragraph. The texts themselves, however, seem less decisive on this question. The *Umm* in one place indeed says that whoever is held back by an enemy desacralizes where he has been held back 'and slaughters a *hady*'. But elsewhere in the text the discussion of the issue is more complicated. After saying that the *muḥṣar* who has no *hady* with him should get hold of one to slaughter so that he can desacralize, the *Umm* then discusses what happens if he cannot get hold of one. Two views are given: one is that the person may not desacralize without offering a *hady*; the other is that there is no obligation if something is impossible. It is then said that some (the partisans of this latter view?) offer a descending scale of obligations for someone who cannot get a *hady* to offer – giving food to poor people or fasting. In each case the obligation is only to the extent that it is possible – *idhā qadira addā* (cf. Shāfiʿī, *Umm*, ii, 238, l. 1 and 241, ll. 10ff.; and cf. the Shāfiʿī Muḥibb al-Dīn al-Ṭabarī, *Qirā* [ed. Muṣṭafā al-Saqqā], Cairo 1970, 584 which also reports the two opinions from Shāfiʿī and declares his preference for the latter). Ibn Ḥazm, in his summary of Shāfiʿī's position, also indicates that two doctrines were known: the first is presented as in the *Umm*. The second is similar to the alternative in the *Umm* but is expressed thus: he desacralizes and the *hady* is a debt which he owes (*dayn ʿalayhi*) – it is also said that he must provide food or fast if he cannot offer a *hady* (Ibn Ḥazm, *Muḥallā* [ed. A. M. Shākir], Beirut 1969, vii, 206, l. 10 from bottom). The distinction between Mālikīs and Shāfiʿīs on this point, therefore, does not seem absolute: the one saying you slaughter a *hady* if you have one, the other in effect saying that you should do your best to offer a *hady* but that there are alternatives which would allow desacralization without one.

[7] Abū Jaʿfar Muḥammad al-Kulaynī, *al-Furūʿ min al-Kāfī* (ed. A. A. al-Ghaffārī), Tehran 1347, iv, 368ff. Shaykh al-Ṭāʾifa al-Ṭūsī, *Tibyān*, Najaf 1957, ii, 153–62 does not use the distinct terminology of al-Kulaynī but nevertheless indicates his preference for the view that the *muḥṣar bi-ʿaduww* is a different case from the *muḥṣar* by any other cause: the former may desacralize at the place where he has been held back, the latter only by the slaughter of a *hady* in the *ḥaram*.

Ibn Ḥazm's position is associated with his view that it is possible to make a condition when entering *iḥrām*. In turn that view is supported by (probably based on) a *ḥadīth*: the Prophet advised Ḍubāʿa bint al-Zubayr, who was anxious to make *ḥajj* but was unwell (and feared that she would be unable to complete it), that she should stipulate as she entered *iḥrām* that her place of desacralization would be wherever God stopped her (*inna maḥillī ḥaythu taḥbisunī*). Ibn Ḥazm apparently understands that to mean that it is open to anyone to make such a stipulation when undertaking to make a pilgrimage, and he relates it to the question of whether the *muḥṣar* is required to slaughter a *hady* when desacralizing at the place where he has been held back. He says that if you have made such a stipulation then there is no duty to offer a *hady*, but if you did not make such a stipulation then a *hady* is necessary. His wording here is uncompromising: 'he owes a *hady* without fail (*lā budda*) ... he may not substitute a fast or anything else for this *hady*; whoever cannot obtain one, the obligation remains (*huwa ʿalayhi dayn*) until he does so'.[8]

* * *

The difficulty of accepting that the differences regarding *iḥṣār* arise mainly from different understandings of Q2:196, as well as the argumentative ingenuity of the scholars and their concern to make it appear that their doctrines are aligned with the Qurʾān, become evident when we look more closely at the way in which some of the positions are argued in the *fiqh* texts. Some of the argumentation is complex, and multiple issues connected with *iḥṣār* are discussed: for example, is it possible for the Meccans or for anyone else who is in the sacred territory of the *ḥaram* to experience *iḥṣār*? The following paragraphs focus on the four main points at issue between the *madhhabs* and summarize only some of the arguments.

1. Is the muḥṣar whose inability to complete has been caused by an enemy a different case from one held back by any other cause?

It is clear that in practice all the *madhhabs* use the words *iḥṣār* and *ḥaṣr* when talking of all cases: the Shāfiʿīs and Mālikīs talk of the *muḥṣar bi-ghayri ʿaduww* as well as the *muḥṣar bi-ʿaduww* and the Ḥanafis include being held back by an enemy as a cause of *iḥṣār* along with things like illness, injury to oneself or one's mount, and running out of funds. Nevertheless, they sometimes argue that *iḥṣār* has a primary meaning which may perhaps be extended to include other meanings and sometimes that, although it might have a general sense elsewhere, in Q2:196 it is limited to one sense only.

[8] Ibn Ḥazm, *Muḥallā*, vii, 203, ll. 6ff., 206, l. 6 from bottom ff. For the *ḥadīth*, see Wensinck, *Concordance et indices de la tradition musulmane*, 8 vols, Leiden 1936–88, s.v. *maḥill*.

For example, the Ḥanafis tend to state that *iḥṣār* is general in meaning and has the same sense as *manʿ*: it covers being held back by any cause. But they are not averse to citing also philologists like al-Kisāʾī and Abū ʿUbayda who claim that *iḥṣār* has the particular sense of being prevented by an illness whereas prevention by an enemy is more correctly *ḥaṣr*.[9] The point is to counter the Shāfiʿī understanding of the word, which claims that *iḥṣār* in connection with Q2:196, refers especially to being held back by an enemy. Against that, the Ḥanafi scholars argue that the word not only has a general meaning but if it does have a more specific sense, it is one which is completely opposed to the claims of their opponents.

It is presumably in this context of inter-school argument too that the otherwise hardly comprehensible sayings attributed to figures such as Ibn ʿAbbās and Ibn ʿUmar are to be understood. These sayings assert, for example, that *iḥṣār* (or *ḥaṣr*) can *only* result from an enemy (*lā iḥṣār/ḥaṣr illā bi-ʿaduww*), something which is inconsistent with the general way in which the *madhhab*s use the words *iḥṣār* and *ḥaṣr* in their discussions.[10]

Ibn Ḥazm clearly shows his impatience with such linguistic niceties. He shares the Ḥanafi view that *iḥṣār* may result from any cause including an enemy but he sees the attempt to distinguish between *ḥaṣr* and *iḥṣār* as completely unfounded. He shares the general acceptance that Q2:196, where the verb (*uḥṣirtum*) from which *iḥṣār* is derived occurs, was revealed when the Prophet was held back by an enemy at al-Ḥudaybiyya, and he points out that Ibn ʿUmar and others used the word in ways which contradict the claim that it primarily refers to being held back other than by an enemy. Furthermore, he draws attention to another Qurʾānic instance of the verb *uḥṣira* (at Q2:273) which also refers (according to the understanding of it which he offers) to being held back by an enemy. He insists, therefore, that *iḥṣār* is completely inclusive and that there is no difference between it and *ḥaṣr*.[11]

All of this gives the impression that these linguistic arguments are secondary – introduced to support already accepted views and to argue against those of the opponents. Fundamentally, the different views do not arise out of semantics.

The Shāfiʿī view that the *muḥṣar bi-ʿaduww* is a different legal category from all other *muḥṣar*s, and that he may desacralize in a way different from that of others, rests on the tradition about what the Prophet did at al-Ḥudaybiyya and on the acceptance that it was in relation to al-Ḥudaybiyya that Q2:196 was revealed. The text of 2:196, furthermore, is also understood by the Shāfiʿīs to offer proof for their view: following the conditional ‘and if you are held back (*fa-in uḥṣirtum*)’ there occurs the phrase ‘and

[9] al-Kāsānī, *Badāʾiʿ*, iii, 1206–7; al-Sarakhsī, *Mabsūṭ* (ed. al-Tūnisī), Cairo 1324, iv, 108, ll. 7ff.
[10] For a selection of such pithy definitions of *iḥṣār*, see Ibn Abī Shayba, *Muṣannaf* (ed. al-Afghānī), Karachi 1987, iv/1, 217 where *ʿidhr* should probably be read *ʿaduww*; Ibn Ḥazm, *Muḥallā*, vii, 203, l. 16.
[11] Ibn Ḥazm, *Muḥallā*, vii, 204, ll. 7ff.

when you are in security (*fa-idhā amintum*)'. It is argued that this implies that the *iḥṣār* had resulted from a lack of security and that would be more fitting regarding restraint by an enemy and inappropriate if the restraining factor were an illness.

In addition to their insistence that the verse, in spite of its association with the Ḥudaybiyya event, has to be understood as having a general application, and their related recourse to philology, the Ḥanafīs counter the Shāfiʿī interpretation of *fa-idhā amintum* by arguing that illness too can be a cause of fear and insecurity and they are able to cite sayings of the Prophet in which he describes something as offering security against a specific illness – for example, 'the common cold gives security against leprosy (*al-zukām amān min al-judhām*)' or 'boils give security against the plague (*al-damāmil amān min al-ṭāʿūn*)'.[12]

2. May the hady *(if there is one) be slaughtered by the* muḥṣar bi-ʿaduww *at the place of* iḥṣār *or must it be slaughtered in the* ḥaram*?*

The Mālikī and Shāfiʿī view on this – that the *hady* may be slaughtered at the place where the pilgrim has been held back by an enemy – is argued above all by reference to what the Prophet did when he was held back by Quraysh at al-Ḥudaybiyya and the generally accepted idea that the Ḥudaybiyya incident was the occasion for the revelation of Q2:196. According to those *madhhab*s, al-Ḥudaybiyya was in whole or in part outside the sacred territory (*ḥaram*), and, if part was inside it, the place where the Prophet caused the *hady*s to be slaughtered was outside.[13]

The Ḥanafī insistence that everyone who is *muḥṣar* and owes a *hady*, including someone who has been held back by an enemy, must cause it to be slaughtered at Mecca, is supported by a number of arguments. One is by reference to Qurʾānic verses: Q2:196 says 'do not shave your heads until the *hady* reaches its *maḥill*', the last word being understood to mean 'place of slaughter'. That the *maḥill* must be the sanctuary at Mecca, the Ḥanafīs argue, is clear from Q22:33, which concerns animal offerings and tells us 'then their *maḥill* is to the Ancient House (*ilā ʾl-bayt al-ʿatīq*)'. *Al-bayt al-ʿatīq* is generally understood as a reference to the Kaʿba.

Perhaps more fundamentally, the Ḥanafī view is based on the conviction that the sanctuary is the proper place for offerings, especially those involving the shedding of blood. Desacralization by the shedding of blood is a *qurba*, an act intended to propitiate God, and such acts require a dedicated time and place – in this case the sanctuary and the days of slaughtering at the end of the *ḥajj* ceremonies. An analogy is made with the blood offering required for desacralization when the pilgrim has taken advantage of

[12] Shāfiʿī, *Umm*, ii, 236; Sarakhsī, *Mabsūṭ*, iv, 107, l. 4 from the bottom ff.; Kāsānī, *Badāʾiʿ*, iii, 1207, ll. 11ff. Neither saying is listed in Wensinck, *Concordance*, s.vv. '*zukām*' and '*dummal*'.

[13] Mālik, *Muwaṭṭaʾ*, in the *Sharḥ al-Muwaṭṭaʾ* of al-Zurqānī, Cairo 1936, ii, 292ff. Al-Shāfiʿī, *Umm*, ii, 236ff. The *Bāb al-iḥṣār bi-ʿaduww* in the *Umm* begins by citing Q2:196 and asserting the al-Ḥudaybiyya event as its occasion of revelation. It then moves to argue that the reports of al-Ḥudaybiyya by the *ahl al-maghāzī* support the understanding of the verse which has been elaborated.

mutʿa (here signifying that he has combined *ḥajj* with *ʿumra* and after completing the latter on arrival at Mecca has come out of *iḥrām* to await the beginning of the *ḥajj*[14]): since the *hady* which is required to compensate for *mutʿa* must be slaughtered in the *ḥaram* so must that which achieves the desacralization of the *muḥṣar*.

In addition to those arguments, it was also necessary to confront the example given by the Prophet at al-Ḥudaybiyya, which was the main prop for the Mālikī and Shāfiʿī view that the *muḥṣar bi-ʿaduww* may desacralize at the place where he has been held back. One possibility was to argue that the Prophet was a special case. He could not be sure, if he sent the *hady*s on into the *ḥaram* with somebody else, that the order to slaughter them there would be carried out (presumably because Quraysh still controlled Mecca) and his decision to have them slaughtered at al-Ḥudaybiyya was dictated by that circumstance. Alternatively, some held that the Prophet did send the *hady*s into the *ḥaram* with Nājiya b. Jundub (who appears in some of the *sīra* accounts of al-Ḥudaybiyya) and that they were slaughtered inside the sacred territory. Another possibility was to argue that al-Ḥudaybiyya itself was in whole or in part within the *ḥaram* and so the decision to slaughter there did not infringe the fundamental principle.[15]

In the *Umm* al-Shāfiʿī responds to the Ḥanafī use of Q22:33 by insisting that the Sunna (as revealed in the Ḥudaybiyya incident) shows that the pilgrim who is held back by an enemy may perform the slaughter outside the *ḥaram* (in the *ḥill*) and that Q22:33 only indicates the desirability, not the obligation, of doing it at the sanctuary. Furthermore, he is able to cite another Qurʾānic verse which, he says, shows that the *hady* of the Prophet failed to reach the *ḥaram* at the time of al-Ḥudaybiyya: Q48:25, understood as referring to the events associated with al-Ḥudaybiyya, says, 'They are those who disbelieved and barred you from *al-masjid al-ḥarām* and the *hady* was held back (*maʿkūf*) from reaching its *maḥill*'. As for the phrase in Q2:196 which al-Shāfiʿī's opponents use to support their view that the *hady* must be slaughtered in the *ḥaram* – '[and do not shave your heads] until the *hady* reaches its *maḥill*'– he merely responds by saying that God knows its *maḥill* best.[16]

It is interesting that the *ḥadīth* used by Ibn Ḥazm in his argument that <u>all</u> *muḥṣar*s, of whatever cause, may desacralize at the place where they have been held back – the report that the Prophet had told his paternal aunt Ḍubāʿa to say *Allāhumma maḥillī ḥaythu taḥbisunī* as she entered *iḥrām* for a pilgrimage she was not sure she would be able to complete – is not cited here by al-Shāfiʿī. He did, however, know the *ḥadīth* and used it to support a conclusion completely opposed to that of Ibn Ḥazm. In his summary of al-Shāfiʿī's views while arguing against them, al-Sarakhsī tells us that

---

14 See Arthur Gribetz, *Strange Bedfellows: Mutʿat al-nisāʾ and mutʿat al-ḥajj*, Berlin 1994.
15 al-Sarakhsī, *Mabsūṭ*, iv, 106–7.
16 al-Shāfiʿī, *Umm*, ii, 238, l. 4 from bottom ff.

al-Shāfiʿī used that *ḥadīth* to support his view that a *muḥṣar* who is sick may not usually desacralize at the place where he has fallen ill but must wait until he has recovered and then go on to Mecca and complete the rituals of an *ʿumra* before he is allowed to desacralize. The only exception is if the *muḥṣar* who falls ill had made the stipulation recommended to his aunt by the Prophet. Such a one may leave *iḥrām* at the place where illness had prevented him from continuing. Whereas Ibn Ḥazm uses the report about the Prophet's words to Ḍubāʿa to support his view that everyone who is 'held back', by whatever cause, may leave *iḥrām* at the place of *iḥṣār* (although those who had not made the stipulation would have to offer a *hady*), al-Shāfiʿī uses it contrarily: the Prophet would not have told his aunt to make the stipulation if it was normally allowed for the *muḥṣar* held back by illness to leave *iḥrām* at the place where they had fallen ill.[17]

The question of whether al-Ḥudaybiyya was or was not in the *ḥaram* is perplexing. There are three basic views – that it was outside, inside, and partly inside and partly outside. My initial assumption was that the idea that al-Ḥudaybiyya was part of the sacred territory, or at least that some of it was, was generated by the Ḥanafī attempt to counter the use of the reports about al-Ḥudaybiyya by their opponents, who considered it legitimate for the *muḥṣar bi-ʿaduww* to slaughter the *hady* at the place of *iḥṣār* even if it was outside the *ḥaram*. By arguing that the Prophet did indeed slaughter his victims at al-Ḥudaybiyya, but that al-Ḥudaybiyya was a part of the *ḥaram*, the Ḥanafīs could argue that the prophetic precedent supported their view rather than that of the Shāfiʿīs. The fact that the Ḥanafīs resort to other defensive stategies – such as arguing that the Prophet sent Nājiya to slaughter the *hady*s inside the *ḥaram*, seems to support the view that on this point they are reacting to the arguments and material used by their opponents.

It is surprising, therefore, to find that the issue is blurred in the *Umm*, where al-Shāfiʿī accepts that part of al-Ḥudaybiyya was inside the *ḥaram* while at the same time he insists that the Prophet ordered the *hady*s to be slaughtered outside. He refers to a mosque at al-Ḥudaybiyya as the place marking the spot where the Prophet had slaughtered the *hady*s and received the oath of allegiance under the tree (outside the *ḥaram*).

The *Muwaṭṭaʾ* does not seem concerned with the issue – so far as one can tell Mālik assumes that al-Ḥudaybiyya was not part of the *ḥaram* or at least that the question was whether the *hady*s have to be slaughtered at the sanctuary itself, not merely, as the later Ḥanafī texts suggest, inside the sacred territory. Nor do the early *sīra* accounts of the events which are connected with al-Ḥudaybiyya seem to address the question of whether it was within or outside the *ḥaram*, although one of Ibn

[17] al-Sarakhsī, *Mabsūṭ*, iv, 107–8.

Hishām's reports from Ibn Isḥāq tells us that the Prophet had pitched his camp outside the *ḥaram* (*fī 'l-ḥill*) but prayed inside it.[18]

On the whole, it seems likely that the argument about whether al-Ḥudaybiyya was or was not a part of the sacred territory arose as a result of an attempt to relate the accounts of the Prophet's behaviour to the question of *iḥṣār*. As the reports about al-Ḥudaybiyya came to be seen as relevant to the question, so the reports were elaborated and interpreted in ways which supported one point of view and undermined another. Another example of this occurs in the following section.

*3. Is there a requirement for eventual fulfilment (*qaḍā'*) of the intended pilgrimage by the* muḥṣar bi-ʿaduww*?*

The Mālikī and Shāfiʿī view that the person who has been held back by an enemy may desacralize at the place of *iḥṣār* and has no obligation to fulfil (*qaḍā'*) the intended *ḥajj* or *ʿumra* (unless the obligatory *ḥijjat al-islām* has not yet been performed) is presented as based on the example of the Prophet at al-Ḥudaybiyya. This is at first sight rather contradictory since the *sīra* reports tell us that the Prophet did make an *ʿumra* in the year after al-Ḥudaybiyya and that *ʿumra* is generally known in the tradition as the *ʿumrat al-qaḍā'*. But the Mālikīs and Shāfiʿīs do not see that *ʿumra* as a required fulfilment of the one aborted at al-Ḥudaybiyya. In the *Muwaṭṭa'* and widely quoted elsewhere, Mālik, after reporting that the Prophet and his companions desacralized at al-Ḥudaybiyya, says: 'And (*thumma*) it is not known that the Prophet ordered any of his companions or those with him to complete (*an yaqḍū*) anything or to return for anything'.[19] It is also argued that there can be no duty of *qaḍā'* because the Qur'ān does not refer to it and that although the *ʿumra* in the following year is commonly called *ʿumrat al-qaḍā'*, that was not because it was an obligatory fulfilment for the aborted one but because God fulfilled on behalf of the Prophet his intention to enter Mecca and perform the rituals at the Kaʿba.[20]

Paradoxically the Ḥanafīs, who have insisted on the general applicability of Q2:196 (even while accepting Ḥudaybiyya as its occasion of revelation), on this point are happy to refer to the reports of the *ʿumrat al-qaḍā'* to show that the Prophet did see *qaḍā'* as obligatory for all who had been prevented from fulfilling an intended pilgrimage.[21] So the Mālikīs and Shāfiʿīs, who generally wish to emphasize the importance of the reports about al-Ḥudaybiyya for the law on *iḥṣār*, now have to defuse an inconvenient detail of those reports, while the Ḥanafīs, who claim to rely on the

---

[18] Ibn Hishām, *Sīra*, ii, 319, ll. 10–11.

[19] In the *Sharḥ* of al-Zurqānī, ii, 293. For *thumma* with this sense of 'and', see Q10:47: *thumma 'llāhu shahīd ʿalā mā yafʿalūna*. Dutton, *Origins*, 95 translates, 'since that time there has been no knowledge that ...'.

[20] al-Shāfiʿī, *Umm*, ii, 238, l. 3, 239, ll. 8ff.

[21] al-Kāsānī, *Badā'iʿ*, iii, 1211, ll. 7f.

general applicability of Q2:196, are now happy to use the Ḥudaybiyya material to support their doctrine.

4. Is it always necessary to slaughter a hady *in order for the* muḥṣar *to come out of* iḥrām*?*

The Malikīs differ from the Ḥanafīs and Shāfiʿīs in allowing the *muḥṣar bi-ʿaduww* to desacralize without offering a *hady* if he does not have one with him. (Ibn Ḥazm also allows that possibility for any pilgrim so long as when he entered *iḥrām* he said, 'O God, my *maḥill* is where you stop me'.)

In the *Muwaṭṭaʾ* Mālik does not make a big issue out of this but seems to accept that not all of those at al-Ḥudaybiyya had a *hady* to offer, so when he discusses where the *hadys* are to be slaughtered he simply uses phrases such as 'if he has one'. Al-Kāsānī, who argues against the Mālikī view, suggests that some justified it by the argument that although the Prophet himself slaughtered a *hady* at al-Ḥudaybiyya, it was not on account of his *iḥṣār* and his need to desacralize as a *muḥṣar*. It was merely that the Prophet had brought a *hady* to slaughter at the end of the *ʿumra* and he did so according to his original intention. So in effect he desacralized as a *muḥṣar* without a blood offering specifically intended for that purpose, and that shows that the *muḥṣar* may come out of his *iḥrām* without a *hady*.[22]

The Shāfiʿī and Ḥanafī insistence that all *muḥṣars* must offer a *hady* is argued with reference to the *fa-in uḥṣirtum fa-mā ʾstaysara min al-hady* of Q2:196. Since the verse does not distinguish between someone who has a *hady* with him and someone who does not, nor between someone who had stipulated, when entering *ihrām*, that if he became 'held back' he would not offer a *hady* and someone who had made no such stipulation, it follows that the words of the verse mean that every *muḥṣar* must offer a *hady* in order to desacralize.

But the argument is also based on considerations other than the words of the verse. For example, it is argued that the possibility of ending the state of *iḥrām* is offered to the *muḥṣar* as a concession, an act of leniency (it is a *rukhṣa*) occasioned by a need, and that inevitably requires the compensation of a *hady*.[23]

The basic problem with which all the schools are concerned is that of how the *muḥrim* may get out of the sacral state of *iḥrām* if it proves impossible for him to fulfil the purpose – performance of *ḥajj* or *ʿumra* – for which he had entered it. That might be judged as a practical problem which would arise in a religion which takes ritual seriously, whether or not it was referred to in scripture. Presumably pilgrims often fell ill, suffered injuries, lost their way, ran out of funds, etc.

[22] al-Kāsānī, *Badāʾiʿ*, iii, 1212, ll. 10 from bottom ff.
[23] al-Kāsānī, *Badāʾiʿ*, iii, 1211, l. 7 from bottom, 1212, ll.10 ff.

The special case envisaged by the Mālikīs and Shāfiʿīs, however – prevention from completion by an enemy – seems to be more of a theoretical possibility. There are some authorities who are reported as holding that there is no *iḥṣār* (*scil.*, as a result of an enemy) in Islam.[24] Although there must have been many times when access to the sanctuary was impossible or difficult because of military and political disturbances, the relevance of the Ḥudaybiyya reports would have been doubtful. For one thing, in Islamic times it is unlikely that many pilgrims travelled to Mecca bringing animal offerings with them: today at least most of them buy their offerings at Mecca. On that point the Ḥanafī view that the *muḥṣar* should either send on his his *hady* to the sanctuary cr send money to purchase one seems more practical than the alternative doctrine that the *muḥṣar bi-ʿaduww*, should slaughter his *hady* at the place of his *iḥṣār*, as the Prophet had done at al-Ḥudaybiyya. Mālik's doctrine that no *hady* is necessary if one is not available may be the most practical of all but was clearly judged by some as failing to provide a proper compensation for what, even if unintentional, was transgression of correct ritual.

* * *

This limited sample of the material on *iḥṣār* shows how difficult it is to assess the precise role of Q2:196 in the debates. The scholars frequently refer to it to support their views and no doubt consider that their views are based on it, but for us that is not so obvious. One text which is notably lacking in references to the Qurʾān in its sections on *iḥṣār* is the *Muwaṭṭaʾ*. There Mālik's view that the *muḥṣar bi-ʿaduww* is a special category which deserves a separate chapter from *man uḥṣira bi-ghayri ʿaduww* is not explicitly explained. The chapter on the former consists of two reports with no analysis or explicit argumentation: a summary account of al-Ḥudaybiyya (without any mention of the *ʿumrat al-qaḍāʾ*) which is introduced only by: *ʿan Mālik annahu balaghahu anna* ...; and a report (Mālik-Nāfiʿ-Ibn ʿUmar) concerning Ibn ʿUmar, who was about to set out for pilgrimage 'in the Fitna', declaring that he would do what the Prophet did in the year of al-Ḥudaybiyya. There is no reference to Q2:196, not even to point out that the Ḥudaybiyya event was its occasion of revelation.[25] It could, of course, be argued that the Qurʾānic material and its relevance was simply assumed to be known and accepted.

The *Muwaṭṭaʾ* deals with all other cases of *iḥṣār* in its *Bāb fīman uḥṣira bi-ghayri ʿaduww*. In this chapter too there are no explicit references to Q2:196 although some of the material alludes to the Qurʾānic phrases *mā ʾstaysara min al-hady* and 'a

[24] E.g., al-Ṭabarī, *Tafsīr* (ed. M. M. Shākir), Cairo 1955ff., iv, 47, ll. 3ff.

[25] al-Zurqānī, *Sharḥ*, ii, 292ff. The *fitna* is identified by al-Zurqānī and others as the struggle between Ibn al-Zubayr and ʿAbd al-Malik, when al-Ḥajjāj was sent to besiege Mecca.

fast of three days in the *ḥajj* and seven when you have returned'. There is no prophetic material in this section – all the reports are about companions and successors such Ibn ʿUmar, Ibn Zubayr, ʿĀʾisha, Ibn ʿAbbās, and Marwān b. al-Ḥakam. In effect, Mālik puts the *muḥṣar bi-ghayri ʿaduww* in the same position as someone who has arrived late for the *ḥajj* (*man fātahu ʾl-ḥajj*).[26]

On this basis one could conclude that it is the Ḥudaybiyya reports which cause Mālik to make a distinction between *iḥṣār bi-ʿaduww* and *iḥṣār bi-ghayri ʿaduww* and there is no observable tension between his views regarding *iḥṣār* and Q2:196, which is of questionable importance for the discussion of *iḥṣār* in the *Muwaṭṭaʾ*.

In the *Umm*, by contrast, the discussion of *iḥṣār* shows more awareness of the Qurʾān and is more concerned to reconcile what is basically the Mālikī position on *iḥṣār* with Q2:196. That may explain why al-Shāfiʿī takes a harder view than the Medinese Imam about the necessity for the slaughter of a *hady* by the *muḥṣar* who has been held back by an enemy: Q2:196 says *fa-in uḥṣirtum fa-mā ʾstaysara min al-hadyi.* We also find al-Shāfiʿī justifying the view that no *qaḍāʾ* is required from the one who has been held back by an enemy by the argument that the Qurʾān makes no reference to it.[27]

As for the Ḥanafī view that there is no difference between types of *iḥṣār*, that the law is the same no matter what the cause of the inability to complete the pilgrimage, again it is difficult to decide how far it depends on Q2:196. Our relatively late Ḥanafī texts do make frequent reference to that verse, but the insistence that all *hady*s have to be slaughtered at Mecca cannot be justified entirely by it, and Q22:33 (*thumma maḥilluhā ilā ʾl-bayti ʾl-ʿatīq*) has to be brought in to support it. Even then, it is unlikely that Q22:33 is the basis of the doctrine that all *hady*s have to be slaughtered at the sanctuary: the desire to associate the central sanctuary with ritual slaughter seems natural. Furthermore, the Ḥanafī view that *qaḍāʾ* is required of all *muḥṣar*s is not based on the Qurʾān but is justified in part by reference to the Ḥudaybiyya reports.

If the relationship between the Qurʾān and Ḥanafī views on the various questions associated with the topic of *iḥṣār* is not clear, there does seem to be evidence of the impact of the Ḥudaybiyya reports upon their views. We have noted, for example, their need to show that the Prophet did slaughter the *hady*s in the *ḥaram* at the time of al-Ḥudaybiyya, and their willingness to justify the need for *qaḍāʾ* by reference to the Prophet's *ʿumrat al-qaḍāʾ*. Like the Mālikīs and the Shāfiʿīs, the Ḥanafīs too accept that Q2:196 was revealed in connection with al-Ḥudaybiyya even though their doctrines on *iḥṣār* (apart from the need for *qaḍāʾ*) are inconsistent with, or irrelevant to, the reports about that incident.

Allowing for some vagueness and uncertainty, the material on *iḥṣār* in works of *fiqh* seems to suggest the following developments.

---

26 al-Zurqānī, *Sharḥ*, ii, 294ff.
27 al-Shāfiʿī, *Umm*, ii, 236, l. 3 from bottom.

The earliest view may be the basic position maintained by the Ḥanafīs – no differentiation between causes of *iḥṣār*, and the need to offer a *hady* at the sanctuary in order to end the state of *iḥrām*. The basic concern was to allow the desacralization of the *muḥrim* unable to complete his *ḥajj* or *ʿumra*, and the most common circumstances envisaged for that were illness, injury to the pilgrim or his mount, shortage of money, etc. Detention by an enemy was probably not envisaged as a likely cause. The solution to the problem was based to some extent on practicality but also on the conviction that the breach of the correct ritual had to be compensated for by an animal offering and that the sanctuary was the place where such offerings should be made. How far the Qurʾān was important in this is difficult to assess.

That position is then disturbed by the awareness of the relevance of the reports about al-Ḥudaybiyya for the question of *iḥṣār*, and perhaps of the growing importance of prophetic example as a source of law. It was now thought important to relate the accounts of al-Ḥudaybiyya, which were an important ingredient in the traditional material on the life of the Prophet, to the issue of the *muḥṣar*. This development led to the view that *iḥṣār bi-ʿaduww* was a special category of *iḥṣār* and that someone held back by an enemy should follow the example of the Prophet at al-Ḥudaybiyya. Although it is possible to imagine that the tension between the account of the Prophet's actions there and the words of Q2:196 was already felt, the *Muwaṭṭaʾ* gives little indication of that.

The third stage would be when it became necessary to reconcile the two conflicting doctrines which had developed – that there is only one sort of *iḥṣār* and one way of desacralization for the *muḥṣar*, and that *iḥṣār bi-ʿaduww* is a distinct type with its own rules for desacralization – with the text of Q2:196 and the reports about al-Ḥudaybiyya. This stage is visible in the developed *fiqh* texts and is marked by use of the Qurʾānic verses (2:196 and others) and the reports relevant to al-Ḥudaybiyya to defend whichever of the two conflicting doctrines was one's own and to weaken the doctrine of the opponents. It also involved greater complexity and sophistication of argument and possibly some shifts in position – as, for example, the Shāfiʿī insistence on the importance of the *hady* for the desacralization of the *muḥṣar bi-ʿaduww* (relative to the Mālikī position on this point), and acceptance of the possibility of making stipulations when entering *iḥrām* which would allow one to desacralize wherever one was held back and possibly even without a *hady*.

The early *sīra* reports about al-Ḥudaybiyya do not seem to reveal any awareness of their relevance for the legal questions related to *iḥṣār*: they do not appear even to use words associated with the root *ḥ-ṣ-r*. The reports collected by Ibn Hishām and al-Wāqidī hardly cite any of Q2:196 or refer to it as having been revealed at the time of al-

Ḥudaybiyya – in contrast with their extensive citations of *Sūrat al-Fatḥ*, which is systematically related to the events connected with al-Ḥudaybiyya.[28]

In the chapter of the *Umm* devoted to *al-iḥṣār bi'l-ʿaduww* al-Shāfiʿī is reported as having begun by quoting the opening words of Q2:196 and then saying: 'I have not heard any of the specialists in exegesis (*ahl al-ʿilm bi'l-tafsīr*) from whom I have learned contradict that this verse was revealed at (*bi*; on the occasion of?) al-Ḥudaybiyya when the Prophet was 'held back' (*uḥṣira*) and the idolaters prevented him from reaching the sanctuary ...'.[29]

It is not clear, however, when it came to be accepted that the verse was revealed in connection with al-Ḥudaybiyya: Ibn Hishām and al-Wāqidī do not provide evidence of it and neither does the *Muwaṭṭa'*. From the time of al-Shāfiʿī onwards it does look as though the connection was generally accepted and it was the desire to incorporate the reports about al-Ḥudaybiyya in legal discussion of *iḥṣār* and find ways of reconciling those reports with Q2:196 which seem to be of primary importance for the material discussed here.

---

[28] The only citation of a part of Q2:196 which seems to occur in the reports about al-Ḥudaybiyya collected by Ibn Hishām and al-Wāqidī appears in the latter's *Maghāzī* (ii, 578) and refers to the story of the infestation of the head of Kaʿb b. ʿUjra. Kaʿb was in *iḥrām* like the other companions at al-Ḥudaybiyya and was therefore forbidden to shave his head until the time of desacralization. He suffered, however, from infestation of lice, or some other malady of the head, and wished to shave before completing his pilgrimage. He asked the Prophet what he should do and it was in connection with that that there were revealed the words which are part of Q2:196: 'whoever of you is sick or has an ailment of his head must provide a compensation (*fidya*; i.e., for premature shaving of the head) of a fast, or alms, or an animal offering (*nusuk*)'. This story occurs frequently in *tafsīr* on that part of the verse – it provides a widely accepted occasion of revelation for the words. But the material of Ibn Hishām and al-Wāqidī does not mention that al-Ḥudaybiyya was the occasion of revelation for the opening words of the verse.

[29] al-Shāfiʿī, *Umm*, ii, 236.

Fiqh for beginners
An Anatolian text on *jihād*

Colin Imber (University of Manchester)

My interest in the early history of the Ottoman Empire seems at first a long way from Norman Calder's interest in the early development of *fiqh* and the formation of Islamic doctrine. Nonetheless, it became clear to both of us during the course of many conversations, that both subjects share a common difficulty. Students of Islam face the problem that the earliest Islamic sources for the emergence of the religion date from about two centuries after the 'historical events' of Muḥammad's mission. The same is true of Ottoman history. The nucleus of the future Ottoman Empire emerged around 1300, but there are almost no indigenous Ottoman sources from before 1400, and it is not until the late fifteenth century that narrative chronicles make their appearance. It is largely on these late sources that historians have based their accounts of both the emergence of Islam and the emergence of the Ottoman Empire.

In his studies of early Islamic texts, Norman Calder pursued a literary method. By examining the format of texts, he reconstituted the process of their composition, and was then able to speculate on the date and circumstances of their compilation and to evaluate their contents. His conclusions were always novel and, for those who share his approach, always persuasive. The victim of his method was conventional history writing. What had formerly appeared to be established facts emerged, more often than not, as literary artefacts. The methods which Norman used to examine early Islamic texts apply equally well to early Ottoman texts and produce similar results. The well-known facts evaporate, and what emerge are separate strands of oral and literary tradition, which by 1500 had been woven together to form a coherent but unhistorical account of the Empire's origins.

Historians of early Islam have constructed not only historical narratives but also, on the basis of these, theories – which Norman Calder viewed with his customary scepticism – to explain the appearance and success of the new religion and of the Islamic conquests which followed. The same is true for early Ottoman history. During the course of the twentieth century competing theories have emerged, on the basis of the traditional narratives, to explain the origins of the Empire. Of these, by far the most successful has been Paul Wittek's theory of the 'ghazi origins' of the Ottomans and of the other Turkish principalities which appeared in western Anatolia at the same period.[1] In his view, the first Ottoman ruler, Osman, and his fellow Turkish emirs, were leaders

[1] See especially Paul Wittek, *The Rise of the Ottoman Empire*, London 1938.

of ghazi brotherhoods, bands of men united by the ideology of holy war and dedicated to the expansion of Islam and the conquest of Christianity. Wittek formulated this theory in the 1930s and it remains, despite challenges, and with slight modifications, the most popular theory of the origins of the Ottoman Empire.

In 1986, about fifty years after the first appearance of Wittek's 'ghazi thesis', Şinasi Tekin announced his discovery of a fourteenth-century Turkish text on holy war[2] which appeared to provide a striking confirmation of Wittek's views. In 1989, he published the full text with an introduction. It is not strictly speaking an Ottoman text, but originated, in Tekin's view, from the emirate of Karasi, a principality which in the first half of the fourteenth century adjoined Ottoman territory in north-western Anatolia. It was therefore, in his opinion, the product of an environment where both the ideology and the practice of holy war flourished. There has so far been no focused analysis of the text, but those who have referred to it imply that it has its origin in the mundane realities of fourteenth-century Karasi. Tekin, for example in the introduction to his edition,[3] comments that the rule on how to remove booty from enemy territory when the Muslim leader has no animals reflects 'a primitive state structure', and regards it as unthinkable that the first Ottoman rulers, Osman and Orhan, would not have possessed the necessary beasts of burden.[4] Elizabeth Zachariadou supports the assertion that: 'In Turkish Anatolia the possibility of expansion by the conquest of Christian territories favoured the formation of military groups under leaders who adopted the ideology of holy war and eventually assumed full political leadership,' with a footnote referring to this text.[5] She also refers to it in an article on the emirate of Karasi: 'One text, the *Hikayet-i Gazi*, which was very probably composed in the Emirate of Karasi at that time reveals the spirit prevailing there. Its author tried to explain the meaning of holy war waged by the Muslims against the infidels and the rules of that war.'[6] Cemal Kafadar, in a somewhat obscure discussion of the work refers to it as 'a code-book of gaza',[7] an activity which, following Tekin, he erroneously differentiates from *jihād*.[8] In short, historians who have commented on this work have found in it proof that the principalities of western Anatolia in the fourteenth century were indeed the creation of active ghazis.The starting point for this interpretation of the text is Wittek's theory of the

[2] Şinasi Tekin, "XIV yüzıla ait bir *ilm-i hal*: Risaletü'l-islam", *Wiener Zeitschrift für die Kunde des Morgenlandes*, 76 (1986), 279–92.
[3] Şinasi Tekin, "XIV yüzılda yazılmış Gazilik Tarikası 'Gaziliğin Yolları' adlı bir eski Anadolu Türkçesı metni ve *gaza/cihad* kavramları hakkında", *Journal of Turkish Studies*, 13 (1989), 139–204. Hereafter 'Tekin'.
[4] Tekin, 148. The text in fact gives a standard rule of *fiqh* in Turkish translation.
[5] Elizabeth Zachariadou, "The Oguz Tribes: The Silence of the Byzantine Sources", *Res Orientales*: VI, *Itinéraires d'Orient. Hommages à Claude Cahen* (1994), 285–9.
[6] E. Zachariadou, "The Emirate of Karasi and that of the Ottomans: Two Rival States", in Elizabeth Zachariadou (ed.), *The Ottoman Emirate, 1300–1389*, Rethymnon 1993, 225–36.
[7] Cemal Kafadar, *Between Two Worlds: The Construction of the Ottoman State*, Berkeley 1995, 64.
[8] Kafadar, *Between Two Worlds*, 79–80. The distinction between *ghazw* (Turkish: *gaza*) and *jihād*, is that *ghazw* normally refers to a single battle, raid or campaign, whereas *jihād* refers to holy war in general.

ghazi origins of the Ottoman Empire: it is the theory which determines the interpretation. Let us, however, follow Norman Calder's example and start not with a theory but with the text itself.

The work survives in two manuscripts, one (ms. P) in Tekin's private collection, and the other (ms. TK) in the Library of the Topkapi Palace, Hazine 201. Tekin has shown from their watermarks that both manuscripts date from the late fifteenth or early sixteenth centuries. The language, however, is clearly archaic and there seems no reason to dispute the fourteenth-century date or Anatolian provenance of the text itself. The attribution to the emirate of Karasi, however, is optimistic. The Introduction to ms. P names the dedicatee as Ya'qub Beg b. Bakhshi. Tekin assumes that the 'Bakhshi', named as the father of the dedicatee, should read 'Yakhshi', and identifies him with a prince of the House of Karasi who bore this name.[9] The first of these assumptions is most probably correct. The difference between Bakhshi and Yakhshi in the Arabic script is a single dot, and the same copyist later makes the same slip in writing *yaşlu* ('wounded') as *başlu*[10] [p. 162 ¶1].[11] The identification of the dedicatee's father with Prince Yakhshi of Karasi is, however, more speculative, given our fragmentary knowledge of the *dramatis personae* of fourteenth-century Anatolia. However, the fact that the dedicatee bears the title *beg* ('lord') and is described as *Khudavend-i a'zam* and *makhdumzade-yi mu'azzam*[12] indicates that he was a member of a royal household and, quite possibly but by no means certainly, of the House of Karasi. What seems certain, therefore, is that it is a fourteenth-century Anatolian – and quite probably western Anatolian – text, compiled for a member of a ruling family, conceivably the House of Karasi.

On the nature of the text itself it is easier to reach a conclusion. First, as Tekin informs us, it is not an independent work, but forms a chapter in a book entitled *Risaletü'l-islam*. This deals with the relative merits of different ways of earning a living, these being, in descending order of worth, holy war, trade, agriculture and craft. Second, as the Introduction to ms. P states, the work is not original but a translation from Arabic, the compiler informing us that, on the order of the dedicatee he had 'collected a few drops from the ocean of the knowledge of God Most High' and 'translated this book (*risalet*) from the Arabic tongue into Turkish'.[13] The sources of the *Risalet* are therefore literary, suggesting that the chapter on holy war reflects Arabic literary learning rather than the Turkish military spirit. Furthermore, the fact that the *Risalet* seems to be a translation and that the chapter on holy war appears not in

---

9 Şinasi Tekin, "XIV üncü yüzyıla".
10 Tekin, 162 ¶1 reads *başlu*.
11 References in square brackets refer to the page and paragraph no. in the edition of the text in Tekin.
12 Şinasi Tekin, "XIV üncü yüzyıla".
13 Şinasi Tekin, "XIV üncü yüzyıla".

isolation but within the framework of a moralistic discussion suggests that it belongs to an established literary genre, and this indeed turns out to be the case.

The problem of how a Muslim may lawfully secure a living is one which, in the Ḥanafī tradition, goes back to *al-Iktisāb fi rizq al-mustaṭāb*,[14] attributed to al-Shaybānī (d. early ninth century). Here the author, with an eye to the rhyming potential of the words, identifies four means of livelihood: trade, renting out, agriculture and craft *(al-ijāra wa'l-tijāra wa'l-zirā'a wa'l-ṣinā'a)* 'all of which are equally licit in the opinion of most of the jurists',[15] and lays out the principles for assessing the moral worth of a trade or profession.[16] The same preoccupation appears in the *Tanbīh al-Ghāfilīn* of Abu Layth al-Samarqandī, where 'The chapter on the merits of earning' (*Bāb faḍl al-kasb*) presents a series of *hadīth* on the question of lawful acquisition.[17] In this chapter al-Samarqandī introduces the notion of holy war as a means of livelihood. He also has separate chapters on the merits of holy war.[18] Some of the material from both these sections appears again in the *Kitāb shir'at al-islām ilā dār al-salām* of Muḥammad b. Abu Bakr al-Sharjī (d. 1177). In this work, however, the author has re-shaped the chapter on lawful acquisition to give it an outline similar to that of the *Risalet*. 'The thirtieth chapter concerning the pursuit of what is licit' (*al-faṣl al-thalāthūn fi ṭalab al-ḥalāl*) ranks professions in terms of merit, beginning with the statement: 'The most meritorious source of gain (*afḍal al-makāsib*) is *jihād* in the path of God Most High, the exalting of the Blessed Word in the pursuit of a daily bread'. There follow sections on the merits of trade, crafts, agriculture and livestock rearing.[19]

This much should make it clear that the contents of the *Risalet* place the work within a tradition of Islamic literature that goes back to the ninth century. This is a point which Tekin himself seems to have noticed, since he points out the similarity between it and a Turkish translation of the parallel section in the *Kitāb shir'at al-islām*.[20] He also mentions the *Tanbīh al-Ghāfilīn* and presents in facsimile a manuscript of a Turkish translation of its chapter on *jihād*.[21]

It is clear therefore that the *Risalet* belongs to the mainstream of Islamic literature. Even though it has not so far been possible to identify the immediate source or sources of which it is a translation, it is nonetheless easy to recognize the starting point of the chapter on holy war. This is at once apparent from the opening passage, where the compiler explains that booty coming from holy war (*gazilikten gelen ganimet*) is legitimate gain, but only provided the Muslim warriors follow certain

---

14 Muḥammad b. Ḥasan al-Shaybānī, *al-Iktisāb fi rizq al-mustaṭāb*, Beirut 1986.
15 al-Shaybānī, *al-Iktisāb*, 40.
16 al-Shaybānī, *al-Iktisāb*, 36.
17 Abu Layth al-Samarqandī, *Tanbīh al-Ghāfilīn* Cairo 1851, 163–4.
18 al-Samarqandī, *Tanbīh*, 178–82.
19 British Library, Delhi Arabic 1760, 45v–49r.
20 Şinasi Tekin, "XIV üncü yüzyıla".
21 Tekin 139, and Appendix.

precepts (*resme*), principles (*erkan*) and conditions (*şart*). If they do not observe these, the gain is illegal [p. 156 ¶1]. The source of this idea is *fiqh*, which treats war against the infidels as a legitimate mode of acquisition, alongside, for example, sale, gift or inheritance. The jurists lay out the rules of warfare which the warriors must observe, and the manner of distributing booty so that it becomes the legal property of the Muslims.

In a work of *fiqh*, the location of this material is always the opening section of the chapter on *al-Siyar*. The jurist al-Marghinānī (d. 1197) defined *siyar* as 'the plural of *sīra*, this being the [right] way of [conducting] affairs. In law, it refers specifically to the *siyar* of the Prophet in his wars (*maghāzī*)'.[22] Like any other jurist, he then goes on to specify the persons whom the law obliges to fight the infidels and in what circumstances, the rules for waging warfare, granting peace and making treaties with the enemy, and the rules for distributing booty. These, with some omissions in detail, form the subject of the chapter in the *Risalet*.

The contents of the chapter therefore are no more than a recapitulation of the rules of warfare as these appear in any comprehensive work of Ḥanafī *fiqh*. A closer examination, however, shows that *fiqh* is the source not only of the substance of the chapter, but also of most of its phraseology. A comparison is easy since, allowing for differences in form and language between sub-genres, works of *fiqh* are stereotypical. They preserve and transmit not only the form and contents of earlier works, but also reproduce, either verbatim or with insignificant variations, the important passages and phrases of their predecessors. These are what appear in Turkish translation in the *Risalet*.

The rules of warfare which the *Risalet* presents correspond closely with the same rules as they appear in the 'abbreviated' works of *fiqh*, as a comparison with *al-Matn* of al-Qudūrī (d. 1029), the *Kanz al-Daqā'iq* of al-Nasafī (d. 1142), and *al-Hidāya*[23] of al-Marghinānī demonstrates. A few examples make this clear. When discussing the mode of warfare, al-Qudūrī writes: 'They should seek the help of God Most High, and fight them. They should set up mangonels against them, set fire to them, send water against them, cut down their trees and destroy their crops.'[24] The same rule appears in the *Kanz*: 'We should seek help in God Most High, and fight them by setting up mangonels, burning them, drowning them, cutting down their trees and destroying their crops.'[25] The *Risalet* differs from these only in the addition of a non-significant phrase and in the order of presentation: 'The Muslims should take refuge in God and seek the help of God and begin fighting. They should set up mangonels,

---

22 al-Marghinānī, *al-Hidāya*, Cairo 1972, v, 434.
23 *al-Hidāya* is a commentary rather than an abbreviated work. However, it is a commentary on its author's own abbreviated work, *al-Bidāya*, and as such contains the text of *al-Bidāya*.
24 al-Qudūrī, *al-Matn*, Cairo 1957, 113.
25 al-Zaylaʿī, *Tabyīn al-Haqā'iq*, Bulaq 1895, 243.

destroy and burn their crops, cut down their trees and drown them in water' [p. 158 ¶1]. Correspondences such as this occur throughout the text. Here, for example, al-Qudūrī lays out the rules for the division of spoil: '[The Imam] should not divide the booty in the Realm of War. [He should not divide it] until he has taken it to the Realm of Islam. If any of the men who take spoil dies in the Realm of War, he has no right in the booty before the division and the sale of the booty. If he dies after its removal to the Realm of Islam, his share goes to his heirs.'[26] The corresponding passage in the *Risalet* reads: 'Whatever they have taken from the territory of the infidel, they should not divide on the territory of the infidel. If anyone from the army dies in the territory of the infidel, that person has no share in the booty. If he dies after they have taken it to the territory of the Muslims, that person has a share and it is given to his heir' [p. 160 ¶3]. Here the correspondence may not be verbatim, but the sense and the sequence of the material are identical in both passages. A closer correspondence occurs in the passage which grants a small share of the booty to women who tend the sick. In *al-Hidāya* of al-Marghināni, this reads: 'A niggardly amount should be given to a woman if she has treated the wounded and tended the sick.'[27] In the *Risalet* this becomes: 'A little something should be given to women if they have tended wounded *ghazis*' [p. 162 ¶1].

In one case the *Risalet's* translation of a passage of *fiqh* is inaccurate. A problem which the jurists raise is who has the right to grant a safe-conduct (*amān*) to the infidels. On this question al-Qudūrī has: 'If a free man or a free woman grant a safe conduct (*ammana*) to an infidel, a group [of infidels], a garrison or a town, their safe-conduct is valid'.[28] The *Risalet* renders the passage as follows, reading the Arabic accusatives as nominatives: 'If the enemy is defeated (*bunalsa*) and seeks *amān*, it is permissible (*reva*) for a Muslim man, woman, group or garrison (*bir kal'e ehli*) to grant a safe-conduct' [p. 159 ¶3]. What seems to have happened is that the Arabic manuscript from which the compiler was working omitted the word 'infidel' (*kāfir*^{an}) from the list of grantees. Since it is the only word in the list to show the accusative case in unvowelled script, the compiler quite reasonably read the remaining accusatives as nominatives and hence the mistranslation.

These few examples are enough to make it clear that *fiqh* is the source of the rules of warfare in the *Risalet*. Much of the text, however, does not present rules so much as explanation or commentary. Here too it is easy to locate the source of the material in *fiqh*, although usually in commentaries, such as Zaylaʿī's on the *Kanz* rather than in abridged works such as the *Kanz* itself. An example of this is the treatment in the *Risalet* of the term 'communal obligation' (*farḍ kifāya*). After defining the phrase, the text gives three examples: 'A communal obligation is one where, if some people are

---

26 al-Qudūrī, *al-Matn*, 115
27 al-Marghināni, *al-Hidāya*, v, 502.
28 al-Qudūrī, *al-Matn*, 114.

fulfilling it, but others are not, no obligation falls on [the latter group], like performing funeral prayers, saying *yarḥamuka'llāh* to someone who sneezes, or returning greetings' [p. 157 ¶2]. The parallel passage in Zaylaʿī's – and other jurists' – commentaries reads as follows: 'When [the obligation] is put into effect through some, it drops from the remainder, like funeral prayer, burying the dead or returning greetings'.[29] Another instance of commentary on a rule, is the passage where the *Risalet* explains why a horseman should receive twice the share of booty allotted to an infantryman: 'Two shares should be given to a horseman, and one to an infantryman, because the horseman both stands firm and pursues, while the infantryman is able only to stand firm' [p. 161 ¶3]. This straightforward explanation is a simplified version of a convoluted argument found in the classical commentaries. The following is an abbreviated version of the equivalent passage in Zaylaʿī: 'One portion goes to a footman and two to a horseman ... because deserts are according to abilities and the horseman's ability is three times that of the footman, because the horseman is for attack, retreat and standing firm, and the infantryman is for standing firm and nothing else ... [However] attack and retreat are of one kind. Retreat is not approved in itself, but only sanctioned for the sake of attack, so [the horseman's] ability is twice that of the footman'.[30] A final example of the correspondences between the *Risalet* and the commentaries concerns the Prophet's share of the booty:

> [The Prophet] – upon him be peace – used to take from the booty something which he had fixed his eye upon ... such as good armour,[31] a good sword or a good slave or slave-girl ... The lords of today are not entitled to take his share. Imam Shāfiʿī – blessings be upon him – said: "Whoever is Caliph in the present time, the Prophet's share belongs to him" [p. 162 ¶3].

The equivalent passage in *al-Hidāya* of al-Marghinānī reads: 'The *ṣafī* is something the Prophet – blessings and peace be upon him – chose for himself from the booty, such as armour, a sword or a slave-girl. Shāfiʿī – may God's mercy be upon him – said: "The share goes to the Caliph."'[32]

These examples indicate that the *Risalet* corresponds with *fiqh* in contents, and phraseology. The same is true of its vocabulary, as a few examples will make clear. Jurists typically place acts within moral categories, ranging from 'forbidden' (*ḥarām*) to 'obligatory' (*wājib*), and the *Risalet* does the same, but attempts to render the Arabic terminology in Turkish, not always with great clarity. The most exact renderings are Turkish *kayurmaz* for Arabic *la ba'ṣ* ('it does not matter') [e.g., p. 158 ¶1] and Turkish *revadır* for Arabic *yanbaghī* ('it is fitting') [e.g., p. 158 ¶3]. In some places the

[29] al-Zaylaʿī, *Tabyīn*, 241.
[30] al-Zaylaʿī, *Tabyīn*, 254.
[31] Turkish *çukal* ('armour'), following ms. P. Tekin has *çub* ('wood'), following ms. TK. *Çukal* is clearly to be preferred, as it corresponds with *dirʿ* ('armour') in the Arabic texts. It is also inherently unlikely that the Prophet would have selected a piece of wood as his share of the spoils of battle.
[32] al-Marghinānī, *al-Hidāya*, v, 507.

compiler introduces the same Arabic term as evidently appears in the original text, but pairs it with a Turkish synonym. Thus he renders the Arabic *silāh* ('weapon[s]') as *bilik ve silāh* [p. 159 ¶2], Arabic *'alaf* ('fodder') as *yem ve 'alef* [p. 161 ¶1], and *yu'addabu* ('he should discipline') as *segide edebleye* [p. 159 ¶3]. Elsewhere he takes care to render Arabic words and phrases as precisely as possible with Turkish paraphrases. Hence Arabic *raḍakha* ('to give a niggardly amount') becomes Turkish *az nesnecik ver* ('to give a little something') [p. 162 ¶1]; the Arabic technical terms *mukātab* ('slave who has contracted with his owner to purchase his freedom for an agreed sum') and *salab* ('the spoil of a slain man which a warrior may legally acquire in battle') become *gendözin bahaya kesmiş kul* ('slave who has agreed a price for himself') [p. 162 ¶1] and *at ve don ve silah* ('horse, accoutrements and weapons') [p. 163 ¶2].

This much should make it clear that most of the *Risalet* is a direct translation from *fiqh*. In the few passages where this does not seem to be the case, the non-standard material usually serves only to illustrate a rule of *fiqh*, or to deduce a rule already implicit in the juristic texts. An example of an explanatory phrase occurs with the rule that, before attacking the infidels, the Muslims should call on them to accept Islam. In works of *fiqh*, the authors usually state laconically: 'They should summon them to Islam.' To this the *Risalet* adds that they should say to the infidels: 'Come on! Become Muslims!' [p. 157 ¶3]. A similar addition occurs when the compiler states the rule which allows the Muslim leader to break a peace that he has concluded with the infidels, but only after he has warned the infidels. The compiler again illustrates the rule by adding that the Muslims should announce to the enemy: 'Be aware! We have broken our truce!' [p. 159 ¶1]. These additions to the juristic texts do not alter or modify their sense. In another case, however, the compiler, or more probably his immediate source, creates a new rule: 'When the lord of the Muslims enters the Realm of War, he should review his army so that he knows his horsemen and his footmen' [p. 161 ¶3]. The reason for this rule is that it is a person's status as horseman or footman at the moment of entry into enemy territory that determines his share of the booty. Even if a horseman loses his mount, or if a footman acquires one, their status as horseman or footman remains unaltered. The *Kanz* expresses the rule concisely: 'What is taken into account [in determining who is] a horseman or a footman is [their status] at the crossing'. To this Zailaʿī adds by way of commentary: 'That is to say, what is considered is his being a horseman or a footman at the time of crossing [from] the Realm [of Islam to the Realm of War.] If he entered the Realm of War as a horseman and his horse is lost and he fights as a footman, he is entitled to a horseman's share ...'[33] The idea in the *Risalet* that the Muslim leader should review his troops just before entering enemy territory

33 al-Zaylaʿī, *Tabyīn*, 255.

arises directly from this rule. The review is necessary so that the commander can establish future shares in the booty.

It should now be clear that this chapter in the *Risalet* presents a juristic view of warfare and does not reflect the spirit of ghazis fighting on the Anatolian frontier. This leaves the question of whether the work has any interest, apart from the purely philological, for historians of fourteenth-century Anatolia. There are two obvious approaches to the problem. The first is to identify any material which appears to have no counterpart in *fiqh* and seems not to emerge from a juristic rule. Any such passage might be an addition of the compiler which represents a contemporary reality rather than a juristic ideal. The second approach is to examine the implications, if any, of the language of the translation.

With regards to the substance of the chapter, departures from *fiqh* are very few. A slightly different way of presenting one rule of warfare might, however, be an indication of the milieu in which the compiler was working. It is an implicit rule in *fiqh* that Muslim troops should not keep booty for themselves before its formal distribution, unless the Muslim leader permits it, or unless the raiding party was less than a full army. However, the jurists do not always state the rule explicitly. The *Risalet*, however, not only states it explicitly, but does so twice: 'The Muslims should not steal or conceal anything of the booty' [p. 158 ¶3], and 'Whenever the army makes a full-scale attack (*tamam akın*) and returns to the Muslims' territory, whatever booty they have with them – right down to things as small as needle and thread – they should bring to the *imam* and hide nothing' [p. 162 ¶1]. The repetition of this usually unstated rule suggests that the compiler was making an effort to educate his audience in this particular point, which in turn suggests that the dedicatee and his followers did make raids into Christian territory but, hardly surprisingly, did not observe the rules for the distribution of booty. Two other non-standard passages perhaps also hint at the type of warfare that they undertook. A rule which appears in the *Risalet*, but apparently not in *fiqh* reads: '[The Muslims] should not cut off the infidels' noses or ears, or gouge out their eyes' [p. 158 ¶3]. The prohibition here might be a reflection of actual practice. It may however be no more than an imaginative re-statement of a *hadīth* which opens Shaybānī's chapter on *jihād*, and which appears as a rule in later works of *fiqh*: ' ... you should not mutilate anybody ...'[34] Another hint of reality emerges from a rule that allows a *dhimmī* a small share of the booty if he acts as a guide on enemy territory. *Al-Hidāya* expresses the rule as follows: 'The *dhimmī* receives a niggardly amount only if he fights or shows the way.'[35] The *Risalet* however adds to this bald statement the comment that *dhimmīs* receive something (*nesne*) from the booty: ' ... if they have helped the Muslims or if they have acted as guides to infidels' villages, or the places where they hide cloth

[34] Majid Khadduri, *War and Peace in the Law of Islam*, London 1955, 21.
[35] al-Marghinānī, *al-Hidāya*, 502.

(*kumaş koyacak inler*)' [p. 162 ¶1]. The reference specifically to villages and cloth are an addition to *fiqh* and might indicate the type of raids that the dedicatee and his followers undertook. If this is the case, it suggests that villages rather than fortified towns were the typical targets of raids, and that, apart presumably from slaves and animals, textiles were the most prized form of moveable wealth.

These three items, however, are all that emerge from the contents of the *Risalet* as conceivably representing realities rather than juristic constructs. The language of the text, however, allows for some further speculation.

Orthodox Islam expresses itself through the medium of Arabic. Arabic is, in particular, the language of *fiqh* through which the jurists have formulated concepts which define the religious law and therefore, to an extent, the religion itself. An Arabic term in *fiqh*, or indeed in any other Islamic science, carries with it a precise definition and often a weight of scholarship. This definition and the scholarly context of the word disappears in translation, except for the reader or listener who knows the Arabic term which the translated word represents. A translation of *fiqh* is therefore at best an approximation of its original sense. A grasp of Islam therefore requires a grasp of the Arabic vocabulary of *fiqh* and the other Islamic sciences, and the degree to which this permeates an Islamic language is one measure of the degree of Islamization of the speakers of that language.

What is striking about the *Risalet* is that the compiler did not expect the dedicatee to be conversant with Arabic terminology. Many of the most basic religious terms are, as they remain today, Persian: for example, *Müslüman*, *namaz*, *oruç*, *Peygamber* for Arabic *Muslim*, *ṣalāt*, *ṣawm*, *Rasūlu'llāh*. This suggests that the most basic of the Arabic religious terms that appear in the *Risalet*, such as *ḥajj*, or *ḥalāl*, had also entered the language via contact with Persian speakers, rather than through formal instruction in Arabic. Many of the terms the compiler renders with Turkish words or phrases; hence 'God' is *Tanri* not *Allah*, 'Islam' is *Müslümanlık* not *Islam*, 'holy war' is *gazilik* not *jihād*, 'religious obligation' is, in one instance *borç* ('debt') [p. 157 ¶2] not *farḍ*. 'A man who [is entitled to take] spoil' the compiler renders, not quite accurately, as *akıncı* ('raider') [p. 162 ¶2] and not as *ghānim*. *Tamam akın* [p. 162 ¶2] presumably represents *ghazw*/*ghazwa* ('campaign, raid by an army'), which legal and historical texts distinguish from *sariyya* ('attack by a small raiding party'). Some Arabic words, such as *mukātab*, the compiler has paraphrased. The text of the *Risalet* suggests therefore that the religious vocabulary in current use was either Turkish, Persian, or Arabic that had entered the language via Persian. This allows two observations, one particular and one general.

The first concerns an item of vocabulary. An essential element in any discussion of *al-Siyar* is the concept of *dhimma*. This is the contract by which a non-Muslim subject (*dhimmī*) receives the protection of the law in exchange for the payment of *jizya*. It is also a concept which the compiler treats in the text in terms which derive from *fiqh*, remarking that if the infidels pay *jizya*, 'their property and blood are protected (*harām*) ...' [p. 157 ¶3]. What the compiler does not do, however, is to use the terms *jizya* or *dhimmi*. For *jizya* he substitutes *kharāj*, and for *dhimmī* he substitutes *kharajguzar* ('*kharaj*-paying, tributary'). In *fiqh*, however, *jizya* and *kharāj* are distinct. *Jizya* is a poll-tax and an element in the contract between an infidel and the Muslim sovereign; *kharāj* is a land-tax due on land which remained the property of infidels at the time of conquest. When the text forces the compiler to make a distinction, he does so not by introducing the term *jizya* but by referring to it as *baş haracı* ('Head *kharaj*'): 'The Muslim ruler should make [the infidels'] lands and vineyards subject to *kharaj* and impose head-*kharaj* on their persons' [p. 160 ¶1]. The omission of the term *jizya* and the use instead of *kharāj* suggest that the practice of imposing *jizya*, or at least the use of the term, were unknown in Anatolia at the time of the composition of the text. Instead, perhaps reflecting Ilkhanid practice, it seems that *kharaj* was the general term for taxes imposed on conquered peoples. It is perhaps significant in this respect that the abridged Turkish translation of the *Ghunyat al-Mughnī* of al-Sijistānī (d. 1240) which Tekin gives in facsimile omits passages which refer to *jizya*, suggesting again that the word and concept were unknown in fourteenth-century Anatolia.

The language of the text also allows a more general conclusion. The compiler clearly assumed that the dedicatee was largely unfamiliar with the Arabic terminology which expresses some of the basic concepts of religion and law. The paraphrasing of *mukātab* and omission of *jizya* are two examples of this assumption. Sometimes he does introduce Arabic vocabulary, but after having first provided a Turkish synonym. His introduction of the terms *imām* and *dāru'l-ḥarb* [p. 161 ¶3] after initially using the Turkish phrases *Müslümanlar begi* ('lord of the Muslims') [e.g., p. 157 ¶3] and *kafirler ili* ('territory of the infidels') [p. 160 ¶3] are examples of this practice. Sometimes he introduces an Arabic word together with a Turkish synonym, as in *güç ve kahrile* ('with strength and force') [p. 159 ¶4], *bölük cema'at* ('group, body of men') [p. 157 ¶2] or *alsa ya'ni feth eylese* ('if he takes, that is, if he conquers') [p. 159 ¶4]. The conclusion from the language of the text is therefore that the dedicatee and his followers were not educated in religion or the religious law. A particular detail reinforces this impression. In law, an idea related to the concept of obligation (*farḍ*) is the notion of sin (*ithm*) which non-performance of the obligation entails. In the case of a communal obligation like holy war, no sin arises provided a group of Muslims are performing the duty, but if no one performs it, then the entire community bears the sin. The compiler presents the notion of a communal obligation, but does not mention the related concept of sin, perhaps because he judged it to be beyond the mental grasp of his audience.

This analysis of the text makes it possible to draw a few general conclusions. First, the *Risaletü'l-islam* includes a chapter on holy war because it is a requirement of this genre of literature. It is not a literary reflection of conditions in fourteenth-century Anatolia. Second, the material in the chapter derives almost entirely from *fiqh* and is almost wholly conventional. It tells us next to nothing about warfare in Anatolia. Third, the language of the text suggests that the dedicatee was unfamiliar with some of the most basic vocabulary and concepts of Islam. Finally, a few passages which do not appear to correspond with juristic texts may be additions by the compiler. Any other conclusions must be extremely tentative.

Let us, nonetheless, speculate. The purpose of the *Risaletü'l-islam* was to educate the dedicatee in the fundamentals of a religion which he professed, but of which he was largely ignorant. Given that he was a member of a ruling house, one may assume that his subjects were as ill-educated as he was in matters of religion. The text was therefore the product of a society in the first stages of becoming Islamic. Certain elements in the chapter on holy war hint that the dedicatee and his followers did make raids into non-Muslim territory; that these were on villages, rather than on towns and fortresses; that textiles were the most prized booty; and that the raiders habitually removed their victims' eyes, noses and ears. This suggests that military organization was minimal, and that military objectives amounted to no more than plundering the countryside. Whether this amounts to a Wittekian 'ideology of holy war' is doubtful, and it would be unwise to draw further conclusions from what are, in any case, remote conjectures. The one thing certain about the text is that it represents an effort to educate an absolute beginner in the rudiments of *fiqh*.

In praise of the few

Etan Kohlberg (The Hebrew University of Jerusalem) [1]

Writing about the Imāmiyya, the Muʿtazilī *qāḍī* ʿAbd al-Jabbār (d. 415/1024–5) observes: 'The books of their masters of old are full of passages in which the many are condemned and the few are praised' (*wa-kutub ruʾasāʾihim al-qudamāʾ mamlūʾa bi-dhikr dhamm al-kathīr wa-madḥ al-qalīl*).[2] The following is an attempt to put ʿAbd al-Jabbār's statement in perspective by tracing the motif of 'blaming the many and praising the few' in some Shīʿī sources.[3]

1 The believers are few

The belief that the many are condemned and the few are praised rests on two assumptions: that belief is praiseworthy and unbelief is to be condemned; and that the number of believers is small while the number of unbelievers is great. The former assumption is shared by all Muslims; the latter is characteristic of minority groups.

The Imāmiyya are a case in point: the assertion that the number of believers is small is often found in early Imāmī texts. According to Jaʿfar al-Ṣādiq, there are angels in the fourth heaven who praise God for having guided 'the few creatures from among the many' to the right religion.[4] Al-Ṣādiq is also reported to have declared: 'A believing woman is rarer than a believing man, and a believing man is rarer than the philosopher's stone; and which of you has seen the philosopher's stone?';[5] 'all men are animals except for a few believers'.[6] In the Imāmī view, this has always been the case: in the world of pre-existence, God demanded of His creatures (*al-khalq*) that they affirm not only His

[1] I am indebted to Frank Stewart, Patricia Crone and Fritz Zimmermann for their helpful comments on this article.

[2] ʿAbd al-Jabbār, *Tathbīt dalāʾil al-nubuwwa* (ed. ʿAbd al-Karīm ʿUthmān), Beirut n. d. [1966–8], i, 212. ʿAbd al-Jabbār refers to the Imāmiyya as 'Rāfiḍa'.

[3] Most of these sources are Imāmī Shīʿī.

[4] Abū Jaʿfar al-Ṭūsī, *Amālī*, Najaf 1384/1964, i, 143 › Muḥammad Bāqir al-Majlisī, *Biḥār al-anwār*, Tehran 1376–94/1956–74 [= *BA*], lxviii, 21, no. 35. Elsewhere, only one angel is mentioned (Rajab b. Muḥammad al-Bursī, *Mashāriq anwār al-yaqīn fī asrār amīr al-muʾminīn*, Beirut n. d., 18 › *BA*, xxvi, 295, no. 57).

[5] *Al-muʾmina aʿazz min al-muʾmin waʾl-muʾmin aʿazz min al-kibrīt al-aḥmar fa-man raʾā minkum al-kibrīt al-aḥmar*: Muḥammad b. Yaʿqūb al-Kulīnī, *al-Kāfī*, Tehran 1375–7/1955–7, ii, 242, no. 1 › *BA*, lxvii, 159, no. 3. For the expression *aʿazz min al-kibrīt al-aḥmar*, see M. Ullmann, *Wörterbuch der klassischen arabischen Sprache*, Wiesbaden 1970–, i, 28 a–b, s.v. *kibrīt*.

[6] *Al-nās kulluhum bahāʾim illā qalīl min al-muʾminīn*: al-Kulīnī, *al-Kāfī*, ii, 242, no. 2 ›*BA*, lxvii, 159, no. 4. For the variant reading *qalīlan* (considered grammatically more correct) see al-Majlisī, *Mirʾāt al-ʿuqūl*, Tehran 1401–11/1981–91, ix, 286. Cf. M. A. Amir-Moezzi, "Seul l'homme de Dieu est humain. Théologie et anthropologie mystique à travers l'exégèse imamite ancienne (aspects de l'imamologie duodécimaine IV)", *Arabica*, 45 (1998), 193–214, at 205 n. 37.

divinity and Muḥammad's prophethood, but also ʿAlī's position as Imam (or legatee);[7] all agreed to the first two demands but, out of pride, rejected the third; the only exception were 'the people of the right' (*aṣḥāb al-yamīn*), who were very few (*nafar qalīl wa-hum aqall al-qalīl*).[8] Abraham was for a time the only believer of his generation; later he was joined by Ismāʿīl and Isḥāq.[9] All prophets had many more enemies than supporters.[10] When Muḥammad declared that those who opposed ʿAlī would not be saved from the fires of hell, his wife Maymūna exclaimed: 'By God, I do not know any of your companions who loves ʿAlī, except a few'; to which Muḥammad replied, 'A few believers are a multitude'.[11] Maymūna identified these loyal Companions as Abū Dharr, Miqdād and Salmān, and added herself to the list.[12]

The believers who are 'rarer than a philosopher's stone' may well be those who, in addition to possessing complete faith, are privy to the secrets of the Imāmī religion and guard these secrets from the uninitiated.[13] They are the perfect believers.[14]

---

[7] See the discussion in M. A. Amir-Moezzi, *Le guide divin dans le shīʿisme originel*, Paris–Lagrasse 1992, 86–8 = *The Divine Guide in Early Shīʿism*, tr. D. Streight, Albany 1994, 33–4; M. M. Bar-Asher, *Scripture and Exegesis in Early Imāmī Shiism*, Leiden 1999, 132–4 (to Q7:172, the 'covenant verse'). In a Shīʿī *qirāʾa* of this verse, ʿAlī is explicitly mentioned as *amīr al-muʾminīn* (Abū ʾl-Naḍr al-ʿAyyāshī, *Tafsīr* (ed. Hāshim al-Rasūlī al-Maḥallātī), Qumm 1380/1960–1, ii, 41, nos 113, 114 ›*BA*, xxxvii, 332–3, no. 72; Hāshim al-Baḥrānī al-Katkānī, *Kitāb al-burhān fī tafsīr al-qurʾān*, Tehran 1374–5/1954–5, ii, 50, no. 32; al-Kulīnī, *al-Kāfī*, i, 412, no. 4 › Sharaf al-Dīn al-Najafī, *Taʾwīl al-āyāt al-ẓāhira fī faḍāʾil al-ʿitra al-ṭāhira*, Qumm 1407/1987, 180, no. 19, al-Katkānī, *al-Burhān*, ii, 47, no. 10; see M. M. Bar-Asher, "Variant Readings and Additions of the Imāmī-Šīʿa to the Quran", *Israel Oriental Studies*, 13 (1993), 39–74, at 58–9.

[8] al-Ṭūsī, *Amālī*, i, 237–8 › *BA*, xxiv, 2, no. 4; Raḍī al-Dīn Ibn Ṭāwūs, *al-Yaqīn bi-ikhtiṣāṣ mawlānā ʿAlī bi-imrat al-muʾminīn* (ed. Muḥammad Bāqir al-Anṣārī and Muḥammad Ṣādiq al-Anṣārī), Beirut 1410/1989, 282 › al-Najafī, *Taʾwīl*, 180–1, no. 20, *BA*, xxxvii, 310–11, no. 41; al-Bursī, *Mashāriq*, 17–8 ›*BA*, xxvi, 294–5, no. 57. For *aṣḥāb al-yamīn* as referring to the initiated believers, see Amir-Moezzi, *Le guide divin* = *The Divine Guide*, index, s.v. A different exegetical tradition to Q7:172 maintains that all of mankind acknowledged the imamate of ʿAlī and the other Imams (ʿAlī b. Ibrāhīm al-Qummī, *Tafsīr* (ed. Ṭayyib al-Mūsawī al-Jazāʾirī), Najaf 1386–7/1966–7, i, 247; in the version of al-Qummī cited by al-Najafī, *Taʾwīl*, 179–80, no. 17, there is an addition to the effect that some acknowledged the Imams only with their tongues, while others did so in their hearts).

[9] al-Kulīnī, *al-Kāfī*, ii, 243–4, no. 5 › *BA*, xlvii, 373, no. 94, lxvii, 162, no. 7.

[10] *BA*, lxvii, 158 (in the chapter entitled *Qillat ʿadad al-muʾminīn*).

[11] *Al-qalīl min al-muʾminīn kathīr*. This sentence also appears independently as a Prophetic tradition: al-Barqī, *Kitāb al-maḥāsin* (ed. Jalāl al-Dīn al-Ḥusaynī al-Muḥaddith), Tehran 1370/1950–1, i, 220, no. 125 › *BA*, ii, 266, no. 26. Cf. the Imāmī reading of Q3:123 ('and God most surely helped you at Badr, when you were utterly abject'), where the *adhilla* of the ʿUthmānic codex is replaced by *qalīl* (variants: *ḍuʿafāʾ*, *ḍiʿāf*). See Abū ʿAbdallāh Aḥmad b. Muḥammad al-Sayyārī, *al-Qirāʾāt* (also known as *al-Tanzīl waʾl-taḥrīf*), ms. Marʿashī no. 1455, fols. 11b–12a, and the references given in Bar-Asher, "Variant Readings", 54.

[12] *Aṣl Jaʿfar b. Muḥammad al-Ḥaḍramī*, in *al-Uṣūl al-sitta ʿashar* (ed. Ḥasan Muṣṭafawī), Qumm 1405/1984–5, 62. See in general E. Kohlberg, "Some Imāmī Shīʿī Views on the Ṣaḥāba", *Jerusalem Studies in Arabic and Islam*, 5 (1984), 143–75, repr. in his *Belief and Law in Imāmī Shīʿism*, Aldershot 1991, art. IX. For *al-aqall* vs. *al-akthar* see further M. A. Amir-Moezzi, "Seul l'homme de Dieu", 196–7.

[13] Concealing secrets (*kitmān*) and not propagating them (*idhāʿa*) are a hallmark of true belief: E. Kohlberg, "Taqiyya in Shīʿī Theology and Religion", in H. G. Kippenberg and G. G. Stroumsa (eds), *Secrecy and Concealment: Studies in the History of Mediterranean and Near Eastern Religions*, Leiden 1995, 345–80.

[14] The term 'perfect believer' or 'perfect belief' (*al-muʾmin/al-īmān al-kāmil*) is used for example by Muḥsin al-Fayḍ al-Kāshānī in his *Rāh-i ṣawāb* (published in *Dah risāla-yi muḥaqqiq-i buzurg-i Fayḍ-i Kāshānī* [ed. Rasūl Jaʿfariyān], Iṣfahān 1371 sh./1992–3, 138), as also by al-Majlisī, *BA*, lxvii, 159, 164. A similar term used by al-Fayḍ is *al-mumtaḥan* (*al-Maḥajja al-bayḍāʾ fī tahdhīb al-iḥyāʾ* [ed. ʿAlī Akbar al-Ghaffārī], Beirut 1403/1983, iv, 372–3); this is found in some of the earliest Imāmī texts (Amir-Moezzi, "Seul l'homme de Dieu", 205). See also the *Kitāb al-haft* ascribed to al-Mufaḍḍal b. ʿUmar al-Juʿfī, ed. Muṣṭafā Ghālib (under the title *Kitāb al-haft al-sharīf*), Beirut 1977, 39. For al-Qāḍī al-Nuʿmān, the *qalīl* referred to in Q38:24 are those who perform acts of righteousness purely for the

There is a second category of believers, comprising all Shīʿīs who acknowledge the unique position of ʿAlī and the other Imams, but who have not been initiated into the secrets of the faith. As Mūsā al-Kāẓim tells his brother ʿAlī b. Jaʿfar, they have a special role: to provide company (*uns*) for the perfect believers, so that the latter will not feel lonely because of their small numbers.[15] Many of these uninitiated believers were criticized by the Imams for various shortcomings and were even described at times as not being true Shīʿīs. In one story, for example, al-Mufaḍḍal b. Qays[16] tells the Imam that there are fifty thousand Shīʿīs in Kūfa. Jaʿfar responds, 'I wish there were twenty-five men in Kūfa who acknowledged our rule and only spoke the truth about us.'[17] In a second account, al-Mufaḍḍal b. ʿUmar al-Juʿfī[18] informs al-Ṣādiq that the Imam has only few followers in Kūfa. When word of this gets to the Kūfans, they defame and threaten al-Mufaḍḍal. Al-Ṣādiq comes to his defence, declaring that they are not true Shīʿīs (*mā hum lanā bi-shīʿa*): Jaʿfar's *shīʿa* are those who avoid controversy, who engage in prayer and supplication and who abstain from the pleasures of this world.[19] There is finally the story of Sadīr al-Ṣayrafī, who tells al-Ṣādiq that it is not proper for him to adopt a quietist policy, given that he has many loyal followers (*li-kathrat mawālīka wa-shīʿatika wa-anṣārika*);[20] had ʿAlī enjoyed the same number of supporters immediately after the Prophet's death, his right to rule would not have been challenged. When the Imam asks him how many supporters (*shīʿa*) he thinks there are, Sadīr first mentions one hundred thousand, then two hundred thousand, then 'half the world'. In response, the Imam suggests that the two of them embark on a journey to Yanbuʿ (on the Mecca–Medina road). On the way they stop to pray and see a young shepherd pasturing kids. Al-Ṣādiq tells Sadīr, 'If the number of my supporters equalled the number of those kids, it would not be proper for me to abstain [from fighting]'. After completing the prayer, Sadīr counts the kids and finds out that there are seventeen of them.[21] What these accounts show, then, is that the number of true believers is far smaller than meets the eye.[22]

---

sake of God (*lillāh*), without expecting a reward, not even from Him: al-Qāḍī al-Nuʿmān, *Kitāb al-himma fī ādāb atbāʿ al-aʾimma* (ed. Muḥammad Kāmil Ḥusayn), Cairo n. d., 101.

15 al-Kulīnī, *al-Kāfī*, ii, 245, no. 7 › *BA*, lxvii, 165, no. 9.

16 For whom see ʿAbdallāh al-Māmaqānī, *Tanqīḥ al-maqāl*, Najaf 1349–52/1930–3, §12,084.

17 *BA*, lxvii, 158–9, no. 2 (from Ibn Bābawayh's *Ṣifāt al-shīʿa*).

18 For whom see e.g. ʿInāyat Allāh al-Quhpāʾī, *Majmaʿ al-rijāl* (ed. Ḍiyāʾ al-Dīn al-Iṣfahānī), Iṣfahān 1384–7/1964–7, vi, 123–31. He was often accused of extremism (*ghuluww*).

19 al-Qāḍī al-Nuʿmān, *Daʿāʾim al-islām* (ed. A. A. A. Fyzee), Cairo 1383/1963, i, 58–9.

20 This is in line with Sadīr's activist tendencies (see the entry on him in al-Māmaqānī, *Tanqīḥ*, §4622). ʿAbdallāh b. ʿAṭāʾ (who is perhaps to be identified as a son of ʿAṭāʾ b. Abī Rabāḥ: see al-Māmaqānī, *Tanqīḥ*, §§6957–61 and the appendix at the end of §6961) is similarly said to have asked al-Bāqir why he did not rebel, given the large number of his supporters in Irak (al-Kulīnī, *al-Kāfī*, i, 341–2, no. 26; Muḥammad b. Ibrāhīm al-Nuʿmānī, *Kitāb al-ghayba*, Beirut 1403/1983, 111 › *BA*, li, 138, no. 8). This is also the question put to al-Ṣādiq by Sahl b. al-Ḥasan al-Khurāsānī (unidentified); Sahl maintains that the Imam has the support of 'one hundred thousand' Shīʿī fighters (Ibn Shahrāshūb, *Manāqib āl Abī Ṭālib*, Beirut 1405/1985, iv, 237 › *BA*, xlvii, 123–4, no. 172).

21 al-Kulīnī, *al-Kāfī*, ii, 242–3, no. 4 › *BA*, lxvii, 160–1, no. 6 (in the chapter *Fī qillat ʿadad al-muʾminīn*). The period of ʿAlī's caliphate (35–40/656–661) is a special case: Imāmī Shīʿī scholars

2 Polemics

The early Imāmiyya, identifying themselves as the *qilla*, maintained that the majority is condemned because it is always wrong and the few are praised because those who are right are always a minority. In polemical exchanges, fraught with danger as they often were, Imāmī Shīʿīs generally restricted themselves to countering the Sunnī argument that the majority is always right. The following examples demonstrate this point.[23]

An early encounter is said to have taken place in Medina between Muʿāwiya b. Abī Sufyān and members of the Banū ʿAbd al-Muṭṭalib, including al-Ḥasan, al-Ḥusayn and ʿAlī's nephew ʿAbdallāh b. Jaʿfar b. Abī Ṭālib. At the meeting, dated to the first year of Muʿāwiya's caliphate (i.e. 41–42/661–662), ʿAbdallāh b. Jaʿfar (d. 80/699) presented the Shīʿī case before the caliph, emphasizing the injustice perpetrated against the Prophet's family.[24] He concluded by identifying ʿAlī, al-Ḥasan, al-Ḥusayn and nine of al-Ḥusayn's descendants as the *ulū ʾl-amr* whom God commanded the believers to obey ('Obey God, and obey the Messenger and those of you who are in authority', Q4:59).[25] Muʿāwiya sent for witnesses, who confirmed that what ʿAbdallāh b. Jaʿfar had said was true. The caliph thereupon told the Banū ʿAbd al-Muṭṭalib that if this was indeed the case, then the entire community had forsaken Islam and would perish, with the sole exception of the *ahl al-bayt* and their supporters. These, however, were but few in number *(fa-ulāʾika fī ʾl-nās qalīl)*. Muʿāwiya's point was that what most people believe is more likely to be true than what only a few believe. ʿAbdallāh b. al-ʿAbbās, who was in attendance, responded:

> God says in His book: 'For few indeed are those that are thankful among My servants' (*wa-qalīl min ʿibādī ʾl-shakūr*, Q34:13); and He says: 'Yet, be you ever so eager, the most part of men believe not' (*wa-mā akthar al-nās wa-law ḥaraṣta bi-muʾminīn*, Q12:103); and He says: 'Save those who believe, and do deeds of righteousness – and how few they are!' (*illā ʾlladhīna āmanū wa-*

---

maintain that he enjoyed large-scale support among the Companions and that his reign was thus legitimate also from a Sunnī point of view. Al-Shaykh al-Mufīd (d. 413/1022), for example, emphasizes that those who fought alongside ʿAlī in the Battle of the Camel included not only the Banū Hāshim but also Muhājirūn, Anṣār 'and other believers': al-Mufīd, *al-Jamal aw al-nuṣra fī ḥarb al-Baṣra*, Najaf 1368/1948–9, 3. Sulaym b. Qays is reported to have given the number of these Muhājirūn and Anṣār as four thousand: *Kitāb Sulaym b. Qays*, Najaf n. d., 187 › *BA*, xxxii, 215.

[22] See also E. Kohlberg, "Imam and Community in the Pre-Ghayba Period", in S. A. Arjomand (ed.), *Authority and Political Culture in Shiʿism*, Albany 1988, 25–53, at 32–3, repr. in *Belief and Law in Imāmī Shīʿism*, art. XIII.

[23] Needless to say, these examples are in no way exhaustive.

[24] Sulaym b. Qays, *Kitāb Sulaym b. Qays*, ed. Najaf, 204–7 = ed. Muḥammad Bāqir al-Anṣārī al-Zanjānī, Qumm 1415/1994, 834–41 › *BA*, xxxiii, 265–8. A version of this report is cited from Sulaym in Aḥmad b. ʿAlī al-Ṭabrisī, *al-Iḥtijāj*, Beirut 1410/1989, 285–8 › *BA*, xliv, 97–102, no. 9. Further sources are listed by al-Zanjānī at 999–1002. For ʿAbdallāh b. Jaʿfar and his relationship with the Umayyads see W. Madelung, "The *Hāshimiyyāt* of al-Kumayt and Hāshimī Shīʿism", *Studia Islamica*, 70 (1989), 5–26, at 18–22, repr. in his *Religious and Ethnic Movements in Medieval Islam*, Aldershot 1992, art. V; *idem*, *The Succession to Muḥammad*, Cambridge 1997, 329.

[25] For the problematic reference to twelve rulers in a work supposedly going back to a disciple of ʿAlī, see E. Kohlberg, "From Imāmiyya to Ithnā-ʿashariyya", *BSOAS*, 39 (1976), 521–34, at 532–3, repr. in *Belief and Law in Imāmī Shīʿism*, art. XIV; Amir-Moezzi, *Le guide divin*, 251 n. 543 = *The Divine Guide*, 213 n. 543.

> *ʿamilū ʾl-ṣāliḥāt wa-qalīl mā hum*, Q38:24); and He says about Noah: 'And there believed not with him except a few' (*wa-mā āmana maʿahu illā qalīl*, Q11:40).[26]

Ibn ʿAbbās went on to mention the Israelites, all of whom worshipped the golden calf with the exception of Aaron, his sons and a small group from among his household (*nafar qalīl min ahl baytihi*); similarly, ʿAlī enjoyed the support of only a small group of believers.[27]

Later in the Umayyad period, another polemical exchange is said to have taken place, this time pitting Zayd b. ʿAlī (put to death in 122/740) against a group of Syrian supporters of the regime. The Syrians argued that since most people rejected Zayd's claim that only members of his family were entitled to rule (*istiḥqāq al-imāma*), this claim had no validity. Zayd's response was to cite Qurʾānic passages showing that truth resides with the few;[28] he then produced an epistle he had written on the subject, which contained many additional Qurʾānic passages praising the few and blaming the many. This work, entitled *Risāla fī madḥ al-aqall wa-dhamm al-akthar*, is no longer extant, but was still available to the Shīʿī scholar Raḍī al-Dīn ʿAlī b. Mūsā Ibn Ṭāwūs (d. 664/1266).[29] The transmitter of this account, Khālid b. Ṣafwān,[30] reports that Zayd's opponents were unable to counter his arguments and regretted having initiated the encounter. But Khālid does not reveal whether the Syrians turned away from their 'false and worn out beliefs'.[31]

---

26 *Kitāb Sulaym b. Qays* (ed. al-Zanjānī), 842. In the version preserved in *BA*, xxxiii, 268, these Qurʾānic passages are cited by ʿAbdallāh b. Jaʿfar, who ends by telling Muʿāwiya, 'The believers among the people are but few' (*al-muʾminūn fī ʾl-nās qalīl*). ʿAbdallāh b. al-ʿAbbās then repeats the Qurʾānic verses (except for Q34:13) and goes on to speak about the Israelites. In the Najaf edition (207), the sentence indicating the switch from ʿAbdallāh b. Jaʿfar to ʿAbdallāh b. al-ʿAbbās is missing. In the version reproduced by al-Ṭabrisī (*al-Iḥtijāj*, 286 › *BA*, xliv, 98, no. 9), the speaker is ʿAbdallāh b. al-ʿAbbās, who cites Q34:13 and 38:24.

27 *Kitāb Sulaym b. Qays*, ed. Najaf, 208 = ed. al-Zanjānī, 843.

28 The verses cited (partially or in full) are Q38:24, 11:116, 4:66, 2:249, 12:103, 6:116, 25:44, 9:34, 5:49 (in this order).

29 Ibn Ṭāwūs, *Saʿd al-suʿūd*, Najaf 1369/1950, 223–5. See E. Kohlberg, *A Medieval Muslim Scholar at Work: Ibn Ṭāwūs and his Library*, Leiden 1992, 319, no. 514. Cf. Rudolf Strothmann, "Das Problem der literarischen Persönlichkeit Zaid b. ʿAlī", *Der Islam*, 13 (1923), 1–52, at 4–5.

30 He is probably to be identified with Khālid b. Ṣafwān b. ʿAbdallāh Ibn al-Ahtam (d. 135/752); see *GAS*, ii, 462–3. Ibn al-Ahtam was a famous preacher (*khaṭīb*) who admonished (*waʿaẓa*) both ʿUmar b. ʿAbd al-ʿAzīz and Hishām b. ʿAbd al-Malik (al-Ṣafadī, *al-Wāfī biʾl-wafayāt*, xiii [ed. M. al-Ḥujayrī], Wiesbaden 1404/1984, 255) and was a table companion of Hishām (Yāqūt, *Muʿjam al-udabāʾ*, Beirut 1411/1991, iii, 274). A Khālid b. Ṣafwān is mentioned by al-Mizzī, *Tahdhīb al-kamāl* (ed. Bashshār ʿAwwād Maʿrūf), x, Beirut 1408/1987, 96, as having transmitted from Zayd; he may well be our preacher.

31 Ibn Ṭāwūs, *Saʿd al-suʿūd*, 225. Zayd appears to have welcomed confrontations of this kind. Maʿmar b. Khaytham who, together with his brother Saʿīd, was a propagandist for Zayd (*min duʿāt Zayd*; see Aḥmad b. ʿAlī al-Najāshī, *Rijāl* [ed. Muḥammad Jawād al-Nāʾīnī], Beirut 1408/1988, i, 408, no. 472 › al-Quhpāʾī, *Majmaʿ al-rijāl*, iii, 115–6), cites Zayd as declaring: 'I vied with Hishām b. ʿAbd al-Malik and tried to outwit him in debate' (*kuntu ubārī Hishām b. ʿAbd al-Malik wa-ukāyiduhu fī ʾl-kalām*) (Muḥsin al-Amīn, *Aʿyān al-shīʿa*, Damascus–Beirut 1354–82/1935–63, xxxiii, 74, citing the *Maqtal al-Ḥusayn* of al-Muwaffaq b. Aḥmad al-Khwārizmī [d. 568/1172–3]). For an example of such a debate see al-Balādhurī, *Ansāb al-ashrāf*, vi, b (ed. Khalil Athamina), Jerusalem 1993, 85–6, no. 163 and the references given by the editor; Ibn ʿAsākir, *Taʾrīkh madīnat Dimashq*, xix (ed. ʿUmar al-ʿAmrawī), Beirut 1415/1995, 471.

The third example, from the early ʿAbbāsid period, is taken from the *Manāqib āl Abī Ṭālib* of Muḥammad b. ʿAlī Ibn Shahrāshūb (d. 588/1192). Here we read of a debate between Abū ʿUbayda al-Muʿtazilī and the Imāmī *mutakallim* Hishām b. al-Ḥakam (d. 179/795).[32] Abū ʿUbayda begins by saying to Hishām, 'The proof (*dalīl*, lit. 'sign') of the correctness of our belief and the incorrectness (*buṭlān*) of yours is that we are many and you are few, even though there are many offspring of ʿAlī and many who claim to be descendants of these offspring.'[33] Hishām replies, 'You cannot be referring to us with these words; your aim is rather to criticize Noah: he stayed among his people for 950 years, calling on them night and day to be saved, "and there believed not with him except a few" (Q11:40).'[34]

There are two difficulties with this text. The first is Abū ʿUbayda's identity: none of the leading figures of the Muʿtazila of the time was known by this *kunya*.[35] It might be suggested that 'al-Muʿtazilī' is a scribal error. A possible emendation would be 'al-Tamīmī' or 'al-Taymī' (though there is no obvious similarity in Arabic script between 'al-Muʿtazilī' and 'al-Tamīmī/al-Taymī'). In this case, two persons come to mind. One is Abū ʿUbayda al-Tamīmī (*fl.* first half of the second/eighth century), the leader of the Ibāḍī 'community of Muslims' (*jamāʿat al-muslimīn*) in Baṣra;[36] the second is the renowned scholar Abū ʿUbayda Maʿmar b. al-Muthannā al-Taymī (d. *c.* 210/825), who was reportedly a Khārijī.[37] Either could have met Hishām b. al-Ḥakam (though there appears to be no record of such a meeting). It is unlikely, however, that the number of Khārijīs (or Muʿtazilīs, for that matter) at the time far exceeded the number of Imāmīs; an argument based on the numerical superiority of the Khārijīs would have made little sense. The identity of Hishām's interlocutor thus remains unknown. The second difficulty concerns Abū ʿUbayda's reference to the great number of descendants of ʿAlī. There seem to be two ways of interpreting his point. The first is that the number of Imāmīs has remained small, even though it includes many of ʿAlī's genuine or spurious offspring. An alternative explanation is that although there are many such offspring, the number of Imāmīs is small because not all these offspring are Imāmīs. Hishām's answer, at any rate, is clear: by pointing to the precedent of Noah he refutes the contention that a small number of adherents is an indication that the cause they support

---

32 For Hishām see J. van Ess, *Theologie und Gesellschaft im 2. und 3. Jahrhundert Hidschra*, Berlin–New York 1991–7, index, s.v. His death-date is discussed at i, 353.

33 Reading *adʿiyāʾihim* (for *iddiʿāʾihim*).

34 Ibn Shahrāshūb, *Manāqib*, i, 274 › *BA*, xlvii, 401, no. 3.

35 There is a reference to Abū ʿUbayda Bakr b. al-Aswad al-Nājī who transmitted from al-Ḥasan al-Baṣrī and Muḥammad b. Sīrīn (both of whom died in 110/728–729) and is counted among the Baṣran Muʿtazilīs (Abū ʾl-Qāsim al-Kaʿbī al-Balkhī, *Maqālāt al-islāmiyyīn* [the section on the Muʿtazila], in *Faḍl al-iʿtizāl wa-ṭabaqāt al-muʿtazila* [ed. Fuʾād Sayyid], Tunis 1406/1986, 97; see also Ibn Ḥajar al-ʿAsqalānī, *Lisān al-mīzān*, Beirut 1407–8/1987–8, ii, 58–9, no. 1697). He is, however, little known (cf. van Ess's observations on the names cited by al-Kaʿbī, *Theologie*, i, 61–2).

36 See van Ess, *Theologie*, index, s.v.

37 See M. Lecker, "Biographical Notes on Abū ʿUbayda Maʿmar b. al-Muthannā", *Studia Islamica*, 81 (1995), 71–100, at 94–7, repr. in his *Jews and Arabs in Pre- and Early Islamic Arabia*, Aldershot 1998, art. XVIII.

is wrong.[38] A similar point is made in a passage near the beginning of the *waṣiyya* which Mūsā al-Kāẓim is said to have addressed to Hishām.[39] This text is preserved in the *Tuḥaf al-ʿuqūl* of al-Ḥasan b. ʿAlī Ibn Shuʿba (*fl.* mid-fourth/tenth century);[40] a somewhat different version of its first part is also reproduced in the *Kāfī* of al-Kulīnī (d. 329/941).[41] In the passage in question, the seventh Imam emphasizes that God in His book condemns the many and praises the few.[42]

The next example, unlike the previous three, does not involve a live debate (whether real or imaginary). It is taken from the *Kitāb al-Īḍāḥ* ascribed to the Imāmī scholar al-Faḍl b. Shādhān al-Naysābūrī (d. Muḥarram 260/Oct.–Nov. 873), of which a number of sections are devoted to polemics against the Murjiʾa.[43] At one point the author takes up the Murjiʾī claim that, since they are the majority (*ahl al-kathra waʾl-jamāʿa*), right must be on their side. He responds that 'we have found that great numbers are condemned in various places of God's book, while small numbers are praised'.[44] There are a number of Qurʾānic passages[45] which, the author states, provide irrefutable support for his view: 'Don't you see that the few are praised? God praises the followers of the truth, even though they are few; God's hand [or: God's mercy] was never with the people of falsehood' (*mā kānat yad allāh ʿalā jamāʿat ahl al-bāṭil qaṭṭ*).[46]

In all four cases, the structure is similar: the anti-Shīʿī side argues that what the majority believes is always right; the Shīʿī response is to cite Qurʾānic verses demonstrating the untenability of this argument. Appeal to *ḥadīth* is strikingly lacking – an indication perhaps of the antiquity of the texts.[47] The one exception is *Kitāb al-Īḍāḥ*,

---

38 This is in keeping with what other sources tell us about Hishām's views; see van Ess, *Theologie*, iv, 657.

39 For this *waṣiyya*, see van Ess, *Theologie*, i, 354.

40 Ibn Shuʿba, *Tuḥaf al-ʿuqūl*, Beirut 1394/1974, 283–97 › *BA*, i, 132–59, no. 30, lxxviii, 296–319, no. 1.

41 al-Kulīnī, *al-Kāfī*, i, 13–20, no. 12.

42 al-Kulīnī, *al-Kāfī*, i, 15; Ibn Shuʿba, *Tuḥaf*, 284 › *BA*, i, 135, lxxviii, 298–9. In al-Kulīnī's version, the Qurʾānic verses cited are Q6:116, 31:25, 29:63 (for *dhamm al-kathra*) and Q34:13, 38:24, 40:28, 11:40 (for *madḥ al-qilla*). Two additional verses adduced as examples of *madḥ al-qilla* (Q6:37, 5:103) are in fact examples of *dhamm al-kathra*. The verses cited in Ibn Shuʿba's version are Q6:116 and 6:37 (*dhamm al-kathra*) and Q34:13, 38:24, 11:40 (*madḥ al-qilla*). Both versions also include the sentence *wa-aktharuhum lā yashʿurūn*, which neither forms part of the ʿUthmānic text nor is attested as a variant reading (cf. the discussion in *BA*, i, 135).

43 For al-Faḍl see *Encyclopaedia Iranica*, s.v. 'Fażl b. Šāḏān' (E. Kohlberg). Doubts concerning his authorship of the *Kitāb al-Īḍāḥ* are expressed by Aḥmad Pāktachī, *Dāʾirat al-maʿārif-i buzurg-i islāmī*, iv, Tehran 1370 sh., 52.

44 al-Faḍl b. Shādhān, *K. al-Īḍāḥ* (ed. Jalāl al-Dīn al-Ḥusaynī al-Urmawī), Tehran 1392/1972, 125.

45 Q6:119, 12:106, 7:17, 2:249, 38:24, 11:40, 34:13, 4:66, 7:187, 2:243, 5:103. Some verses are cited in their entirety, others only in part.

46 Ibn Shādhān, *K. al-Īḍāḥ*, 126. See also Hamid Enayat, *Modern Islamic Political Thought*, London–Austin 1982, 20.

47 That the absence of *ḥadīth* does not necessarily reflect an early date has been demonstrated by M. Cook, *Early Muslim Dogma*, Cambridge 1981, 141.

where the reference to God's hand not being with the people of falsehood implies an acquaintance with the Prophetic tradition *yad allāh maʿa/ʿalā ʾl-jamāʿa*.[48]

3 Some later developments

Following the onset of the Greater Occultation (*al-ghayba al-kubrā*) in 329/941, the motif of *dhamm al-kathra wa-madḥ al-qilla* began losing much of its appeal. Several factors combined to bring this about. In the first place, the early esoteric tradition, with its emphasis on a small spiritual elite, gradually gave way to a more rationalistic approach.[49] Secondly, once the Imāmīs acquired the backing of the Buwayhid rulers they stopped feeling like a minority, whatever their actual numbers.[50] According to ʿAbd al-Jabbār, they now adopted the arguments of their opponents. The Ḥanbalīs, ʿAbd al-Jabbār says, used to contend that they were many (and therefore right) and that the Rāfiḍa (i.e. Imāmiyya) were few (and therefore wrong). The Rāfiḍa replied by insisting that God condemns the many and praises the few. Yet starting in the 350s/960s (i.e. with the consolidation of Buwayhid power), they began using the same argument against the Ḥanbalīs which the Ḥanbalīs had used against them, namely that truth lies with great numbers.[51] A final point to consider is the Imāmī attitude to consensus. In Devin Stewart's view, from the late fourth/tenth century Sunnī *ijmāʿ* was gradually incorporated by Imāmī jurists into their legal theory.[52] If this was indeed the case, the theme of *dhamm al-kathra wa-madḥ al-qilla* would no longer have been a viable proposition.

This theme did not, however, disappear altogether: it was kept alive by the Akhbārī branch of Imāmī Shīʿism. The Akhbārīs, who wished to cleanse Imāmī legal theory of all Sunnī accretions, were fiercely opposed to the incorporation of Sunnī *ijmāʿ*;[53] *dhamm al-kathra wa-madḥ al-qilla* provided them with effective ammunition in their struggle. In the final chapter of his *al-Fawāʾid al-ṭūsiyya*, the leading Akhbārī

---

48 For this tradition see e.g. al-Nasāʾī, *Sunan*, Cairo 1348/1930, vii, 92 (*Kitāb taḥrīm al-dam, bāb qatl man fāraqa ʾl-jamāʿa*), al-Tirmidhī, *Ṣaḥīḥ*, Cairo 1350–3/1931–4, ix, 10, 11 (*abwāb al-fitan, bāb mā jāʾa fī luzūm al-jamāʿa*). See al-Qāḍī al-Nuʿmān, *Ikhtilāf uṣūl al-madhāhib* (ed. Muṣṭafā Ghālib), Beirut n. d., 131–2 (insisting on a metaphorical interpretation of *yad*), and the discussion in D. Gimaret, *Dieu à l'image de l'homme*, Paris 1997, 192–4.

49 Cf. Amir-Moezzi, *Le guide divin*, 319–35 = *The Divine Guide*, 133–9.

50 I owe this point to Patricia Crone.

51 ʿAbd al-Jabbār, *Tathbīt*, i, 211. Though ʿAbd al-Jabbār's statement may be true, I have not come across the argument in question in Imāmī sources.

52 D. J. Stewart, *Islamic Legal Orthodoxy*, Salt Lake City 1998, 111–73. For a critique, see W. Madelung's review of Stewart's book, in *JAOS*, 120 (2000), 111–4.

53 Stewart, *Islamic Legal Orthodoxy*, 175–208. The Akhbārīs, following early Imāmī scholars, held that the only valid *ijmāʿ* was that which incorporated the views of the Imam as laid down in *ḥadīth*: M. J. McDermott, *The Theology of al-Shaikh al-Mufīd* [d. 413/1022], Beirut 1978, 287–8; W. Madelung, "Authority in Twelver Shiism in the Absence of the Imam", in *La notion d'autorité au Moyen Age: Islam, Byzance, Occident*, Paris 1982, 163–73, at 164, repr. in his *Religious Schools and Sects in Medieval Islam*, London 1985, art. X; *Encyclopaedia Iranica*, s.v. 'Ejmāʿ' (D. J. Stewart). This view of consensus was criticized by ʿAbd al-Jabbār: *al-Mughnī*, xvii (ed. Amīn al-Khūlī), Cairo 1382/1963, 204. For contemporary Imāmī views see H. Modarressi, *An Introduction to Shīʿī Law*, London 1984, 3. See further van Ess, *Theologie*, iv, 654–60.

scholar Muḥammad b. al-Ḥasan al-Ḥurr al-ʿĀmilī (d. 1104/1693) contends that consensus has no binding authority (*ḥujjiyya*), as its legitimacy derives from the agreement of the many (*kathra*); since the many are condemned in numerous traditions and Qurʾānic verses, consensus must be rejected as an *aṣl*.[54] Al-ʿĀmilī does not cite any traditions, but adduces over fifty verses. These verses (which make up the bulk of the chapter) mostly refer to small groups of believers or to a majority of unbelievers.[55] Finally, al-ʿĀmilī points to the lessons of history: enquiry and investigation *(al-tatabbuʿ waʾl-istiqrāʾ)* show that in every generation, the men of falsehood are the majority and the men of truth are only few.[56] A somewhat different argument is put forward by another celebrated Akhbārī scholar, Muḥsin al-Fayḍ al-Kāshānī (d. 1091/1680). He quotes Qurʾānic passages (Q2:170, 43:22–23) which in his view show that unbelievers appealed to consensus in rejecting the prophets.[57] His point is thus that consensus was used by the majority as a tool to further the cause of evil.[58]

In the non-Imāmī Shīʿī world, the proposition that it is among the few that truth is to be found was upheld in a creed known as *Tāj al-ʿaqāʾid wa-maʿdin al-fawāʾid* composed by ʿAlī b. Muḥammad Ibn al-Walīd (d. 612/1215), the fifth Yemeni missionary (*dāʿī*) of the Ṭayyibī Ismāʿīlīs.[59] The sixty-eighth tenet, entitled 'Truth lies with the small group', opens with the statement: 'It must be believed that truth always lies with the small group and with the elite, while falsehood and error are found among the many and the masses' (*wa-yuʿtaqad anna ʾl-ḥaqq abadan fī ʾl-firqa al-qalīla waʾl-khawāṣṣ min al-nās wa-anna ʾl-bāṭil waʾl-ḍalāl fī ʾl-kathra waʾl-ʿawāmm*).[60] In support of this statement, Ibn al-Walīd adduces five Qurʾānic passages, all of which were used by early Imāmī polemicists.[61] Though these passages deal with specific events, Ibn al-Walīd obviously takes them to reflect a universal truth.

In addition to quoting from the Qurʾān, Ibn al-Walīd cites ʿAlī as declaring: 'The people of truth are the [real] community, though they be few, and the people of falsehood are the people of unbelief and division, though they be many' (*ahl al-ḥaqq hum al-jamāʿa wa-in qallū wa-ahl al-bāṭil hum ahl al-kufr waʾl-furqa wa-in*

[54] al-Ḥurr al-ʿĀmilī, *al-Fawāʾid al-ṭūsiyya* (ed. Mahdī al-Lājiwardī al-Ḥusaynī and Muḥammad Durūdī), Qumm 1403/1983, 552. Elsewhere in the *Fawāʾid* (e.g. in a number of passages in *fāʾida* no. 91, pp. 402–16), al-ʿĀmilī provides further arguments against *ḥujjiyyat al-ijmāʿ*.
[55] al-Ḥurr al-ʿĀmilī, *al-Fawāʾid al-ṭūsiyya*, 552–7.
[56] al-Ḥurr al-ʿĀmilī, *al-Fawāʾid al-ṭūsiyya*, 557. This is a recurrent Shīʿī theme; see *Encyclopaedia Iranica*, s.v. 'Evil (in Shiʿism)' (E. Kohlberg).
[57] Muḥsin al-Fayḍ, *Rāh-i ṣawāb*, 130–1. See also Stewart, *Islamic Legal Orthodoxy*, 188.
[58] Citing some of the verses adduced by earlier writers (Q34:13, 38:24, 29:63, 6:37, 12:103, 6:116, 12:106, 7:179), al-Fayḍ further maintains that those who are rightly guided (*ahl-i hidāyat*) have always been few (*Rāh-i ṣawāb*, 135); he underscores this point by reproducing (in Persian translation) a number of traditions from the chapter *Fī qillat ʿadad al-muʾminīn* in al-Kulīnī's *Kāfī* (*Rāh-i ṣawāb*, 136–7).
[59] This work was first brought to the notice of Western scholars when W. Ivanow published an English summary of it in his *A Creed of the Fatimids*, Bombay 1936. See further I. K. Poonawala, *Biobibliography of Ismāʿīlī Literature*, Malibu 1977, 157; Delia Cortese, *Ismaili and Other Arabic Manuscripts*, London 2000, 79.
[60] Ibn al-Walīd, *Kitāb tāj al-ʿaqāʾid wa-maʿdin al-fawāʾid* (ed. ʿĀrif Tāmir), Beirut 1967, 125.
[61] They are Q12:103, 11:40, 2:249, 38:24 and 34:13: Ibn al-Walīd, *Tāj al-ʿaqāʾid*, 125, 126.

kathurū).[62] There is also an excerpt from a speech of ʿAlī beginning with the sentence: 'Those are the least in number, yet the greatest in God's esteem'(*ulāʾika ʾl-aqallūn ʿadadan al-aʿẓamūn ʿinda ʾllāh qadran*).[63] This sentence (or variants thereof) is also found in a sermon which ʿAlī reportedly addressed to his disciple Kumayl b. Ziyād al-Nakhaʿī;[64] but the rest of the excerpt cited by Ibn al-Walīd does not correspond to any version of the sermon known to me. The chapter ends with an exchange between an Imam and one of his followers. The follower complains that the Shīʿīs are few and suffer at the hands of the masses (*ʿawāmm*, i.e. the Sunnīs). The Imam explains that when Iblīs realized he could not bring the Shīʿa over to his side, he turned the masses against them; the fact that the Shīʿa are few does not reflect unfavourably on them; indeed, they are the most excellent (*lubb*, lit. 'the best part') of humankind.[65]

For Ibn al-Walīd, then, the number of believers has always been small; God praises the believers; hence He praises the few. Conversely, the number of unbelievers has always been great; God condemns the unbelievers; hence He condemns the many. What was true for the Imāmiyya in the first centuries of Islam also held for the small Ṭayyibī community in the sixth/twelfth century.[66]

4 Numbers are irrelevant

So far, the main point at issue has been the significance to be attached to the number of believers. There were those, however, who dismissed the entire question of numbers as irrelevant. Though they were not Imāmī Shīʿīs, what they argued is instructive in that it

62 Ibn al-Walīd, *Tāj al-ʿaqāʾid*, 126.

63 Ibn al-Walīd, *Tāj al-ʿaqāʾid*, 126.

64 Ibrāhīm b. Muḥammad b. Saʿīd al-Thaqafī, *al-Ghārāt* (ed. ʿAbd al-Zahrāʾ al-Ḥusaynī al-Khaṭīb), Beirut 1407/1987, 91; Aḥmad b. Abī Yaʿqūb al-Yaʿqūbī, *Taʾrīkh*, Beirut 1379/1960, ii, 206; Ibn Shuʿba, *Tuḥaf*, 119; Ibn Bābawayh, *al-Khiṣāl*, Najaf 1391/1971, 171, no. 257; *idem*, *Ikmāl al-dīn wa-itmām al-niʿma*, Najaf 1389/1970, 285; al-Sharīf al-Raḍī, *Khaṣāʾiṣ amīr al-muʾminīn*, Najaf 1368/1948–9, 82; al-Shaykh al-Mufīd, *al-Irshād*, Beirut 1399/1979, 122, tr. I. K. A. Howard, London 1981, 169; al-Ṭūsī, *Amālī*, i, 20; Saʿīd b. Hibat Allāh al-Rāwandī, *Minhāj al-barāʿa fī sharḥ nahj al-balāgha* (ed. ʿAbd al-Laṭīf al-Kūhkamarī), Qumm 1406/1985–6, iii, 320; Ibn Abī ʾl-Ḥadīd, *Sharḥ nahj al-balāgha* (ed. Muḥammad Abū ʾl-Faḍl Ibrāhīm), Cairo 1378–83/1959–64, xviii, 347; Amir-Moezzi, "Seul l'homme de Dieu", 213. Commentators are divided over the identity of the *aqallūn* to whom ʿAlī referred: al-Rāwandī maintains that these are the legatees of whom, since the Prophet's death, there is only one in each generation: *Minhāj al-barāʿa*, iii, 325. Here al-Rāwandī relies on an Imāmī exegesis of Q56:13–14 ('A multitude of those of old, and a few [*qalīl*] of those of later time'), where *qalīl* is glossed as 'one', namely ʿAlī (see al-Najafī, *Taʾwīl*, 643, no. 7 › *BA*, xxxv, 333, no. 7, al-Katkānī, *al-Burhān*, iv, 276, no. 1. Al-Najafī's source is the commentary of Ibn al-Juḥām [alive in 328/939–940; cf. E. Kohlberg, *Muslim Scholar*, 369–71, no. 623]). Ibn Abī ʾl-Ḥadīd, in contrast, cites 'our colleagues' (*aṣḥābunā*) as identifying the *aqallūn* with the saints known as *abdāl: Sharḥ nahj al-balāgha*, xviii, 351. The identity of the *aṣḥāb* depends on Ibn Abī ʾl-Ḥadīd's affiliation; he may have been a Zaydī, but the issue has not yet been conclusively resolved; see *EI2*, s.v. 'Ibn Abi 'l-Ḥadīd' (L. Veccia Vaglieri).

65 Ibn al-Walīd, *Tāj al-ʿaqāʾid*, 126.

66 The belief that the followers of truth are few and the followers of falsehood are numerous is upheld by Naṣīr al-Dīn al-Ṭūsī (d. 672/1274) in one of his most important Ismāʿīlī works, the *Rawḍat al-taslīm*, also known as *Taṣawwurāt*, ed. and tr. W. Ivanow, Leiden 1950, chapter (*taṣawwur*) 18, pp. 70–2 (Persian) = pp. 79–81 (English). It remains to be investigated how widespread this belief was among Ismāʿīlī scholars.

represents an alternative strategy for defending the few; furthermore, some of their arguments are based on texts also used by the early Imāmiyya.

In his *Faḍl al-iʿtizāl*, ʿAbd al-Jabbār responds to claims that the Muʿtazila are not part of the community, that they are opposed by the majority of Muslims (*al-jamʿ al-ʿaẓīm min al-muṣaddiqīn li-Muḥammad*) and are few in number in comparison with the *jamāʿa*.[67] ʿAbd al-Jabbār insists that the term *jamāʿa* refers to those who agree on the truth, regardless of their number. In support of this, he quotes ʿAbdallāh b. Masʿūd as declaring: '*Jamāʿa* means whatever conforms with obedience to God, even if it is one person' (*al-jamāʿa mā wāfaqa ṭāʿat allāh wa-in kāna rajulan wāḥidan*).[68] ʿAbd al-Jabbār also cites Qurʾānic verses (Q11:40, 38:24, 4:66, 7:102, 6:116, 52:47) where, he says, God praises the few and condemns the many.[69] How could one rely on *kathra*, when those who followed Noah and the other prophets were only few? It is known that the many may err while the few may be right (*al-kathīr qad yaqaʿ minhum al-khaṭaʾ wa-min al-qalīl al-ṣawāb*).[70] God calls on the believers to obey those in authority (*ulū ʾl-amr*), not those who are many (*ulū ʾl-kathra*).[71]

Texts of the type adduced by ʿAbd al-Jabbār are also found in Shīʿī sources. We have already encountered Ibn al-Walīd's citation of ʿAlī's pronouncement about the people of truth; a variant thereof is cited by ʿAbd al-Jabbār.[72] In several Imāmī sources, the Prophet is reported to have defined the community (*jamāʿat al-umma*) as those who uphold the truth, 'even though there are (or: even if there were) [only] ten of them' (*wa-in kānū ʿashara*),[73] and to have declared: 'My community are the people of truth, even though they are few/even if they were few' (*jamāʿat ummatī ahl al-ḥaqq wa-in qallū*).[74] For the early Imāmīs (and for Ibn al-Walīd), these traditions proved that the few are always in the right; ʿAbd al-Jabbār would presumably have seen in them proof that the community of believers comprises those who are in the right, regardless of whether they are few or many. These divergent interpretations derive from the

67 ʿAbd al-Jabbār, *Faḍl al-iʿtizāl*, in *Faḍl al-iʿtizāl wa-ṭabaqāt al-muʿtazila*, 185.

68 ʿAbd al-Jabbār, *Faḍl al-iʿtizāl*, 186. ʿAbd al-Jabbār's source for Ibn Masʿūd is *Kitāb al-maṣābīḥ* of Muḥammad b. Yazdād (for whom see van Ess, *Theologie*, index, s.v.). Ibn Yazdād probably died in the first half of the fourth/tenth century (*Theologie*, i, 62 n. 22). ʿAbd al-Jabbār repeats this argument in his *Tathbīt*, i, 211. See also the discussion in Uri Rubin, *Between Bible and Qurʾān: The Children of Israel and the Islamic Self-Image*, Princeton 1999, 141 (with further attestations of the saying of Ibn Masʿūd). Cf. al-Naẓẓām's view that consensus means every teaching based on a solid argument (*ḥujja*), even if it is the teaching of a single person (see al-Ghazzālī, *al-Mustaṣfā min ʿilm al-uṣūl*, Cairo 1356/1937, i, 110, tr. van Ess, *Theologie*, vi, 182 [text 251]; *idem*, *Theologie*, iii, 386).

69 ʿAbd al-Jabbār, *Faḍl al-iʿtizāl*, 186. See also *idem*, *al-Mughnī*, xvii, 209.

70 ʿAbd al-Jabbār, *Faḍl al-iʿtizāl*, 188.

71 ʿAbd al-Jabbār, *Faḍl al-iʿtizāl*, 189. For ʿAbd al-Jabbār, the *ulū ʾl-amr* are the scholars (ibid.).

72 '*Jamāʿa* means joining the people of truth, though they be few; division means following the people of falsehood, though they be many' (*al-jamāʿa mujāmaʿat ahl al-ḥaqq wa-in qallū waʾl-furqa mutābaʿat ahl al-bāṭil wa-in kathurū*): *Faḍl al-iʿtizāl*, 186.

73 al-Barqī, *al-Maḥāsin*, i, 220, no. 124; Ibn Bābawayh, *Maʿānī ʾl-akhbār*, Najaf 1391/1971, 151, no. 2 › *BA*, ii, 266, no. 22.

74 al-Barqī, *al-Maḥāsin*, i, 220, no. 123; Ibn Bābawayh, *Maʿānī ʾl-akhbār*, 151, no. 1 › *BA*, ii, 265, no. 21. See further al-Shaykh al-Mufīd, *al-Ifṣāḥ fī imāmat ʿAlī b. Abī Ṭālib*, Beirut 1409/1989, 25–7. Cf. Ibn Bābawayh's statement: *al-jamāʿa ahl al-ḥaqq wa-in qallū*: *al-Khiṣāl*, 552, cited in Rubin, *Between Bible and Qurʾān*, 142; Niʿmat Allāh al-Jazāʾirī, *Zahr al-rabīʿ*, Beirut 1411/1990, 356.

ambiguity of *wa-in*: for the Shīʿīs a factual assertion is being made in the concessive clause ('even though there are only ten of them') while for ʿAbd al-Jabbār the clause is hypothetical ('even if there were only ten of them'), no stand being taken on the question of whether what is postulated in this clause is true or not.

Another prominent representative of the position that numbers are irrelevant is the Fāṭimid al-Qāḍī al-Nuʿmān (d. 363/974).[75] His views on this subject are set out in the *Ikhtilāf uṣūl al-madhāhib* (composed after 343/954), in the context of a lengthy discussion of consensus. Like the early Imāmiyya, al-Nuʿmān rejects consensus of the Sunnī type as having no basis in either Qurʾān[76] or *ḥadīth*.[77] He next mentions two questions about which Sunnī scholars disagree. One is, who are the members of the group whose consensus must be followed?[78] If the answer to this first question implies that the members of the group constitute less than half of the community, then the second question arises: in that case, is their consensus sufficient in itself to bind the whole community? Here al-Nuʿmān distinguishes two rival doctrines. The first proceeds from the assumption that in case of disagreement (*ikhtilāf al-umma*), truth lies with the majority of the whole Muslim community (*al-jumhūr al-akthar wa'l-sawād al-aʿẓam*). The basis for this are traditions such as *yad allāh ʿalā 'l-jamāʿa*, with *jamāʿa* being understood as synonymous with *umma*. The *ijmāʿ* of the group in question is thus binding only when it represents the opinion of the majority. Al-Nuʿmān identifies those who subscribed to this view as *akthar al-ḥashwiyya wa'l-nawāṣib*, 'most traditionalists and anti-Shīʿī Sunnīs'.[79]

The second doctrine has it that the consensus of the relevant group is binding even when its members are a minority of the *umma*. Upholders of this position are 'those who claim to use reasoning' (*ahl al-naẓar bi-zaʿmihim*), by which al-Nuʿmān is in all likelihood referring to the Muʿtazila.[80] Basing themselves on scripture (Q7:187, 12:103, 10:83, 11:116),[81] they argue against the proposition that truth must be with the majority. They also cite *ḥadīth*, for example that odious innovations will spread to cover most of the community (thus reducing the believers to a minority).[82]

---

[75] A list of sources and studies on al-Nuʿmān is provided in F. Daftary, *The Ismāʿīlīs: Their History and Doctrines*, Cambridge 1990, 651–2 n. 266.
[76] al-Nuʿmān, *Ikhtilāf*, 81–103.
[77] al-Nuʿmān, *Ikhtilāf*, 103–4.
[78] al-Nuʿmān, *Ikhtilāf*, 105–8. This is one of the issues discussed by al-Ghazzālī in his detailed analysis of *ijmāʿ*; see his *al-Mustaṣfā*, i, 110–27, summarized in H. Laoust, *La politique de Ġazālī*, Paris 1970, 158–61. See also Wael B. Hallaq, "On the Authoritativeness of Sunni Consensus", *International Journal of Middle East Studies*, 18 (1986), 427–54, at 441–4, repr. in his *Law and Legal Theory in Classical and Medieval Islam*, Aldershot 1994, art. VIII.
[79] al-Nuʿmān, *Ikhtilāf*, 108–9. For the notion of *al-sawād al-aʿẓam*, see Rubin, *Between Bible and Qurʾān*, 127–8 and index, s.v.
[80] Al-Nuʿmān himself restricts the use of *naẓar* to cases where no answers are to be found in either Qurʾān or tradition; see *Ikhtilāf*, 137–54.
[81] These passages, however, refer to a minority of believers among a majority of unbelievers, not to a minority of believers within the *umma*.
[82] al-Nuʿmān, *Ikhtilāf*, 109.

In his response, al-Nuʿmān concentrates on the issue of numbers. If great numbers are an indication (*ʿalāma*) of truth, then the prophets and their small bands of followers were in the wrong, and the unbelievers, who formed the majority, were in the right.[83] If, in contrast, truth resides with the few, then the *umma* would have to follow a deviant minority (*man shadhdha minhum wa-fāraqahum*). Once most members of the community adopt the position of the deviators and only a minority adheres to its original position, the majority will have to revert to the view of this minority.[84] Al-Nuʿmān's own view is that numbers are irrelevant and that truth can only be established by proof (*wa-fī dhālika ʾl-bayān ʿalā anna ʾl-ḥaqq lā yathbutu biʾl-kathra mimman ittabaʿahu wa-lā biʾl-qilla*[85] *minhum wa-innamā yathbutu biʾl-ḥujja*).[86] The use of the term *ḥujja* is significant: in Fāṭimid Ismāʿīlism, it denotes not only 'proof' as an abstract notion, but also the Imam or his representative.[87] For al-Nuʿmān, *ijmāʿ* is based on the Qurʾān and on the words of Muḥammad and the Imams;[88] the community (*jamāʿa*) which follows the true Imam (*imām al-ḥaqq*) is the one whose opinions are binding, irrespective of number (*qallat aw kathurat*).[89]

It would thus appear that al-Nuʿmān's is a position intermediate between the Muʿtazila and the Imāmiyya: he concurs with the former that numbers are irrelevant, while following the latter in his insistence on the crucial position of the Imam as the repository of truth.

5 Conclusion

It is only natural for small communities to try to put an acceptable gloss on their inferior numbers. Early Imāmī Shīʿīs did so by using the theme of *dhamm al-kathra wa madḥ al-qilla* in an apologetic context: being the majority, they argued, does not mean being right. At the same time, the notion of the select few was central to their faith: only a handful of believers preserved the truth when the Prophet died; only few believers know the secrets of the religion; the perfect believers are a minority even within their own community. The changes in the political fortunes of the Imāmiyya from the mid-fourth/tenth century and the gradual abandonment of the esoteric tradition caused the theme in question to be largely discarded. It was, however, brought back by the Akhbārīs in the context of their struggle against consensus.

---

83 al-Nuʿmān, *Ikhtilāf*, 109–10.
84 al-Nuʿmān, *Ikhtilāf*, 110. This is an instance of *ilzām (reductio ad absurdum)*; for further examples see S. Stroumsa, *Freethinkers of Medieval Islam*, Leiden 1999, index, s.v.
85 Reading thus for *li qilla*.
86 al-Nuʿmān, *Ikhtilāf*, 110.
87 Cf. Daftary, *The Ismāʿīlīs*, 127–8. See in general *EI2*, s.v. 'Ḥudjdja (in Shīʿī terminology)' (M. G. S. Hodgson).
88 al-Nuʿmān, *Ikhtilāf*, 129–30.
89 al-Nuʿmān, *Ikhtilāf*, 133. Cf. al-Nuʿmān's *Sharḥ al-akhbār fī faḍāʾil al-aʾimma al-aṭhār* (ed. Muḥammad al-Ḥusaynī al-Jalālī), Beirut 1414/1994, i, 367.

The problem of numerical inferiority can also be resolved by denying any significance to the number of adherents. This line of argument was pursued by al-Nuʿmān but – as shown in the case of Ibn al-Walīd – was not shared by all Ismāʿīlīs. Among the Muʿtazilīs, its most eloquent spokesman was the *qāḍī* ʿAbd al-Jabbār.

Can rights co-exist with religion?

Oliver Leaman

There is an Enlightenment view which establishes a sharp distinction between human rights and religion. The Enlightenment saw itself as representing a new direction in thought, forging new ideas and relationships, and religion was definitely seen as the enemy. Religion stood for reaction and superstition, and if it was to survive within an Enlightenment environment it had to change into a rational system which is self-consciously in accordance with the principles of reason. This was nowhere as strongly felt as in moral and political philosophy, where the doctrine of natural rights, rights which we have by virtue of our humanity, relies on nothing more than that humanity. The idea of basing rights on religion is equivalent to basing reason on religion, or the principles of clear rational thought on superstitious tradition. The slogan 'Dare to know' is clearly set up in opposition to the ways in which religion throws doubt on the ability of human beings to know, and argues that we need to rely on tradition to inform us of what we can know, by contrast with the efforts of our reason alone. Rights then exist outside religion, even in opposition to religion, and there is no way on the Enlightenment view that religion can be used to support human rights. On the contrary, if anything is acceptable in religion, it must be because it does not interfere with human rights, or accords with those rights. There is a right to hold religious beliefs, however misguided these are, but no need for religious sanction for such right. The direction of justification is definitely from the notion of rights to the notion of religion, and only an etiolated form of religion at that, a rational religion which serves to represent in transcendental form the principles of reason themselves.

Yet there seems to be nothing on the surface incompatible between rights and religion. Why should a religion not embody rights for individuals and groups within its structure and teachings? Islam, for example, does give different religious groups, such as the *ahl al-kitāb*, specific rights, and many religions express their views in terms of political ideals. For example, many South American Catholics interpret Christianity as a revolutionary doctrine on the side of the poor, and several important Anglican clerics have similar, although perhaps less radical, views. Religious believers have often been in the forefront of those defending the idea of rights, and they would regard those rights as stemming from the religion.

But it is in this question of the basis of the rights that the real problem lies. What do rights rest upon? For the liberal, rights are part of the basis of what it is to be human, and need to be recognized at the same time as the inalienable humanity of creatures is also recognized. Some would even extend those rights to non-humans, in particular animals, or even parts of the living and non-living environment. The idea is that the individual as an individual has a set of rights which exist as a result of her individuality, and the leading issue of politics and morality is how to reconcile her rights with the rights of others, since clearly in a world in which everyone has rights there is going to be potential conflict between different people all trying to assert their rights to act freely in defence of their own beliefs, wants and needs.

Liberal thinkers thus spend a lot of time discussing how to reconcile the rights of some with the rights of others in a way which is mutually acceptable, or at least not morally objectionable. Whether they can bring off this reconciliation satisfactorily is not at issue here, but we need to examine the alternative to liberalism, what might be called communitarianism. This sees rights as not being embodied in individuals, but in institutions or communities, since individuality is too weak and narrow a notion to serve as a basis of rights. The communitarian objects to the idea of the individual as the basis of ethics, and the nature of morality as stemming from the potential conflict between rational egoists since this is an entirely inappropriate foundation for ethics. Individuals do not just happen to come together and form institutions, but it is their coming together and forming institutions which is the basis of morality itself. The liberal notion of the individual subject as initially independent of society is incapable of providing an explanation for the growth of social phenomena such as a shared moral consciousness and common ethical reactions. This is not just a comment on causality, since no one really thinks that historically the individual of liberalism functioned independently of everyone else and then got together with others to carry out certain common purposes. The point is that the idea of the individual as existing even theoretically without any social characteristics, but only with a basic notion of individuality, is not the idea of a perfectly free and rational individual, but rather the idea of an empty individual, an individual who is incapable of developing even theoretically in character and moral depth in the ways in which we do develop socially.

There is no doubt that these sorts of objections to liberalism are powerful, but they founder on the difficulty of explaining precisely what notion of community is the notion which has to lie at the foundation of morality. Is there a notion of community which is generally acceptable and which cannot be challenged by any alternative conception of morality? If so, then the liberal cannot get his argument started. There does not seem to be. It is always possible for an individual like Diogenes the Cynic to perform unusual and strange practices in pursuit of what he says is how we ought to live, in an environment which is not mediated by a concept of community which he accepts, and for this to be a viable option. Can we rule out from the start such a lifestyle as possibly acceptable? According to liberalism we cannot rule it out, and

Mill argued that we should see alternative lifestyles as similar to experiments, each of which is trying to determine what the best way of living might be. We cannot rule out an experiment just because we think it is not going to work. We can only rule it out if we think that it is obvious for some reason that it is not going to work, and the strength of liberalism is that we do not seem to be able to rule out *a priori* any lifestyle, however apparently disastrous or unviable it might seem to be.

This is where religion comes in. Religion fits in with communitarian accounts of morality, in the sense that it identifies morality with a particular set of beliefs and practices which are part of a community, perhaps a community which the religion itself has established. What counts as right within a religion is specified by the religion, and many theologians would argue that there is no possibility of discovering what is right without first accepting the teachings of religion. Only God is able to establish the principles of morality, and unless we follow God's law, we shall not manage to adhere to those principles, however much we might try to. In any case, what counts as ethical behaviour is derivative on adherence to the religion, so the sorts of activities which liberals commend are only commendable if they are carried out within the context of the appropriate religion, here standing for the appropriate community.

Can we not work out what sorts of behaviour ought to be pursued by ourselves, using reason alone? Not according to the communitarian view of religion's role in morality. What makes morality morality is its accordance with faith, since only God is able to say what morality is. This is not to suggest that the only possible religious view is that what is good is good because God says it is good. It is perfectly possible to argue that what is good is good because it is good, and God confirms its goodness through his law. Even on this view, though, what counts as right might only make sense within some sort of community, and even a religious community, since only such a community could educate us in moral behaviour.

This positioning of rights within the structure of a religious community is what makes the practice of such rights so fragile, of course. Since rights are secondary, secondary to the religion, it is easy to abandon them in what are taken to be the interests of the religion. In the words of John Gray, a contemporary liberal, 'Do Muslims defend their traditions on the grounds of fairness and parity in a tolerant society? If so, we have to agree to them. But if they defend them because they are "true", then we have to resist their claim and assert the fundamental values of liberalism. And if necessary we have to be authoritarian in doing so' (*The Independent* 4 March 1996). What is useful about the liberal notion of rights is that they commit the state to respecting the space which surrounds us as primarily private space, not to be interfered with except for the purposes, generally, of preventing one set of rights interfering with the rights of others. Within the context of the religious state, by contrast, all crime becomes crime against God (*fasād*, or 'deviation' is the common name for anti-social behaviour in the Islamic Republic of Iran) and so it is easy for the state to disregard what might otherwise be regarded as the inalienable rights of individuals. That is, if the private space of the individual is only accepted as private within the context of the religious community in which the individual lives, then it is not really private at all, and may be invaded at any time if the interests of the community, or the religion, require such intervention.

Religion manages to do this by its function of reducing what might be regarded as the polarities of our normal lives. Our lives are characterized by a number of important polarities, which define the sort of people we are. These include:

private	public
self	others
internal	external
individual	communal
particular	general
personal	universal
philosophy	religion
rational	emotional
culture	nature
nomos	*sharīʿa*
awe	prayer
intellectual	practical
scarcity	plenty
wisdom	virtue
rationality	religion

According to many versions of liberalism, the concepts on the right are generally constructed out of those on the left, and *vice versa* for the communitarian. If we identify religion with communitarianism, as we should, then it looks as though religions will always interpret rights as secondary to the truths of the religion, as deriving their force from the religion. After all, within the context of religion everything derives its significance from the religion, from the fact that we live in a world created by God, and there can be no notion of rights that is independent of our relationship with God, the most important relationship in our lives. At this stage the normal move would be to present arguments for thinking that the liberal conception of rights is preferable to the communitarian view, or the reverse, and it is easy to see what sorts of arguments would be employed here. The liberal would argue, entirely plausibly, that the main problem with basing rights on some common set of beliefs and values is that there is no common set of beliefs and values which cannot itself be questioned, and so it is difficult to see how that set of propositions can be called common. The communitarian often argues that the liberal conception of the individual is far too impoverished to make sense of decision-making, and that the notion of coming to the construction of values out of an initial absence of values is futile.

Rather than rehearse the familiar arguments yet again, there might be scope to use the notion of religion to investigate whether there might be ways of bridging what seems to be a wide chasm between these standard philosophical positions.

What we could use here is an important principle established by Ibn Rushd (Averroes), the principle that it is possible to come to the same truth in a variety of different ways. Ibn Rushd argued that religion and philosophy, by which he meant a rational way of establishing truth which is not based on revelation, are two paths to the same destination. They are two different ways of doing the same thing, as it were, and the differences are important in that they are appropriate to different kinds of people. For those who are capable of reasoning theoretically, philosophy is an appropriate way of seeking to establish the truth. For those who are less gifted theoretically, or perhaps not interested in working in that way, religion is the right method to follow. This is not to disparage religion, but to point out that (in Ibn Rushd's view) religion is available to everyone, while philosophy is only available to a minority.

We tend to identify this sort of argument with Ibn Rushd, but in a different form it was also used by his philosophical opponent, Ibn al-ʿArabī. The latter argued that we tend to think of the notion of *tawḥīd* in ways which do not really make it impinge on our own lives. But if the notion of *tawḥīd* is taken seriously, it implies that we do not really exist apart from God, that there is not really any 'us' at all, there is just God. When we look around the world we see what we take to be different and discrete things, but really there is nothing except God, on the notion of *tawḥīd*, and Ibn al-ʿArabī goes into great detail on how we might acquire the ability to see both ourselves and the rest of the world (as we say) as part of God. So we can see the world both as it normally appears, and as an aspect of God. Both ways of seeing the world are correct, in the sense that there is truth in both these positions. Although in reality there only exists one thing, God, it is not the case that we are mistaken in experiencing the world as existing separately from God, or in a differentiated way. We can experience the world in this way, God has made this possible, and we do not get it wrong if we think of ourselves as separate from God, since to a degree we are separate from God. We are separate in the sense that we can regard ourselves as separate, and indeed it is difficult for us to regard ourselves as really part of the deity. Here again we have the idea of there being different routes to the same truth. What the ordinary person believes in his unreflective way is not wrong, but it is not a complete description of the truth either. It embodies the complete truth in a way which makes it possible for him to live his ordinary life, but the philosopher and the mystic know of another way of attaining the truth which is more remote from our notion of the ordinary life. As a result of that gap it raised the important political question, which we shall not be addressing here, as to whether the philosophers and mystics were capable of living an ordinary life, whether, that is, they could be acceptable members of the *umma*. What is important here is the idea that there are different ways of doing the same thing, and different paths to the same destination, an idea which has been refined over a long period in Islamic philosophy.

We tend to think of religions as fairly rigid structures consisting of fixed doctrine and accompanying practices, and we tend, mistakenly in my view, to use language like 'the Christian approach to x' and 'the Islamic approach to y'. But religions are in every sense loose and flexible institutions, and the doctrines which go along with them share in that looseness and flexibility. Like everything else, religions which do not adapt and change, do not survive. Religions are about everything, yet to be a believer does not mean that one shares with the religion all its beliefs nor that one uses the religion to structure the whole of one's view of reality. On the contrary, it is up to the participants in religion to define for themselves how far they are going to go in following religion. There are perhaps principles which have to be accepted before we can accept that someone is actually a believer in a particular religion, but we should stress the 'perhaps' here. So we should not think that when we embody rights within a religion we are necessarily fixing them within a straitjacket which is going to control their role strictly.

On the other hand, the important feature of such rights is that their ultimate justification is in terms of something other than either themselves or the individuals who claim them, but in the religion. Yet what the religion provides is a way of looking at the world, a way in which rights feature as topics. Rights delimit comparative relationships within a view of the world in which God has indicated that human beings ought to relate to each other in particular ways. The religious view of the world provides a context within which such a repertoire of rights makes sense. Religion provides the account of the basis of the rights which helps us understand how those rights link up with the rights and duties of others, and where those rights acquire their ultimate justification. They make the rights language comprehensible, in the sense that they provide that language with its context. To take an entirely different sort of example, what makes a particular piece of human behaviour comprehensible is the way in which it fits in with a wider context. If an apparently healthy and wealthy individual kills herself, we need to provide such surprising behaviour with a context if we are going to be able to understand it. And we can usually provide such a context, since we are not usually prepared to accept that behaviour is inexplicable. If it really is inexplicable, then we suggest that the agent was not really in control of herself when she acted, but had to do what she did, since there could have been no reason for it.

From a religious point of view, what gives rights their meaning is their role in how God wishes us to live. In the language of the communitarian, rights are thus provided with a context within which they make sense. Although as we know only too well, it is easy in practice for a state which uses religion or the language of religion as its state ideology to abandon rights for religious reasons when it is useful to do so, there is nothing specifically religious about this policy. A liberal state which upholds the sanctity of individual rights may also come to abandon some in order to increase others, and one could hardly use such examples to challenge the idea of liberal rights themselves. One of the leading problems of liberalism is that when rights come into conflict there is no obvious way of reconciling them. According to the third paragraph of article 18 of the UN Covenant:

> Freedom to manifest one's religion or beliefs may be subject only to such limitations as are prescribed by law and are necessary to protect public safety, order, health, or morals or the fundamental rights and freedoms of others.

So human rights may be in conflict with each other (acknowledged again in article 29 of the UN Universal Declaration of Human Rights). This suggests that the liberal account of the justification of rights is no more insulated against the danger of being co-opted by some larger cause than is the case with rights in religion.

But how are we to understand rights where the individual right holder does not accept the view of religion with respect to his rights? This may be because he does not accept the religion and its revelation (if there is one), or because he does not think that his rights are based on the religion. He just believes that he has an inalienable right to do something, a right which requires no further justification than the fact of his humanity. Perhaps it would not matter, since it might be argued that he does not understand the real basis of his rights, but they are his rights nonetheless. We need to bring in here Ibn Rushd's argument that it is possible to get to the same truth in different ways. The believer thinks that the basis of his rights lies in God, and the non-believer thinks it lies in his individuality. They both believe something which is true, that the individual has rights, but they explain these rights in different ways.

Surely this is not correct, though. What these two theories deal with are accounts of which theory of rights is true. They cannot both be true (although they could both be false), and they are each suggesting that they represent the true position on the nature of rights. How can they be different routes to the same truth? Well, exactly the same problem arises when we consider the contrast between philosophy and religion, or between mysticism and common sense. These are also different ways of representing what is true, and they argue for their own view as the true view, not as one view among many of the true view. But according to Ibn Rushd they are wrong to do so, since they are compatible with each other. What we need to ask is whether liberalism and communitarianism are similarly compatible. There are good arguments for thinking that they are. They both stress different things. Liberal theory stresses the fact that it is an individual who ultimately is the right holder. Communitarian theory stresses the fact that rights exist within some institutional framework. They are clearly compatible, so long as they do not incorporate claims to represent the whole basis of rights separately. This is entirely similar to the link between religion and philosophy on the account provided by Ibn Rushd. Religion and philosophy stress different aspects of the truth. Religion concentrates on presenting the truth in a way accessible to everyone, while philosophy restricts it to those few who can grasp it. But do not both religion and philosophy claim the right to describe exclusively the nature of reality? Sometimes they do, but if they do they are mistaken, since it is feasible to represent them as being compatible.

The problem which appears to be created by contrasting rights and religion is a problem which arises when we take too seriously the polarities which dominate much philosophy and political theory. It is surely the point of religion to reject such polarities, to present a view of humanity which reconciles these apparent contradictions in our lives. If the message of religion is accepted, then one knows how to reconcile the contradictions, since body and soul, the public and private, the personal and the political, and so on all become united in one view of the nature of reality. The communitarian view also has the advantage that it points to someone who has duties in response to our rights. It is often argued that rights and duties are correlative, and yet if we have positive rights it is difficult to see who has the duty to satisfy them. For example, if there is a positive right to match desert with reward, then someone has to provide the appropriate reward. According to Kant, it is because of problems like this that it is only rational for us to seek to act morally if we presuppose the idea of divine justice (eventually) characterizing our lives. On a communitarian approach, God can represent the duties correlative with the rights, and in the next world he can compensate us for our undeserved sufferings in this world. The liberal view tends to become quite conservative, since it is often difficult to specify whose duties match positive rights to things like education, sustenance and so on. Religion can represent these duties as at least in principle in existence somewhere, even if not in this world.

Is there really no separate notion of rights in religion? After all, there often seems to be no concept of negative liberty in religion. Negative liberty is the notion of being free from interference, and is the standard concept of freedom in liberalism. Positive liberty, by contrast, is the freedom to do something, in particular to realize oneself, to act in accordance with the ways in which we ought to act. Positive liberty sees human beings as being defined in a particular way, and their freedom to act is then describable in terms of that definition. From the point of view of religion, of course, how we are defined is expressed in the religion, and so it would be regarded as unimportant at best if there was no freedom to behave in ways which go against the recommendations of the religion. Rights are involved in this sort of approach, of course. Within the context of a religion, can we have a right to act in ways which are contrary to the faith? Once one joins a club, does one have the right to act in contravention of the constitution of the club? One does not, and on joining many clubs one has to sign a document saying that one will uphold the rules and regulations of the club. In the *Crito* Plato argues that just by virtue of the fact that he is an Athenian citizen, and did not leave the city when he was at perfect liberty to do so, he is obliged to suffer whatever penalties the city wishes to impose on him. There is no private space which he is entitled to occupy by contrast with the public space established by the law and constitution of Athens. One might argue, though, that from the point of view of the truths of religion even the choice which Plato considers in the *Crito* is rather too free. It is not so much a matter of leaving a club, more a matter of abandoning the truth and choosing hell. Actually, Plato describes the consequences of going against the law in much the same way, arguing that such illegal action would be equivalent in going against everything his life has been about up to that point.

Here we have to consider what is involved in being in a religion, or accepting a religion. Does this necessarily involve accepting or committing oneself to accept a specific set of rules and facts? It might, but even if it does one would probably have to accept that what one calls a religion, and the lifestyle attached to it, is relatively loose and subject to alteration. Even the leading principles of a particular faith are interpretable in a wide variety of ways. So even if the notion of rights is embodied in religion, there is no reason to think that that notion is thereby unduly constrained in its scope and effectiveness.

But does that not mean that the religion really has no control over the notion of rights which might go with it? This may succeed in rescuing the notion of rights, but at the cost of emasculating religion. It looks as though religion will be made to fit in with whatever notion of rights one might otherwise support. But surely this is what in fact happens. That is, someone who is committed to the equality of men and women will interpret religious texts in such a way as to establish support for such equality, however unlikely the text is to support such a position, and even if there are religious texts which seem to rule out such equality explicitly supplementary arguments or principles, or even *aḥādīth*, will be constructed and applied to defend the right. Some believers will disapprove of this strategy, arguing that this is to stretch the text too far, and then there can be a debate about what might be regarded as part of the faith and what may not. The way we should regard religion here is as the language in which the debate takes place, in the sense that it represents the application of concepts surrounding the debate. The debate only makes sense if we use the appropriate language, but language does not constrain the debate. On the contrary, language makes the debate itself possible.

It will be argued that basing rights on religion is inevitably to make rights secondary to something else, and hence ultimately vulnerable to the ways of interpreting that something else. It has been argued that this is not necessarily going to be damaging to rights and their holders, although it must be admitted that basing rights on religion historically tends to lead to their implementation becoming weakened. Yet it is also the case that basing rights on nothing more than individuality has also resulted, on occasion, in their being disregarded, since one then has to balance different rights when they come into conflict, and there are no general principles which tell one how to get the balance right apart from the bare notion of individuality. This notion is not sufficiently rich, many would argue, to help determine the resolution of such conflicts and so it is not difficult to argue for the restriction of some rights on the basis of the protection or the development of others. The liberal is then in no better position to defend rights as compared with the communitarian.

The standard criticism which the liberal brings against the communitarian is that communitarianism is an inherently conservative position. The communitarian is obliged to argue, the suggestion is, that the community is the basis of rights, and so the values of the community itself cannot be criticized in terms of the rights language which it itself establishes. The problem with this, of course, is that it insulates the values of the community itself from that language, but it is surely always open to us to criticize those values, since we can always ask whether what is taken to be the basis of our rights is itself morally acceptable. The outstanding problem which naturalism in ethics has to overcome is that there appears to be no natural definition of what a human being is which will satisfy everyone, or at least no definition which really is a definition. It is always open to others to challenge what we might think the purpose of human life is. No doubt some of these challenges are rather strange, in that it might be thought that given our biological structure there are some answers to how we ought to live, yet there is no determinate and complete set of answers to that question which would have to satisfy everyone. The communitarian, in insisting on a particular concept of the community as basic to ethics, suggests that such a concept is so basic that it cannot itself be challenged. And that is very much the difficulty which the religious form of communitarianism appears to get itself into, in arguing that rights are embodied in the religion it suggests that the religion itself is beyond challenge.

But as we know religions are not above challenge. If it is possible not to accept the message of a particular religion, then does that mean that the rights which that religion seeks to establish are not accessible to the non-believer? This does not follow. It is perfectly feasible to accept the right and yet go wrong in what its basis is. One might think that the right is merely based on our humanity, and that would be erroneous, according to the communitarian, but not seriously erroneous, since the right holder would use it within the context which gives the right its meaning, but without noticing that context. The right holder would correctly identify the right, but not what its application presupposes, so he would have grasped the truth that there is a right, but not the way to establish it. To give an example from a different area of knowledge, some people can solve quickly mathematical problems, yet not say how the solution works. Would we have to deny that they knew the answer, say, to 1256 x 4329? Clearly the person who knows the explanation for why the mathematics works knows more than the other person who does not have this explanation, but they both know the same thing. Here we have the case yet again of there being two different routes to the same truth.

However, it will be said, this is not a plausible example, since in the case of mathematics there is complete certainty, while in ethics there is debate and disagreement. We cannot challenge mathematics in the same way that we can challenge religion. But what does it mean to challenge religion? It might mean to challenge the facts or alleged facts of revelation, the prophecy of particular individuals, and so on. But how important are these to religion? They are very important for many believers, yet for others they are not important, they are just vivid and imaginative accounts that are designed to bring out to the widest possible constituency how they ought to live and behave. The stories themselves are not important, what is important is what they imply. If people find it easier to work out how to behave through thinking of a religion being literally true, then there is no reason why they should not think in that way and if some people find it easier to work out how to behave through thinking of a religion as not being literally true, then there is no problem in their thinking in that way either. It is not the truth of the stories which are associated with religion which gives the religion its force, but its ability to connect up with our lives and plans, to help us relate to the meaning of the world.

We might even see the view that liberals have of rights as the possessions of autonomous and independent individuals as similar to the stories which make up religion. That is, the notion of the individual which liberalism holds dear as primarily existing outside of a social framework or community can be seen as a largely romantic concept. The whole idea of the pre-social being is after all generally not supposed to represent an actual state of affairs, but rather a theoretical starting point which allows us to place rights on a rational ethical foundation. Critics of this starting position claim that the individual who is thus placed within a pure context of choice exists in such rarefied conditions that there is nothing relevant which can be derived from such an hypothesis, even from such a theoretical hypothesis. But the idea of the entirely free individual taking upon himself various obligations and establishing links with other individuals is a valuable idea. It shows how even if we start with entirely egoistic motives we might end up wishing to restrain our egoism to take account of the interests of others. This notion of the individual is regarded by Hegel as tragic, since that individual realizes that one right comes up against another right, he appreciates for the first time that the world is a place in which there are a multiplicity of obligations which require mediation, rather than a natural realm in which we feel entirely at home in our environment.

The argument here has not been that it is wrong to base our behaviour on an account of human rights, nor that there is anything wrong on basing our behaviour on religion. These are both acceptable conceptual environments within which human morality may flourish. Let us return to the idea that there can be two different ways of reaching the same truth. The truth in question here is how we ought to behave. We can tell two sorts of stories about this truth. According to one, what makes morality possible is the fact that we each possess rights on the basis of our individuality, on the basis of our common membership of humanity. According to the other story, we are in a world which is created by a deity who means us to live in a certain way, and as a result we should realize our essence by following divine law. These stories are different stories, but they are not incompatible. They both have a happy ending, they both explain how it is possible for us to live morally. Liberalism answers the question of *who* has rights, while communitarianism answers the question *why* they have such rights. The liberal might try to counter the approach of the religious arguments for rights by claiming that they restrict our autonomy, as though the association of rights with anything apart from themselves might result magically in their losing their power. The religious account of morality rejects the independence of rights for similar motives, as though if there existed an independent source of value then the force of the religion is restricted. We should bring these views closer together and then we can see what they share, as compared to concentrating on what they exclude. Rights can co-exist with religion, and religion can co-exist with rights.

Bibliography

W. Chittick, "Ibn al-ʿArabī", in S. Nasr and O. Leaman (eds), *History of Islamic Philosophy*, London–New York 1996, 497–509

R. Dworkin, *Taking Rights Seriously*, London 1977

O. Leaman, *Averroes and his Philosophy*, Richmond 1997

O. Leaman, "Is there a Concept of Liberty in Medieval Jewish Philosophy?", *Rivista di storia della filosofia*, I (1997), 141–51

O. Leaman, (1998) "Philosophy of Religion", in O. Leaman (ed.) *The Future of Philosophy*, London 1998, 120–33

M. Sandel, *Liberalism and the Limits of Justice*, Cambridge 1998

Researching Muslim minorities
Some reflections on fieldwork in Britain

Seán McLoughlin (University of Leeds)

Introduction

This paper is about some of the problems and possibilities of researching the Muslim minority in contemporary Britain. In particular, my reflections are based on the experience of living amongst, and writing about, the 50,000-strong Muslim population of Bradford, a city in the north of England long noted for its now largely redundant woollen textiles industry.[1] Muslim men first came to Bradford to work in this and other low-paid sectors of the economy during the post-war boom of the late 1950s and 1960s. They arrived mainly from Mirpur district in Pakistani-administered 'Āzād' Kashmir, but also from other parts of Pakistan, as well as Bangladesh and India. Since the 1970s economic restructuring has hit these communities particularly hard, with male unemployment amongst Pakistanis in Bradford running at over 25 per cent.[2] Nevertheless, having reunited their families and built up institutionally complete and culturally vibrant communities, Muslims now consider themselves to be here to stay. Moreover, a majority of the population today is British-born.

In January 1989 however, Bradford's Muslims came to international attention in such a way that their belonging to the British nation was to be called seriously into question. A copy of Salman Rushdie's novel *The Satanic Verses* – said to defame the character of the Prophet of Islam and his family – was burnt by members of the Bradford Council of Mosques.[3] This was followed, one month later, by Ayatollah Khomeini's *fatwā* calling for the death of Rushdie for blasphemy. In the wake of these events a dominant discourse emerged amongst the liberal establishment which produced

[1] This paper draws on data collected for a PhD in Social Anthropology awarded by the University of Manchester in 1997. I would like to thank the University and the Economic and Social Research Council (award: R00429424215) for their support between 1992 and 1996. An adjusted version of my thesis is to be published (by Pluto Press) as, *Representing Muslims: Religion, Ethnicity and the Politics of Identity*, London 2001.

[2] In 1991, based on the 'ethnic' question asked at the census, it was found that of one million or so Muslims estimated to be living in Britain, approaching 460,000 were Pakistanis. Relative to the majority 'white' population, Pakistanis (along with Bangladeshis) experience some of the highest levels of deprivation in the country. In many cases, this can be seen as a consequence of migration from places like Mirpur, which have a long history of political marginalization and socio-economic underdevelopment. See M. Anwar, *Muslims in Britain: 1991 Census and other Statistical Sources*, Centre for the Study of Islam and Christian–Muslim Relations (CSIC) Papers, No. 9, Selly Oak Colleges, Birmingham 1993.

[3] The Bradford Council of Mosques was instituted during 1981 as a forum for the representation of Muslim concerns in the city. For an account of its work see P. Lewis, *Islamic Britain*, London 1994. For useful commentaries on the Rushdie Affair see M. M. Ahsan and A. R. Kidwai (eds), *Sacrilege versus Civility* (The Islamic Foundation), Leicester 1989, and L. Appignanesi and S. Maitland (eds), *The Rushdie File*, London 1989.

Muslims as fanatical, intolerant and ignorant 'outsiders' who should either embrace the 'responsibilities' that come with 'a British way of life' or make their homes elsewhere.[4]

This then was the context when late in 1993 I began a year's fieldwork in Bradford to collect material for a doctorate in anthropology. Mine was an attempt to explore the different ways in which Muslims were representing their identities, both to each other and to wider society, in a post-Rushdie context. Given the size and diversity of Bradford's Muslim communities, this meant that I had to draw upon a number of methodological approaches to carry out my work. Nevertheless, while I consulted historical and contemporary sources and analysed quantitative data sets, my main research tools remained broadly anthropological. Following the pioneering ethnographer, Bronislaw Malinowski (1884–1942), most anthropologists have sought to actively immerse themselves in the lives and languages of distant 'exotic' cultures by taking up residence *in situ*.[5] In common with anthropologists who have worked overseas, my methodological approach combined participant observation with unstructured interviews. I also recorded my observations, reflections and any developing theories in a field diary. However, working at home did make a difference to the conduct of my research. The people whom I was studying were in the process of reconstructing their world views in a pluralistic context dominated by English culture and language, the 'habitus' within which I myself have been socialized. Moreover, as the Rushdie Affair illustrated, Muslims' calls for greater recognition of their religious beliefs and practices represent an active challenge to just what it means to be 'British' in a multi-ethnic society.

Undertaking fieldwork 'at home' in an urban setting is just one of the things I want to write about in this paper. In what follows, I begin with a general overview of the new Islamic presence in Western Europe. Thereafter, I come to a series of reflections on the practicalities of making contacts with Muslim communities in Bradford. As we shall see, my work was conducted mainly in English with Muslim leaders and youth. I met people in public spaces such as mosques, community centres, schools and colleges, although it was, of course, easier to gain access to some of these contexts than others. This discussion is followed by a consideration of the role of my own subjectivity in the process of collecting data. Given a widespread recognition amongst social scientists that no knowledge is 'value-free', it is important to locate the way in which I was positioned in the field *vis-à-vis* my respondents. Finally, in the

---

[4] A *fatwā* is a formal opinion in Islamic law promulgated by a specialist, a *muftī*. However, there is now some doubt as to whether, technically speaking, Khomeini did in fact issue a *fatwā* in this context. An article in *The Guardian* (13 November 1996) has argued that it was Western observers who first used the term in relation to Rushdie's book.

[5] For a recent introduction to the anthropology of religion, with useful references to Islam, see C. Bennett, *In Search of the Sacred: Anthropology and the Study of Religions*, London 1996.

wake of well-established critiques of western scholarship on Islam, I briefly examine the possibilities for representing Muslims after Orientalism.

Reconstructing Islam in Western Europe: global and local contexts

A recent volume edited by two anthropologists with an interest in Muslim society, Ahmed and Donnan, begins by insisting that Islamic Studies today must change, 'in response to the fact that the lives of many ordinary Muslims have been changing, and as a reflection of the equally dramatic changes taking place in the world more generally'.[6] Partly, but only partly, in sympathy with Said's polemic on the essentialism of 'Orientalist' scholarship – to which we shall return in the final section – their statement contains an implicit critique of what many have traditionally seen as a textually based field of study, one which has not much concerned itself with the everyday practice of Islam.[7] Of course, this is just the sort of critique that one might expect from anthropologists who tend to examine the working of things from the 'bottom up'. Such an approach, of course, has its own problems. However, what is perhaps most important about Ahmed and Donnan's intervention is that, even as two established social scientists, they still want to (re)claim Islamic Studies as their own field.[8] For them, Islamic Studies is broadly construed as multi-disciplinary; it is bounded only by an interest in 'the study of Muslim groups and their religion Islam'.[9] This, I think, is significant and moreover captures the spirit of an increasing number of publications that seek to explore contemporary Muslim societies. While sacred texts often remain a central focus of attention, not least in terms of the commodification of Islamic culture, themes such as travel, space and the media have begun to organize interesting volumes on ordinary Muslim lives.[10] They have in common the insistence that religious identities are always fluid, contextual and contested. Moreover, in most of these works, where there is a shift in scholarly emphasis to include cultural practices as

6 A.S. Ahmed and H. Donnan (eds), *Islam, Globalization and Postmodernity*, London 1994, 1.

7 E. Said, *Orientalism*, London 1978.

8 According to B. S. Turner (*Orientalism, Postmodernism and Globalism*, London 1994), few social scientists were working on Islam in the 1970s. Brief reflection on why interest has renewed since the 1980s suggests a number of explanations including: (1) the Islamic resurgence, following the failure of secular-nationalist regimes to deliver significant social, economic or political development in the Muslim world; (2) the decline of Communism in the late 1980s which, it has been argued, rightly or wrongly, leaves Islam as the only 'world system' that currently offers an 'alternative', or indeed a 'threat', to the cultural and economic hegemony of the West; and (3) the fact that during the 1980s postmodernism and globalization became established as significant, if controversial, trends in contemporary social theory. I say more about both of these later on in my paper.

9 Ahmed and Donnan (eds), *Islam, Globalization and Postmodernity*, 1.

10 See for example, D. F. Eickelman and J. Piscatori (eds), *Muslim Travellers: Pilgrimage, Migration and the Religious Imagination*, Berkeley-Los Angeles 1990; M. Fischer and M. Abedi, *Debating Muslims: Cultural Dialogues in Postmodernity and Tradition*, Wisconsin 1990; B. Metcalf (ed.), *Making Muslim Space in North America and Europe*, Berkeley–Los Angeles 1996; and D. F. Eickelman and J. W. Anderson (eds), *New Media in the Muslim World*, Indiana 1999.

well as classical texts, there is also an interest in the margins of the Muslim world, as well as its centre. The study of Muslim minorities appears to have come of age.

Around seven million Muslims now live in Western Europe.[11] This figure compares with the eleven and a half million Muslims in the former Soviet Union who trace their roots to the medieval empire of the Mongols, and the five million Muslims in the Balkans (Yugoslavia, Albania, Bulgaria and beyond) whose heritage is marked by Ottoman interests in that area. While there were of course historical centres of Islamic civilization in Sicily and Andalusia until the eleventh and fifteenth centuries respectively, the Muslim population of Western Europe today has only recently been established. Muslims have come mainly as economic migrants and political refugees from North Africa, the Middle East and South Asia, settling in several nations including Spain and Italy in the south, and Norway and Denmark in the north. However, by far the largest concentrations of Muslims have been in the following countries: France (2.619 million), especially from Algeria, Morocco, Tunisia and Turkey; Germany (2.012 million), especially from Turkey; and Britain (1 million), especially from Pakistan, Bangladesh and India.[12]

The notion of migration (*hijra*) has a prominent place in the history of the Islamic community, given the Prophet's journey from Mecca to Medina in 622 CE. Although migration leading to a life under non-Muslim rule is quite a different matter, it is interesting to note that historically, the permissibility of travelling and trading in Christendom, as Muslims have done for many centuries, prompted only minor debates in Islamic law.[13] This changed somewhat during the colonial period when many Muslims around the world found themselves ruled by non-Islamic governments such as the British in India. The main issue under these circumstances was whether it was desirable for Muslims to migrate to lands still ruled by their co-religionists.

In any case, there is no precedent for the numbers of Muslims that have voluntarily sought a life 'amongst the unbelievers' in the modern period.[14] For the majority, men who came to work in low-paid sectors of western labour markets from the late 1950s onwards, the most common justification for their migration was economic necessity (*ḍarūra*). Debates about the status of migrants in Islamic law were, therefore, never uppermost in their minds. Nevertheless, many ordinary Muslims have tirelessly sought to reconstruct the institutional, ritual and customary 'life support

[11] S. Vertovec and C. Peach (eds), *Islam in Europe: The Politics of Religion and Community*, Basingstoke–London 1997, 14. See also T. Gerholm and T. Lithman (eds), *The New Islamic Presence in Western Europe*, London 1988, and J. Nielsen, *Muslims in Western Europe*, 2nd edn, Edinburgh 1995.

[12] Vertovec and Peach, *Islam in Europe*, 14.

[13] See B. Lewis and D. Schnapper (eds), *Muslims in Europe*, London 1994.

[14] Lewis and Schnapper (eds), *Muslims in Europe*.

systems' of Islam in the West, most especially since families began to be reunited in the 1970s. Yet, as Werbner has observed of this process, Muslim settlers

> do not simply share a culture deriving from their place of birth; the taken for granted features of this culture are no longer natural and self-evident. They have to be renewed and relocated in this new context.[15]

So, as contexts change, so too do interpretations and styles of religion. Indeed, Metcalf considers that the transformation of contemporary Islamic symbols and institutions is probably most evident, and perhaps most innovative, at the margins of the Muslim world.[16]

Starting more or less from scratch then, Muslims have taken a number of steps towards establishing themselves in the West, both in terms of building up their own community organizations and institutions, and negotiating with the authorities for a greater recognition of their public needs. For example, across Western Europe, mosques, madrasas and religious associations have been instituted to provide facilities for prayer, education and a wide range of other community functions. The *ḥalāl* meat trade is well established within the European Union, which currently exempts both Jews and Muslims from stunning animals before ritual slaughter. The question of regulation remains an issue however, as does concern about the open-air slaughtering of animals during *ʿīd al-aḍḥā*.[17] Reflecting more their interactions with wider society, Muslims have lobbied for accommodations within the workplace and public institutions with regard to religious holidays, prayer rooms and the availability of *ḥalāl* food. State schools have perhaps received most attention, with concessions sought by Muslim parents in terms of the availability of single-sex schools and modest uniforms for girls, Islamic collective worship and multi-faith religious education. In many schools there is now more attention to Muslim concerns about the curriculum in sport, art and music and in some countries there are state-funded Muslim schools. In other areas of public life, some diasporized Muslims would like a separate system of personal law, most especially in respect of marriage, divorce and the custody of children. However, like the calls for state-funded Muslim schools, such claims have been met with the charge of separatism. A state's system of law is routinely seen, again like its schools, as providing a common and, as such, integrating reference point, for the nation's diverse ethnic

---

[15] P. Werbner, *The Migration Process*, Oxford 1990, 1.

[16] Metcalf (ed.), *Making Muslim Space*. Indeed, it has been argued that the novelty of the circumstances in which diasporized Muslims find themselves 'has facilitated changes in religious institutions and practices at least as important as those inspired by earlier generations of elite Muslim intellectuals in the Middle East and the Indian subcontinent', Eickelman and Piscatori (eds), *Muslim Travellers*, 5.

[17] *The Muslim News*, 25 December 1998.

groups.[18] Finally, although many dead are still sent 'home' for burial overseas, there are an increasing number of Muslim bodies being buried within Western Europe. Negotiations with the authorities have sought to ensure that, according to Muslim custom, the deceased are laid to rest in a cloth shroud as soon as possible after death.

While Muslims have been broadly successful in reconstructing many of the main features of their religious worlds in Western Europe, levels of institutional completeness and public recognition do, of course, vary within and between nation-states. Muslims have been most successful in areas where there are large enough numbers to demand concessions from the local state. However, given the proliferation of Muslim organizations following migration, many serving fairly discrete ethnic constituencies, organizing single bodies to make representations on a national level has proved more difficult.[19] Moreover, in contexts where 'race' and culture, as well as religion, mark their 'difference' from majority populations, Muslim leaders have often been required to rationalize Islamic religious beliefs and practices to wider society. This is by no means commonplace in majority Muslim countries where Islam, for the most part, remains taken for granted as part of the overall cultural context.[20]

The status of religion and minorities can also vary greatly in the pluralized secular democracies of Western Europe. In England, for example, most Muslim migrants and their families have always been 'citizens' of the nation although there is a head of state who is head of the established Anglican Church too. Islam therefore has no official status as a religion but the integration of Muslims is encouraged on a communal basis. In contrast, while Muslims in Germany have been able to secure a degree of recognition from the state, a biological rather than a political construction of national belonging has impeded this process. Until very recently, Muslims – even those born in Germany – were seen not as citizens but as 'guest workers'.[21] In France, where

[18] For a discussion of the situation in England see S. Poulter, *Ethnicity, Law and Human Rights*, Oxford 1998. Poulter argues that the very diversity of Islamic law would make an accommodation difficult to achieve.

[19] For example, during 1994, Conservative Home Secretary Michael Howard advised Muslim organizations to 'speak with one voice' if they wanted to have more influence on government policy-making in Britain (*Q-News*, 25 March 1994). Muslims responded when, in November 1997, a new umbrella organization, the Muslim Council of Britain, was inaugurated with the specific objective of representing 'Muslim issues' to the (now Labour) government (*The Muslim News*, 26 December 1997).

[20] That said, there is highly charged political contestation over the signifier 'Islam' throughout the Muslim world and for some 'Muslim' minorities especially, such as the 'Alawīs from Turkey or the Aḥmadīs from Pakistan, migration to the West allows much greater freedom of religious expression. See Metcalf (ed.), *Making Muslim Space*.

[21] *The Muslim News*, 25 December 1998, reports that the new German government has announced a revision in the nationality laws, which will allow all immigrants to become citizens, should they fulfil various criteria. One such qualification is being able to demonstrate economic self-sufficiency. This rules out the 25 per cent of Turkish settlers who are currently unemployed. Accounts of Muslims in Germany can be found in Gerholm and Lithman (eds), *The New Islamic Presence in Western Europe*; Eickelman and Piscatori (eds), *Muslim Travellers*; Nielsen, *Muslims in Western Europe*; Lewis and Schnapper (eds), *Muslims in Europe*; Metcalf (ed.), *Making Muslim Space*; Vertovec and Peach (eds), *Islam in Europe*.

the state recognizes, and seeks to integrate, the individual rather than the group, the situation is different again. Given that religion and the state are formally separated, expressions of religious identity in the public sphere have been interpreted as an unwelcome challenge to the cherished French principle of laicity. For example, in 1989 three Muslim girls were banned from wearing Islamic headscarves to a state school in Creil.[22]

Islam in the contemporary West must therefore be seen as the product of complex and ongoing interactions between Muslim minorities and the states and societies in which they now reside. However, the continuing influences of migrants' homelands and international Islamic currents are also important. Such links are facilitated by the ever-expanding possibilities of rapid communication across the boundaries of contemporary nation-states, that is, globalization.[23] The impact of globalization has undoubtedly been rather contradictory, most especially in terms of the power geometry, which constitutes the relationship between 'the West' and 'the Rest'. Nevertheless, technological innovations, such as affordable international air travel, satellite media systems and the Internet, have had the effect of increasing contact between people around the world in such a way that many are experiencing the globe as a 'time–space combination' in common. Of course, the circulation of languages, people, goods, capital and ideas is nothing new, not least within the Muslim world or, indeed, its relationship with the West.[24] However, there is little doubt that the revolution heralded by modern communications technology has accelerated the rate, and highlighted the significance, of these social, cultural, economic and political processes. For example, elite Muslim organizations can reproduce their ideas and imagine global communities as never before, both in terms of speed and coverage. Notably, the Muslims in Britain who lobbied for Rushdie's book to be banned in 1989 were first alerted to its contents when photocopies, faxes and telexes were sent to Britain by a network of Islamic activists based in India.[25]

So it is then that Muslim migrants, apparently on the periphery of the Islamic world, can not only maintain linkages with 'old' Muslim centres in their homelands, but also create multiple 'new' Muslim centres of their own. The globalization of Muslim

---

[22] For accounts of Muslims in France see the listings for Muslims in Germany above.
[23] S. Hall, "The Question of Cultural Identity", in S. Hall, D. Held and T. McGrew (eds), *Modernity and Its Futures*, Cambridge–Oxford 1992, 273–325. On the one hand, it has been argued that globalization has given rise to a process of cultural homogenization where the consumer-capitalism of the West has been exported worldwide to such an extent that it is now routinely considered 'universal'. On the other hand however, some have maintained that because globalization has had the effect of relativizing notions of cultural discreteness, it has also given rise to a revivalist defence of particularistic identifications by national, ethnic and religious groupings.
[24] There is, of course, a credible argument that Islamic civilization played a significant part in the formation of modern Europe. See, for example, N. Matar, *Islam in Britain 1558–1685*, Cambridge 1998.
[25] C. Bhatt, *Liberation and Purity: Race, New Religious Movements and the Ethics of Postmodernity*, London 1997.

communities does not suggest some united or undifferentiated *umma* however.[26] As noted above, unity on a national or even local level is difficult enough to sustain, and the diversity of all Muslim communities can be enumerated in the many different ways that religious identity is qualified and crosscut by identifications of sect, region, language, gender, ethnicity, generation and class. So, while many Muslims may increasingly 'imagine' their religious communities globally, they have to contextualize them locally. Moreover, if we take the idea of a locally contextualized Islam seriously we should be wary of measuring the 'new' margins of the Muslim world against 'norms' determined by 'old' Islamic centres. Urban communities such as those I studied in Bradford are no more or less representative of 'Muslim society' than the villages of Mirpur in 'Āzād' Kashmir from which many of my respondents' families originate. Finally, it is surely a matter of note that, as Voll has observed, this implosion of the local and the global is also gradually breaking down some of the boundaries which have traditionally made for a radical separation of scholarly Western 'selves' and objectified Muslim 'others'.[27] The fact of 'the Rest *in* the West' rather than 'the West *and* the Rest', as Hall has put it, has created the conditions of possibility for scholars such as myself to write about the realities of researching 'Islamic Britain' or 'Britannia's Crescent'.[28]

Going to the field: encountering British-Muslim communities in Bradford

Beginning my fieldwork in Bradford, I found a bewildering number of 'texts' competing to represent Muslims, most especially in public spaces. These were not communities waiting to be 'discovered' by some intrepid anthropologist. Produced by the state, media, civil society, academia and, ever increasingly, Muslims themselves, such 'texts' were diverse in terms of the medium of their production, the patterns of their consumption and their ideological perspectives and goals. Indeed, all of the following were available to me in supplementing material collected through participant observation and unstructured interviews: state policy-making documents on minority issues; minutes of local council meetings concerning Muslim affairs; educational syllabi for a multi-cultural society; oral history projects recording the formation of Asian communities in Bradford; television and radio programmes, newspapers and magazines including those produced by Muslims for Muslims; desk-top published tracts distributed by competing Muslim movements; tourist information leaflets selling

[26] For further discussion see my paper, "In the Name of the *umma*: Globalization, 'Race' Relations and Muslim Identity Politics in Bradford", in W. A. R. Shadid and P. S. van Koningsveld (eds), *Political Participation and Identities of Muslims in non-Muslim States*, Kampen 1996, 206–28.
[27] Cited in T. Sonn (ed.), *Islam and the Question of Minorities*, Atlanta 1996, 23–5.
[28] Hall, "The Question of Cultural Identity". See also Lewis, *Islamic Britain*, and D. Joly, *Britannia's Crescent*, Aldershot 1995.

'Bradford's flavours of Asia'; and novels by authors such as Salman Rushdie and Hanif Kureishi who have written about the experiences of being Asian and Muslim in Britain.

Of course, one of my main concerns in Bradford was to find out just what ordinary Muslims themselves made of these various representations of their identity. Given the size and scale of the urban field site, public religious and cultural events were the single most useful way of meeting people when I first arrived in the city. Regular fairs, talks, camps, conferences, exhibitions, plays, films and charity dinners all provided opportunities for occasional conversations with British-Muslims and allowed me to begin to gauge what issues people really felt were important. It was quite usual then for me to check local libraries, shops, community centres and restaurants for posters and flyers advertising events in the inner-city ward where I chose to live.

After a few weeks of rather general activities involving, for the most part, fleeting contact with a wide range of people, I was keen to immerse myself in more specific projects that would provide me with opportunities for in-depth participant observation. In this regard, I found that public meetings organized by the local Racial Equality Council and Inter-Faith Centre were the most important ones for the progress of my research. At discussions of the educational 'underachievement' of minorities, council funding cuts or the new Agreed Syllabus for Religious Education in schools, I met the local 'community leaders' who eventually became some of my key informants. They held positions of influence in local mosques, voluntary organizations and schools so I quickly learned the importance of being in regular contact with them. Indeed, establishing relationships with some ordinary Muslims might well have been impossible without the co-operation of these 'brokers'. The state's attempt to manage racialized and ethnicized minorities through immigration legislation and the monitoring of welfare benefits has created – not surprisingly – some suspicion of 'outsiders' without established *bona fides*.

In all of the field sites I was eventually to work in, I sought, as far as possible, to write about the way in which different contexts brought together the discrepant representations of Muslim identity made in turn by the state, community leaders and 'ordinary' people themselves. Given this concern, freedom of movement between contexts and groups of people was essential. Certainly, I can understand why involving oneself in reciprocal relationships confined to a limited range of contexts has brought all sorts of benefits to traditional anthropological practice. However, when in the 1970s the anthropologist Verity Saifullah-Khan 'became a female relative' in an extended Pakistani-Muslim family in Bradford, she had to accept all sorts of restrictions on her activities.[29] For example, her adopted 'parents' prevented her from taking a role in a

[29] V. Saifullah-Khan, "Pakistani Villagers in a British City", (unpublished doctoral thesis, University of Bradford 1974).

local play as they saw it as an 'unrespectable' activity. By contrast with Saifullah-Khan, I had neither the hindrance of such restrictive relationships nor, by the same token, the benefit of such intense reciprocal connections.

I did hope, nevertheless, to be able to 'give something back' to the people I wanted to work with. As we shall see in the next section, such a statement reflects a general move away from impersonal and dispassionate approaches to fieldwork in anthropology. It begins to summarize the ethical difficulty of 'observing' respondents without 'participating' in some sort of mutually agreed 'project' with them. Even in the 1970s, Anwar notes that he made good contacts with Pakistani-Muslims in Rochdale because he helped and advised people on a range of community affairs.[30] In any case, as we shall see now, three of the main projects I settled on produced quite different results. I sometimes failed in securing the participant-observer status I was so keen to develop, often for reasons far beyond my control.

One of the issues that many Muslims suggested would be a useful focus for my research was the call for Islamic schools to be funded by the British state. Fortunately, during the period of my research in Bradford, Feversham College, a Muslim girls' school, put in an application for financial assistance from the government.[31] However, when I spoke to both the headteacher and chair of governors, it soon became clear that I would not be given permission to participate in, or observe, the life of the school. They were quite happy to give me interviews, as were other key figures involved in the application process. Moreover, I did eventually visit the school for an 'open evening' in October 1994. Nevertheless, it is worth exploring briefly why my proposed presence at the school was not welcomed. My gender was certainly an issue; the call for Muslim schools is in large part an expression of the desire amongst many Muslim parents for their daughters to be educated in a single-sex environment and I was, after all, a single white male. However, there was also the question of whether I could be trusted. Although Feversham College had welcomed a number of (mainly female) visitors in the past, not least to try and underline that the institution was not simply 'separatist', this has not always had positive effects. Some have written less than complimentary accounts of their visits to the school.[32] So, given that an important application for state funding was in progress, the school's representatives could not, understandably, afford discrepant accounts of their project to emerge unchecked.

York Road mosque proved to be a more successful focus for intensive fieldwork because a ready-made role emerged for me at the institution. For nine

[30] M. Anwar, *The Myth of Return: Pakistanis in Britain*, London 1979.
[31] See S. McLoughlin, "A-part of the Community? The Politics of Representation and a Muslim School's Application for State Funding", *Innovation: The European Journal of the Social Sciences*, 11.4 (1998), 451–70.
[32] See, for example, S. Khanum, "Education and the Muslim Girl", in G. Saghal and N. Yuval-Davis (eds), *Refusing Holy Orders*, London 1992, 124–40.

months, every Sunday afternoon from 2 p.m. to 4 p.m., I taught the basics of English and maths to a group of around a dozen Muslim boys. I was paid £12 per week for my work as the mosque was part of a study support network of schools and community centres organized by Bradford Local Education Authority (LEA). The aim of the network was to assist Muslim children with their homework and exam revision at a time when their 'underachievement' at school had become very high profile in the city.[33] Indeed, I was first introduced to the President of the mosque over lunch at a large conference organized by Bradford LEA to explore ethnic minority underachievement. It was there that he invited me to become one of two tutors on the study support scheme. My teaching, and in particular the friendly relationship I developed with the President, secured the opportunity to meet the parents of children attending the mosque and the freedom to observe the day-to-day functions of the institution.[34]

In the summer of 1994 I began fieldwork on another in-depth project. Having become aware that the LEA was encouraging inter-cultural exchanges between schools in Bradford and Pakistan, I was told that Belle Vue Boys' School, which has a 90 per cent Muslim intake, was interested in organizing such a project. Unfortunately, no LEA funding was available so the school had to take on the funding of their visit to Pakistan themselves. Making my first visit to Belle Vue on the occasion of an *ʿīd* party, I met with the students and staff involved in planning for the trip, which was to include a cricket tournament at Karachi Grammar School. The students, who were about to go into sixth form, soon involved me in organizing various activities which eventually raised £2600 towards the cost of sending a 'team' of thirteen overseas. The plan was to go first to Karachi to play cricket, and then up to Mirpur and the Punjab, to visit students' families and see the sights. During our fundraising activities I built up strong relationships with the 'cricketers' and was able to observe them and question them about their identities as British-Pakistani-Muslims. Indeed, it was my intention to accompany the tour to Pakistan and explore how my respondents 'played' out their multiple identities both 'home' and 'away'. However, due to the prolonged, violent expression of ethnic tensions in Karachi, and the threat that this posed to personal safety, parents and teachers decided that the tour – and with it my research plans – would have to be postponed indefinitely.[35] As I learned the hard way, the experience of fieldworking can be very unpredictable.

[33] Figures released as a part of the government's controversial secondary schools' league tables in 1993 indicated that when it came to GCSE examination results, Bradford came seventy-fifth out of 108 local authorities (*The Bradford Telegraph and Argus*, 17 November 1993).

[34] See S. McLoughlin, "The Mosque-Centre, Community-Mosque: Multi-functions, Funding and the Reconstruction of Islam in Bradford", *The Scottish Journal of Religious Studies*, 19 (1998), 211–27.

[35] I did eventually travel to Pakistan and, together with a colleague from Manchester University, recently published the following: S. McLoughlin and V. S. Kalra, "Wish You Were(n't) Here: Discrepant Representations of Mirpur in Narratives of Migration, Diaspora and Tourism", in R. Kaur and J. Hutnyk (eds), *Travel-Worlds: Journeys in Contemporary Cultural Politics*, London 1999, 120–36.

Partial connections: reflexivity and the researcher[36]

> According to ethnographies written in the classic mode, the detached observer epitomizes neutrality and impartiality. This detachment is said to produce objectivity because social reality comes into focus only if one stands at a certain distance. When one stands too close, the ethnographic lens supposedly blurs its human subjects.[37]

In recent years, with the 'postmodern' turn in anthropology and various developments in feminist theory, there has been an increasing recognition that no method of academic enquiry is 'value-free'. Lyotard, for example, describes 'the postmodern condition' in terms of a pervasive incredulity towards the grand-narratives of legitimation such as 'science' which hold a modernist view of the world in place.[38] The universal claims of post-Enlightenment thinking are therefore seen as giving way to more contingent and fragmentary, more local and particular, constructions of knowledge. In anthropology, this crisis of certainty can be linked to the work of Asad, Said and others who have shown that anthropological representations of 'other cultures', wittingly or unwittingly, helped to justify Western colonial hegemony.[39] The limitations of Said's critique are briefly considered in my final section, but for present purposes he very clearly anticipates the methodological root of the postmodern predicament:

> No one has ever devised a method for detaching the scholar from the circumstances of life, from the fact of his involvement (conscious or unconscious) with a class, a set of beliefs, a social position or from the mere activity of being a member of a society. These continue to bear on what he does professionally.[40]

Having sought to deconstruct the authority of the author, 'postmodernists' have encouraged various new strategies for 'writing culture' in anthropology. For example, the incorporation of the voice of the 'other' into ethnographies is almost taken for granted today, while a greater reflexivity amongst anthropologists, in terms of writing themselves more explicitly into (rather than out of) their texts, is also common.[41] I have certainly supported the former strategy in my own ethnographic work but it is the latter

[36] An earlier, much shorter, reference to some of the issues mentioned in this section can be found in S. McLoughlin, "An Underclass in Purdah", *BJRULM*, 80 (1998), 89–106.
[37] R. Rosaldo, *Culture and Truth: The Remaking of Social Analysis*, London, 1993, 168.
[38] J. F. Lyotard, *The Postmodern Condition: A Report on Knowledge*, Manchester 1984.
[39] A. Grimshaw and K. Hart, *Anthropology and the Crisis of Intellectuals*, Cambridge 1993. See also T. Asad (ed.), *Anthropology and the Colonial Encounter*, Atlantic Highlands, NJ 1975.
[40] Said, *Orientalism*, 10. Even Malinowski, who at the beginning of the twentieth century claimed to have pioneered 'scientific' ethnography, has now 'come to be seen as a purveyor of fiction and a fraudulent self-publicist whose fieldwork diaries posthumously revealed the strain between his professional and private personalities' (Grimshaw and Hart, *Anthropology and the Crisis of Intellectuals*, 14–7).
[41] See A. S. Ahmed and C. N. Shore (eds), *The Future of Anthropology*, London 1995.

– reflexivity – that I want to focus on in this section. Strathern maintains that a reflexive alertness to one's own subjectivity during research can begin to reveal and assess the effects of a methodology in practice.[42] Attention to subjectivity illuminates, of course, that fieldworkers, as well as respondents, 'speak' from a variety of identification positions, all of which are context bound and implicated in relations of power. So it is then that I now want to make explicit some of the ways in which my own subjectivity, as a white, male, university student of Irish-Catholic descent, impacted on the fieldwork I undertook amongst Muslims in Bradford. In particular, I consider how I was positioned *vis-à-vis* my respondents and the partial connections I was able – and unable – to make with them.

Not all ethnographers who have written about the Muslim presence in Britain mention the role of their own subjectivity in their work. However, those that do have added an important dimension to their studies in terms of contextualizing the way in which knowledge is negotiated between the observer and the observed, the outsider and the insider. For example, writing about fieldwork amongst Bengali-Muslims in Bradford, Barton reports that he was variously understood to be 'a friend of the *imām*'; 'a journalist'; 'a Christian priest'; 'a student'; 'a police officer'; 'a new convert to Islam' and 'a Home Office representative'. Each ascribed identity predisposed potential respondents to him in very different ways. As Barton himself observes, 'few people were indifferent to a stranger'.[43] Elsewhere in the literature, Jeffrey notes how she and her husband became engaged in obligations to 'fictive kin' during her work with the Pakistani Christians and Muslims of Bristol.[44] She recalls how respondents creatively associated their surname, Jeffrey, with *Jaʿfarī*, denoting 'honorary' descent from the sixth Shīʿite *imām*, Jaʿfar al-Ṣādiq (d. 765). With respect to her study of Manchester, Werbner prefaces her work with the recognition that she is a migrant herself and that this gave her a deep affinity with the experiences of her Pakistani respondents.[45] In contrast to these 'outsider' accounts, Anwar acknowledges the importance of contacts he established as a result of his 'ethnic' identity as a Pakistani, his Islamic 'orthodoxy' and his membership of the local Community Relations Council in Rochdale.[46]

My own experience of fieldwork in Bradford was made up of precisely these sorts of partial connections with the people I got to know. Indeed, it was the dynamics of particular relationships that shaped the depth and detail of the data I was able to collect. I usually introduced myself to respondents as a 'university student' and 'part-

42 M. Strathern, "The Limits of Auto-anthropology", in A. Jackson (ed.), *Anthropology at Home*, London 1987, 16–37.
43 S. Barton, *The Bengali Muslims of Bradford*, Community Religions Project, Department of Theology and Religious Studies, University of Leeds 1986, 16.
44 P. Jeffrey, *Migrants and Refugees: Muslim and Christian Pakistani Families in Bristol*, Cambridge 1976.
45 Werbner, *The Migration Process*.
46 Anwar, *The Myth of Return*.

time teacher' with an interest in Muslim communities in Britain – both very much 'outsider' categories. However, in some contexts, I was able to re-negotiate the way in which I was initially perceived and go on to establish the sort of close relationships necessary for producing in-depth accounts of personal and communal identity. For example, one morning, I found myself sitting in a sixth-form common room for the first time, talking with a group of teenagers. Introductions were going well when suddenly another group of students returned from classes, only to aggressively enquire, 'What's he doin' here?' My new acquaintances answered, 'It's ok; the *gorā* (white man) is safe', a reply that at once supported my presence but clearly marked my continuing 'outsider' status.

Some of my most productive research activity in Bradford was the result of interactions with young British-born Muslims. They were the group of respondents with whom I usually had most in common. It was therefore fairly easy to identify interests we shared such as contemporary music, football or computers. Indeed, contacts such as those made at Belle Vue Boys' School often 'snowballed', leading on to invitations to students' homes to meet their parents, to family weddings, to afternoon and evening parties at local night clubs, to local pool halls and to football matches. However, I soon realized that nothing was to be gained by hastily asking new respondents about 'being Muslim in Bradford'. When, early on in my research, I announced to an assembled class of students that I would be happy to meet with anyone interested in talking about 'Muslims in Britain', the only response I received was from an enthusiastic young woman who promptly advised me that, 'Everyone else, they're part-time Muslims – you don't need to talk to them 'cos they know nothing.' On a number of occasions like this then, I had to be wary of associating myself exclusively with a 'loud and proud' minority of religious activists. I did not want to be alienated from the 'silent majority' whose religious identity was routinely 'ethnic' and relatively unconscious. Both groups were of equal interest to me as both represent important trends in British-Muslim identity formation.

As the issue of identity was at the forefront of what I wanted to explore, one way of gently raising the subject in conversation was to talk about my own experiences. So it was then that I routinely presented the fact that my family are economic migrants from Ireland, and was able to recount experiences of my own that I anticipated might generate some discussion amongst respondents. For example, I shall never forget visiting my uncle's farm in Ireland as a teenager and being met with the salutation, 'Welcome, Englishman'. Having grown up in Britain with a profound ambivalence about 'belonging' – if not living – 'here', I could have had no more uncomfortable mode of greeting from a relative at 'home' in Ireland. This was an experience that some of my younger respondents and I had in common. Many had visited Pakistan or 'Āzād'

Kashmir and had their 'difference' objectified for them by relatives. For example, Shamas, a young man studying at Belle Vue Boys' School, recalled how relatives in Mirpur had called him a '*wilāyatī* chicken', a 'foreign' weakling unable to undertake the strenuous daily tasks that rural people might routinely do. Others reported being 'ripped off' by locals who always charged *wilāyatī* visitors over the odds: 'They see you coming; the way you walk, dress and talk and they're supposed to be your own people.' It was not surprising then that while walking down Allama Iqbal Road, Mirpur's main street, I made instant links with people that I could not have made in Britain where being 'white' is unremarkable. With the simple greeting, 'All right mate', my similarity was produced by those on holiday who wanted to make a 'British-connection'. Indeed, my hotel room became a place for fellow (male) '*wilāyatīs*' to escape the boredom of village life and catch up on the latest football results via satellite or maybe tuck into a plate of 'English' fish and chips. However, when I spent some time with older British-Pakistanis whom I knew well from Bradford, in a place rather less well used to white British visitors than Mirpur – Gujjar Khan – I was constructed in a rather different way. They parodied the (dis)respect that a *gorā* still routinely 'commands' in the subcontinent by playfully referring to me as 'Seán *ṣāḥib*' whenever we were out and about in the town, a measure of the unease that we all felt now that the context of our relationship had changed.

I would not, therefore, want to essentialize my migrant heritage as a point of connection with my Muslim respondents. It was very much dependent on the situation. In other contexts 'being Irish' was crosscut by the experience of racism in contemporary Britain. For example, when I spoke to the headteacher of Feversham College about the possibility of me undertaking fieldwork at the school, I naturally enough attempted to put the case for my involvement. I naively thought that we had a point of connection when she referred to a speech that she had recently listened to from an Irish-Catholic councillor at a meeting about state-funded religious schools. Catholics, of course, have had such schools for decades. However, despite some commonalities with the councillor, the headteacher had found his argument that, 'We understand what you are going through' unconvincing. Indeed, she met my own equally banal platitudes with a gracious lesson in the politics of identity. In my field-notes I wrote up the following clumsy reflections:

> She explained the difference between us. I was not, she said, 'brown', 'black' or a 'Paki' and I did not wear *shalwār qamīs*. I spoke English as a first language and I was white. My colour and culture marked the boundary that divided us. Here was a Muslim woman, strong and pious – *in shā'a Allāh* (God-willing) she would say, time and time again as we chatted – who recognised the nature and need for politically constructed identities. She was 'black' because I was 'white', because 'white' people in Britain had categorised her as such.

As noted in the previous section, my failure to gain access to Feversham College can also be explained in terms of my gender. Jeffrey considers that during her fieldwork in Bristol her gender allowed her access to spheres of life not usually open to male researchers.[47] Indeed, it should be no surprise that women researchers, Muslim and non-Muslim, have produced the best accounts of Muslim women in Britain.[48] By contrast, Anwar witnesses to the fact that the social segregation of Muslim women and men in Rochdale restricted his access to female respondents even though, in many respects, he was an 'insider' in the local community.[49] While, in time, he was able to speak to some women, in general he had very little contact with them, at least in domestic contexts. This was certainly my experience. Nevertheless, while it is fair to say that my work often reflects the experiences of men more than women, I did find that meeting and talking with young women in schools and colleges was usually as straightforward as meeting and talking with young men, so long as conversations were held in a group situation. I was also able to meet professional women who were activists and professionals in 'community' and related arenas. All such women were, of course, used to formal face-to-face relationships with men on a daily basis.

Factional divisions along the lines of religious sect and *barādarī* ('brotherhood', a patrilineal intermarrying caste grouping) have become tropes in the literature on South Asian Islam in Britain.[50] For example, Barton, writing about his work with Bengali-Muslims, and in particular the role of the *imām* (prayer leader and religious functionary), warns the researcher against associating with just one religious 'sect'.[51] He argues that this is likely to restrict mobility beyond that circle, as was his own fate. While, as noted above, I was wary of associating exclusively with religious activists for fear of alienating 'ordinary' Muslims from my research, for a number of reasons I experienced none of Barton's particular problems during my time at York Road mosque, a Barelwi institution.[52] Firstly, a majority of Muslims in Bradford are Kashmiri Barelwis so I was routinely working amongst the largest Muslim constituency in the city. Secondly, I attempted to establish close relationships with no other mosques, preferring to confine myself to a single institution where I could

47 Jeffrey, *Migrants and Refugees.*
48 See, for example, A. Shaw, *A Pakistani Community in Britain*, Oxford 1988; Werbner, *The Migration Process*; Saghal and Yuval-Davis, *Refusing Holy Orders*; and K. Knott and S. Khokher, "Religious and Ethnic Identity among Young Muslim Women in Bradford", in *New Community*, 19 (1993), 601–22.
49 Anwar, *The Myth of Return.*
50 See Shaw, *A Pakistani Community in Britain* and P. Werbner, "Factionalism and Violence in British Pakistani Communal Politics", in H. Donnan and P. Werbner (eds), *Economy and Culture in Pakistan*, London 1991.
51 Barton, *The Bengali Muslims of Bradford.*
52 Barelwis seek to defend the popular Sufi beliefs and practices of Muslims from the Indian subcontinent including the intercessionary power of a *pīr* and visitation at the shrine of such a 'saint'. Their main detractors, of course, claim that Barelwi practices must be seen as *bidʿa* (heretical innovation). See F. Robinson, *Varieties of South Asian Islam*, Centre for Research in Ethnic Relations, University of Warwick 1988.

concentrate on specific aspects of its everyday life. Thirdly, my work did not involve me in continuing close contact with the *imām*, the figure at any mosque that is most likely to court sectarian controversy. In fact, I was most interested in the funding of the institution's various functions, something that was not overseen by the *imām*. Finally, and perhaps most crucially, it struck me that many 'ordinary' Muslims, old and young alike, did not really identify with sectarian labels. Most did not have a conscious sense of being 'Barelwis' or indeed anything else – they were just 'Muslims' or 'Sunnīs' or, when pressed, 'not Wahhabis'.

Issues of religious affiliation were rather more important when, over a period of a couple of months, I began to attend meetings organized by Young Muslims UK. This revivalist organisation with a national profile has a vibrant branch of activists in Bradford.[53] While I had made the nature of my presence and interest as a university student known to key figures in the movement, and so attempted to dispel the initial impression that I was a 'brother Muslim', other members occasionally challenged my motives for being present at events. Some may have become weary of a 'hanger-on' whose interest did not translate into conversion to Islam. Indeed, the fact that I presented myself as being of 'Irish Catholic heritage', but, when engaged in debate, was rather too woolly and liberal about 'what I believed', probably did not help matters. Others may have been concerned about the alleged 'undercover' surveillance of Muslim organizations, given that Britain is one, increasingly important, node in the network of Islamist organizations worldwide. Finally, on one occasion I was asked whether I worked for the Church of England and, as such, was the 'right-hand man' of so and so who had become known to Muslims in Bradford for his work on Islam in Britain.

---

[53] Young Muslims UK is the youth wing of UK Islamic Mission which in turn can be located within the tradition of political Islam represented by Jamā'at-i Islāmī in Pakistan. See Lewis, *Islamic Britain*.

Representing 'Muslim voices' after Orientalism[54]

In this final section I want to reflect very briefly on the significance of contemporary debates about Orientalism for undertaking research on Muslims (including Muslim minorities). Said, of course, maintains that, during the colonial period, the quest for an ever more systematic knowledge of the East by Orientalists, consciously or unconsciously, legitimated the Western will to power.[55] Although the authority of Western scholarship seems to have been relativized in the post-colonial world, not least by the rise of a global mass media, Said's work still raises important questions about how the academy should seek to represent Islam today.[56] This is a problem that Said himself does not choose to address. Having deconstructed Western representations of the Orient, he does not put forward a new or more positive representation of the East or Islam and, as such, has been taken to task for failing to give voice to the ways in which 'Orientalized' peoples themselves have sought to resist Western stereotyping.[57] Of course, Said was very much influenced by Foucault's argument that every representation reveals only a representer, so it seems that for him to try and represent Islam would have associated him with just the essentialism that, he argues, is so characteristic of Orientalism.[58]

In adopting this position Said falls into the most extreme of postmodernist traps, that is, deconstructing himself into silence. However, not everyone has been as reticent as Said when it comes to putting forward accounts of Islam after Orientalism. Given that traditional Orientalist scholarship seemed to generalize far too readily about the 'unchanging' characteristics of Muslim society, another postmodernist strategy – one that was mentioned in the previous section – has been to deconstruct Islam and emphasize the plural and contested nature of particular 'Muslim voices'. The importance of this approach is underlined by the following quotation from Fischer and Abedi's introduction to their account of contemporary Muslim identities:

> There are times, increasingly, when we need touchstones, reminders and access to the humanism of others. The following essays are intended to explore genres of access. The opening essay is a response to requests for reading material on the lives of people in the Middle East, lives that can reach through the numbing opaqueness of news accounts of confrontation, ideological war, and endless

[54] This section is necessarily brief. For a more elaborate form of my argument, see McLoughlin, *Representing Muslims*.

[55] Said, *Orientalism*.

[56] See Ahmed and Shore (eds), *The Future of Anthropology*. For example, they consider that some of the most informative books written recently on India and Pakistan have been not by academics but by journalists such as Mark Tully.

[57] For recent critiques of Said on a wide range of fronts, see B.S. Turner, *Religion and Social Theory*, 2nd edn, London 1991; B. K. Smith, "After Said, After Ayodhya: New Challenges for the Study of Indian Religions", *Religion*, 26 (1996), 365–72; B. Sayyid, *A Fundamental Fear: Eurocentrism and the Emergence of Islamism*, London 1997; J. J. Clarke, *Oriental Enlightenment: The Encounter Between Asian and Western Thought*, London 1997; R. King, *Orientalism and Religion: Postcolonial Theory, India and 'The Mystic East'*, London, 1999.

[58] For an account of the influence of Foucault on Said, see King, *Orientalism and Religion*.

> killing; through the reifying opaqueness of histories of political regimes, kings, dictators, coups, and revolutionary masses; through the idealizing opaqueness of theologies of Islam or symbolic analyses of ritual. Lives that make narrative sense, that are not just sentimental soap operas, that do not tell us that people everywhere are the same.[59]

Nevertheless, there are some residual theoretical difficulties with this perspective, as we shall see now.

El-Zein, for example, takes the notion of the plurality of Islam to its logical conclusion. He maintains that because of the variety of cultural forms and meanings that 'Islam' assumes around the world, we should cease to use such a 'unified' category at all.[60] In its place, he suggests the term 'islams' which is, of course, in the plural and without capitalization, and so can be seen as a simple but helpful way of deconstructing the notion that there is only one way of being Muslim, and that one interpretation of Islam has more intrinsic value than another. Unfortunately, as Sayyid comments,

> the problem with El-Zein's account is that he believes that by demonstrating the multiplicity of the uses of Islam he can refute the orientalist idea that Islam is one entity ... anti-orientalists mark not so much a break from orientalism, as its reversal ... Whereas Islam occupies the core of the orientalist explanations of Muslim societies, in anti-orientalist narratives Islam is decentred and dispersed.[61]

So, El-Zein tends to ignore the fact that there is a certain 'unity in diversity' about 'Muslim voices'; they do actually share 'fundamental' symbols in common, such as the Qur'ān and the Prophet Muḥammad. Indeed, it is these symbols that have facilitated an imagined continuity of experience amongst Muslims through time and across space for nearly fourteen hundred years. Moreover, as Cohen maintains in his study of the symbolic construction of community, it is the form rather than the content of symbols that people hold in common.[62] So, for example, the general sacredness of the Qur'ān for all Muslims does not require uniformity in its interpretation. Indeed, symbols are effective in constructing a broadly recognized sense of community precisely because they have a general elasticity, because they allow people to supply part of the meaning.[63]

Another residual problem with a postmodern emphasis on the plurality of 'Muslim voices' is that, having criticized the essentializing discourses of Orientalism, one might have expected that the essentializing discourses of Muslims themselves would be subject to criticism. However, because a naive reading of postmodernism

---

[59] Fischer and Abedi, *Debating Muslims*, xix.

[60] A.H. El-Zein, "Beyond Ideology and Theology: The Search for the Anthropology of Islam", *Annual Review of Anthropology*, 6 (1977), 227–54.

[61] Sayyid, *A Fundamental Fear*, 37–8.

[62] A. P. Cohen, *The Symbolic Construction of Community*, London 1985.

[63] Cohen, *The Symbolic Construction of Community*.

routinely suggests that our knowledge of the world can only ever be culturally relative, such moral and political interventions are often left well alone.[64] Of course, ideologies of, say, Islamic 'purity', cannot be assumed to be coercive or authoritarian. One cannot prejudge where and how the social effects of a particular discourse will be concentrated.[65] Nevertheless, exclusionary, and even exterminatory, practices continue to be pursued in the name of religious 'authenticity', and mere deconstruction does not, of course, dissolve their efficacy.

The engaged anthropologist must surely make an intervention then, and position herself or himself carefully, when confronted with a situation where there is a perceptible imbalance of power. This question of standpoint epistemology is taken up in a roundabout, but very pragmatic, way in the recent report into 'Islamophobia' in Britain by the Runnymede Trust.[66] The report recognizes that while the British government officially seeks to include Muslims in the nation, pervasive 'closed views' of Islam as uniquely monolithic, threatening and unchanging, have been central to the exclusion of Muslims from the mainstream of public life. Very much in the Orientalist tradition, 'closed views' continue to see Islam as 'the other', the total inverse and opposite of 'the West'. In contrast, more 'open views' of Islam point to the profound heritage shared between the two. Nevertheless, the report is quite clear that it is legitimate to remain 'open' to disagreeing with, and even criticizing, Islam and Muslims in certain situations, and not to be forever hamstrung by the charge of 'eurocentrism'. For me, this is an important point. I was confronted with all sorts of dilemmas about how I would finally represent the variety of 'Muslim voices' when my fieldwork was completed. The relations of power between actors, Muslim and non-Muslim, shifted around all the time as contexts changed. Accordingly, as these closing remarks from my field diary reveal now, I was always being challenged to define and redefine what, for me, was 'acceptable' in the name of Islam:

> It is one thing to advance the argument that mosques are 'safe spaces' from the racism of wider society, but something else to maintain this when a young woman confronts you with her anger at being excluded from such institutions. It is one thing to valorise the 'voices of the people' *vis-à-vis* the reified representations of community leaders, but a rather different matter when the latter are trying to make themselves heard by the powerful state bureaucracy. It is one thing to consider Islamism disruptive of the universalisation of Western modernity but when the same discourse is deployed to disparage the beliefs and practices of ordinary Muslims or members of other faiths, one has to think again.

---

64 Turner, *Religion and Social Theory.*

65 For an elaboration of this argument about 'strategic essentialism', see D. Fuss, *Essentially Speaking: Feminism, Nature and Difference*, New York–London 1989.

66 *Islamophobia: A Challenge For Us All*, The Runnymede Trust, London 1997 (available from 133 Aldersgate Street, London, EC1A 4JA).

Jāmī's re-contextualization of biographical traditions 'The biography of Anṣārī' in the framework of the *Nafaḥāt al-uns**

Jawid A. Mojaddedi (University of Exeter)

I

In the introduction of his *Nafaḥāt al-uns*, ʿAbd al-Raḥmān Jāmī (d. 1492)[1] acknowledges two precursors in the sufi *ṭabaqāt* genre.[2] He states that the genre originated with Muḥammad al-Sulamī's (d. 1021) Arabic work, the *Ṭabaqāt al-Ṣūfiyya* which was later introduced into the Persian literary tradition in the form of Anṣārī's *Ṭabaqāt al-Ṣūfiyya*.[3] Furthermore, Jāmī acknowledges his incorporation of a redaction of the latter work, which he identifies as the immediate precursor. That redaction constitutes the first major section of the *Nafaḥāt*, representing the early members (*mutaqaddimān*) of the diachronic sufi community (i.e. those who lived before Anṣārī). Jāmī explains that he has updated it as far as his own time, by the addition of the biography of Anṣārī along with those of his contemporaries (*muʿāṣirān*), followed by those of the Sufis who came after them (*muta'akhkhirān*). ʿAbdallāh Anṣārī (d. 1089), his predecessor in Sufism from Herat, therefore holds a position of central importance in Jāmī's structuring of the past. The precise role which his biography fulfills, as part of the middle, or *muʿāṣirān*, section of the *Nafaḥāt*, as well as the historical implications of the source material which Jāmī draws upon for its compilation, represent the main topics of the following discussion.

Although the main sequence of biographies in the *Nafaḥāt* is not divided formally into separate 'sections' as such, nonetheless their order of presentation corresponds closely to the aforementioned sequence of three chronological groups (*mutaqaddimān* – [Anṣārī and his] *muʿāṣirān* – *muta'akhkhirān*). Moreover, since

* This paper draws in part on research which was carried out while I was completing my doctoral thesis under Norman Calder's supervision ("Reworking Time Past: The Sufi *ṭabaqāt* Genre from al-Sulamī to Jāmī"). The British Academy is to be thanked for providing me with a studentship, and the British Institute of Persian Studies for helping me to visit the Tehran University Manuscript Library. However, my greatest debt by far is to Norman, my teacher and mentor from my first year as an undergraduate to the submission of the thesis on Thursday 12 February 1998 (immediately after he had read and commented upon the final draft).

[1] For further biographical information see ʿA. A. Ḥikmat, *Jāmī*, Tehran 1941, chs 1 and 2.

[2] See Jāmī, *Nafaḥāt al-uns min ḥaḍarāt al-quds* (ed. M. ʿĀbidī), Tehran 1991 (henceforth *Nafaḥāt*), 1.7–2.22.

[3] This work is not only called 'Anṣārī's *Ṭabaqāt al-Ṣūfiyya*', but is also usually assumed to be a work that can be ascribed to Anṣāri, by both traditional and modern scholars. However, its structure suggests that it should not be classified as the product of a single author (see J. A. Mojaddedi, *The Biographical Tradition in Sufism: The Ṭabaqāt Genre from al-Sulamī to Jāmī*, Richmond 2000 [henceforth *BTS*], ch. 3).

this broad division has been outlined by Jāmī himself, it may serve as a useful basis for an initial analysis of this collection of over 600 biographies.[4]

To begin with, it is necessary to identify the sections representing these three chronological groups, since there are no demarcations in the text itself to indicate where one section ends and the next one begins. As already mentioned, the *Nafaḥāt* begins immediately with a redaction of Anṣārī's *Ṭabaqāt al-Ṣūfiyya* (henceforth the '*Ṭabaqāt of Herat*') – its first biography is that of Abū Hāshim al-Ṣūfī, who was included in the same position for the first time in the precursor. The demarcation of this first *mutaqaddimān* section from the next, which represents Anṣārī and his *muʿāṣirān*, is relatively straightforward. This is because the parameters of the *mutaqaddimān* section are clearly defined, by virtue of the fact that it is a redaction of the *Ṭabaqāt of Herat* which preserves the latter's overall format. Therefore, the final biography which corresponds to the *Ṭabaqāt of Herat*, namely that of Abū ʿAlī al-Daqqāq, marks the end of the *mutaqaddimān* section and the beginning of the *muʿāṣirān* section (see Fig. 1 below).[5]

The point of demarcation between the *muʿāṣirān* section and the subsequent *mutaʾakhkhirān* section of the *Nafaḥāt*, however, is not as self-evident. The organisational structures of the *Nafaḥāt* themselves suggest that the transition takes place with the first of a series of cohesive 'clusters' of juxtaposed biographies whose subjects lived between the twelfth and fifteenth centuries. The members of these clusters are inextricably linked together, such that they cannot be separated from each other by classification into different sections of the *Nafaḥāt*, and since virtually all of them lived indisputably beyond the lifetime of Anṣārī, it would seem appropriate to consider them as representing the *mutaʾakhkhirān* (see Fig. 1). For example, Yūsuf Hamadānī (d. 1140) is the first member of the first of these clusters, which consists of a total of nineteen juxtaposed biographies representing an unbroken line of transmission of the 'Naqshbandī' order of Sufism as far as Jāmī's own teachers in the late fifteenth century.[6]

---

4 The *Nafaḥāt* also possesses an appendix, consisting of the biographies of thirty-four sufi women. However, it is only the main sequence of biographies (according to the earliest manuscript, which serves as the main text for Maḥmūd ʿĀbidī's excellent edition), that is discussed in this study.

5 The biography of Abū ʿAlī al-Daqqāq is in fact the 322nd Biography in the *Nafaḥāt*. Approximately 80 per cent of those which precede it correspond to biographies already provided in the *Ṭabaqāt of Herat*.

It is worth pointing out that there is an unfortunate case of mistaken identity in the article on Jāmī in the *Encyclopaedia of Islam* (second edition), where the authors state that his *Nafaḥāt* was based on 'Aṭṭār's *Tadhkirat al-awliyāʾ*'; 'Anṣārī's *Ṭabaqāt al-Ṣūfiyya*' must surely have been intended; see *EI2* s.v. 'Djāmī' (Cl. Huart/[H. Massé]). In fact, the *Nafaḥāt* remarkably contains no evidence of the use of 'Aṭṭār's *Tadhkira* whatsoever, in spite of the fact that Jāmī shows that he is familiar with the work by mentioning it in the biography of its author (*Nafaḥāt*, 596). When considered alongside his identification of 'Anṣārī's *Ṭabaqāt al-Ṣūfiyya*' as the immediate precursor of the *Nafaḥāt*, this seems to indicate that Jāmī (accurately in my opinion) did not consider the *Tadhkira* as belonging to the same (*ṭabaqāt*) genre.

6 See *Nafaḥāt*, 408.5–410.7 (Kāshgharī); 410.8–416.4 (Aḥrār). Whilst it is Kāshgharī of Herat who is recognized in most sources as Jāmī's teacher in Sufism, it is the Central Asian Aḥrār, positioned immediately after the former at the culmination of the Naqshbandī cluster, who is given priority here. This is probably on account of his higher status in the wider Naqshbandī order of Khurasan and Central Asia, which was acknowledged also by Jāmī, not only by means of this biography, but also in

It is followed by similar clusters (of up to thirty biographies), each of which, in turn, represents in approximately chronological order Sufis living within the parameters of the same time-span (twelfth to fifteenth century) (see Fig. 1).[7]

According to the dates provided, virtually all of the approximately seventy biographies located between those of Daqqāq and Hamadānī are devoted to individuals living in the eleventh and early twelfth centuries, appropriately for a section purporting to represent 'contemporaries' (*muʿāṣirān*) of Anṣārī.[8] The most obvious function of this relatively short section within the overall framework of the *Nafaḥāt*, which consists in total of approximately ten times as many biographies, is to cement together the two sections on either side of it. In this way, selected contemporaries of Jāmī in the *muta'akhkhirān* section, with precedence being given to his own (Naqshbandī) teachers, are linked as far back as the early members of the diachronic sufi community (*mutaqaddimān*), whose authority had already been securely established (see Fig. 1). First of all, Jāmī's contemporaries are linked through the lineage structured by their own particular cluster back to its first member (e.g Yūsuf Hamadānī for Jāmī's teachers), and then the *muʿāṣirān* section bridges the gap between that individual and the authoritative *mutaqaddimān*. The structuring of continuity from the late fifteenth century as far back as the eighth century (and implicitly even further back to the time of the Prophet)[9] serves to legitimize the authority of those contemporaries of Jāmī whom he has included.[10]

The cohesion between the *mutaqaddimān* and *muta'akhkhirān* sections appears to have been further enhanced by the inclusion of suitably qualified biographies at either extremity of the *muʿāṣirān* section (see Fig. 1). For instance, Aḥmad al-Ghazālī (d. 1126), the very final member of the *muʿāṣirān* section, and Abū ʿAlī Fārmadī (d. 1084), who precedes him (separated only by the latter's named teacher Abū Bakr Nassāj [d. 1094],[11] and his brother Muḥammad Ghazālī [d. 1111]), fulfil the bridging role at the interface between the *muta'akhkhirān* and *muʿāṣirān* sections; these two individuals are the ones to whom each of the first members of the clusters in the *muta'akhkhirān* section are linked back (e.g. Yūsuf Hamadānī is linked back to

his dedication of one of his *Mathnawī*s (entitled *Tuḥfat al-Aḥrār*) to him. One of the later manuscripts, perhaps in an attempt at harmonization, even implies a close association between Jāmī and Aḥrār, through the latter's deputy in Bokhara (*Nafaḥāt*, 415.21–416.4)

7 Representational diagrams of the major clusters of the *muta'akhkhirān* are provided in *BTS*, Appendix, Figs 2–5.

8 See below concerning the Chishtī family cluster, which includes the notable exceptions to the rule.

9 Jāmī incorporates into the introduction of the *Nafaḥāt* ʿAbd al-Karīm al-Qushayrī's well-known demonstration of the continuity between the eighth-century representatives claimed by the sufi tradition and the *salaf* generations of the Prophet's immediate successors (*Nafaḥāt*, 23).

10 Those of Jāmī's immediate predecessors from the fifteenth century who are included are all from the vicinity of Herat where he himself was based, in itself implying exclusivity. The *Nafaḥāt* also conspicuously lacks representation of the sufi traditions that are associated with Shīʿī Islam (see further *Nafaḥāt*, Editor's Introduction, 38–40).

11 *Nafaḥāt*, 379.10.

Fārmadī [see Fig. 1]).[12] Ghazālī and Fārmadī in turn are linked back to two specific individuals included towards the very beginning of the *mu'āṣirān* section, namely Abū 'l-Qāsim al-Gurgānī and Abū 'l-Ḥasan al-Kharaqānī.[13] In turn, each of the latter pair is linked back to an illustrious member of the *mutaqaddimān*; the introduction of Gurgānī's biography locates him at the end of a continuous chain of succession stemming from Abū 'l-Qāsim al-Junayd,[14] while the introduction of Kharaqānī's (d. 1034) biography states that he was not only a spiritual successor of Abū Yazīd al-Basṭāmī (d. 865), but was also trained by him, and all in spite of the fact that he was born long after Abū Yazīd had already died (*intisāb-i Shaykh Abū 'l-Ḥasan dar taṣawwuf bih Sulṭān al-'Ārifīn Shaykh Abū Yazīd Basṭāmī-st wa tarbiyat-i īshān dar sulūk az rūḥāniyyat-i Shaykh Abū Yazīd-ast wa wilādat-i Shaykh Abū 'l-Ḥasan ba'd az wafāt-i Shaykh Abū Yazīd bih muddatī-st*).[15] The logistics are irrelevant here; what is important to observe is that pairs of suitably qualified biographies have been positioned at either extremity of the *mu'āṣirān* section in order to enhance the links with the *mutaqaddimān* and *muta'akhkhirān* sections, like steel reinforcements which serve to enhance the cohesion between adjacent walls of a building.

[12] *Nafaḥāt*, 380.21–2 (*intisāb-i way dar taṣawwuf bi-Shaykh Abū 'Alī Fārmadī-st*).

[13] Whilst Fārmadī is linked back directly to both Gurgānī and Kharaqānī, Aḥmad Ghazālī is linked back through one intermediary, his teacher al-Nassāj, to Gurgāni alone (see *Nafaḥāt*, 379.10; 373.9–12).

[14] *Nafaḥāt*, 312.

[15] *Nafaḥāt*, 303.18–21.

Figure 1
The **muʿāṣirān** *section within the overall framework of the* **Nafaḥāt al-uns**

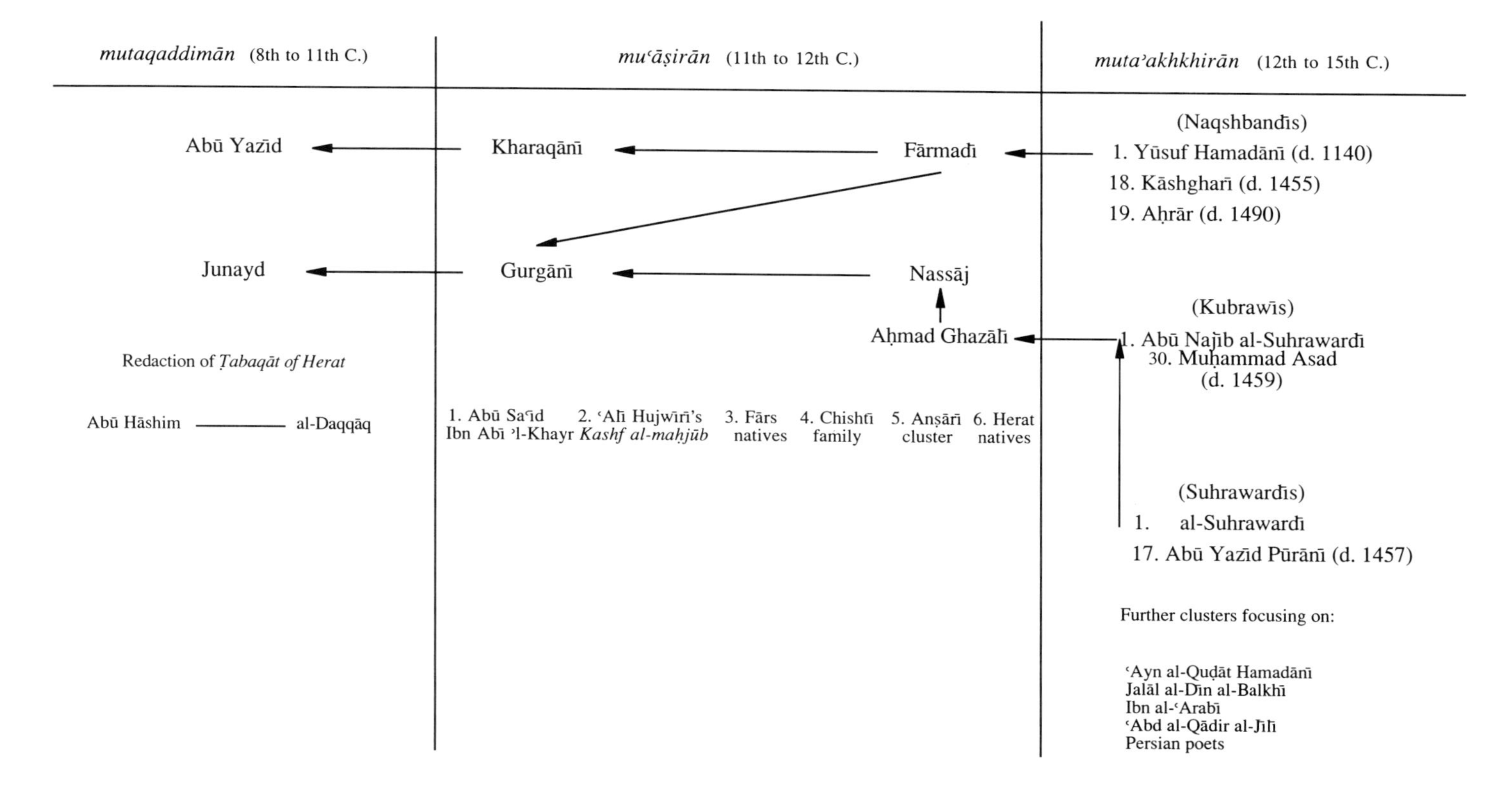

II

Whilst the *mu'āṣirān* section of the *Nafaḥāt* may serve primarily the function of cementing together the *mutaqaddimān* and *muta'akhkhirān* sections, nonetheless its structure and content deserve attention in their own right as products of Jāmī's labour and savoir-faire'.[16] In this regard it is of comparable value to the *muta'akhkhirān* section, since neither of them is based on a single source; they both stand in contrast with the *mutaqaddimān* section, which, as a whole, is modelled closely on the *Ṭabaqāt of Herat*.[17] Whereas the organizational structures and content of the *mutaqaddimān* section are consequently determined to a considerable extent by that work, the subsequent two sections in the *Nafaḥāt* take over from where it finishes, with no single precursor to follow as a model.

As I have already suggested, the *muta'akhkhirān* section consists essentially of a series of clusters of biographies which are coeval in that each of them, in turn, represents a linear advance through the same time span.[18] That is to say, whilst the *muta'akhkhirān* section as a whole does not depict a chronological advance from the very beginning of the section to the end, each of its component clusters in turn structures such an advance. As shown above, the *mu'āṣirān* section represents a chronological advance through only one generation, by virtue of the specific pairs of biographies positioned at either extremity, from the immediate successors of the *mutaqaddimān* to the immediate predecessors of the *muta'akhkhirān*. The remainder of its constituent biographies have been juxtaposed to form clusters according to their sources and the mutual associations between their subjects.

The most clearly defined cluster of the *mu'āṣirān* section is also its sole example which structures a sufi lineage. It consists of six juxtaposed biographies, the first of which introduces its subject, Abū Isḥāq Shāmī, as a successor (through three named intermediaries) of Ibrāhīm b. Adham, one of the 'mythical' founders of Sufism.[19] Shāmī is said to have visited the Khurasanian town of Chisht, where he met his successor Abū Aḥmad Abdāl Chishtī (d. 355), who is the subject of the subsequent biography. Abū Aḥmad is the first of a sequence of five members of the same family who are presented as the transmitters of the sufi tradition of the Syrian Shāmī. Thus, Abū Aḥmad's son and successor Muḥammad is listed next, followed in turn by his

---

[16] P. Ricoeur, "The Narrative Function" in his *Hermeneutics and the Human Sciences: Essays on Language, Action, and Interpretation* (ed. J.B. Thompson), Cambridge–New York 1981, 293.

[17] I do not wish to imply that Jāmī's creativity is not evident at all in his redaction of the *Ṭabaqāt of Herat*, but rather that it can only be appreciated there after a comparison with its source. For such a comparison, see *BTS*, ch. 6.

[18] Three of these clusters depict a complete lineage stretching as far as the late fifteenth century, whilst the remaining (five) clusters represent only a portion of that time span. See further *BTS*, ch. 6.

[19] *Nafaḥāt*, 328.1–6. With regard to the portrayals of Ibn Adham as a 'frontier ascetic' in sources prior to his adoption by the sufi tradition, see M. Bonner, *Aristocratic Violence and Holy War*, New Haven 1996, 125–34.

nephew and successor Yūsuf. Succession from father to son is then resumed by the presentation of Yūsuf's son Quṭb al-Dīn Mawdūd (d. 527), who is followed in turn by his own son and successor Aḥmad.

The Chishtī family cluster is particularly cohesive not only because it structures a linear transmission of Sufism, but also because the contents of its biographies share a distinctive narrative style. Moreover the transition from one biography to the next is achieved smoothly and consistently by the provision of introductions and dates of death at the start and conclusion respectively of each biography. The cluster therefore seems to have been imported as a whole into the *Nafaḥāt*. It should be noted also that, although most of the Chishtī cluster would qualify as 'contemporaries' of Anṣārī by virtue of the overlap between their lives and his, this does not apply to the earliest and final members. Those members seem to have been included as well in this section, in order to preserve the integrity of the original source. That would probably have been a local collection of biographies devoted to the sufi tradition of this particular family from Chisht. That no such source has yet been traced is probably due to the fact that it would have been superseded by its incorporation into the *Nafaḥāt*.

Further clusters can be identified in the *muʿāṣirān* section, beginning with the first dozen biographies, most of which are associated with Abū Saʿid b. Abī ʾl-Khayr al-Mayhānī (d. 1045), the subject of the seventh biography.[20] (As previously mentioned, this initial cluster also includes both Kharaqāni and Gurgānī, neither of whom is explicitly associated with Abū Saʿīd in the *Nafaḥāt*.)

Muḥammad al-Sulamī, the aforementioned author of the first work of the sufi *ṭabaqāt* genre, is amongst those included here, qualifying apparently by virtue of the material in his biography that is introduced as a narration by Abū Saʿīd, who is also said to have received a cloak of initiation (*khirqa*) from him.[21] Sulamī is closely followed by his fellow scholars ʿAbd al-Karīm al-Qushayrī (d. 1072) and ʿAlī Hujwīrī (d. *c*. 1074), both of whom are included in a cluster of juxtaposed biographies for which the latter's work, the *Kashf al-maḥjūb*, is the principal source.[22] Another well-known eleventh-century scholar Ibn Bākuwayh (d. 1050) is included amongst fellow Sufis from Fārs, immediately before the Chishtī family cluster.[23]

Immediately following the Chishtī family cluster is the longest cluster of this section. It includes the biography of Anṣārī, in relation to whom the whole *muʿāṣirān* section is supposed to have been compiled. In view of the stress that Jāmī places on the importance of Anṣārī as his precursor, and this cluster's own importance both within the framework of the *Nafaḥāt* as well as for the traditional biography of its main subject, attention will now focus on its structural characteristics and their significance.

---

20 *Nafaḥāt*, 305–12. See Fig. 1.
21 *Nafaḥāt*, 316.10–16. See Fig. 1.
22 *Nafaḥāt*, 318, 319. See Fig. 1.
23 *Nafaḥāt*, 325. See Fig. 1.

III

The biography of Anṣārī in the *muʿāṣirān* section of the *Nafaḥāt* marks the start of a cluster of twenty-three juxtaposed biographies, the contents of which appear to have been derived almost entirely from a single source.[24] Just as the members of the Chishtī family cluster are made up of the same distinctive type of material, so too are the constituent biographies of this cluster. They consist of juxtaposed segments of material presented, under the rubric *Shaykh al-Islām guft*, as narrations by Anṣārī himself. Furthermore, the source of this particular cluster seems to have been 'multi-layered', originally having taken the form of a monograph biography of Anṣārī, but eventually becoming transformed into twenty-three biographies by the time of its incorporation into the *Nafaḥāt*. Its transformation can be detected most clearly from the material found at the very beginning and the very end of the cluster; it starts as one would expect with an introduction to Anṣārī, the subject of the first biography,[25] but curiously the cluster also ends, ostensibly after twenty-two further biographies, with a conclusion to the biography of Anṣārī.[26] In other words, the beginning and end of the biography of Anṣārī seem to have been separated by the intervening biographies. This is only ostensibly the case because most of the twenty-two intervening biographies consist of no more than a couple of statements indicating their subjects' associations with Anṣārī, as in the following examples:

> Abū ʿAlī Zargar:
> Shaykh al-Islām said, 'Bu ʿAlī Zargar was one of my teachers (*pīr*), amongst the best of them. He was a Sufi, a disciple of Abū 'l-ʿAbbās Qaṣṣāb Āmulī, and he transmitted segments (*ḥikāyat kard*)[27] about him.'
>
> Abū ʿAlī Būtahgar:
> Shaykh al-Islām said, 'He was also one of my teachers. He was a generous man, and he had seen Shaykh Ḥuṣrī and transmitted segments about him.'
>
> Shaykh Abū Naṣr Qabbānī:
> Shaykh al-Islām said, 'He made many worthwhile journeys and saw many shaykhs; he had seen Shaykh Abū ʿAmr Akkāf and served him as a disciple (*khidmat*) in Jordan, and he had also seen Abū ʿAmr Nujayd. Shaykh Abū Naṣr also had seen, in Arraghān in Fārs, ʿAbdallāh Mānik, a student of Shiblī. He transmitted segments about them to me.'

---

24 It can be argued that the 'cluster' of juxtaposed biographies with mutual associations extends beyond these parameters, for the first member, Anṣārī himself, is preceded by Aḥmad b. Abī Rajāʾ (d. 857), a precursor in Ḥanbalism from Herat (*Nafaḥāt*, 335.12–24), whilst the final member is followed by further biographies that include material attributed to Anṣārī (see below, and *Nafaḥāt*, 355.21–358.11)

25 *Nafaḥāt*, 336

26 *Nafaḥāt*, 355.16–20. Included here are precise dates for the death of Anṣārī.

27 For further discussion of this interpretation of the term *ḥikāya*, see *BTS*, ch. 3.

> Shaykh Ismāʿīl Naṣrābādī:
> Shaykh al-Islām said, 'He was the greatest of the sons of Shaykh Abū 'l-Qāsim Naṣrābādī. I have *ḥadīth* from him as well as segments about his father.'[28]

The segments of material presented above would not in themselves be inappropriate for the context of a biography of Anṣārī, as they effectively represent his own credentials in the form of a list of the teachers and associates from whom he obtained authority. It is only their demarcation by the use of headings, as four separate biographies, which creates an irreconcilable conflict. They are representative of a large proportion of the material in this cluster which similarly gives the impression of having originated as part of a biography of Anṣarī, before eventually becoming labelled as separate biographies by a later redactor. It looks as though their demarcations had been introduced systematically at the mention of the name of each individual, without due concern about the consequences for the original monograph biography of Anṣārī.

Whilst the above 'biographies' are typical of the majority in this cluster in that they each consist of only a couple of statements, there is also a significant number which are more extensive; they contain biographical segments about their subjects which are not directly relevant to Anṣārī, as if the introductory statements about them had over time attracted additional material.[29] A relatively short example of the latter is presented below:

> Shaykh Muḥammad Abū Ḥafṣ Kūrfī:
> Shaykh al-Islām said, 'Shaykh Muḥammad Abū Ḥafṣ Kūrfī was a major figure, a great leader of his time, and also one of my teachers.'
>
> Once [Shaykh Muḥammad] was sick. People came to him and the conversation started. Someone made a false claim about himself in front of him and he couldn't stand it. His sense of honour *(ghayrat)* overwhelmed him, and he jumped up and said, 'Truth, truth, truth (*ḥaqq*).' An hour later he returned to his senses and said, 'I seek God's forgiveness, I seek God's forgiveness, I seek God's forgiveness (*astaghfiru 'llāh*)! I had become weak.' Then he apologized.[30]

The biography presented above is taken up mostly by a narrative illustrating Muḥammad Kūrfī's sense of honour (*ghayrat*), such that he could not bear to hear false claims being made. Since it is not directly relevant for a biography of Anṣārī, it would have been an odd ingredient of a monograph biography devoted to him. It could therefore represent growth of the text after an initial biography of Anṣārī. Such material would almost justify demarcation as a separate biography, even if it had originally grown out of a biography of Anṣārī. It could have encouraged the introduction of

28 *Nafaḥāt*, 347.16–348.8
29 Five biographies fit into this category, the longest of which is that of Yaḥyā ibn ʿAmmār al-Shaybānī (*Nafaḥāt*, 339.16–340.19).
30 *Nafaḥāt*, 349.1–6.

further demarcations, for all other digressions (however short) about newly mentioned individuals.

It is not necessary to look too far for a possible source of this cluster. Both the characteristics of its basic unit of material, and its traces of growth and interpolation followed by a relatively careless redaction, make this material remarkably similar to the *Ṭabaqāt of Herat*. That work is similarly made up of discrete segments presented under the rubric *Shaykh al-Islām guft*, and it has also been shown to have undergone a process of 'organic growth', as well as (a sequence of) redactions.[31]

The most conspicuous signs of growth and redactions in the *Ṭabaqāt of Herat* are its inclusion of thematic 'chapters' (uniquely for the sufi *ṭabaqāt* genre) and 'repeat biographies'. On closer inspection these anomalies can be seen to be 'outgrowths' of the biographies that immediately precede them; over time they seem to have acquired their own headings and introductions, presumably as the length of their digressions made them seem like separate chapters/biographies in their own right. For instance, the biography of Junayd in the *Ṭabaqāt* is followed ostensibly by one of the anomalous thematic 'chapters' as well as a 'repeat biography'. The former, entitled *Mas'ala fī al-tawḥīd*, begins with a segment presenting an utterance attributed to Junayd about *tawḥīd* (unity), which is followed by several folios/pages of material appropriately about *tawḥīd*.[32] However, this merges seamlessly with a resumption of Junayd's biography, starting with the following segment:

> Shaykh al-Islām said, 'Junayd said, "People imagine that I am a student (*shāgird*) of Sarī al-Saqaṭī. [However] I am a student of Muḥammad 'Alī Qaṣṣāb."'[33]

The above segment, whilst being relevant for a biography of Junayd, is unrelated to the issue of *tawḥīd*, the topic of the 'chapter' in which it is actually located, according to the headings provided. In fact, it signals the start of a sequence of biographical segments about Junayd (together with commentary attributed to Anṣārī), none of which is related to *tawḥīd*. This gives the distinct impression that the so-called chapter about *tawḥīd* has grown out of an original biography of Junayd, splitting it into two parts,[34] in the same way as the intervening outgrowth biographies in the *Nafaḥāt* divide the biography of Anṣārī.

Biographical segments about Junayd in the *Ṭabaqāt of Herat* have accumulated beyond the parameters of both his biography and the aforementioned thematic chapter. They continue as far as the 'repeat biography' devoted to Abū 'l 'Abbās ibn al-Surayj

---

[31] See *BTS*, ch. 3.

[32] For precise details about the start of this section, see *BTS*, ch. 3.

[33] al-Anṣārī, *Ṭabaqāt al-Ṣūfiyya* (ed. 'A. Ḥ. Ḥabībī), Kabul 1967 (henceforth *TabH*), 182.3–4.

[34] Regarding the other thematic chapters in the *Ṭabaqāt of Herat*, see J.A. Mojaddedi, "Anṣārī's *Ṭabaqāt al-Ṣūfiyya*: A Literary Approach", in C. Melville (ed.), *Societas Iranologica Europaea: Proceedings of the Third European Conference of Iranian Studies*, Wiesbaden 1999, ii, 162–4.

(d. 918), the Shāfiʿite jurist based in Baghdad who was eventually counted as one of the *mujaddids* (revivers) of that *madhhab*.[35] The sole segment which actually refers to Surayj in that entire 'repeat biography' is presented below:

> One day [Surayj] passed by the edge of Junayd's circle, listened and then went on his way. Someone asked him, 'What did you think of Junayd?' He answered, 'I may not know anything about the symbolic language (*rumūz*) of this group (*qawm*), but I still recognize that this shaykh has an awe-inspiring presence (*ṣawla*) which is different to that of the vain.'[36]

The above segment seems to be more relevant for a biography of Junayd than one of Surayj, since it functions to attribute to the former the approval of the eminent Shāfiʿite jurist. In fact, the narrative motif of a religious scholar expressing his approval of a Sufi is fairly common, further examples being present in the biographical tradition of Junayd itself (including a variant involving Surayj).[37]

The 'biography' of Surayj in which the above segment is located is a 'repeat biography' because the *Ṭabaqāt of Herat* already includes a biography devoted to him – one that actually contains relevant material about Surayj.[38] It therefore seems that the segment presented above, which is located shortly after the biography of Junayd, was in fact intended to be a continuation of the latter, but eventually acquired, in a relatively short-sighted redaction, a heading and introduction that labels it as an independent biography of Surayj.

The *Ṭabaqāt of Herat* shows many other such indications of growth and interpolation, and that it reached its final form after a sequence of redactions. It is written in an ancient dialect of Herat,[39] and, on the evidence of its many formal inconsistencies and the contrasting methods of presentation used, it seems to have been completed with the participation of a number of compilers, interpolators and redactors who belonged to an ongoing tradition in that city. Whilst the *Ṭabaqāt* is ascribed to Anṣārī, the individual whom the tradition that produced the work looked back upon as their inspiration and founder, the text itself alludes to a number of sources, including notes taken down in study and discussion sessions by both Anṣārī and his students, as well as the latter's own collection of written segments (*ḥikāyāt, juz'hā*) and 'diary writings' (*rūznāmahā*). Similar references can be found in the cluster of the *Nafaḥāt* under discussion.[40]

---

35 See *EI2*, s.v. 'Ibn al-Suraydj' (J. Schacht).
36 *TabH*, 184.16–185.3.
37 See al-Qushayrī, *al-Risāla* (ed. M. ʿA. Maḥmūd and A. Ibn Sharīf), Cairo 1972–4; (repr.) Tehran n. d., 72.10–6.
38 See *TabH*, 311–2.
39 See further, W. Ivanow, "Tabaqat of Ansari in the Old Language of Herat", *JRAS*, 1923, 1–34 and 337–82.
40 *Nafaḥāt*, 338.8, 339.2. For a discussion of the implications of these types of sources on the 'authorship' of the work, see further Mojaddedi, "Anṣārī's *Ṭabaqāt al-Ṣūfiyya*", 160–2.

IV

There is of course already a strong link between the *Nafaḥāt al-uns* and the *Ṭabaqāt of Herat*, by virtue of the fact that a redaction of the latter has been included as the first major section of Jāmī's work. An examination of the way in which he redacts the *Ṭabaqāt of Herat* may offer an indication of Jāmī's own reading of and attitude towards its multi-layered form. For instance, it is worth observing how, having read closely its actual contents, Jāmī deals with the biography (and chapter) headings which seem out of context. Whereas he maintains most of those headings and introductions provided for 'outgrowth' biographies, he eliminates those provided for the anomalous thematic 'chapters' and 'repeat biographies'. He therefore seems to follow a fairly liberal approach in his accommodation of problematic material from that work, but one which draws the line at the worst cases. For instance, whilst in the *Ṭabaqāt of Herat* the biography of Junayd is followed by outgrowths, such as the aforementioned thematic 'chapter' on *tawḥīd* and the 'repeat biography' of Surayj, Jāmī eliminates both of them in his redaction of it; he prefers to remove the headings and introductions that had been inserted there, to include (a selection of) their contents within the parameters of his own biography of Junayd, from which they had originally grown out. This critical aspect of Jāmī's redaction has been applied consistently throughout, with all the other thematic 'chapters' and 'repeat biographies' of the *Ṭabaqāt of Herat* similarly having been eliminated.

Since the source of the cluster under discussion seems to have had the same distinctive characteristics as the *Ṭabaqāt of Herat*, one might well expect Jāmī's redaction of it to reveal a similar method as the *mutaqaddimān* section of his *Nafaḥāt* which after all is based on the latter work. As already mentioned, the *Nafaḥāt* includes twenty-two 'outgrowth' biographies, which intervene between the initial and final parts of the biography of Anṣārī. However, since none of these constitutes a 'repeat biography' (i.e. a biography that had already been included in the *Nafaḥāt*), and there are no thematic 'chapters', their preservation does not strike the reader as being out of character. It is therefore all the more significant then that two substantial 'outgrowths' can be identified within this cluster which are deprived of their own headings, even though they are considerably longer than many other such outgrowths which have been converted by precisely that means into separate 'biographies'. These two outgrowths which lack their own headings consist of lengthy sequences of segments about Abū ʾl-Ḥasan al-Kharaqānī and Ibn Bākuwayh respectively, both of whom are already represented by biographies in the the *Nafaḥāt* (see above).[41] Since the redactor of the

[41] *Nafaḥāt*, 340.22–341.18 (Kharaqānī), 342.23–343.4 (Ibn Bākuwayh). The traditional identification of Kharaqānī as Anṣārī's teacher in Sufism is supported by the material presented here, which

source for this cluster had demarcated other (much shorter) 'outgrowth biographies' relatively indiscriminately, it seems more than likely that he would have at least done the same for these two substantial outgrowths. Their lack of separate headings, with the consequence that they are included, almost 'disguised', as mere continuations of the biographies which precede them, suggests the influence of Jāmī's preference to eliminate repeat biographies – he has probably removed headings that had already been provided for these outgrowths in his source. It would have been only as a result of the new context in which they had been embedded (i.e. in the *Nafaḥāt*) that these two sequences of segments became stripped of the labels that would have identified them as the biographies of Kharaqānī and Ibn Bākuwayh respectively.

The cluster of the *Nafaḥāt* under discussion appears to have been based on a source that possessed the distinctive characteristics of the same ongoing tradition of Sufism that produced the *Ṭabaqāt of Herat* and looked back upon Anṣārī as its authoritative founder. It even attributes to him its contents in the same distinct way 'autobiographically', as if they were dictated to the compiler directly by the *Shaykh al-Islām*. The cluster includes two references to the *jāmiʿ-i Maqāmāt-i Shaykh al-Islām*, once towards the beginnning and once at the end. This is most probably a reference to the 'compiler' (*jāmiʿ*) who had originally gathered appropriate segments from amongst those accumulated by the tradition in Herat, for the purpose of preparing a monograph biography of Anṣārī, the overall format of which can still be distinguished.

V

Arthur J. Arberry has shed further light on this cluster in the *Nafaḥāt* by his discovery of the *unicum* of a separate work that overlaps significantly with its contents. In 1963, he published an edition of a manuscript which he identified as Jāmī's (previously lost) biography of Anṣārī.[42] This work possesses the overall format of a monograph biography of Anṣārī, thereby determining Arberry's classification, and it corresponds closely with the aforementioned cluster of biographies in the *Nafaḥāt*, in that over half of its component segments are also found there in exactly the same order. Whilst it is more extensive than the cluster in the *Nafaḥāt*, it also includes hallmarks of Jāmī's method of redaction, including the manner in which additional citations from relatively late sources, such as ʿAbdallāh al-Yāfiʿī's (d. 1367) *Mirʾāt al-jinān*, are incorporated.[43] Moreover, Arberry found this manuscript amongst a number of

illustrates a relationship of mutual respect between teacher and precocious student. Included amongst these segments are variants, signifying the importance material about this relationship had in the eyes of those who compiled it (e.g. see *Nafaḥāt*, 340.25–1, 341.8).

42 A. J. Arberry, "Jāmī's Biography of Anṣārī", *Islamic Quarterly*, 7 (1963), 57–82.

43 *Ibid.*, 58.

recognized works by Jāmī, and he interprets a reference in its colophon to the 'author' by the *laqab* (honorific) *Ḥaḍrat-i Makhdūmī* (used by senior Naqshbandī Shaykhs, including, on occasion, by Jāmī), as confirmation that this was indeed his work.[44]

There seems to be little doubt as to the correctness of Arberry's identification of this *unicum* as Jāmī's biography of Anṣārī, the loss of which had been lamented by his predecessors.[45] However, one significant qualification to Arberry's classification is necessary, for it needs to be pointed out that the manuscript which he has discovered is only a monograph biography in its overall form. A close inspection of Arberry's manuscript reveals that, whilst it does not possess any headings that demarcate further biographies within it, nonetheless it includes the same outgrowths that have been represented as separate biographies in the corresponding *Nafaḥāt* cluster (and more besides).[46] In other words, it contains the same effects of growth and interpolation, only without the headings to demarcate them.

Furthermore, whilst this so-called monograph biography may be longer than its counterpart, unlike the cluster in the *Nafaḥāt* it fails to reach a conclusion where the reader might expect to find the details of the death of Anṣārī. The copyist (apparently in 1517) explains that it was left incomplete by the author (*ittimām nayāfta...wa samt-i ikhtitām napadhīrufta*).[47] This would suggest that it is not necessarily older than the corresponding cluster in the *Nafaḥāt*, as Arberry implies, let alone its source. Rather, each of the texts, Arberry's *unicum* and the corresponding cluster in the *Nafaḥāt*, may have been derived from a common source produced by the same tradition in Herat that produced the *Ṭabaqāt*. Moreover they each possess the hallmarks of redaction by Jāmī, in addition to evidence of a long process of development before having reached him.

The differences in their form are most likely attributable to the contrasting contexts for which Jāmī has redacted them. Whilst Jāmī may have preferred to preserve (most of) the demarcations of outgrowth biographies in the redaction which he incorporated into the *Nafaḥāt*, in the preparation of a monograph biography of Anṣārī it would have been appropriate to eliminate them as the first step. The fact that he did not remove the outgrowth segments of material that had generated the demarcations in the first place may be simply because the work was left incomplete. Arberry's manuscript would thus represent Jāmī's attempt to create his own monograph biography of Anṣārī on the basis of the same source that he had already used for a cluster of biographies in the *Nafaḥāt*. After reading it closely for that purpose, one might expect him to have

---

[44] *Ibid.*, 58, 80 (Arabic text, colophon).
[45] Arberry, "Jāmī's Biography of Anṣārī", 57; S. de Laugier de Beaurecueil, "Esquisse d'une biographie de Khwaja ʿAbdallah Ansari", *MIDEO*, 4 (1957), 97.
[46] E.g. Arberry, "Jāmī's Biography of Anṣārī", 70–1, paras 44–8 (Arabic text) (cf. *Nafaḥāt*, 347.16–349.6).
[47] *Ibid.*, 57, 80 (Arabic text, colophon).

recognized that the source had originated as a monograph biography of Anṣārī, and therefore already lent itself conveniently to a redaction back into that format.

The subjects of the 'outgrowth biographies' that have been preserved in this *Nafaḥāt* cluster are all associates of Anṣārī, and therefore also fellow natives of Herat. Both of these factors could have made their inclusion, ostensibly as independent biographies, seem worthwhile; not only does it help to underline the importance of Anṣārī himself, Jāmī's named precursor as the reputed 'author' of the *Ṭabaqāt of Herat*, but it also serves to build up a local tradition of Sufis associated with the city, where four centuries later Jāmī also was based. One need look no further for corroboration than the biographies which follow immediately after it, as they are also devoted to individuals from Herat, starting with further associates of Anṣārī.[48] The longest of these by a considerable margin, is in fact devoted to Aḥmad Nāmiqī Jāmī (better known as Shaykh Aḥmad-i Jām), Jāmī's most celebrated predecessor from the same place of origin.[49]

VI

The priority given to the depiction of Herat as a centre of major importance for Sufism is also evident in the other main sections of the *Nafaḥāt*. To begin with, the *mutaqaddimān* section takes the form of a redaction of the *Ṭabaqāt of Herat*, which is written in an ancient dialect of that city and is attributed to its most celebrated sufi authority, who is referred to even today simply as *Pīr-i Harāt*. As a result of having been been based on that precursor, the *mutaqaddimān* section also includes a high proportion of natives of Herat amongst its selection of the Sufis of the past, with a disproportionately significant presence of those who were associated directly with Anṣārī.

As already mentioned, the *muta'akhkhirān* section represents Sufism between the twelfth and fifteenth centuries in the form of coeval clusters. These clusters culminate with individuals who were not only contemporaries of Jāmī, but who also lived in Herat and its surroundings. The starting-point for Jāmī's compilation of these clusters was evidently his own direct experience as a Sufi based in Herat. That is to say, Jāmī structured lineage clusters for his selection of the Sufi orders that were represented in its environs during his lifetime. Furthermore, the incorporation of the additional clusters, focusing on Rūmī, ʿAyn al-Quḍāt al-Hamadānī and ʿAbd al-Qādir al-Jīlī respectively (see Fig. 1 above), is probably a reflection of their importance in the eyes

[48] See *Nafaḥāt*, 355–73. In fact, the first four biographies have been derived from the *Ṭabaqāt of Herat*. They appear to have become displaced from the remainder of the redaction of that work inadvertently, although it is surely no coincidence that they have been relocated specifically to this point, immediately after the only other portion of the *Nafaḥāt* which has been based on material with the same distinctive characteristics.

[49] *Nafaḥāt*, 363–71. Note that Aḥmad-i Jām is also referred to as *Shaykh al-Islām Aḥmad*.

of the contemporary sufi tradition where he was based, in common with the wider tradition in the eastern Islamic territories.[50] Jāmī's own specific preferences are revealed by the inclusion of the cluster devoted to Ibn ʿArabī and his followers, as well as the final cluster which is devoted (innovatively for this genre) to the major poets who wrote in Persian.[51] After all, Jāmī himself was both a highly regarded commentator on the works of the former, as well as a respected poet in his own right.

The scope for creativity available to a compiler of a *ṭabaqāt* work has been exploited in these ways by Jāmī to fulfil his objectives. Through his criteria for inclusion and his arrangement of component biographies, he not only structures the past of Sufism in such a way as to exaggerate the influence of the Sufis associated with Herat, but he also manages to depict his own Naqshbandī order as the pre-eminent tradition. This order's lineage as far as his own teachers is not only presented in the form of the first cluster of the *muta'akhkhirān* section, but it also possesses (uniquely) its own conclusion in glorification of the order.[52]

The *Nafaḥāt al-uns* has often been regarded by both traditional and modern scholars, in common with other works of the *ṭabaqāt* genre, as a convenient source of facts for the period of history which it depicts.[53] This seems to be influenced by its quantity of biographies, the numerous sources from which it has drawn as well as the seemingly broad selection of entries. Unfortunately, such an approach disregards entirely the fact that this work is a literary representation of the past, written specifically about the author's own religious tradition (i.e. Sufism) and within the constraints and conventions of an established genre. The form of this kind of work, with a specific emphasis on structuring continuity through the generations as far as one's own specific teachers, and redefining the identity of the diachronic community by a process of selection, arguably contains a more significant message than its actual contents. For instance, whilst Jāmī's choice of entries may at first seem relatively broad and comprehensive, devoting considerable space to some of the more controversial figures in the sufi tradition (e.g. Ibn ʿArabī, ʿAyn al-Quḍāt al-Hamadānī), as well as those whose association with Sufism is dubious (a fact readily admitted by Jāmī himself, for instance, with respect to the poet Ḥāfiẓ),[54] it can hardly be considered all-inclusive.[55] Moreover the order in which biographies are presented is not based solely on an

---

[50] See *Nafaḥāt*, 417–20, 459–71, 507–33.

[51] See *Nafaḥāt*, 539–63, 593–611.

[52] In addition to a list of the main principles of the order, the conclusion also contains praise and glorification, including the famous poem that is still popular with the Naqshbandī order, which begins with the *bayt*: *Naqshbandiyya ʿajab qāfila sālārān-and / kih burand az rāh-i pinhān bi-ḥaram qāfila-rā* ('The Naqshbandīs are such amazing caravan-leaders / That they can guide the caravan to the sacred precinct through a hidden route') (*Nafaḥāt*, 417.5). This represents special treatment for Jāmī's own order, since none of the other sufi lineage clusters possess their own separate conclusion.

[53] E.g. J. S. Trimingham, *The Sufi Orders in Islam*, Oxford 1971.

[54] *Nafaḥāt*, 612. 1–3.

[55] See note 10 above.

'arbitrary' criterion, such as chronology, but has been established according to Jāmī's own preferences and requirements.

The cluster in the *Nafaḥāt* which includes the biography of Anṣārī has already been recognized as one of the richest sources for the latter's biographical tradition, second only to Arberry's *unicum*. Although it is no longer possible to accept the latter's interpretation of the presentation of segments under the rubric *Shaykh al-Islām guft* as meaning that they were obtained 'direct from the saint's lips',[56] the material nonetheless remains of value. It represents the depiction, by the ongoing tradition which had produced the original source, of their most esteemed predecessor. Beginning with the variant accounts of the prognostication of his birth, through the signs of his precocious childhood to the noble and miraculous feats of his later life, the use of such *topoi* of religious biography illustrates the priorities and aspirations of this specific tradition of Sufism, the only one which concerned itself with providing extensive details about the life of Anṣārī. In this way it represents a continuation of the *Ṭabaqāt of Herat*, which they had also produced.[57] For Jāmī, a few centuries later, it served his need to structure a continuity between the sufi orders of his own time and the authoritative early generations, whilst at the same time underscoring the importance of Herat, through the biography of its favourite son.

[56] Arberry, "Jāmī's Biography of Anṣārī", 58.

[57] The biography of Anṣārī was maintained as a separate work to the *Ṭabaqāt of Herat*, probably because it took the form of the biography of the individual to whom that work had been ascribed. However, other works of this genre have included the biographies/obituaries of their 'authors' (e.g. Ibn Saʿd's *Ṭabaqāt*).

The exegetical literature of abrogation
Form and content

Andrew Rippin (University of Victoria, Calgary)

I

The sub-discipline of *ʿulūm al-Qurʾān* known as *al-nāsikh waʾl-mansūkh* ('the abrogator and the abrogated [in the Qurʾān]') is represented in a surprisingly large number of works.[1] This impression is especially clear when the inventory of texts is compared to the number of books in other sub-disciplines such as *asbāb al-nuzūl*, a type of material sometimes considered more important in exegetical terms.[2] There are probably fifteen or so well-known classical texts which deal with *al-nāsikh waʾl-mansūkh*. However, by searching through various bibliographical sources, manuscript catalogues and inventories of printed books, it is possible to produce a list that quickly expands to a total of over forty works. This total includes only those works in Arabic written before the nineteenth century. It does not include works which simply treat abrogation as a part of their subject (i.e., general *ʿulūm al-Qurʾān* works). Neither does it include works which are said to have existed at some point but of which there is no trace today (i.e., all these books actually exist in either published or manuscript form although some are unidentified as to author).[3] These classical texts range from massive tomes of over 200 printed pages or manuscript folios to texts of under two handwritten pages. Some works are simple listings of verses, the abrogated verse countered by its abrogator with no discussion whatsoever; others are substantial texts which are more interested in the discussion of the issues arising from the possibility of abrogation than in the actual documentation of the Qurʾānic phenomenon.

---

1 The writing of this essay has stretched over a long period of time, incorporating work completed during two sabbatical fellowships, one at the School of Oriental and African Studies, London, and the other at the Maison Méditerranéenne des Sciences de l'Homme, Aix-en-Provence. Research trips to consult various manuscripts in London, Dublin, Berlin, Cairo, Istanbul and Manisa were funded by the Social Sciences and Humanities Research Council of Canada. Many colleagues have helped with various aspects of this study; I would like to thank especially David Powers (Cornell), Avraham Hakim (Tel Aviv) and Claude Gilliot (Aix-en-Provence) for sharing various resources with me.

2 See my "The Exegetical Genre *asbāb al-nuzūl*: A Bibliographical and Terminological Survey," *BSOAS* 48 (1985), 1–15, for a list of nineteen works which includes some only said to exist and of which there is no exact information. As an addendum to that list, it should be noted that the text by Ibn Ḥajar al-ʿAsqalānī (see 9, no. 14) has now been discovered and has been published (in two volumes) under the title *al-ʿUjāb fī bayān al-asbāb*, Dammān, Saudi Arabia 1997.

3 Knowledge of the texts (and the number of them) has increased substantially over the last thirty years. When Muṣṭafā Zayd wrote his classic book on abrogation in the Qurʾān, *al-Naskh fīʾl-Qurʾān al-Karīm*, Cairo 1963, he was able to list fifteen books on the topic in his bibliography and actually analysed only nine, a number which includes the listing of abrogated verses compiled by al-Suyūṭī in his *al-Itqān fī ʿulūm al-Qurʾān*. Al-Ḍāmin's introduction to his edition of Qatāda's text on abrogation, published in 1980 (see below, text no. 1) manages to list seventy-five texts including many which are said to have existed but of which there is no trace in the form of actual tangible texts.

The following is a list of classical texts on *al-nāsikh wa'l-mansūkh* which have been available to me for consultation in this study. I have attempted here to provide sufficient information to describe and facilitate access to the texts without endeavouring to provide a comprehensive list of all the manuscript copies or printed editions in each and every case. Neither is this a complete list of all the books which exist; a significant number are available in manuscript[4] and perhaps printed form[5] to which I have not had access. This study has been carried out under the presumption, however, that the list produced would at least provide a representative sample of the genre.

1) Qatāda b. Diʿāma al-Sadūsī (d. 118/ 736), *al-Nāsikh wa'l-mansūkh.*
See *GAS*, i, 31, Nachträge in viii, 263. The text was first published by Ḥātim Ṣāliḥ al-Ḍāmin in *al-Mawrid* 9.4 (1980), 479–506, and then separately, Beirut 1984, as volume 1 of the series *Silsilat kutub al-nāsikh wa'l-mansūkh.* The edition is based on the ms. Ẓāhiriya 7899, fols 65–7. The ascription of the text is doubtful.

2) al-Zuhrī, Abū Bakr Muḥammad b. Muslim b. ʿUbayd Allāh b. ʿAbdallāh b. Shihāb (d. 124/742), *al-Nāsikh wa'l-mansūkh.*
See *GAS*, i, 280–3. The text was first published by A. Rippin, "Al-Zuhrī, *naskh al-Qur'ān* and the Problem of Early *tafsīr* Texts", *BSOAS*, 47 (1984), 22–43 (text on 27–37); Ḥātim Ṣāliḥ al-Ḍāmin subsequently published the text in *Majallat al-majmaʿ al-ʿilmī al-ʿIrāqī*, 38.2 (1987/1407), 305–33, and separately (Beirut 1988), as *Silsilat kutub al-nāsikh wa'l-mansūkh*, iv. The ascription of the text is doubtful; the association of the text with the Ṣūfī al-Sulamī is based on a misunderstanding by the manuscript copyist (cf. *GAS*, i, 674, no. 18). The only original copy of the text which exists is Princeton Yehuda ms. 228.

3) Ibn Wahb, ʿAbdallāh (d. 197/812), *al-Jāmiʿ: bāb al-nāsikh wa'l-Nāsikh min al-Qur'ān.*
See *GAS*, i, 466. The text has been published by Miklos Muranyi as *Al-Gāmiʿ: Die Koranwissenschaft*, Wiesbaden 1992, fols 13b–20b, [40]–[57] of the facsimile, 235–52 of the printed text (in reverse order).

4 There are especially a number of late medieval works of which I have not availed myself, although they are reasonably accessible. These would include the works of al-Nājī (d. 900/1495), *Jawāb al-Nājī ʿan al-nāsikh wa'l-mansūkh* (Cairo, Taymūr *mujāmiʿ* 207) and al-Karmī (d. 1033/1624), *Qalā'id al-marjān fī 'l-nāsikh wa'l-mansūkh min al-Qur'ān* (Princeton Yehuda 1246 and 3399; Berlin 480). Other texts which may be valuable for a study such as this are found in manuscript collections in Baghdad and Sana'a, for example, but these have not been available to me.

5 The following texts, along with some others mentioned below which I have consulted in manuscript form, have reputedly been printed but I have not been able to obtain a copy of them: Jalāl al-Dīn al-Maḥallī (d. 864/1459), *Kitāb al-nāsikh wa'l-mansūkh*, see *GAL* Sii, 140, published Delhi 1305; Muḥammad b. Muḥammad b. Muḥammad [Aḥmad] b. Zankī al-ʿIrāqī al-Shuʿaybī al-Isfarā'inī, *al-Nāsikh wa'l-mansūkh*, see *GAL* Sii, 205, printed Istanbul 1290.

4) Abū ʿUbayd, al-Qāsim b. Sallām (d. 224/838), *al-Nāsikh waʾl-mansūkh.*
See *GAS*, i, 48; viii, 81–7. A facsimile edition of the manuscript Ahmet III 143 (209ff.) was published by F. Sezgin, Frankfurt 1985. That manuscript was edited with commentary by John Burton, Cambridge 1987; it was also edited by Muḥammad al-Mudayfir, Riyadh 1990. See A. Rippin, "Abū ʿUbaid's *Kitāb al-nāsikh waʾl-mansūkh*", *BSOAS*, 53 (1990), 319–20, for details on the manuscript fragment, Türk ve Islam Eserli Müzesi 7892. For an outline of the text, see Burton's edition, 55–6; also see John Wansbrough, *Quranic Studies: Sources and Methods of Scriptural Interpretation*, Oxford 1977, 193–4, 198.

5) al-Zaʿfarān, ʿAbdallāh b. al-Ḥusayn b. al-Qāsim b. Ibrāhīm al-Ḥasanī al-Zaydī (d. *c.* 300/912), *Kitāb al-nāsikh waʾl-mansūkh.*
See *GAL*, i, 191–2; Si, 334; *GAS*, i, 42. Burton has examined ms. Berlin 10226 (fols 5–45) and has provided a table of contents and description of the text in the introduction to his edition of Abū ʿUbayd's *naskh* text (see no. 4 above), 44–5.

6) al-Naḥḥās, Abū Jaʿfar Aḥmad b. Muḥammad (d. 338/950), *al-Nāsikh waʾl-mansūkh.*
See *GAL*, i, 132; Si, 201; *GAS*, i, 49; viii, 242–3, and Nachträge in ix, 318. The text was published in Cairo, 1323/1905 (Maṭbaʿat al-Saʿāda) from a manuscript dated 724/1323, and published again in 1938 (ed. Zakī Mubārak); both include Ibn Khuzayma (text no. 12 below) at the end. The latter edition is cited here. Recent commercial prints proliferate, some including Ibn Khuzayma's text, others omitting it. A newly edited version has appeared, without Ibn Khuzayma at the end, *al-Nāsikh waʾl-mansūkh fī kitāb Allāh (azza wa-jalla) wa-ikhtilāf al-ʿulamāʾ fī dhālika*, ed. Sulaymān b. Ibrāhīm b. ʿAbdallāh al-Lāḥim, Beirut 1991, in three volumes.

7) Ibn al-Azharī, Abū ʿAbdallāh Muḥammad b. Aḥmad (d. 370/980), *Risāla fīʾl-nāsikh waʾl-mansūkh.*
There is some doubt regarding the identification of Ibn al-Azharī. He is likely the same as *GAL*, i, 129; Si 197, and *GAS*, i, 18; viii, 204, although this person is named Abū Manṣūr rather than Abū ʿAbdallāh; this specific work is not listed in any of these entries. Cf, however, *GAL*, i, 191 for this work by a vaguely identified author Muḥammad b. Aḥmad al-Zuhrawī with the same date of death; this may suggest some cataloguing confusion. The catalogue of the Hamidiye collection (in the Sulaymaniye Library, Istanbul) also indicates this death date for the author. I have examined the manuscript Hamidiye 196, fols 1b–5b. The Hamidiye catalogue lists both mss 196 and 197 as this text, but number 197 is, in fact, a copy of Hibāt Allāh, *al-Nāsikh waʾl-mansūkh* (see no. 8 below), as Sezgin lists, *GAS*, i, 48. The copy of the text in ms.

Hamidiye 196 is structured as follows: fol. 1b, *tafsīr* on Q2:106, and Q3:5. From then the text provides a simple listing of abrogated verses organized by topic: fols 1b–2b, *jihād* (43 verses); fols 2b–3a, *qibla* (2 verses); fol. 3a, *zakāt* (9 verses); fols 3a–b, *ṣalāt* (1 verse); fol. 3b, *ḥajj* (1 verse); fols 3b–4a, *nikāḥ* (6 verses); fol. 4a, *ṭalāq* (2 verses); fol. 4a–b, *mīrāth* (2 verses); fol. 4b, on various legal rulings (8 verses); fols 4b–5b, on strengthening and lightening of legal rulings; fol. 5b, conclusion.

8) Hibāt Allāh, Abū ʾl-Qāsim b. Salāma (d. 410/1019), *al-Nāsikh waʾl-mansūkh.*
See *GAS*, i, 47–8 (with an extensive list of manuscripts). The text has been published many times, frequently on the margin of al-Wāḥidī, *Asbāb nuzūl al-Qurʾān*, as used here in the edition of Cairo 1400. It has also appeared separately e.g., Beirut–Damascus 1986 (ed. Zuhayr al-Shārwīsh and Muḥammad Kanʿān). An English translation exists: Anwarul Haqq, *Abrogation in the Qur'an*, Lucknow [1925]. Etan Kohlberg, *A Medieval Muslim Scholar at Work: Ibn Ṭāwūs and his Library*, Leiden 1992, item 467, 297–8, points out that the manuscript tradition of this text seems to suggest that at least two recensions of it exist; further study of the manuscripts is needed to establish the exact dimensions of the divergences.

9) al-Isfarāʾinī, Abū ʿAbdallāh Muḥammad b. ʿAbdallāh al-ʿĀmirī [al- ʿĀmidī?] (d. fifth/eleventh century), *al-Nāsikh waʾl-mansūkh.*
See *GAL*, Sii, 987, no. 41 (probably the same text as *GAL*, Sii, 983, no. 3). The author quotes his teacher Abū Isḥāq Ibrāhīm b. Muḥammad al-Isfarāʾīnī who died in 418/1027 (see *GAL*, Si, 667), making a fifth-century death date likely. A number of manuscripts of the text are readily accessible: Chester Beatty 5246/2, fols 69b–94a; India Office Catalogue number 1180 (Delhi Arabic 79; India Office 4313), fols 1a–37a; British Library OR 12608 (fols 1b–37a). According to Ḥ. Ṣ. al-Ḍāmin, in his edition of Ibn al-Bārizī, 7 n. 8 (see text no. 19 below), this work has been published with al-Suyūṭī, *Lubāb al-nuqūl fi asbāb al-nuzūl*, perhaps Cairo 1954, but al-Ḍāmin was not explicit about the publication details; Muṣṭafā Zayd, *al-Naskh*, in his bibliography 855, no. 19, also cites the text as published but does not provide a publisher or date. Some of the text is published in Aḥmad Nagarī (d. after 1180/1766), *Dustūr al-ʿulamāʾ*, Arabic translation by ʿAbdallāh al-Khālidī, Beirut 1997, 902–6 (corresponding roughly to fols 3a–5b of British Library OR 12608). *GAL*, Sii, 205 cites a *naskh* text by another al-Isfaraʾīnī, d. 747/1346 (Istanbul 1290), but I have not been able to locate a copy in order to compare it.

10) al-Baghdādī, Abū Manṣūr ʿAbd al-Qāhir b. Ṭāhir (d. 429/1037), *al-Nāsikh waʾl-mansūkh.*

See *GAL*, i, 385. The text has been published (ed. Ḥilmī Kāmil Asʿad ʿAbd al-Hādī), Amman 1987, based upon the mss Berlin Petermann 555 (a somewhat broken copy) and Beyazit 445. A third significant manuscript exists, Manisa 178, written in the eighth century, 101 fols. On the text, see Wansbrough, *Quranic Studies*, 199.

11) Makkī al-Qaysī (d. 437/1045), *al-Īḍāḥ li-nāsikh al-Qurʾān wa-mansūkhih.*
See *GAL*, i, 406; Si, 718. (Edited by Aḥmad Ḥasan Farḥāt, Riyadh 1976.)

12) Ibn Khuzayma, Abū Manṣūr Muẓaffar b. al-Ḥusayn b. Zayd b. ʿAlī al-Fārisī (d. 490/1097), *Kitāb al-mūjiz fīʾl-nāsikh waʾl-mansūkh.*
See *GAL*, Si, 201 (i.e., the entry for al-Naḥḥās). The text has been printed at the end of al-Naḥḥās, *al-Nāsikh waʾl-mansūkh* (see above text no. 6), Cairo 1905, 1938 and frequently reprinted. The printing of the text along with the work of al-Naḥḥās may well stem from a manuscript tradition. For example, the copy in Ambrosiana X67 (Griffini 28; catalogue no. CCLXIV) consists of al-Naḥḥās, fols 1–65 and Ibn Khuzayma, fols 66–69a. On the identification of this author, see Claude Gilliot, "Textes arabes anciens édités en Égypte au cours des années 1985 à 1987", *MIDEO*, 19 (1989), 306, no. 26, and "Textes arabes anciens édités en Égypte au cours des années 1987 à 1990", *MIDEO*, 20 (1991), 368–9, no. 86. The identification of Ibn Khuzayma as Abū Manṣūr helps in bringing together a substantial number of manuscript copies of texts on *naskh*. It would seem, however, that there are several recensions of the text existing in various manuscripts and that these have been ascribed in a variety of ways in manuscript catalogues (including to al-Baghdādī, text no. 10 above, who is also Abū Manṣūr), although there can be little doubt that all should be attributed to Ibn Khuzayma. There seems to be a large number of manuscripts of this work, many of them misidentified. As examples, attention may be paid to Princeton Yehuda ms. 3137, identified in the manuscript catalogue as 'Abū Manṣūr, probably ʿAbd al-Qāhir b. Ṭāhir al-Baghdādī', but it is, in fact, this text. This is also true of Berlin 479 and 483, and Aya Sofya 291/1 with some variation (at the very least, the printed text has omitted some of the text towards the end of some of the manuscript copies). Inspection of Chester Beatty 3883, fols 209–226a, catalogued under Najm al-Dīn al-Nīsābūrī (d. *c.* 550/1155) shows that it, too, is the work of Ibn Khuzayma.

13) Ibn Barakāt, Abū ʿAbdallāh Muḥammad b. Hilāl b. ʿAbd al-Wāḥid al-Ṣūfī al-Saʿīdī al-Naḥwī (d. 520/1126), *Kitāb al-Ījāz fī maʿrifat mā fī ʾl-Qurʾān min mansūkh wa-nāsikh.*
See *GAL*, Sii, 987, no. 45 (author unidentified as to date). Manuscript copies include Princeton Yehuda 228, fols 9b–50a (catalogue no. 140); Cairo Dār al-Kutub Taymūr *tafsīr* 148, 34–68, under the title *Mukhtaṣar fī ʿilm maʿrifat al-nāsikh waʾl-*

mansūkh. Ḥ. S. al-Ḍāmin has announced his intention to publish this book but, as far as I have been able to determine, it has not yet appeared.

14) Ibn al-ʿArabī, Abū Bakr Muḥammad b. ʿAbdallāh b. al-ʿArabī al-Ishbīlī al-Maʿāfirī (d. 543/1148), *al-Nāsikh waʾl-mansūkh fīʾl-Qurʾān*.
See *GAL*, I, 412–3, although this work is not listed. Published [Rabat] 1988; 2nd edn, Cairo 1992 (ed. ʿAbd al-Kabīr al-ʿAlawī al-Madgharī), based on one manuscript from Rabat and another from the Qarawīyīn in Fez. See C. Gilliot, "Textes arabes anciens édités en Égypte au cours des années 1992 à 1994", *MIDEO*, 22 (1995), 304–5, no. 52.

15) Ibn Ḥazm, Abū ʿAbdallāh Muḥammad (d. likely 584/1188), *Fī maʿrifat al-nāsikh waʾl-mansūkh*.
The ascription of this work has created a good deal of confusion. Muṣṭafā Zayd, *Naskh*, 324 and n. 3 (and other writers) attributed it to Abū ʿAbdallāh Muḥammad b. Aḥmad b. Ḥazm (d. 320/932). In *GAL*, i, 400; Si, 696 (and other writers) it was attributed to Abū Muḥammad b. Ḥazm al-Ẓāhirī (d. 456/1064) but this is clearly incorrect and not at all in keeping with Ibn Ḥazm al-Ẓāhirī's ideas on *naskh* (see R. Arnaldez, *Grammaire et theologie chez Ibn Ḥazm de Cordoue*, Paris 1956, 238–45). The identification suggested here relies on the observation (already noted in A. Rippin, "al-Zuhrī", 26 n. 38; also J. Burton, edition of Abū ʿUbayd, *al-Nāsikh*, 44 n. 56) that the introduction to this text is identical (word for word) with certain sections of the introduction to the text of al-Ḥāzimī, Abū Bakr Muḥammad b. Mūsā b. Ḥāzim (d. 584/1188), *al-Iʿtibār fīʾl-nāsikh waʾl-mansūkh min al-āthār*, Hyderabad 1359 (further prints and editions of this work exist – see Claude Gilliot, review of Burton's edition of Abū ʿUbayd, *Arabica*, 38 [1991], 398), 5 line 21 to 7 line 4. This is the same as the present text as published on the margin of *Tafsīr al-Jalālayn*, Cairo 1924, ii, 151, line 27 to 153 line 26. An edition of the text has appeared separately (ed. ʿAbd al-Ghaffār Sulaymān al-Bandārī, Beirut 1986), and the text has also appeared, in some prints, with the pseudo-Ibn ʿAbbās text *Tanwīr al-miqbās*.

16) Ibn al-Jawzī, Jamāl al-Dīn Abū ʾl-Faraj ʿAbd al-Raḥmān (d. 597/1200), *Nawāsikh al-Qurʾān*.
See *GAL*, i, 500–6; Si, 918. Published many times, including reprint, Beirut [1986].

17) Ibn al-Jawzī, Jamāl al-Dīn Abū ʾl-Faraj ʿAbd al-Raḥmān (d. 597/1200), *al-Muṣaffā bi-akuff ahl al-rusūkh min ʿilm al-nāsikh waʾl-mansūkh*.
See *GAL*, i, 500–6; Si, 918. Published by Ḥātim Ṣāliḥ al-Ḍāmin, *al-Mawrid*, 6.1 (1977), 195–216, and separately as *Silsilat kutub al-nāsikh waʾl-mansūkh*, ii, Beirut 1984, on the basis of two Baghdad manuscripts.

18) Shuʿla, Shams al-Dīn Abū ʿAbdallāh Muḥammad al-Mawṣilī al-Ḥanbalī (d. 656/1258), *Ṣafwat al-rāsikh fī ʿilm al-mansūkh wa'l-nāsikh*.
See *GAL*, Si, 859, no. 9a. Edited by Muḥammad Ibrāhīm ʿAbd al-Raḥmān Fāris, Cairo 1995. See C. Gilliot, "Textes arabes anciens édités en Égypte au cours des années 1994 à 1996," *MIDEO*, 23 (1997), 320–1, no. 47.

19) Ibn al-Bārizī, Hibāt Allāh b. ʿAbd al-Raḥmān b. Ibrāhīm Sharīf al-Dīn b. al-Bārizī al-Hamawī (d. 738/1338), *Nāsikh al-Qur'ān al-ʿazīz wa mansūkhih*.
See *GAL*, ii, 86; Sii, 101. Edited by Ḥātim Ṣāliḥ al-Ḍāmin, first published in *Majallat al-majmaʿ al-ʿilmī al-ʿIrāqī*, 33.1 (1982), 265–317 and then published separately, as *Silsilat kutub al-nāsikh wa'l-mansūkh*, iii, Beirut 1983; edited on the basis of Damascus ms. Ẓāhirīya 5881, fols 88–94.

20) al-Hamdhānī, ʿAbdallāh b. Shihāb al-Dīn (d. 786/1383), *Kitāb al-nāsikh wa'l-mansūkh*.
See *GAL*, Sii, 311, almost certainly the same as *GAL*, Sii, 985, no. 19. I have consulted India Office ms. catalogue no. 1181, ms. no. 4314 (matches Delhi Arabic 981b), fols 253b–4a (the complete text).

21) Ibn al-ʿAtā'iqī, ʿAbd al-Raḥmān b. Muḥammad b. Ḥillī (d. ca 790/1388), *al-Nāsikh wa'l-mansūkh*.
Edited by ʿAbd al-Hādī al-Faḍalī, Najaf 1970.

22) Ibn Mutawwaj, Aḥmad al-Baḥrānī (d. 836/1432), *al-Nāsikh wa'l-mansūkh*.
Edited by Muḥammad Jaʿfar Islāmī with a commentary in Persian by ʿAbd al-Jalīl al-Ḥusaynī al-Qārī (d. 976/1569), Tehran [1387].

23) al-Ujhūrī, ʿAṭīyat Allāh b. ʿAṭīya al-Burhānī al-Shāfiʿī, (d. 1190/1776), *Irshād al-raḥmān li-asbāb al-nuzūl wa'l-naskh wa'l-mutashābih min al-Qur'ān*.
See *GAL*, ii, 329; Sii, 456; ms. Cairo Dār al-kutub *tafsīr* 42 (among others), a simple listing of abrogated verses in *sūra* order, interwoven with *asbāb al-nuzūl*; see A. Rippin, "Exegetical Genre", 11, no. 17.

24) [pseudo-al-Jaʿbarī], *Mukhtaṣar asbāb al-nuzūl wa-ziyādatuhu al-nāsikh wa'l-mansūkh*.
Ms. Berlin Staatsbibliothek 3578; see A. Rippin "Exegetical Genre", 6–7, no. 10. The text has *asbāb al-nuzūl* alternating with *naskh* in *sūra* order.

25) al-Dimashqī, ʿAbd al-Raḥmān b. Muḥammad (d. ?), *Risāla [fī] al-nāsikh wa'l-mansūkh.*
See *GAL*, Sii, 984, no. 8. I have consulted a copy printed at the end of *Tafsīr al-Jalālayn* (Delhi 1893). *GAL* lists this as also published on the margin of *Tafsīr al Jalālayn* (Delhi 1311).

II

All of the texts on abrogation listed above deal with a large number of verses in the Qur'ān which are, according to their authors, liable to be considered abrogated. The maximum total tends to be around 250 verses, which is fairly substantial when one remembers that a total of 500 verses is often considered the sum of legal verses in the whole of the Qur'ān. Virtually all of the texts (the exceptions are primarily the very early ones) start with a discussion of what are known as the 'modes of abrogation' which clarifies the way in which these verses are considered to be abrogated.[6]

There is a series of verses, and even entire *sūra*s, which are, according to various reports, said to have been removed from the Qur'ān during Muḥammad's lifetime. According to a report from Anas b. Mālik, for example, a *sūra* used to be recited in the Qur'ān, equal in length to *sūra* 9; of it he remembered only one verse, 'Even if a man had two valleys of gold, he would desire a third, and if he had the third, he would desire a fourth, and nothing but earth can fill the belly of man. God forgives whoever repents.'[7] This type of abrogation is known as *naskh al-ḥukm wa'l-tilāwa*, abrogation of the ruling and the recitation (although the legal impact of the previously mentioned omitted verse is not clear, it must be admitted).

Another mode of abrogation exists, connected most frequently to the penalty for adultery but also to the number of times that a child may be suckled before creating a bar to marriage. Both are instances of the type of abrogation which displays a verse missing from the Qur'ān but a ruling which remained, *naskh al-tilāwa dūna 'l-ḥukm*. Such verses exercised the minds of some Muslim thinkers in the classical period, mainly for reasons of working out the relationship between the *uṣūl*, the sources of the law, in such cases.

However, the majority of the books dealing with abrogation in the Qur'ān do not bother with such niceties except to raise the topic of the modes of abrogation in theory in their introductory discussions. The concern of these books is always with the

---

6 See John Burton, *The Sources of Islamic Law: Islamic Theories of Abrogation*, Edinburgh 1990, for a full treatment of the 'modes' of abrogation. One of the few exceptions to the tripart division of *naskh* is to be found in Makkī's work (text no. 11 above), which suggests a sixfold division.

7 Hibāt Allāh (text no. 8; margin of al-Wāḥidī, Cairo 1400), 10–11; also see David S. Powers, "The Exegetical Genre *nāsikh al-Qur'ān wa mansūkhuhu*", in A. Rippin (ed.), *Approaches to the History of the Interpretation of the Qur'ān*, Oxford 1988, 125; Ibn al-Jawzī, *Nawāsikh* (text no. 16), 33–4, provides a list of a series of passages, including whole *sūra*s which were 'removed' from the Qur'ān.

third, and most common, type of abrogation in which the ruling of one Qurʾānic verse is seen to be in conflict with another. An example is found in *sūra* 8, verses 65–66, where the command is first given, 'If there are twenty disciplined men among you, they will overcome two hundred, while if there are a hundred of you, they will defeat a thousand of those who disbelieve', suggesting that warriors should be prepared to fight against 10 to 1 odds in a battle. This was replaced, in legal terms, by the next verse, 'Now God has lightened things for you; He knows how much weakness exists among you. If there are a hundred patient men among you, they will overcome two hundred, while if there are a thousand of you, they will overcome two thousand with God's permission'; thus the required odds were reduced to 2 to 1. This is subsumed under a mode of *naskh* known as *naskh al-ḥukm dūnaʾl-tilāwa*, in which the ruling has been abandoned but the recited verse has remained in the text of scripture.

While all the books share a common subject material, an initial observation which must be made about the books, one which has already been noted by Wansbrough,[8] is that within the genre there are two different ways of approaching the material. We can, in fact, talk about two separate groups of texts. One group places the material within the *tafsīr* tradition by following the order of the text of the Qurʾān (subject to certain classificatory systems to be discussed below). The other, much smaller group deals with the material within the context of *ḥadīth* and *fiqh*, indicated by the influence of legal topics in the order of presentation. This very fact is significant, because it immediately raises questions over how we understand and approach matters of the 'genre' of works within the classical Muslim religious fields of study. It also poses the issue of understanding the historical significance of those texts which contravene the majority patterning.

The first and most common type of book on abrogation is structured essentially in two parts: first, an introduction, and second, a *sūra* by *sūra* treatment of the phenomenon of abrogation with a varying amount of explicatory material for each verse, following Qurʾānic order in its presentation.[9]

That these works are the result of diligent study of earlier sources is stated in several of the texts. For al-Dimashqī (text no. 25), it would appear to be the process of compilation and condensation of these earlier sources which was of utmost concern. He writes:

> I have written [this treatise] by shortening six books on the knowledge of [the principles of] abrogation, arranging it according to the order of the Qurʾān and leaving out the mention of the causes of the abrogation and the occasions of

[8] John Wansbrough, *Quranic Studies: Sources and Methods of Scriptural Interpretation*, Oxford 1977, 198.

[9] The main exception here is the texts of al-Zuhrī (text no. 2) which puts the passages together in seemingly random order, leading mainly to questions concerning its compositional history; see A. Rippin, "Al-Zuhrī, *naskh al-Qurʾān* and the Problem of Early *tafsīr* Texts", *BSOAS*, 47 (1984), 22–43.

> revelation [connected to the abrogation]. I have formulated the issue of abrogation precisely and [indicated] how it is proven, as well as [detailing] the disagreement about it and the methods of its transmission. To this I have added mention of the number of *sūra*s in which there are no abrogators or abrogated verses, those in which there are abrogators but no abrogated, those in which there are abrogated verses but no abrogators.[10]

The process of abbreviation was not the only one employed in order to proliferate the number of books on the topic, however. In the case of Ibn al-Jawzī, his dissatisfaction with previous works led him to write not one but two books on the subject, one an abbreviation of the other. Consider his statement at the beginning of his larger work, *Nawāsikh al-Qur'ān* (text no. 16):

> Anyone who looks at the book of abrogation by al-Suddī will see the incredible confusion and whoever looks at the book of Haybāt Allāh will see many terrible mistakes. But people still lap these works up because of their concision, but they do not understand the subtleties that lie at the root [of the subject].[11]

This sort of polemic should not be taken too seriously. It is common to read disparaging remarks about one's predecessors – this is as true in modern works of scholarship as it is in classical Muslim works of *tafsīr* – but the issue certainly provides an explanation for the proliferation of books on abrogation.

One tendency in many of these books is to list a great deal of information in the introduction, displaying a mania for classification:[12] which *sūra*s do and do not have abrogated verses, which verse abrogates the greatest number of verses (always *āyat al-sayf*, Q9:5, 'When the hallowed months have slipped away, then fight the polytheists wherever you find them'), which verse remained legally binding the longest before being abrogated, which individual verses contain both the abrogator and the abrogated, which individual verses have a valid legal ruling between two abrogated segments and, finally, which abrogated verses precede their abrogator within the text of the Qur'ān. All of this reflects a basic encyclopaedic–taxonomical impulse on the part of the authors with the likely ultimate purpose of easy memorization of the material.[13]

Some of the texts search for a way of classifying all of the abrogated and abrogating verses. Ibn al-Bārizī (text no. 19) and Ibn Khuzayma (text no. 12) both separate the verses using the terminology of 'abrogation by exception or implied in the

---

[10] al-Dimashqī (text no. 25), 509–10. Note that the other possibility, that there are both abrogators and abrogated in one *sūra*, is not mentioned.

[11] Ibn al-Jawzī, *Nawāsikh* (text no. 16), 12; there is no trace of the book of al-Suddī. For similar statements, see Makkī (text no. 11), 40.

[12] As noted by D. S. Powers, "Exegetical Genre", 121.

[13] On the notion of a basic human drive towards the creation of taxonomies, see Tom McArthur, *Worlds of Reference: Lexicography, Learning and Language from the Clay Tablet to the Computer*, Cambridge 1986, ch. 5, who argues that the basic order of society and the view of the world simply carried over into scribal classrooms from ancient times, producing this taxonomical impulse, and resulting in lists and orderings of data of all sorts, mostly for the purpose of facilitating memorization of the material. Also see Jack Goody, *Domestication of the Savage Mind*, Cambridge 1977, ch. 5, "What's in a list?".

meaning', *bi 'l-istithnā' aw mā fī 'l-ma'nā* (in which the interpretational context of a passage plays a large role in the determination that abrogation has occurred) and 'abrogation following from the order of the arrangement of the Qur'ānic text', *'alā'l-naẓm*. Abrogated verses where an exception to the ruling comes immediately after the verse or phrase in question are listed in a sequence in Ibn Khuzayma (providing a list of 23 verses) followed by a listing of 102 verses abrogated by a later verse.[14] This is preceded by a list of the 113 verses abrogated by *āyat al-sayf* and the 9 verses by *āyat al-qitāl* (Q9:29, 'Fight those who do not believe in God or the last day'). Ibn al-Bārizī follows a similar setup, with almost identical numbers, but he structures his text to give a *sūra* by *sūra* treatment. Within each *sūra*, he first lists verses abrogated by *āyat al-sayf*, then ones by *āyat al-qitāl*, then verses 'by exception or meaning', then verses abrogated by later verses.

As well as providing these sorts of collocations of information, the introductions found in these works generally cover a fairly standard range of topics, some of which reflect issues of contention in the classical Muslim scholastic community. There is no doubt that the idea of abrogation in general became one which generated considerable debate in Islam, especially with regard to the actual possibility of it occurring (and it certainly continues to be a topic a great interest, judging by the number of books being published on the subject today).[15] It created a theological problem as well as a juridical one, and each of the texts displays to varying degrees some concern with the issue.

The argument seems to have two points of origin. One is to be located in *uṣūl* arguments, ultimately bearing on the relationship between the Qur'ān and the *sunna* as sources of law. The figure of Abū Muslim al-Iṣfahānī (d. 322/933)[16] is always cited as someone who denied the possibility of abrogation altogether (a position rejected as non-Muslim by many authors). Sometimes there is a sense that Abū Muslim's position was required to provide appropriate symmetry to the overall arguments and positions rather than necessarily representing the historical argument of a specific individual. However, Fakhr al-Dīn al-Rāzī,[17] for example, quotes extensively from Abū Muslim in his discussions on various points about abrogation in a manner which suggests the reality of the position.

The arguments about the possibility of abrogation may also have had their origin in inter-religious polemic; at the very least, the arguments are paralleled by discussions in that area. *Naskh* means both intra-Qur'ānic abrogation and inter-religious

14 Edition at the end of al-Naḥḥās, Cairo 1938, 267–8.

15 Without making any particular effort to collect books on the topic, I have gathered seven such books in my library, including the work of Muṣṭafā Zayd mentioned above. The form of these books is not that of the classical model; rather, they tend to be interested primarily in the material from the angle of jurisprudential theory.

16 See *GAS*, i, 42–3, ix, 188–9.

17 al-Rāzī, *al-Tafsīr al-kabīr*, Tehran n. d., iii, 229 (ad Q2:106).

supersession. These meanings are often confused to some extent and the polemical aspect of the meaning never seems to be far from the minds of many authors (with the Jews being held to deny all abrogation in legal matters as an extension of the position of denying the possibility of inter-religious supersession). Lying behind this, then, is the doctrine of *taḥrīf*: the notion that the scriptures of the Jews and the Christians have been altered. The Muslim books on abrogation are implicitly arguing for the integrity of their own scripture despite the presence of contradictory verses which might suggest some sort of indecision on the part of its author, that not being a trait that can be ascribed to God, of course; the fear is that such contradictory verses might be taken as a suggestion of a non-divine origin for the book. In the introduction to many of the texts on abrogation this issue arises in the discussion of the relationship between *naskh* and *badā'*, the mutability of the divine will, which was generally treated by Sunnī Muslims as something different than abrogation. Abrogation is understood as changing the law for the benefit of humanity, as, indeed, God recognized would be necessary, given the changing conditions in the world. Abrogation, therefore, does not imply that God's will has actually changed. That, at least, was the way in which al-Naḥḥās argued the subject.[18]

Other issues raised in the introduction to books on abrogation are more technical ones, including the actual definition of *naskh*,[19] the modes of *naskh*, in which type of verse *naskh* occurs, the difference between 'abrogation', *naskh*, and 'specification', *takhṣīṣ* (which is used as a organizational principle in the work of Ibn al-ʿArabī [text 14]), and the merits of learning the science of *al-nāsikh wa'l-mansūkh*.[20]

In the body of the books, where we generally have the listing of the verses abrogated, we are faced with a fair degree of unanimity on the basic principles of the subject. Opinions certainly varied in individual cases, however, with the result that we have texts which arrive at greatly differing numbers of abrogated verses. The subtlety of the author will have played a role here. One can see in a text such as that of Ibn al-Bārizī the results of a simple gathering together with minimal consideration of all of the implications of the process or the value of what was being undertaken. For example, there are less than a dozen cases in the book, out of just under 250, in which the author mentions the possibility (usually saying *wa-qīla*) that the verse is not abrogated according to some opinions; similarly, only once does he suggest a difference of opinion over which verse was the abrogator. Clearly, this is a case of either a real desire

[18] al-Naḥḥās (text no. 6; Cairo 1938), 10–11.
[19] See John Burton, "The Exegesis of Q. 2:106 and the Islamic Theories of *naskh*", *BSOAS*, 48 (1985), 452–69.
[20] Usually spoken of in reference to ʿAlī and the Kufan preacher; see al-Naḥḥās, Cairo 1938, 5–6; Hibat Allāh (margin of al-Wāḥidī, Cairo 1400, 5–8); al-Baghdādī, 33–4; al-Isfarā'īnī, ms. British Library OR 12608, fols 1b–2a; Ibn Barakāt, ms. Princeton Yehuda 228, fol. 11a–b; Ibn Khuzayma (in al-Naḥḥās, Cairo 1938, 259); Muḥammad b. Ḥazm (on the margin of *Tafsīr al-Jalālayn*, Cairo 1924, ii, 150–1). Also see the introduction provided by al-Ḍāmin to his edition of Qatāda for a summary of many of these aspects.

to eliminate complexity in the subject or, less plausibly, to create an argument for the lack of difference of opinion within the subject of abrogation. Other books are quite different in this regard, as, for example, with Ibn al-Jawzī, who, while he treats a large number of verses, expresses much reservation about a substantial portion of the supposed cases of abrogation. Of course, it may be that some of the variation in the number of verses does reflect changes in legal positions over the ages. Thus it might be possible to trace the treatment of a verse or legal point chronologically through all these texts to observe shifting emphases, reflecting the changing needs and concerns of each school of law. However, the fact remains that these texts dealing with abrogation are peripheral to that actual legal task. The discussions on the actual points of law are taking place in *fiqh* works – and, even then, it would seem that only the final ramifications of the discussions are exposed in those texts in most instances.

Another aspect of the general nature of many of these books relates to the method of listing the actual verses abrogated with minimal commentary. The text of Muḥammad b. Ḥazm (text no. 15) is representative of one type, for it provides a listing of some 200 verses simply juxtaposed, abrogator followed by abrogated. This text is at least preceded by a fairly full introduction on all the technical matters previously mentioned, but the same cannot be said for the seemingly more trivial texts, such as that from al-Hamdānī (text no. 20). This consists simply of a listing of some twenty verses with their abrogator. The only expansion on the topic which al-Hamdānī gives is to cite the authority from among the companions according to whom the verse is abrogated.

A clear way of providing some measure of clarification as to the differences between all these works is to consider the extent to which explicatory material is appended.[21] A text such as that of al-Naḥḥās (text no. 6) gives extensive treatment of each verse, studying its implications and the opinions on it, in contrast to the text just mentioned of Muḥammad b. Ḥazm with its simple juxtaposition of abrogated verses with the abrogator. Many of the other books fall somewhere in between this simple listing and the expansive treatment of each instance of abrogation as found in al-Naḥḥas, in Ibn al-Jawzī's longer work (text no. 16), and, to a lesser extent, in Makkī al-Qaysī (text no. 11). Hibāt Allāh (text no. 8), Ibn al-Jawzī (text no. 17, his briefer work) and al-Isfarā'īnī (text no. 9) all provide a small measure of clarification, but generally limit the explanatory material to an absolute minimum. In the case of Ibn al-Bārizī, we very seldom find any exegetical comments; these only occur where it seems clear that, in order to defend the position of abrogation, the author must adopt a certain interpretation of the verse in question. It is significant, however, that there seems to be no sense of chronological development through the series of texts to correspond with this appending of clarifying material. If anything, there is a tendency towards

21 As noted in Powers, "Exegetical Genre", 122.

simplification of the material as time goes on. This provides a certain clarification to Norman Calder's insightful understanding of the nature of *tafsīr* texts in general as being 'fundamentally acquisitive'.[22] In the case of a genre such as *al-nāsikh wa'l-mansūkh*, such texts are, indeed, acquisitive in terms of the number of verses brought together, but not necessarily in the accompanying discussion. It would seem that the encyclopaedist impulse is combined with a desire for simplification (probably for the purposes of memorization, which itself would be considered a means of demonstrating mastery of the field of study). The end result of this is a proliferation of barely distinguishable books.

Wansbrough has suggested that the works on abrogation of this type were written to demonstrate the actual presence of the phenomenon in the Qur'ān.[23] The reasons for doing this were twofold. First, such listings provided a polemical defence of the text of scripture, its integrity and cohesiveness (both proving and demonstrating it, as well as, in an earlier period, perhaps establishing it). Second, the texts were designed to prove the scriptural sanction for the doctrine itself, allowing its application to the full range of legal materials in Islam, as well as, perhaps, its application in inter-religious polemic. The peripheral nature of most of these texts to the actual process of the legal sciences and of legal derivation within Islam then comes as little surprise; their actual concern is not with that field at all, although they do, of course, provide a certain documentary support to the work of the jurists.

Concerning issues of scriptural integrity[24] (whether that be thought of in terms of inter-religious polemic or internal Muslim establishment of the canon of the Qur'ān), it is apparent that these books are not consciously arguing the point. The 'facts' of scriptural integrity are, after all, already well established by the time of the writing of almost all of these books. However, it might be said that these books represent a continuation of the taxonomical impulse designed to prove the point. As a result, the works provide an illustration of the conservative nature of the exegetical enterprise. They are following a pattern which has been established in earlier centuries which had a purpose in the beginning but which no longer has any relevance. Such reasoning could provide a further explanation for the proliferation of these texts.

[22] Norman Calder, "*Tafsīr* from Ṭabarī to Ibn Kathīr: Problems in the Description of a Genre, Illustrated with Reference to the Story of Abraham", in G. R. Hawting, A.–K. A. Shareef (eds), *Approaches to the Qur'ān*, London 1993, 101–40, esp. 133.

[23] See *Quranic Studies*, 196.

[24] Also see John Wansbrough, *The Sectarian Milieu: Content and Composition of Islamic Salvation History*, Oxford 1978, 109.

III

The second group of books within the genre of *al-nāsikh wa'l-mansūkh* is substantially smaller. These books do not follow the pattern of an introduction and a *sūra* by *sūra* treatment of their subject. The two best examples of this more distinctive type are those by Abū ʿUbayd al-Qāsim b. Sallām (text no. 4) and ʿAbd al-Qāhir al-Baghdādī (text no. 10). In both instances, it is clear that the elaboration of the law is their primary focus of attention, although each approaches the matter in a different way. Their interest is in abrogation as a juridical principle and its implications; they wish to show what happens to the law when such a tool is applied.[25] The texts are theoretical justifications of a juridical principle and its attestation in both the Qur'ān and the *sunna*. For these texts, abrogation is a device whereby scriptural support is found for laws whose source is likely to be other than scripture and for which scripture already provides evidence, at least according to one's co-religionists of different legal persuasion, for a different point of view.

Abū ʿUbayd's approach to the subject appears to reflect a time when issues were not settled in Islamic law in general and abrogation specifically; here we have a work which is undoubtedly adding to the ongoing discussion of the topic. Abū ʿUbayd's work follows a *muṣannaf* pattern, being divided into twenty-seven legal chapters including prayer, almsgiving, fasting, marriage, divorce, *jihād*, booty, prisoners, inheritance, orphans and so forth. Each chapter deals with abrogation in both the Qur'ān and the *sunna*, where applicable. The book contains the normal introductory material of the works in the genre, including citing the anecdote about ʿAli and the preacher, and discusses the meaning of the word *naskh*. Abū ʿUbayd's interest in abrogation is legal but also ultimately theological. In keeping with his views on *īmān*,[26] abrogation can be seen to be a means for God to provide a temporary inducement to people for them to join Islam by the temporary exclusion of other duties. This needs to be viewed in contrast to other competing views of faith in early Islam, for example that associated with the name of Abū Ḥanīfa which held that faith was not to be judged on the basis of works.

The form of the text by Abū ʿUbayd continued to have some presence in later writings, as within the work of al-Zafarʿān (text no. 5), who, as Burton observes, follows his predecessor's model quite closely. However, even this general approach by legal topics can be made trivial, as in the work of Ibn al-Azharī (text no. 7). There, the form indicates a primary concern for the legal implications of verses, but the text provides only a simple listing as found in the great majority of the books in the genre. After a brief introduction discussing the understanding of the theoretical verses related

[25] See Wansbrough, *Quranic Studies*, 196.
[26] See W. Madelung, "Early Sunni doctrine concerning Faith as Reflected in the *Kitāb al-īmān* of Abū ʿUbayd al-Qāsim b. Sallām (d. 224/839)", *Studia Islamica*, 32 (1970), 233–54.

to abrogation, Q2:106 and Q3:5, Ibn al-Azharī divides his book into a series of chapters and within those chapters simply lists the verses and gives the basic point that abrogation has occurred. His classification system gives the appearance of legal concern but the text itself performs only the listing function.

The work by al-Baghdādī is, in one respect, like the vast majority of the texts already discussed. It, too, starts off with an introductory section covering mostly the same topics as the other books, with no particular distinction in his treatment, although it certainly provides a serious discussion of the issues. Then, however, the author proceeds with the main body of the text in which significant differences are to be noted. The book is divided into eight chapters: (1) Explanation of the meaning of the word *naskh*; (2) Explanation of the conditions of *naskh* and the rules by which it works; (3) Interpretation of Q2:106, the verse which provides the scriptural support for the doctrine; (4) Chapter on abrogated verses where there is agreement on their abrogation and their abrogator; (5) Chapter on abrogated verses where there is difference of opinion about their abrogation; (6) Chapter on abrogated verses where there is general agreement on their abrogation but disagreement on their abrogator; (7) Chapter on what is abrogated in the *sunna* and what abrogates it; (8) Explanation of the distinction between the abrogator and the abrogated where there are doubts about it.

The structure of al-Baghdādī's book indicates a different prioritization of the data. The juridical concepts of disagreement (*ikhtilāf*) and agreement (*ijmāʿ*) are used to classify the material initially. That concern with explicitly religious and legal issues is then reflected in the actual treatment of the verses. Within this text, abrogation is, in fact, a matter not of great concern in and by itself; what is of concern is the status of the law in the individual schools of law and how they have dealt with the ramifications of the abrogation. Al-Baghdādī lived two centuries after Abū ʿUbayd and after the establishment of what had become the common form of the genre of *al-nāsikh waʾl-mansūkh*. That may suggest that we are witnessing an attempt by al-Baghdādī to reformulate the genre. This observation is in keeping with George Makdisi's remarks[27] regarding al-Baghdādī's general significance (but ultimately marginal influence) in the fields of *kalām* and *fiqh*. In his treatment of what he calls the 'three theologies' (*kalām*, *uṣūl al-fiqh*, and *uṣūl al-dīn*), Makdisi shows that al-Baghdādī, in writing his *Kitāb uṣūl al-dīn*, made an attempt to incorporate *fiqh* principles within the structure of what he called *uṣūl al-dīn*. This was an attempt to bring those disciplines together and to demonstrate that *uṣūl al-fiqh* was a subordinate part of *kalām*. Furthermore, while earlier scholarship has portrayed al-Baghdādī's *Kitāb uṣūl al-dīn* as being a significant stage within the history of the development of theological reflection, Makdisi argues that when the book is viewed within a larger historical context, it is in fact a marginal

[27] George Makdisi, *Ibn ʿAqil: Religion and Culture in Classical Islam*, Edinburgh 1997, 76–8. Also see my review of this book, *BSOAS*, 63 (2000), 110–1.

contribution (because its project is ultimately unsuccessful), since *kalām* had been excluded from *uṣūl al-fiqh* within the curriculum of the guilds of law by that time and no effort was able to overcome that stance. When considered in the light of al-Baghdādī's overall intellectual efforts, including that manifested in his book on abrogation,[28] this is a fascinating observation. The polemical aspect of his work on sects in Islam, *al-Farq bayna'l-firaq*, has frequently been noted, making clear his attempt to define 'orthodoxy' in the Islam of his time. Al-Baghdādī's other major extant work (although still unpublished, I believe), *Kitāb tafsīr asmā' Allāh al-ḥusnā*, is dedicated to mediating the understanding of the attributes of God within the context of the 'theologians, grammarians and literary critics' according to the opening paragraph of the text.[29] Al-Baghdādī's works, then, are not simple explications or statements; they each appear to be a part of an overall attempt to define and circumscribe intellectual disciplines, all of which would be under the authority of the rationalist Ashʿarī jurist within a single discipline. *Fiqh* and *tafsīr* should be combined disciplines, al-Baghdādī appears to be arguing, given the evidence which we have in the composition of his work on abrogation. Ultimately, however, that was a position which was to prove unsuccessful.

IV

Towards the end of his book *Studies in Early Muslim Jurisprudence*, Norman Calder drew attention to the question of the interrelation between literary form and social context.[30] In the case of this study, too, it seems that only through such considerations is it possible to account fully for the existence of the mass of texts which are the focus of our attention. The role of learning and of books in medieval society becomes our central concern; the cultural situation in which these books would be employed needs to be determined.

The ideal education in medieval Islamic society, according to Franz Rosenthal, was the acquisition of some learning in all the branches of useful knowledge.[31] However, as a result of the tremendous literary activity in Arab civilization, the fact is that there were simply too many books to read in one's own field of specialization, let alone for it to be possible to gain even a partial knowledge of many fields. It is worth noting how this situation produced the polemical notions that certain fields were the most essential ones in order to understand any given subject. In *tafsīr*, knowledge of the 'occasions of revelation', for example, is touted by al-Wāḥidī in his introduction to

[28] Notable, too, is a significant overlap in the introductory comments in his *Kitāb al-nāsikh wa'l-mansūkh* and a section of his *Kitāb uṣūl al-dīn*, Istanbul 1928, 226–8.
[29] Ms. British Library OR 7547, fol. 1b.
[30] N. Calder, *Studies in Early Muslim Jurisprudence*, Oxford 1993, 161.
[31] F. Rosenthal, *The Technique and Approach of Muslim Scholarship*, Rome 1947, 61.

his book as the crucial element for understanding the Qur'ān.[32] On the other hand, in virtually every text dealing with abrogation one finds the anecdote concerning ʿAlī and the Kufan preacher which suggests that one should not talk about the Qur'ān if not versed in the doctrine of abrogation.[33] The end result of this tendency was the perception that there was a need to master many fields of study. This then led to a high demand for concise textbooks on a range of subjects in order to cope with the demands. The simple fact of limited book circulation in medieval times and the need for ready reference material must account for the existence of some of these books, along with the students' desire for material which can easily be memorized.

The search for an understanding of the existence of so many books on abrogation then leads to consideration of the audiences for which the material was destined. In the general field of *tafsīr*, there are two situations which immediately come to mind in the contemplation of the location of any commentary on the Qur'ān. One is an intellectual situation, located in a scholastic setting devoted to study of the Qur'ān in its many aspects; the other is a popular situation, where a preacher uses the Qur'ān for edification of his audience. Of the former type, there are of course many examples, for it is hard to see any of the bulky and/or technical *tafsīr*s which have become so well-known as having much use except in that setting. However, the text of the *tafsīr* of Muqātil b. Sulaymān, for example, would appear to be designed for the second situation. There is also an intermediate level, perhaps, one which does not neatly fit into either of these stereotyped situations, but rather which seems to locate itself somewhere in between. Perhaps we can conceive of another, less scholarly but yet semi-learned situation, one which would work on a fairly local level to produce people sufficiently familiar with the Qur'ān such that they might become respected individuals within their own communities. This latter 'in-between' group may account for the existence of some of the simpler texts within a genre such as abrogation.

The final implications of this observation may well be that we should not take every text which we encounter as carrying equal weight in representing the thought of the classical Islamic world. Not all the texts which have come down to us through chance or circumstance will have had any particular intellectual impact. The popularity of a text may be the result of a concern for reasonable concision combined with comprehensiveness; thus we can point to the greater popularity of Hibāt Allāh (given the number of existing manuscript copies and the proliferation of prints of it) as compared to al-Naḥḥās, which must be judged a far more serious text. Contemporary scholarship is often tempted to treat every work which still exists as equally significant; in light of the proliferation of texts and the contemplation of the purposes of their composition, it is doubtful that this can be justified.

[32] al-Wāḥidī, *Kitāb asbāb nuzūl al-Qur'ān*, Cairo 1400, 3–4.
[33] See above, note 20.

Creativity and intellectual acumen certainly had their place in medieval Muslim scholasticism alongside an appreciation of the important role of direct memorization. According to al-ʿAskarī (d. 395/1005), 'memorized knowledge is the most difficult and, at the same time, the most useful and rewarding kind of knowledge that swims with you when your ship sinks'.[34] Such approaches to the role of learning manifest themselves in the different works on abrogation. Those authors whose goal was to facilitate the memorization of knowledge produced a certain type of book. Those interested in creativity and acumen produced another. That we find the latter more significant today should not seem surprising, for we can see even more clearly with the benefit of hindsight the 'milestone' texts and what they added to the body of material on the subject. Both types of texts are interesting in their own, but different, ways. One type is sociologically significant, but its content may well not repay much devoted attention; the other is more intellectually significant, but one should not be tempted to see such works as representative of the entire culture of medieval Islam.

Another aspect which this survey of texts allows us to conclude relates to the danger of a simple acceptance of the established 'genre' classifications. These 'genres' are primarily of late medieval construction; in the instance of *al-nāsikh wa'l-mansūkh*, al-Suyūṭī's (d. 911/1505) division of the overall subject called *ʿulūm al-Qur'ān* into 'topics' under the keyword *nawʿ* has proven pivotal to the creation of this and other 'genres'. One of Norman Calder's significant contributions to the field of *tafsīr* studies was his attention to the structural definition of the *tafsīr* genre, which, he noted, was still open for manipulation even in medieval times.[35] In his work, he built upon the observations of Wansbrough, whose separation of the first four centuries of *tafsīr* into its five constituent parts illustrates the diverse nature of the form, contents and approach of all those works which we tend to group (misleadingly) under the keyword *tafsīr*.[36] Detailed studies of the specific texts incorporated within the 'genres', with specific attention to form, structure, purpose and audience, are the only remedy to generalizations built upon superficial aspects (such as book titles), and the consequent glossing of significant differences between the texts.

34 Franz Rosenthal, *Knowledge Triumphant: The Concept of Knowledge in Medieval Islam*, Leiden 1970, 282.
35 Calder, "*Tafsīr* from Ṭabarī to Ibn Kathīr", 133–4.
36 Wansbrough, *Quranic Studies*, part IV.

From case to case
Notes on the discourse logic of the Mishnah*

Alexander Samely (University of Manchester)

The Mishnah is probably the earliest document of the rabbinic legal discourse, as well as one of the most important. It stands at the beginning of the development that leads to the Babylonian and Palestinian Talmuds and has defined the legal (halakhic) agenda of Judaism up to our time. This paper is devoted to some questions concerning the Mishnah as a *text*. We are going to examine aspects of the thematic coherence of the Mishnah. We shall do this using the tools of discourse analysis and other related, synchronic, disciplines.[1] We shall, however, also have to be interested in the relationship between presentational coherence and substantive legal coherence. To what extent does thematic coherence point to (otherwise largely tacit) principles of Mishnaic law? We are thus labouring in a field which, in its Islamic manifestations, was close to Norman Calder's heart. I owe a personal debt to him for our frequent discussions of such topics in the last eight years of his life. Among the conversations I remember very clearly is one which concerned the general problem of law or halakhah as a *religious* expression, and how one might recover what he called in another context, its 'sensibility'.[2] In that conversation, we confronted the possibility that modern scholarship might be incapable of providing a full understanding of legal discourse as worship or devotion.[3] Such questions concern the nature of modern historical scholarship itself. But answers to them are provided not merely in theoretical clarification; they are also found in the practice of scholarship. In reflectiveness as well as practice, Norman Calder's work is exemplary. His presence is felt in the following also for another reason. His intellectual personality has given important features to the ideal scholarly reader whom I take into view when I write.

---

* I am indebted to Julian Abel with whom I first explored some of the ideas in this article and who commented on the halakhic aspects in an earlier draft. Julian is very gratified to be able to have made some contribution towards Norman's cherished memory.

1 For a first orientation in the general parameters for such an analysis, see T. van Dijk, *Text and Context. Explorations in the Semantics and Pragmatics of Discourse*, London 1977, 106–8; R. de Beaugrande and W. Dressler, *Introduction to Text Linguistics*, London–New York 1981, 95ff. See also notes 5 and 50 below.

2 Cf. his paper "The *ʿUqūd rasm al-muftī* of Ibn ʿĀbidīn", posthumously published in *BSOAS*, 63 (2000), 215–28.

3 J. Neusner put the question thus: 'How can the Mishnah be deemed a book of religion, a program for consecration, a mode of sanctification?' (*Formative Judaism: Religious, Historical, and Literary Studies*, Chico, CA 1982, 111).

1 The Mishnah as text

The Mishnah is the earliest detailed statement of rabbinic religious law, or *halakhah*. Its final redaction is usually dated to the early third century CE. This large document, comprising about 800 pages in an English translation, was incorporated and expounded in the Babylonian Talmud (sixth/seventh century CE), which in turn became the dominant articulation of Judaism from the middle ages to modern times. We shall here deal with the Mishnah as a text. That is, we shall treat it not as an uncontrolled, or spontaneous expression of a subject matter, but as a literary representation. As such, its formal features will either testify to deliberately chosen compositional techniques or to socially embedded conventions of how to verbalize and textualize halakhic topics. Some of them may well have arisen in non-literary contexts of presentation.[4] But it is important to note that even in an oral format decisions or conventions exist *both* for the choice of words within each sentence and for the manner in which sentences hang together or follow each other (the *textualization*). They thus comprise language and verbal formulation, thematic range, selection of information (or sources), as well as the constitution, arrangement and progression of textual units. So by saying that such decisions or conventions are embodied in the text we do not exclude an oral prehistory of the document. We do however exclude the possibility that the Mishnah resulted from a purely accidental accretion or accumulation of smaller units of texts into a large jumble of sentences.[5]

Following standard methodology in the study of collective documents that have a history of growth, we shall accept that textual inconsistencies may point to different original settings for neighbouring segments of text; and we shall view the retention of formal differences in the final document as part of a *compilatory* dimension, which co-exists with a *compositional* dimension.[6] The assumption of a

[4] For a descriptive project devoted among other things to this link, see N. Calder, *Studies in Early Muslim Jurisprudence*, Oxford 1993.

[5] Cf. A. Goldberg, "Der Diskurs im babylonischen Talmud", in his *Rabbinische Texte als Gegenstand der Auslegung: Gesammelte Studien II*, Tübingen 1999 (original *FJB*, 11 (1983), 1–45), 263–96, here at 266 [= 5f.]. Goldberg's paper illustrates some general points in the synchronic study of rabbinic texts, and rehearses a number of standard elements of analysis as adapted to the study of certain talmudic passages. Partly due to the differences in the material, however, Goldberg's terms of the analysis are quite different from the one presented here.

[6] For some aspects of such a distinction, see A. Goldberg, "Distributive und kompositive Formen: Vorschläge für die descriptive Terminologie der Formanalyse rabbinischer Texte", in *Rabbinische Texte als Gegenstand der Auslegung* (note 5 above), 107–11; first published in *FJB*, 12 (1984), 147–53. My thinking on the Mishnah as text is of course indebted to the pioneering and programmatic work of Jacob Neusner. Having been stimulated by and having learned from his publications, I find myself nevertheless applying a rather different type of analysis to Mishnaic passages. Still, many of the questions raised in this article were first raised as part of Neusner's scholarly agenda. See in particular his *History of the Mishnaic Law of Purities*, xxi, *The Redaction and Formulation of the Order of Purities in Mishnah and Tosefta*, Leiden 1977. A very clear basic summary of his work on the Mishnah from this period is found as chapter 9 ('The Mishnah as Literature') in his *Formative Judaism* (note 3 above), 109–50. Cf. further *History of the Mishnaic Law of Purities*, xxii, Leiden 1977; "History and Structure: The Case of Mishnah", *JAAR*, 45 (1977), 161–92, and *Judaism: The Evidence of the Mishnah*, Chicago–London 1982.

mix of compilatory and compositional characteristics is also appropriate for the overall thematic arrangement and coherence of the Mishnah. However, each passage needs to be investigated on its merits with regard to this question. Thematic coherence is only one Mishnaic type of textual coherence.[7] In this context we need to mention the divisions of the text into tractate (*massekhet*), chapter (*pereq*) and individual paragraph (*mishnah*). These often coincide with thematic or formal points of transition and thus embody a view on thematic coherence. Paragraph and chapter divisions can fluctuate and are likely to constitute a first layer of commentary on the original thematic arrangement. As for the tractates, they seem to reflect a more fundamental division of the text into larger units.[8] It is clear from the way the sixty-three tractates relate to each other that the thematic coherence between them (certainly if they are considered as *wholes*) is often distinctly weaker than the thematic coherence within them. And yet, the overall distribution of themes within the Mishnah is not predictable on the basis of the thematic structure of tractates. Not all aspects of a topic whose main seat in the Mishnah is a given tractate are always treated in that tractate; and conversely, not everything that is found within a tractate can necessarily be brought under the heading of *one* overarching theme. So while there is clearly *some* thematic coherence to tractates, they are not the control centre for the presentation of a given theme throughout the Mishnah. It is thus the whole of the document which must be taken into view. Yet, the whole document can only come into view if we start with the smallest grammatically autonomous units, the sentences. We must probe for coherence structures on each level, from these smallest units of text to the whole of the work.

The reason for this lies partly in the total absence of an explicit account of the overall thematic order in the Mishnah (or even of its tractates). Thematic connections between separate text parts can be created in a number of ways, including signal key words, dedicated patterned language, explicit cross-reference or the explicit projection of a thematic order. In a text as complex and long as the Mishnah the latter would achieve greatest clarity. But clear signals for the thematic similarity of distant parts of the text are rare, if they occur at all, although some weak marking of divisions is achieved implicitly by verbal or grammatical repetition.[9] If passages are only weakly

---

[7] Cf. for example the list in Neusner, *Formative Judaism*, 118. Other coherence principles in the Mishnah could be added to that list, for example the presentation of a long series of actions in their temporal (but not narrative) sequence, as in mYoma.

[8] Neusner, *Formative Judaism*, 118f.; *History of the Mishnaic Law of Purities*, xxi, chapter one; note that Neusner uses the word 'chapter' also for intermediate Mishnaic divisions as defined by his analysis, not only as defined by the *pereq* found in prints or manuscripts (*op. cit.* 113, 117). See generally Ch. Albeck, *Einführung in die Mishna*, Berlin–New York 1971; G. Stemberger, *Introduction to the Talmud and Midrash*, tr. M. Bockmuehl, 2nd edn, Edinburgh 1996, section II/1.

[9] But even in the case of verbal repetition or quotation, the possible functions of text-articulation are not made explicit. The recurrence of a formulation is often not acknowledged as such, let alone accompanied by a pointer to the earlier occurrence(s). And as we said above, the Mishnah also takes no cognizance of its own divisions and topography. The cross-referencing of non-contiguous parts of the text is one of the indispensable functions of the commentaries to the Mishnah. See also note 32 below.

or rarely connected by signals spanning a textual distance, textual contiguity or proximity becomes paramount for coherence. Contiguous units of text are connected by virtue of position alone: no extra words need to be expended on linking them. They thus provide a textual default structure for the encoding of *thematic* connectedness. Therefore similarity or continuity found in contiguous passages becomes the prime target in the search for thematic coherence in the Mishnah. Since the limits and types of thematic coherence cannot be determined in advance, each textual unit encountered in the sequence of units has the potential for thematic continuity or discontinuity, i.e. the start of a new theme. In order to determine the boundaries of coherence we thus must work our way outwards from any smaller literary unit which has a unified topic, or articulates a theme.[10] In most cases our starting point must be the simple sentence or complex sentence. Starting from this smallest unit we test how far its thematic focus travels, or is developed through neighbouring sentences. A systematic investigation of the whole of the Mishnah yields a (synchronic) map of thematic concentrations, their extent, frequency and position in the Mishnah.[11]

What we have said so far already implies that the relationship between neighbouring units is rarely *hierarchical*: the sequence of units only occasionally expresses a relationship of 'more general' to 'more specific', in the sense that later information simply fills in the details of a picture already given in the opening sentences.[12] More often than hierarchy (or hypotaxis) we find a *paratactic* arrangement of halakhic material, or 'agglutination'.[13] Self-contained items of information are connected with each other not by subordination, but by similarity. Thus thematically connected units tend to be on the same level of generality, they do not form structures of conceptual inclusion or nesting. Yet some contiguous passages

[10] Our concern here partly corresponds to Neusner's interest in establishing 'intermediate divisions' of Mishnaic chapters; his results with regard to the Mishnaic order of Tohorot are summarized in chapter 2 of *The Memorized Torah: The Mnemonic System of the Mishnah*, Chico, CA 1985. These intermediary units are defined for Neusner in the main by: (a) stretches of contiguous text in patterned language; (b) contiguous units with thematic coherence; or (c) a combination of both (most cases). However, he seeks such units on an abstract level, not in specific structures. For a full description of their textual coherence, these larger divisions depend on further, apparently ad hoc categories. Among the latter one finds 'catalogue', 'set', 'group', descriptions of syntactic patterns, or phrases like 'balanced apocopated sentences' (p. 32) or 'matched item for item' (p. 33). Cf. also his *History of the Mishnaic Law of Purities*, xxi, chapter 2. More directly parallel to our project is A. Goldberg's form-analysis, which is concerned with texts as *Gestalt* and examines the relational structures which essentially establish what we here call coherence or 'textuality'; see e.g. his "Form-Analysis of Midrashic Literature as a method of Description", in *Rabbinische Texte als Gegenstand der Auslegung* (note 5 above), 80–95, first published in *JJS*, 36 (1985), 159–74.

[11] Neusner uses the image of the text of the Mishnah written onto one long scroll without any marks for divisions (*Formative Judaism*, 118f.). This important programmatic statement is however only partially realized in Neusner's work on smaller literary units (see preceding note). Segmenting a text is an essential step in ascertaining unknown literary forms, see D. Lenhard, *Die Rabbinische Homilie: Ein formanalytischer Index*, Frankfurt am Main 1998, 10.

[12] Some types of lists, in particular those appearing as openings of tractates, *prima facie* create such hierarchies; however, they often turn out to be only partial expositions of the overall theme. See also section 8 below.

[13] This apt word is used by Neusner ('agglutination of these particular topics'), *Formative Judaism*, 110; *History of the Mishnaic Law of Purities*, xxi, 301.

form tightly knit larger units of thematic discourse. They provide a benchmark of strong thematic coherence in the Mishnah, and to one type of such larger unit we now turn.

2 Thematic progress and the case schema

There are several important types of sentences which are self-contained articulations of a topic in the Mishnah. Prominent among these are the general rule[14] and the list.[15] A crucial role is played furthermore by the conditional sentence. The conditional sentence contains a hypothetical legal case and is a special kind of norm. We shall refer to it henceforth as *case schema*. The case schema consists of the mention of salient features of a situation on the one hand, and the halakhic evaluation of that situation on the other. This halakhic evaluation can be a legal category from which certain actions follow ('clean'–'unclean', 'liable'–'free', etc.) or it can specify an act as permitted or prescribed. The situation and the evaluation are related to each other in a conditional structure, presented in approximately the following form: if P is the case, action A is required.[16] Here is an example:

> mYev. 3:1
> **(i)** [In the case of] four brothers, two of them married to two [women who are] sisters [to each other]: [if] the two married to the sisters died [childless],
> > behold these [widows and siblings] perform *Ḥalitsah* and are not taken in levirate marriage [by the two surviving brothers].

The obligation of levirate marriage is incumbent on the two surviving men from the moment of the deaths of their brothers; and it ties each of them to *both* sisters equally.[17] However, since they are sisters to each other, no one could take *either* in marriage (cf. Lev. 18:18) and so it is decided that the two surviving brothers must go through a procedure which cancels the bond created by the obligation of levirate marriage, that procedure being called *Ḥalitsah*.[18] Since the format of the case schema, as in our example (i), is conditional and concerns a theoretical situation, the

---

[14] For example: 'All circumlocutions used for vows are [as binding] as the vows themselves', mNed. 1:1 (cf. mNaz. 1:1).

[15] For example: 'These are said [only] in the holy tongue: the recitation of first-fruits, the *Ḥalitsah*, the Blessings and Curses, the Priestly Blessing ...', mSoṭ. 7:2. See note 12 above.

[16] See in particular Jacob Neusner, *The Memorized Torah* (note 10 above). For the wide range of grammatical structures used to present this dependency, see M. Azar, "The Conditional Clause in Mishnaic Hebrew", in M. Bar-Asher (ed.), *Studies in Mishnaic Hebrew (Scripta Hierosolymitana xxxvii)*, Jerusalem 1998, 58–68, in particular 67f.

[17] The Gemara uses the expression זיקה, 'tie/chain', for this relationship (e.g., bYev. 26a and 17b); but the notion that such a relationship (before actual performance of levirate marriage or betrothal) is assumed in our passage is also contested in the Gemara.

[18] This is the ritual of taking the shoe off (חליצה) the surviving brother's foot, and exposing him to shame for his refusal (here imposed by the rabbis) to perpetuate the name of his deceased brother by marrying his widow. Cf. Deut. 25:5ff., and mSoṭah, chapter 12.

underlying structure is both hypothetical and general.[19] Units such as (i) are *explicitly* marked as catering for an eventuality. The topic is not a real situation that once obtained in its unique unrepeatability[20] but the *schema* of a potentially infinite repetition of real situations. Textual units which convey one complete case schema are very common in the Mishnah. They tend to be compact, often consisting of one extended sentence as above. They are by no means fully autonomous, in the sense that they could be taken from their textual environment and placed somewhere else without loss of information. Nevertheless – and partly because of their explicit conditional limitation – they have a fairly high degree of thematic independence. Case schemata also often form the point of textual attachment for other small literary structures which can be 'docked on' such as scriptural proof-texts, rival halakhic opinions, generalizations, or clauses giving reasons.[21]

We said that the case schema consists of a situation (usually comprising a plurality of situational factors) on the one hand, and a halakhic evaluation, permission or obligation on the other. Using terminology which has been applied in biblical and Mishnaic studies we shall refer to these two parts as protasis (the 'if' part in case of a conditional sentence) and apodosis (the 'then' part). In our presentation of example (i) above the apodosis (starting with the word 'behold') is marked by indentation. Law which is presented or conceived by way of 'cases' in this way is often referred to as 'casuistic'.[22] In investigating the Mishnah as a text we shall not take the 'casuistic' nature of its halakhah for granted; instead we shall confront it afresh as a textual phenomenon. Our textual analysis is thus not disconnected from the question of what are the substantive features of this sort of law.

Because of their frequent occurrence throughout the Mishnah case schemata need to be considered as prime carriers of thematic identity. The self-contained balance between protasis and apodosis raises a delimited halakhic topic and also gives it a closure. Within the case schema it tends to be the protasis, not the apodosis, which carries the most specific markers of the topic. Permission, obligation or halakhic evaluation as contained in the apodosis tend to be couched in fairly general and

[19] On the important and interesting link between the conditional ('hypotheticals') and the general ('generics'), see W. Frawley, *Linguistic Semantics*, Hillsdale, NJ–Hove–London 1992, 405f.

[20] In this respect, the case schema is the opposite of the so-called 'precedent' (מעשה), which takes into view a singular occurrence, and is basically a rudimentary *narrative* form.

[21] I have addressed the resulting structures in a companion paper to the present article, entitled, "Delaying the Progress from Case to Case: Redundancy in the Halakhic Discourse of the Mishnah", in G. Brooke (ed.), *Jewish Ways of Reading the Bible* (JSSS, 11), Oxford, forthcoming. We shall return to the question of general rules or reasons in section 9 below.

[22] In contrast to statute law, for example. See *s.v.* 'statute law' (p. 1184) and 'case law' (p. 190) in D. M. Walker, *The Oxford Companion to Law*, Oxford 1980. In the biblical context the main distinction is not along the lines of 'case law' *versus* 'statute law', but 'casuistic' *versus* 'apodictic'. See for example, Y. M. Clark, "Law" in J. H. Hayes (ed.), *Old Testament Form Criticism*, San Antonio 1974, 99–139, here at 105–16; Albrecht Alt, "The Origins of Israelite Law", in *Essays on Old Testament History and Religion*, tr. R. A. Wilson, Oxford 1966, 79–132 (German original 1934); E. Gerstenberger, "Covenant and Commandment", *JBL*, 84 (1965), 38–51; cf. also D. Patrick, *Old Testament Law*, London 1986, 21ff.

standardized terms, i.e. terms which can be found also in other halakhic contexts; while the terms of the envisaged situation are often much more concrete (but see section 6 below). This leaves a choice of two main options for any attempt to arrange case schemata thematically. One option is to place together case schemata which have the same or similar apodoses, or to unfold the differences between apodoses. We shall deal with this arrangement below in section 8. The second option is to group case schemata according to the thematic connection between their protases. For this we can find clear and quite frequent examples. In many larger thematic units created from the juxtaposition of case schemata, the protases of neighbouring units are closely related.

The strongest type of thematic coherence found between the protases of neighbouring case schemata in the Mishnah can be described in the following way. Every two neighbouring case schemata will have protases which are as similar to each other as possible *without resulting in the same apodosis*. In other words, each member of a pair will differ from the other in its apodosis; for example the one requires a certain action while the other prohibits it. But they will differ only slightly in the situational features they envisage in the protasis. We shall refer to this as the principle of *minimal potentially critical difference between neighbouring protases*. The word 'critical' here means: making a difference for the apodosis. This literary format creates a conceptual structure in which the contiguous protases stand in a relationship of *variation* while the corresponding apodoses stand in *opposition*. That opposition can hold between binary alternatives or between mutually exclusive members of a halakhic paradigm.[23] The result of varying protases in minimal ways while contrasting apodoses is to make manifest a regularity of law. By modifying the situation only in one factor at a time the effect of an underlying halakhic rule is exhibited in a totally controlled and schematic manner.[24] This, the exhibition of a rule of law, could be called the discourse *function* of the literary *form* 'pair of case schemata' or 'series of case schemata'. A 'series' is thus defined as a sequence in which any pair of neighbouring cases exhibits a relationship defined by the principle of minimal potentially critical difference. As far as the meaning of the word 'potentially' is concerned the Mishnaic continuation of our passage (i) above provides a good illustration:

> **(ii)** If they [the surviving brothers] had already consummated [levirate marriage],
> they must send [the women] away.

[23] On the role of halakhic paradigms and opposition in the Mishnaic treatment of biblical texts, see chapter 11 of my *Rabbinic Interpretation of Scripture in the Mishnah*, Oxford, forthcoming.
[24] We shall address the schematic character of the protasis in more detail below in section 6.

It is clear that the text in (ii) presupposes the text in (i), in that all the other situational factors envisaged in (i) still hold:[25] four brothers, two of them married to two sisters, the latter two brothers die childless. In other words, the situational factors are the same as in (i) except for one additional parameter: the two surviving brothers have created a *fait accompli* by marrying the pair of widows. A comparison of the apodoses in (ii) and (i) shows that they are very similar: no levirate marriage is allowed. Why then do we have case (ii) here, and does this not show that the difference between protases does not have to be 'critical' at all? The wider Mishnaic co-text gives an answer to this: in mYev. 2:6 and 2:7 we find cases in which the *fait accompli* of marriage does make a difference, and there are also other areas of halakhah in which the deed, once done, is acceptable. Our case (ii) is likely to hark back to mYev. 2: it addresses an expectation created by other cases and shows that it does not apply here. Case (ii) is there to show that the *potential* of the situational factor '*fait accompli*' to change the apodosis is not activated.

What then is the opposite of 'critical', or 'potentially critical'? Imagine the following case schema in place of our Mishnaic case (ii), i.e. as continuation of our passage (i):

> If they [the surviving brothers] had put on weight after the deaths of their brothers,
>
> they must send [the women] away.

This is a strange case schema, but why? Obviously because the situational factor 'putting on weight' is simply irrelevant for a halakhic prohibition; yes, they still are barred from taking the women in levirate marriage as in case (i). But in contrast to case (ii) that apodosis is not *informative* here. Given the background concerns of rabbinic halakhah the question of weight of the levir is most unlikely to make a material difference, in particular where a prohibition due to family ties is concerned. It is neither a critical nor, to judge from the wider Mishnaic discourse, a potentially critical difference to the protasis in (i). If we found *such* variations throughout the Mishnah on a grand scale, the character of the document would be totally different from the one we actually have and what we have called 'series' or 'pair' would be a much rarer literary form. Instead our pre-theoretical experience with the document Mishnah makes us start from the assumption that any change in the situation singled out for Mishnaic articulation is going to be *relevant* to the halakhic outcome, even if only by addressing the potential for critical difference.[26] That is why the literary

---

[25] We need to distinguish the fact that the situational factors envisaged are largely the same from the manner in which the Mishnah presents the two cases. It can do so by verbal repetition of the same factors, or by ellipsis, as happens in our passage (ii). See further section 4 below.

[26] See on this also my "Delaying the Progress from Case to Case", section 2 (the 'zero-sum condition'), and example (14) there. Sometimes such disappointed expectations are marked in the text of the protases by the expression אף על פי ('despite the fact that') or the word אפילו ('even').

forms 'pair of case schemata' and 'series of case schemata' as defined above are of such strong representative value for the Mishnaic presentation of case schemata in general. But they are linked to a much wider principle of economy in the presentation of information. There are many (actually, unlimited) variations of a basic situation which have absolutely no bearing on the halakhic evaluation and the Mishnah does not list them as separate case schemata with identical apodosis, nor could any finite text. (And an infinite text is probably a *contradictio in adjecto*.) This also implies that any one case schema (certainly if part of a pair or series) stands for a whole cluster of basically similar – i.e. non-critically different – situations. And this means that due to the economies of relevance the *absence* of certain situational variations from the Mishnaic series can become meaningful or informative. The Mishnah, by not even *saying* that putting on weight makes no difference shows its utter irrelevance; conversely, by *saying* that creating a *fait accompli* makes no difference in case (ii) it grants that it might have done, i.e. that it belongs to the halakhic categories that are in principle relevant. Thus both the words 'critical' and 'potential' imply that the cases selected for presentation in pairs or series are linked to the background concepts of the halakhic discourse.

Our passages (i) and (ii) clearly form a 'pair' of closely related hypothetical cases. Such pairs of neighbouring case schemata are quite frequent. However, the Mishnah also offers examples of larger structures of this type. We shall refer to passages consisting of more than two closely related case schemata as a thematic *series*. Case schemata 'in series' are selected and arranged in such a way that each neighbouring two form a pair according to the principle of minimal potentially critical difference. How frequent such series of case schemata actually are in the Mishnah is difficult to say before the whole of its text has been scrutinized with this structure in mind. Really large ones (say, with more than ten case schemata) are certainly rare. Still, despite their scarcity it is these larger series which show most clearly the textual relationships also underlying the shorter series or even mere pairs of case schemata. We shall now therefore turn to an example consisting of seventeen case schemata in series.

3 Arranging case schemata in series: an example

The series we are going to explain in some detail starts with the pair of two cases we have encountered above. Here they are again, next to each other:

> [mYev. 3:1]
> (**i**) [In the case of] four brothers, two of them married to two [women who are] sisters [to each other]: [if] the two married to the sisters died [childless],
> behold these [widows and siblings] perform *Ḥalitsah* and are not taken in levirate marriage [by the two surviving brothers].

(ii) If they [the surviving brothers] had already consummated [levirate marriage],
they must send [the women] away.

We shall use the following conventions for presenting the case schemata: the cases are sequentially numbered by lower case roman numerals; the apodosis is marked by indentation and further amplifying material (e.g. rival apodoses) is marked by further indentation;[27] explanatory text is added in square brackets. Our translation follows manuscript Kaufmann, while the *mishnayyot* are numbered according to the popular prints where our series corresponds to mYev. 3:1–7.[28] We shall quote each case schema separately and comment briefly on the way in relates to the preceding one, thus explaining in detail the coherence or the thematic progression. All seventeen case schemata are presented together at the end of this article as Appendix.

Before we look at the structure of the text[29] we need to say a word about its subject matter. The following ingredients go into the halakhic mix: the obligation to marry the widow of a brother who died childless which in the view of the rabbis imposes an immediate marriage-like tie on the surviving brother(s); the prohibition of marrying a woman and her sister at the same time (linked to Lev. 18:18); the parallel status of a woman and her co-wife with regard to sisterly relationship (also Lev. 18:18); and the prohibition to marry (or 'uncover the nakedness' of) relatives articulated throughout Lev. 18 and in more restrictive, rabbinic rules. Sometimes when levirate marriage is disallowed (or refused by the surviving brother) the above-mentioned procedure of *Ḥalitsah* is performed which cancels the bond tying the widow to her brother-in-law. These normative structures are presupposed in the formulation of our case schemata and set up the problems to whose solution the series is devoted. But the Mishnah does not articulate or summarize these basics at the outset of our unit (more on this in section 9 below). Here is the complete text of (ii) incorporating extra material relating to a rival apodosis, followed by case (iii):

(ii) If they [the surviving brothers] had already consummated [levirate marriage],
they must send [the women] away.
R. Eliezer says: As far as the House of Shammai is concerned, they can continue [the marriage]; and the House of Hillel say: They must send [them] away.

[27] See my "Delaying the Progress from Case to Case".
[28] The Kaufmann text is taken from G. Beer (ed.), *Faksimile-Ausgabe des Mischnacodex Kaufmann A 50*, The Hague 1930 (reprint Jerusalem, 1968). I have also compared the popular printed text and the base text of Maimonides' *Commentary* (ed. Y. Qafih, *Mishnah ʿim peyrush rabeynu Mosheh ben Maimon, Seder Nashim*, Jerusalem 1965).
[29] What we consider to be a series of seventeen case schemata (plus one, see below) has been analysed as one 'triplet' – our cases (i) to (v) – plus a 'six-entry construction' – our cases (vi) to (xviii) – by Neusner, *A History of the Mishnaic Law of Women*, i, *Yebamot*, Leiden 1980, 9; 58ff. It is clear that the principles of segmentation are different in these two projects of description.

[3:2] (**iii**) If one of them [the widows] was forbidden to one [of the surviving brothers] by reason of the biblical norms of incest,[30]
he is forbidden to her but allowed to her sister,
and the second [brother] is forbidden to both of them.[31]

All the previous situational features mentioned in (i) continue and are tacitly presupposed: four brothers, two married to two sisters, the two married ones die childless. The factor freshly introduced in (ii) is not continued but one new factor is added instead, namely that one of the sisters is forbidden to one of the brothers. This is relevant in that it means that that brother is not tied to her by the duty of levirate marriage that has come into force at the death of his brother. Not being tied by the link of levirate marriage to both sisters at the same time (because one of them is forbidden to him) he is free for the other one.

(**iv**) [If by reason of] the rabbinic norms of incest or priestly marriage constraints,
they [the widows] perform *Ḥalitsah*, and are not taken in levirate marriage.

Here the extra factor of (iii) is varied: what if the relationship is only forbidden according to extra rabbinic norms, not according to scripture? Treated together with this is the case of a priest for whom certain extra categories of women are also forbidden. The apodosis shows that the difference in severity between the two sets of incest rules makes a critical difference: a brother may not marry the one widowed sister (who also must perform *Ḥalitsah*) if the other sister is forbidden to him only by virtue of rabbinic or priestly rules.

[3:3] (**v**) If one of them [the widows] was forbidden to one [of the surviving brothers] by reason of the biblical norms of incest, and the second [widow] was forbidden to the other [surviving brother] by reason of the biblical norms of incest,
the one forbidden to the first is allowed to the second,
and the one forbidden to the second is allowed to the first.
This is what they have said (cf. mYev. 2:3): If the sister is [also] her sister-in-law, she may either perform *Ḥalitsah* or be taken in levirate marriage.

30 The term here translated as 'biblical norms of incest' is אסור ערוה, literally 'prohibition of nakedness' (the latter expression alluding to the wording of incest laws in Lev. 18). As linked to scripture, it is put into opposition to the additional *rabbinic* rules on forbidden relations, called אסור מצוה (lit. 'prohibition of commandment'). The latter term is accordingly translated as 'rabbinic norms of incest' in case (iv) below. On both of these, and the term אסור קדושה, denoting special constraints on priestly marriage, see M. Jastrow, *A Dictionary of the Targumim, the Talmud Babli and Yerushalmi, and the Midrashic Literature*, Philadelphia 1903 (and later reprints), 53b.

31 This time the apodosis consists of two parts, as the two brothers have to be treated differently.

Here we have the basic structure of (iii), but in duplicate: not just one but both sisters are forbidden to each of the two surviving brothers. The amplification attached to the apodosis declares it compatible with a rule treated as known.[32]

> [3:4] (**vi**) [In the case of] **three** brothers, two of them married to two [women who are] sisters, (**vii**) or to a woman and her daughter, (**viii**) or to a woman and her daughter's daughter, (**ix**) or to a woman and her son's daughter,[33] and [if] the two who were married to the sisters died [childless],
> behold, they must perform *Ḥalitsah* with him [the surviving brother] and are not taken in levirate marriage.
> R. Shim'on exempts [them, even from performing *Ḥalitsah*].

Here we leave the numerical constellation introduced in case schema (i). We envisage not two surviving brothers, but only one. The surviving brother, again because of his automatic ties to two women who are related to each other, would violate relationship rules if he were to marry them. The protasis however is extended to accommodate a list of further situations: not just sisterhood, but three further relationships between the two widows concerned are taken into consideration. This is a very economic way to summarize in one protasis–apodosis unit four different case schemata which have the same apodosis and it is found very frequently in the Mishnah.[34] It is in fact consistent with other Mishnaic passages to assume that throughout all our protases the relationship 'sister' can be replaced by these other relationships, and others besides these.[35] It now also becomes clear that, within the series of case schemata concerned with two sisters married to two brothers, cases (i) to (v) form a sub-group (four brothers) and that another sub-group (three brothers) is treated as a relevant variant.

> (**x**) If one of them was forbidden to him by reason of the biblical norms of incest,
> he is forbidden to her and allowed to her sister.

The complicating extra factor of family ties which make levirate marriage impossible is added to the basic structure give in (vi). It conforms to our principle of minimal critical difference in being only one new situational feature; and it is not totally new as it is here applied for the second time in the series. We have encountered an application of the 'incest' relation to the 'four brothers' case in (iii)–(v); now we see it applied to the 'three brothers' case. The overlap say between cases (x) and (iii), could be taken to be unnecessary and therefore as betraying the editorial combination of two

32 That rule is in fact mentioned elsewhere in the same tractate (mYev. 2:3) – but one would not know this from the formula by which it is introduced. The phrase, 'this is what they said', does not acknowledge a co-textual relationship, and is not accompanied by a cross-reference. See note 9 above.

33 The remainder of this protasis is absent from ms. Kaufmann, and the apodosis is an exact repetition of the apodosis of (i).

34 To mention just one further, and very striking example, see mQid. 2:3 (and 2:2). See further section 8 below, on lists.

35 Cf. bYev. 3b, 13b. The three relationships here selected by the Mishnah are those mentioned in Lev. 18:17.

pre-existing units of diverse origin. This is how Neusner interprets the relationship;[36] but such a diachronic conclusion depends entirely on the expectation that the (synchronic) textual coherence of case schemata conforms to some such principle as 'minimal potentially critical difference'.

> (**xi**) If forbidden by reason of the rabbinic norms of incest or priestly marriage constraints,
> they perform *Ḥalitsah* and are not taken in levirate marriage.

Here the Mishnah deals with relationships prohibited by rabbinic norms and priestly constraints; in placing this case after (x) it thus explores the same halakhic difference as between cases (iii) and (iv) above.

> [3:5] (**xii**) [In the case of] three brothers, two of them married to two [women who are] sisters, and one [brother] unmarried: [if] one of the husbands of the sisters died [childless], and the unmarried brother betrothed[37] her, and thereafter his second brother died,
> the House of Shammai say:[38] his wife remains with him and the other one is released by reason of the 'sister of his wife' (משום אחות אשה); [39]
> and the House of Hillel say: he sends away his wife by bill of divorce and *Ḥalitsah*, and the wife of his [deceased] brother by *Ḥalitsah*.
> This is the one about whom they have said (cf. mYev. 13:7): Woe to him because of his wife, and woe to him because of the wife of his brother.

The marital status of the third brother is not mentioned in cases (vi) to (xi); here it is specified as unmarried. This prepares the contrast with the succeeding case schemata (where he is married to an unrelated woman). Our protasis in (xii) introduces a *time* factor into the situation: the sequence of events (i.e. deaths) matters. We shall return to the dynamic nature of such protases below.

> [3:6] (**xiii**) [In the case of] three brothers, two of them married to two [women who are] sisters and one [brother] married to a woman who is not related [to the two sisters]: [if] one of the husbands of the sisters died [childless] and the one married to the woman who is not related consummated marriage with his [deceased brother's] wife and [then] died,
> the second [wife] is released by reason of the 'sister of his wife', and the first [unrelated wife] [is released] by reason of [having been] her 'co-wife'.[40]

---

36 *History of the Mishnaic Law of Women* (note 29 above), i, 62. See further text by note 52 below.

37 Literally, 'made an utterance' (עשה מאמר, Danby [*The Mishnah*, Oxford 1933] and Neusner render 'bespoke'). This is a technical term for a betrothal, in particular for the verbal commitment to levirate marriage from the side of the surviving brother; cf. Jastrow, *A Dictionary* (note 30 above), 723a.

38 On this format of a dispute, producing a bifurcation of the apodosis, see my "Delaying the Progress from Case to Case"; cf. also Neusner, *History of the Mishnaic Law of Purities*, xxi, 166f.

39 This expression alludes to a biblical formulation, in Lev. 18:18 (ואשה אל־אחתה לא תקח), and is used as the Mishnaic name of a norm (see under sign 'π' in chapter 4 of my *Rabbinic Interpretation of Scripture in the Mishnah*, note 23 above).

40 The word for co-wife, צרה, ('rival') also has a link to Lev. 18:18 (cf. 1 Sam. 1:6); for the halakhic principle, see mYev. 1:1. Ms. Kaufmann offers a variant here, probably due to scribal error: its apodosis is identical with the apodosis of (xv) below (as represented both in Kaufmann and the other sources).

Here the existing unrelated wife of the third brother is introduced as a complicating factor. From the moment this woman's husband takes one of the sisters in levirate marriage she is considered to enter into a quasi-relation even to the other sister, under the halakhic category 'co-wife of a sister'. Therefore she is 'released' from levirate marriage with the surviving brother. The tractate of Yevamot opens with a list articulating the levirate status of such co-wives.

> (**xiv**) If he [only] betrothed her and [then] died,
> the woman who is not related performs *Ḥalitsah* and is not taken in levirate marriage [by the surviving brother].

Cases (xiii) and (xiv) explore the difference between consummation and betrothal. As far as the widowed sister is concerned the validity of apodosis (xiii) is tacitly presupposed.

> [3:7] (**xv**) [In the case of] three brothers, two of them married to two [women who are] sisters and one [brother] married to a woman who is not related: [if] the one married to the woman who is not related died [childless] and[41] one of the husbands of the sisters consummated marriage with his wife and died,
> the first wife [of the latter] is released by reason of the 'sister of his wife', and the second by reason of [having been] her 'co-wife'.

The basic features of the situation are those of (xiii) but the sequence of deaths is inverted: now it is the husband of the unrelated woman who dies first, his wife becomes co-wife to one of the sisters and then is widowed again.

> (**xvi**) If he [only] betrothed her and [then] died,
> the woman who is not related performs *Ḥalitsah* and is not taken in levirate marriage.

Again we are rehearsing the difference between consummation (xv) and betrothal (xvi), as in the transition between (xiii) and (xiv).

> (**xvii**) [In the case of] three brothers, two of them married to two sisters and one married to a woman who is not related: if one of the husbands of the sisters died and the one who is married to the unrelated woman consummated marriage with his widow, and the wife of the other brother [i.e. the second sister] died and afterwards the [brother] married to the unrelated woman died,
> behold this woman [the surviving sister] is forbidden to him [the only surviving brother] for ever,
> since she was forbidden to him for one hour.

The critical consequence of another combination of deaths is explored here: what if by the time the surviving brother is under levirate obligation to one of the sisters (who is twice widowed), he is a widower himself? He would by marrying her not entertain

[41] Ms. Kaufmann here and in a number of other passages has no 'and' connecting the different parts of the protasis.

marital ties to the two sisters simultaneously. The case schema answers this (unstated) question[42] in the following manner: although this factor *looks* as if it might make a difference to the general apodosis 'not to be taken in levirate marriage', it does not do so. He is still not allowed to take her. So (xvii) addresses the *potential* for critical difference in the slightly modulated situation. The apodosis is amplified by a reason which enunciates a rule ('since she was forbidden to him for one hour') and similar rules can also be found in other areas of Mishnaic halakhah.[43]

> (**xviii**) [In the case of] three brothers, two of them married to two sisters and one married to a woman who is not related: if one of the husbands of the sisters divorced his wife, and the one married to the woman who is not related died, and the divorced man consummated marriage with her [the unrelated woman] and died,
>
> > this is the [woman] about whom they have said (cf. mYev. 1:1): And all of them, if they died (or exercised their right of refusal)[44] or were divorced, their co-wives are permitted [to be taken in levirate marriage].

Here a structure similar to (xvii) is addressed but two features of the situation are modified at the same time: the sister is divorced not deceased; and the divorce precedes the first death. The result is that one sister is removed from the equation: the unrelated woman married to the divorced husband was never her co-wife, and therefore not the co-wife of a sister of the wife of her prospective levirate husband. She may therefore be taken in levirate marriage by the surviving brother.

Here in (xviii) our format of minimal critical difference between neighbouring protases is not applicable: two factors change from (xvii) to (xviii). Yet the difference is hardly noticeable at first reading. So let us see what the shift of two parameters at the same time means for coherence. It is the following. Without additional knowledge of the background rules it is not clear which of the two differences is actually 'critical' for the apodosis. Only after the halakhic background merely alluded to in (xviii) – namely in the general rule quoted towards the end – is clarified does it become clear that the timing factor alone is decisive. (Had the sister in [xvii] died before the first brother's death occurred the surviving brother could have married her.) In other words the modification of two situational parameters at the same time in this protasis breaks the self-sufficiency of the series: information from outside the series becomes necessary to understand what is the rationale which links the apodosis to the protasis.[45] This reveals what it is that underpins the strong coherence of a pair or series of case schemata: the halakhic regularity behind the cases. Modifying only *one* factor at a time the series can display this principle with maximum clarity, without

42 We shall address the importance of unstated questions in section 7 below.
43 See mNed. 11:9, quoted below in section 9 below.
44 The words in brackets are absent from ms. Kaufmann.
45 One could also say: the quotation of the general rule (found in mYev. 1:1) is meant to illuminate both cases (xviii) and (xvii).

having to articulate it. But as soon as two factors simultaneously change between two neighbouring protases there may still a close thematic relationship but the principle of law is not exhibited with the same definiteness.

This also gives us a criterion to grade different types of coherence at least with regard to neighbouring case schemata. Intuitively speaking (xviii) is related intimately to (xvii); and yet it does not satisfy our principle of minimal potentially critical difference. So with regard to the distinctness with which a legal rule manifests itself between neighbouring case schemata the format of minimal potentially critical difference is simply the strongest option. It avoids ambiguity concerning an underlying halakhic rule more than any other manner of composing case schemata. The absence of a 'serial' relationship as between (xviii) and (xvii) is not the absence of coherence. Rather a different coherence relationship governs which, *for definiteness of underlying principle*, is less effective than the series or pair. But clarity of underlying legal principle is obviously only *one* function of textual coherence between contiguous case schemata in the Mishnah. Not all neighbouring case schemata form a 'pair' as defined by potentially critical difference. As we said above that definition ties a literary *form* (contiguous case schemata) to a discourse *function* (exhibition of a halakhic regularity). The same form can and does make other functional contributions also; and the same function is likely to be realized also in other, very different, Mishnaic literary forms (e.g. the direct expression of a rule). Any non-reductive text of substantial length[46] is bound to confront us with a plurality and continuum of literary forms and functions and the Mishnah is no exception. As for Mishnaic literary forms they are quite flexible in certain respects, they adapt to the substance to be conveyed, interact with each other, and are subject to variation due to both inner-textual and extra-textual factors. They can therefore neither be defined nor recognized as variations of a base form without also linking them to a discourse function, which function is an obviously *ideal* element of the description. [47]

Let us return to our series of cases in mYev. 3. Immediately following case (xviii) the Mishnah pursues a topic arising from the quotation of mYev. 1:1. When the presentation of case schemata is resumed (in mYev. 3:9) their themes are not directly continuous with the preceding: one case deals with three wives not related to each other (but again a series of deaths); one with only two brothers, but similar to (xvii)

[46] Examples of what I mean by 'reductive' texts include documents which do not use whole sentences (such as a telephone book) or use a non-linguistic code (e.g. a computer program). The Mishnah presents its material in a highly restricted number of different formats (a fact often stressed in Neusner's work, e.g. *History of the Mishnaic Law of Purities*, xxi, 164ff.). And yet, compared with these other types of texts it is a rich reservoir of variation.

[47] And so is the definition of the literary form itself. A. Goldberg has addressed the 'ideal-typical' nature of the description of literary forms several times in his publications, e.g. "Form-Analysis of Midrashic Literature" (note 10 above), 85 ([=164]. See also the nuanced exposition by D. Lenhard, "Document or Individual Homily? A Critical Evaluation of Neusner's Methodology in the Light of the Results of Form-Analysis", *JSQ* 4 (1997), 339–56; cf. her *Die Rabbinische Homilie* (note 11 above), Introduction.

above; and one with an exchange of two brides between the times of betrothal and consummation. Thereafter (at the beginning of mYev. 4) the Mishnah turns to the question of pregnant widows. In other words the serial relationship holding between cases (i) to (xvii) weakens in (xviii) and peters out thereafter. There is no sudden, dramatic switch of topic and yet the links between contiguous or proximate case schemata are of a different order.

If we now take into view the whole of this series of case schemata we can provide something of a tree structure for its thematic progress.[48] Fig. 1 shows quite clearly that there is a *directionality* to the case schemata. The discourse works its way through about six levels of complication or differentiation. All seventeen case schemata share the situational feature 'two brothers married to two sisters' (used as a heading in Fig. 1). As we go down the levels we have further quasi-hierarchical relationships. For all the cases from (vi) to (xviii) for example, the situational feature 'one further brother' (in contrast of two, as in (i)–(v)) remains constant. In placing new situations onto this shared foundation two principles are at work: the *addition* of new situational features, or the *replacement* of one situational feature by a new one. Our principle of minimal (potentially) critical difference amounts to saying: in a 'pair' or 'series' only one new situational feature is added or replaced at a time. Table 1 gives a picture of the number of factors the Mishnah mentions in sketching out each of the situations. It shows both principles of variation. The *number* of factors (or 'length' of the protasis) is expressed as the point in the table where the letter A (for apodosis) appears. Case (i) involves four such points, case (ii) five, and cases (iii)–(v) seven. In other words a basic situation is varied by the addition of new factors. Within the group (iii)–(v) on the other hand, the variation takes the form of replacing situational factors, thereby keeping constant the total of factors or the 'length' of the protasis. Two sets of family ties alternate with each other in the case of one widow related to one levir and one of them is also applied to the case of two widows related to two levirs. Addition and replacement together also account for the variation of the subsequent case schemata in the series. Overall, there is an increase in the number of factors which are taken into consideration; this is manifest in the movement of the letter A (point of apodosis) from the middle of Table 1 to its right margin for cases (xii) to (xviii).

It may be useful to point out that an order of cases according to minimal relevant variation is unlikely to be comparable with an order reflecting probability of occurrence. If the arrangement started with the most likely or frequent case in the

48 This is in fact rather rare. More usual than a tree structure (i.e. a hierarchy), is a Mishnaic concentration of variation on the same level of generality. I suspect most series of case schemata have only one or two 'levels', and a greater differentiation within these levels. For an example, see mGiṭ. 1:1–3, which I have analysed as the first passage in my "Delaying the Progress from Case to Case".

Figure 1

mYev. 3:1–7
Two brothers married to two sisters

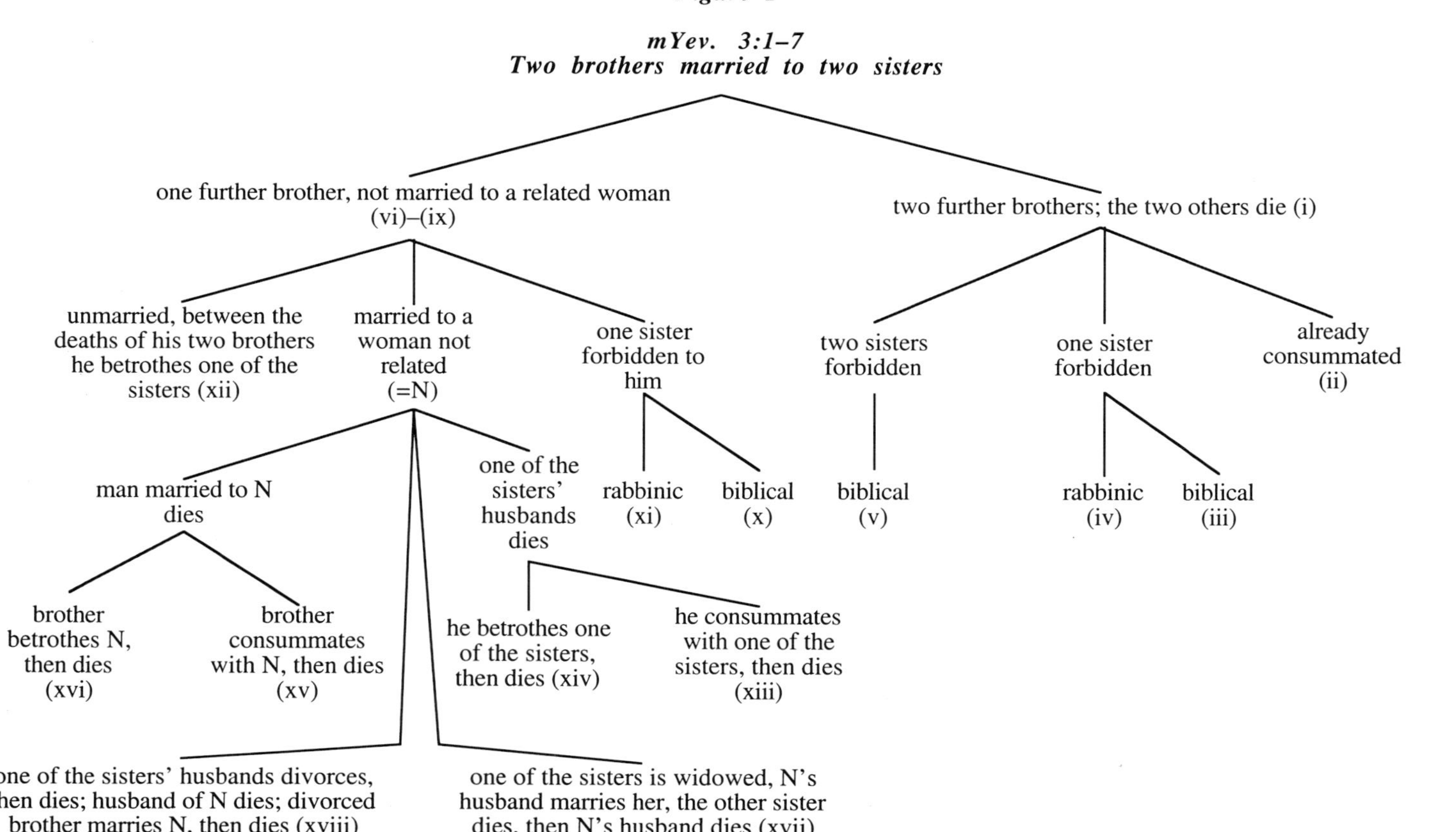

experience of the rabbis and ended with the least likely case (or *vice versa*) a different sequence would be almost certain to emerge. Situations in real life do not come sorted according to the quantity of such complicating factors as are named in the headings of Table 1. Social realities on the ground are likely to cut across what is ultimately a conceptual scheme of distributive or progressive differentiation, at least one as long as our example in mYev. Which of the cases (i) to (xviii) occurred most frequently (or whether they are all fairly theoretical)[49] cannot be deduced from their position in the series.

Despite the fact that the earlier protases seem in some sense to 'contain' the later ones (i.e. provide their most basic form) there is no relationship of subordination for case schemata as wholes. For the earlier apodoses do not 'contain' or directly determine the later ones. As we said above an oppositional relationship of apodoses cuts across the progression of protases. For the protases are (in a 'pair' or 'series' as defined above) *selected* in such a way that apodoses are not identical to, nor wholly predictable from those in the preceding case schema. There is no conceptual hierarchy expressed in the series of case schemata. If subsequent cases in a textual chain of case schemata were increasingly complicated versions of a basic situation presented initially but led to the same apodosis (without addressing an expectation to the contrary), then progressive differentiation would go hand in hand with subordination or hierarchy. But this is not what we find. The apodosis of case number (xvii) cannot be understood as a sub-category of the apodosis of number (i); one cannot infer that the two apodoses are related as general and particular just because the two protases are so related.

Yet as we said before, there are principles of law embedded in the sequence. For the *sequence* of case schemata makes for progressive differentiation of a basic situation (two brothers married to two sisters) and their *selection* makes for a difference between the apodoses which needs to be construed as opposition. A systematic if implicit link is being established between situational features and halakhic decisions. The protasis changes from case to case and so does (mostly) the apodosis. What remains stable is the rationality of a *connection* between them or the logic of law. For the apodosis follows in a regular, not in an arbitrary manner from the protasis; and the regularity or regularities that are embodied in the connection make the coherence of a pair and of a series possible. But the series discloses underlying principles rather than articulating them. We shall investigate below in section 5 some of the conceptual distinctions which point to such regularities of law and in section 9

[49] From time to time it becomes very obvious, even without elaborate consideration of historical likelihood, that an inherent and abstract 'logic' of halakhah alone is responsible for the creation of a series, as in mYev. 10:5.

we shall address the implicit character of this disclosure. First however we should explore the verbal economies of our series.

4 Ellipsis

The importance of ellipsis for textual coherence is obvious and the same goes for the use of pro-forms, be it pronouns or suffixes (such as 'one of *them*' in (iii)). Instead of repeating information a passage presupposes the continued validity of some information mentioned earlier. If isolated from the position in which it is found in the text such a passage will be *incomplete* in some sense. Ellipsis therefore increases the interdependence of parts of the text and the Mishnah uses ellipsis regularly.[50] Table 1 shows to what extent such textual economies are made in our series of case schema. Where a situational feature is not spelled out again the letter E appears. The following picture emerges. In cases (i) to (x) we have a rather high proportion of ellipsis. But after (xii) there is much verbal repetition; the basics of the situation are spelled out again and again. So while the principle of minimal critical difference between protases holds, it finds no direct expression in textual economies. I think the main reason for this is the fact that from case (xii) onwards we are concerned with situations which incorporate an element of time: we have two deaths, and the sequence in which they occur matters, even where the resulting situtation is the same.[51] As soon as there is a temporal dynamic in the relevant features of the situation the opportunities for ellipsis are reduced. All the personages envisaged in the protasis may be the same from one case schema to the next but if the temporal relationship of their acts changes, then they have to be mentioned again specifically (not by pro-forms) if ambiguity is to be avoided. This accounts for the elaborate repetition of a description like 'the one married to a woman who is not related'. So economy is sacrificed to clarity. At least this is the most plausible way to explain why the point at which elaborate verbal repetition begins in our series coincides with the first case which takes account of the genesis of a situation as well as its final state.

A phenomenon related to ellipsis but not identical with it is the set of variations presented in cases (vi)–(ix). They treat together as requiring the same apodosis as sisterhood, a number of other family relationships between the two widows. What interests us here is not the economies made in presenting these cases

[50] For a general treatment, see e.g. Beaugrande and Dressler, *Introduction to Text Linguistics* (note 1 above), 66ff.; D. Crystal, *A Dictionary of Linguistics and Phonetics*, 2nd edn, Oxford–New York 1985, 107f.; K. Malmkjaer, "Text Linguistics", in *idem* (ed.), *The Linguistics Encyclopaedia*, London–New York 1991, 461–71, here at 463f.; G. Brown and G. Yule, *Discourse Analysis*, Cambridge 1983, 191ff. For the Mishnah, see in particular van Uchelen, *Chagigah: The Linguistic Encoding of Halakhah*, Amsterdam 1994.

[51] The Babylonian Gemara queries the necessity of the presence of both of these case schemata in the series, bYev. 30a; cf. also bYev. 32a concerning the similarities between our case (xvii) and one of the case schemata offered after the end of our series.

together in one larger protasis–apodosis structure but the fact that the same variation of the family relationship 'sister' may well be assumed for *all* cases in the series. This is not conveyed in the series itself. It would be strongly implied if these alternative family ties were mentioned at the very beginning of the series. As it is they are mentioned at the beginning of a new sub-section of the series, namely the constellation 'two brothers plus one brother'. Thus it is at least possible that their continued validity for the subsequent cases is meant to be implied if by no means obvious. But the *preceding* cases are difficult to include in such tacit textual continuity. Ultimately our synchronic method finds a limit here. We find information in case (vi) whose pervasive validity for the whole series seems required by halakhah, but would be implied in the textual arrangement only if it appeared in case (i). This points to a disparate historical origin for the two sub-sections of the series.[52]

Ellipsis between case schemata does not work without regard to a proper understanding of the substance of the law. For information that has become irrelevant is also not mentioned again. Some situational features drop out of the picture by being dropped from the text; while others are, by the same mechanism *qua* ellipsis, taken to be continuous. In our Table 1 the transition from case (ii) to (iii) can be seen to illustrate this. Creating a *fait acompli* is not mentioned in again in (iii) because it is not in fact part of the situation in (iii). We have indicated this fact in the table by using the word 'off'. *This* failure to repeat information means: it is not valid in (iii). Rather case (iii) goes back to the basic structure in (i) and presupposes only *its* features through ellipsis (four brothers, two married to two sisters, the two husbands die). So we have two types of non-mentioned features in the same protasis, those which are 'switched off' and those which are 'continuous'. At this point the reader is expected to be able to revert to the starting protasis in (i) as somehow basic and decode the protases (iii) to (v) by adding their new features to the basic situation, not to the expanded version in (ii). For our case at least it seems that variation achieved through the addition (rather than the replacement) of factors (see above) can be ignored for the purposes of ellipsis. In any case the user of the Mishnah is educated to expect a rhythm of expansion and contraction between the situational features of neighbouring case schemata where the halakhah requires it. The scope for repeated experiences with this structure within the Mishnah is provided by its large size and its relatively homogeneous literary nature. However, the same training in reading the Mishnah can also be achieved by instruction provided within the context of its use.

As we just saw ellipsis creates ambiguity. But it also makes a positive contribution to the task of understanding the progression of cases. According to the

52 Different origins are assumed for different coherence reasons by Neusner, *History of the Mishnaic Law of Women*, i, 62; see also note 36 above. Also, cases (i) and (ii) recur elsewhere in the Mishnah (mEd. 5:5), and case (xii) is identical with mEd. 4:9.

Table 1
mYev. 3:1–7: Parameters from case schema to case schema

Case schema	No. of brothers	No. of brothers married to related wives	No. of related wives; nature of relationship	Person dying first	Levirate marriage performed (earlier marriage dissolved)	No. of women related to surviving brother(s)	Nature of that relation	Person dying second	Status of 3rd brother
(i)	4	2	2 sisters	2 sisters' husbands	A				
(ii)	E	E	E	E	consummation	A			
(iii)	E	E	E	E	(off)	1	biblical	A	
(iv)	E	E	E	E	(off)	E	rabbinic	A	
(v)	E	E	E	E	(off)	2	biblical	A	
(vi)	3	2	2 sisters	2 sisters' husbands	A				
(vii)	E	E	woman + daughter	E	(A)				
(viii)	E	E	+ daughter of daughter	E	(A)				
(ix)	E	E	+ daughter of son	E	(A)				
(x)	E	E	E	E		1	biblical	A	
(xi)	E	E	E	E		E	rabbinic	A	

(xii)	3	2	2 sisters	one sister's husband	betrothal		2nd sister's husband	unmarried	A
(xiii)	3	2	2 sisters	one sister's husband	consummation		husband of non-related woman	married to non-related woman	A
(xiv)	E	E	E	E	betrothal		E	E	A
(xv)	3	2	2 sisters	3rd brother	consummation		new husband of non-related woman	married to non-related woman	A
(xvi)	E	E	E	E	betrothal		E	E	A
(xvii)	3	2	2 sisters	one sister's husband	consummation		the other sister	married to non-related woman	A
(xviii)	3	2	2 sisters	3rd brother	divorce of one of the sisters		new husband of non-related woman	married to non-related woman	A

E = ellipsis; A = point at which the apodosis appears

principle of minimal potentially critical difference the user of the Mishnah is expected to scrutinize two neighbouring case schemata for the crucial difference in the situation. Ellipsis helps in this process precisely because the situational features which remain the same are not verbalized again. In other words there is less text which needs to be scrutinized. In extreme cases of ellipsis *only* what is different in the protasis is at all represented by text of the subsequent case schema of which our units (ii), (iv), (xiv) and (xvi) are good examples. Ellipsis is not merely a presentational means of economy; it can direct a spotlight on the minimal difference and thus on the progress from case to case.

5 Progressive differentiation: the conceptual input

The situational features mentioned in neighbouring protases vary according the difference they make for the apodosis – that defines the Mishnaic form with which we are concerned here. What then *are* these variations in more abstract terms? If we start from the example in mYev. 3 we can identify the following situational parameters (in the sequence of their appearance, cf. Table 1): numbers of persons involved; their family status; death as an event, and acts (of marriage, betrothal, divorce) performed. Variation occurs within these parameters and is strictly defined according to a fairly small number of conventions or categories. This restriction leads us to the core of our question, for it is this restriction which excludes irrelevant acts like 'gaining weight' mentioned above.

Family ties between the persons in our case schemata are obviously crucial to the whole thematic framework, and so is the event 'death'. In what sense is death actually contributing to mYev. 3:1–7? Only one aspect of death is treated, namely that the death of a brother creates in the rabbinic view *ipso facto* a marriage-like relationship between the widow and the surviving brother. So the topic of death is placed within the theme of levirate ties.[53] Other family ties turn up at several nodal points of the tree structure: the two brothers themselves; their wives; any pre-existent relation of the widows to the surviving brother(s), in (iii)–(v) and (x)–(xi); and the separation of rabbinic definitions of family ties from biblical ones. As for the actions taken, they are strictly limited to those directly linked to the thematic framework of family ties. Only three different acts are considered: betrothal, consummation of levirate marriage, and divorce, the latter only appearing in (xviii). Consummation appears first in case (ii) and betrothal in (xii). Fig. 1 shows that the differences between these two pairs of categories: consummation *versus* betrothal, biblically

[53] There are a number of diverse and important halakhic effects of death, for example in the realms of impurity, inheritance law, mourning rites, etc. These other effects are totally excluded from mention in mYev. 3, a manifestation of its strict thematic focus.

versus rabbinically prohibited incest, account for the distinguishing factor in about half of the case schemata in the series. The opposition between the members of these pairs thus accounts for many of the oppositions in neighbouring apodoses. They are in fact conceptually fixed binary oppositions and as such have the potential of recurring elsewhere in the Mishnah, including other case schema series. The general importance of binary oppositions and other paradigms of opposition in the structure of Mishnaic halakhah goes beyond their role in the arrangement of case schemata.

Let us turn to those elements in the situation which do not depend on fixed legal categories. Here we come to the numerical constitution of hypothetical situations. In our example we find what looks like the *smallest* set of numbers which will express the problems. The case schemata envisage two brothers married to two sisters: no smaller number of either would allow the main problem to appear, namely that the two widows whom a person might be obliged to marry are already related *to each other*. The nature of the problem is set up by the *obligation* to marry a deceased brother's widow (if he died childless). Our whole series explores what is supposed to happen when two norms come into conflict due to circumstances: the prohibition to marry two sisters and the obligation of levirate marriage. First two surviving brothers then one surviving brother is assumed; again the numbers are the minimum necessary for each halakhic problem. In other words, if we assumed cases with larger numbers, say three brothers married to three sisters, it is suggested that their apodoses could be ascertained with the help of the principles embodied in the 'two-brother-two-sister' cases as given. Two things emerge from this. First, the series of case schemata chooses the lowest numbers necessary for exhibiting the logic of halakhah.[54] Second, purely numerical variations (or multiples) are not presented.

We said above that the progression is not hierarchical. It also does not have a natural point of completion or a *telos*. At which point a series of case schemata comes to an end is not determined by the literary form itself unless it is generated by the mathematical permutation of a number of fixed situational parameters.[55] Very likely some sort of judgement is involved on the side of the Mishnaic author in terminating the series that all the main halakhic principles and categories have been sufficiently exhibited, singly or in their interaction. Further complicating factors can in principle always be added to the current end-point of any series or placed at the nodal points of a tree structure such as presented in Fig. 1. We observed at the start of our investigation that the grammatically complete case schema is a semi-independent literary unit. The open-ended nature of a series consisting of case schemata is directly linked to this independence. A case schemata can appear at any point in the series,

---

[54] For an example of a case schema series whose progress is regulated by a numerical progression in the protases, see mBer. 7:3.

[55] More on this below, in section 8.

including its end, without necessarily changing its format. As far as its formulation is concerned each complete case schema is its own end-point, the beginning and end of a self-contained conditional structure. This self-sufficiency accounts for much of the character of the Mishnaic text with the case schema providing a basic component for agglutinating structures or textual parataxis.[56]

6 General and particular in the case schema

The case schema itself tends to produce a see-saw movement between the specific and the general. The protasis envisages a concrete situation and enumerates the relevant features of that situation. To be sure these features are already highly schematized and selected as the preceding section illustrated. Persons are reduced to halakhic roles (brother, sister, unrelated wife); events are reduced to specific halakhic consequences (death); actions are restricted to a very small universe of related categories (betrothal, consummation, divorce). All of these situational parameters are reduced to the bare minimum. And yet the number of factors to be taken account of in the protases is quite substantial, even in its most basic form as in case (i). And once the factor of timing (of multiple deaths) is introduced the picture given in the protasis is fairly complex. To the (increasing) complexity of the protases, the apodoses provide a *basso continuo* of simplicity. Not only are the apodoses comparatively brief, their categories remain largely continuous within the same halakhic field. They tend to be either special terms belonging to that field such as 'to take in levirate marriage', *Ḥalitsah*, 'to consummate', 'bill of divorce' or 'to send away'. Or they are terms with a near-universal function in the Mishnaic discourse such as 'forbidden' and 'allowed' (אסור and מותר) in case (iii). In general apodoses are not necessarily shorter and more constant in their concepts than protases, but for pairs or series of case schemata this seems to be the case.[57] The complexity of the situational factors, already simplified to meet abstract requirements is thus reduced further when it comes to the halakhic categories which the apodosis pronounces. The contrast between the complexity of the protasis and the briefness and generality of the apodosis is often more pronounced than in our series, in particular where binary oppositions such as 'forbidden–allowed' or 'clean–unclean' provide the main terms for the apodosis.[58] Through their apodosis

[56] It thus also provides an ideal structure for 'docking on' further material, because their own shape need not be modified to accommodate amplifications. On this see my "Delaying the Progress from Case to Case". On textual agglutination, see above note 13.

[57] Sometimes, one protasis is given *several* apodoses to show what its consequences are across a range of different halakhic topics. An example of this may be found in mḤal. 1:8 where a certain type of dough (= protasis) is judged to be liable to dough offering (= apodosis). But then further apodoses are attached to the same protasis, determining the status of that dough with regard to Sabbath laws, blessings, the preparation of food on a holiday and the Passover laws.

[58] Note the simplicity as well as regular *alternation* of the terms 'liable' and 'free' in the apodoses of mB.Q. 3:5, quoted below in section 8, and note 68.

specifically, hypothetical legal cases impose an order on complex facts. Ultimately, the halakhic categories can take care of all eventualities; and every new case schema confirms that nothing under the sun escapes the halakhic order.[59] From this perspective the academic nature of many case schemata gains a new dimension apart from showing that a principle may be developed for its own sake (see above). The far-fetched case – if appreciated as such by the reader – also demonstrates emphatically, by the very improbability of its occurrence, the depth of penetration of the halakhic order. Apodoses provide standard conceptual pigeon-holes into which reality – tendentially all reality – can be sorted. The comprehensive power of this order is one of the implicit messages of the series of case schemata and generally a message of the case schema as a pervasive form in the Mishnah. In it, the crucial role of conceptual categories in the halakhic description of a world comes to the surface, as it does in that other important format of halakhah, the list (see section 8 below).[60]

There is an infinite number of possible situations. But there is only a finite number of halakhic categories ordering these situations. The number is in fact very small in comparison with the complexity of the world as reflected in ordinary language. The identity and number of possible apodoses is fixed by the halakhic system; it is fixed in advance of any increase or future variation of protases, of which modern phenomena such as electricity or life-support machines provide examples. Electricity (say in the context of Sabbath laws) introduces a new term into the language of protases thus creating new case schemata. But it does not effect a corresponding increase in the terms of apodoses. The power of order increases and becomes more restrictive over time for the same reason. If new apodoses are being introduced into the system at all, they are not subject to the laws of contingent variation. The ordering imposed on the world by halakhah depends on the fact that the categories are dramatically fewer than the possible facts (and it is the *possible* facts that the case schemata deal with). This is also the reason why it can be less

[59] Perhaps that is the underlying sense of the demonstrative 'behold' (הרי) which introduces several apodoses in our series. On the Mishnah's suggestion of comprehensive order, cf. Neusner, *Formative Judaism*, 126f.; 129f.; *History of the Mishnaic Law of Purities*, xxi, 311f.

[60] Neusner has often emphasized the imposition of order achieved through the patterned language of the Mishnah (e.g. *Formative Judaism*, 123–5; *Memorized Torah*, note 10 above, 111ff.; *History of the Mishnaic Law of Purities*, xxi, note 6 above, 307f., 311f.). However, from early on Neusner treats this implicit ordering as philosophical in nature (*Memorized Torah*, 146f.; *History of the Mishnaic Law of Purities*, xxii, e.g. p. xii), and speaks of Mishnaic 'philosopher-legislators' (*History of the Mishnaic Law of Women*, i, p. x; see also *History of the Mishnaic Law of Purities*, xxi, pp. xii, 308). But in philosophy conceptual *explicitness* plays a crucial role. And, while any sustained verbalization of reality is bound to have philosophical or 'ontological' implications of one sort or another, that fact alone does not make all discourse philosophical ('language becomes ontology', *Memorized Torah*, 128; cf. *History of the Mishnaic Law of Purities*, xxii, 97f.; 109; 133). In order to provide an explicit, conceptual account of the Mishnaic 'truths' (*op. cit.*, 261), Neusner needs to speak a wholly different language from that of the Mishnah itself. His rendering is indeed profoundly influenced by the language of Western philosophy and science, using terms such as 'system', 'unity', 'human will', 'purpose of man', 'fact', 'truth', 'power of the decisive and uncompelled mind of man', 'rational meanings', and 'irrational compulsions' (all found within one paragraph, *ibid.*). We shall address the implicitness of principles in the Mishnah further in section 9 below.

straightforward to arrange case schemata according to their apodosis than according to their protasis. For normally many more protases go with one apodosis than apodoses (in distinct halakhic fields) with one protasis (see below section 8). On the other hand, a series of case schemata as defined by our principle of minimal potentially critical difference provides such order directly.

When stressing the reductive ordering achieved by the apodosis we should recall that the protasis itself is already a schematic and abstract view of reality, heavily selective in its features and presenting them in the most basic terms possible. Also we should note that each case schema stands in for a large number of slight variations of the same basic situation, etc. In fact the halakhic categories already permeate the way the situation is described not merely its normative treatment: the basics to which the situation is reduced in the protasis are its features as relevant in halakhah.

7 The case schema as problem and question

There is a basic tension in all such claims of order, whether implicit or explicit. The imposition of order is a dynamic cultural activity in which any new situational factor to be envisaged is something of a challenge or a problem.[61] The halakhic discourse can in fact be conceived of as problem-oriented, somewhat parallel to the way in which modern scientific discourse is problem-oriented. For instance case (xii) above presents a situation whose selection seems designed to raise and answer a specific problem (and this is how we explained it in section 3 above). But the problem-based approach is not restricted to single cases. The underlying question of our series is: how can the obligations of levirate marriage be reconciled with pre-existing family ties which might have the effect of prohibiting marriage? The whole series is devoted to this tension or intellectual challenge. It addresses a problem, namely that of potentially contradictory effects of following two accepted norms, by selecting cases in which these norms come into play simultaneously. Cases in which there is no conflict of norms do not come into view. Our series shows how the halakhic categories provide a decision for many of the theoretically possible cases (embodying basically the principle that the incest laws take priority over the obligation of levirate

[61] The notion that the Mishnah's discourse is in major parts formed by a 'generative problematic' is pervasive in Neusner's work; see for example "History and Structure: The Case of Mishnah" (note 6 above), 163–5. And he correctly stresses the Mishnah's interest in the 'moment of disorder' (*Formative Judaism*, 134). However, he distinguishes 'theme' from 'problematic' (thus differentiating elements which are combined in our notion of 'coherence'). He defines 'problematic' as a non-biblical principle running through the whole Mishnaic treatment of the theme and thinks there can be tractates which are 'defined by theme and not by problematic' ("History and Structure", 169f.; see also 172, 175; *History of the Mishnaic Law of Purities*, xxii, 88f.; *History of the Mishnaic Law of Women*, i, 3.

marriage).[62] Many cases in the Mishnah embody such an approach to halakhah as solving problems or regulating the problematical interaction between laws. Another problem-generating dynamic is the exploration of entities in the world which fall between two legal categories (for example, the *ṭumṭum*, i.e. the person of uncertain sex).[63] Again the concern is with the *problematical* case. In emphasizing this aspect we position Mishnaic halakhah in a matrix of some importance for the history and comparison of cultures or discourses.[64]

Many case schemata thus testify to an attitude which selects the *problem* as the main driving force of the discourse. This means they can in principle be read as anticipating an objection or answering an unspoken challenge. The voice which speaks in the Mishnah can be interpreted as being both the problem-poser and the problem-solver. This internal dialogical nature which of course requires alert and active participation of the reader,[65] is again quite typical of certain types of modern scholarly discourse. In the Mishnah the bipolar perspective of problem-solving does not remain implicit. It manifests itself for example by a separation into different voices when a dispute is presented. The frequent use of questions (raised and answered by the main voice of the Mishnah) also serves to create a texture of multiple inner perspectives. There is thus an underlying connection between the Mishnaic preference for the case schema on the one hand and a number of polyphonic or dialogical[66] text structures on the other.

8 The series of case schemata and the list

Increasing the differentiation of the situational factors in the protasis is only one way of arranging case schemata in a thematically coherent manner. Another principle which produces series of usually four case schemata is the permutation of two situational parameters. An example of this appears as sub-set in our tree structure for mYev. 3:1–7 (see Fig. 1). All combinatory possibilities are tested for two pairs of parameters: one of the sisters' husbands dies first *versus* the brother married to the unrelated woman dies first; and: the surviving party betroths *versus* consummates.

---

62 Cf. the second principle articulated by Maimonides in his *Commentary* (tr. Qafih, ad mYev. 1:1, p. 7; see note 28 above).

63 The *ṭumṭum* plays the role of complicating additional factor in a series of case schemata at mB.B. 9:2, for example. The frequent Mishnaic concern with (awkward) timing is also geared towards producing similar borderline cases.

64 I have only indirectly encountered that matrix, which is located in a contemporary discourse influenced by ethnology, cultural history, discourse analysis and philosophy. Cf. the distinction between 'problematic' and 'theorematic' in G. Deleuze and F. Guattari, *Nomadology.:The War Machine*, tr. B. Massumi, New York 1986, 19.

65 Cf. Neusner, *Formative Judaism*, 128f.

66 The dialogical nature of rabbinic literature is even more explicit in later texts; see for example A. Goldberg, "Stereotype Diskurse in den frühen Auslegungsmidrashim", *FJB*, 16 (1988), 23–51; now reprinted in Goldberg, *Rabbinische Texte als Gegenstand der Auslegung* (note 5 above), 242–62.

The four possible combinations provide a mini-series consisting of cases (xiii) to (xvi). There are many instances of such combinatory sets in the Mishnah which exhaust the combinatory possibilities offered by situational parameters subject to binary variation.[67] Here is another example:

mB.Q. 3:5
(i) The one [person] comes with his jar, and the other comes with his beam: if the vessel of the one was broken by the beam of the other,
 the latter is free [from liability],
  for the one had the right of way and the other had the right of way.
(ii) If the owner of the beam was first [if one walked behind the other], and the owner of the jar second, and the jar was broken by the beam,
 he [the owner of the beam] is free.
(iii) If the owner of the beam stood [suddenly],
 he is liable.
(iv) If he said to the owner of the jar, 'Stand' [before stopping]
 he is free.
(v) If the owner of the jar was first and the owner of the beam second, and the jar was broken by the beam,
 he [the owner of the beam] is liable.
(vi) If he owner of the jar stood [suddenly],
 he [the owner of the beam] is free.
(vii) If he said to the owner of the beam, 'Stand!'
 he [the owner of the beam] is liable.

After all we have said so far, the serial nature of this textual progression stands out clearly and requires no explanation as such. What interests us here is the division of the series into two symmetrical sub-sections from (ii), depending on whether the owner of the beam (ii) or the owner of the jar (v) goes first. These two sections are further subdivided for another situational parameter: whether or not the accident occurred in movement or whether the person going first suddenly stopped. And in turn, both of these situations – cases (iii) and (vi) – are further modified by one additional factor, namely whether a warning was spoken or not thus yielding cases (iv) and (vii). The overall structure is only partly one of progressive differentiation, i.e. achieved by the addition of new situational factors. More basic to the understanding of the series is the *permutation* of the two basic binary oppositions 'person causing/suffering the damage' and 'person walking first/second'. The resulting series is of mathematical clarity.

In this context it may be worth supplementing our remarks on ellipsis and pronouns in section 4 above. It is clear from a series such as mB.Q. 3:5 that the use of non-specific pronouns or pronominal suffixes can be taken far in such Mishnaic passages. Determining which of the two persons is the English 'he', which represents a

[67] Such sets of case schemata also play an important role in integrating scriptural information into the halakhic discourse of the Mishnah. See on this chapter 4 in my *Rabbinic Interpretation of Scripture in the Mishnah*, note 23 above (the Topic2 resource). See also the first passage discussed in my "Delaying the Progress from Case to Case".

similar pronominal structure in the Hebrew, is quite impossible in some sentences unless its position in the sequence is 'read' as part of their meaning. So the logic of the series is presupposed in this ambiguous employment of pronouns and pro-forms[68] just as it is presupposed for the proper decoding of ellipsis.

Case schemata enter into coherence relationships not just with other case schemata but with a variety of other Mishnaic literary forms. Perhaps the most important among them is the list.[69] In cases (vi) to (ix) quoted above (mYev. 3:4), a number of alternative protases are linked to the same apodosis. This is in effect a list structure, placed into the framework of a protasis–apodosis dependency. But a large number of Mishnaic lists have no formal link to the case schema at all and yet are related to it by way of the type of information that is conveyed. Lists of this type start with a halakhic evaluation, categorization or consequence, i.e. the material which we have seen contained in the apodosis. This 'apodosis' component of the list names the class whose members are listed or functions as a list heading. The items grouped together under that heading on the other hand can be understood as short descriptions of situations, i.e. they correspond to so many protases. Looking at the following passage will help us understand this correspondence.

> mTer. 1:1
> Five [persons] cannot separate a heave offering, and if they did separate [it], their heave offering is no heave offering: the deaf-mute, the imbecile, the minor, he who gives heave offering from what is not his, and the non-Jew [...].

The list says that heave offering separated by persons falling under one of the enumerated categories is invalid. If we transform this information into a conditional structure we obtain:

> If a deaf-mute, an imbecile, a minor, a person offering from what is not his, or a non-Jew [...] separate heave offering, their separation is invalid.

At this point we have something resembling cases (vi) to (ix) of our main series above, dealing with levirate marriage (mYev. 3:4). If we now spell out the individual case schemata we obtain the following:

> (i) If a deaf-mute separates a heave offering,
> his separation is invalid.
> (ii) If an imbecile separates a heave offering,
> his separation is invalid.

68 The terms 'free' and 'liable' are such more general pro-forms; for serial apodoses in the Mishnah, they can function like 'to do' in English, i.e. stand in for much more specific verbs or messages mentioned only at the beginning of the series; on 'to do', cf. Beaugrande and Dressler, *Introduction to Text Linguistics* (note 1 above), 62f.

69 It is largely due to the work of Neusner that the importance of lists in the Mishnaic discourse is now recognized (although the phenomenon is far from being comprehensively understood, I think); see for example his "The Mishnah's Generative Mode of Thought: *Listenwissenschaft* and Analogical-Contrastive Reasoning", *JAOS*, 110 (1990), 317–21; cf. also his *History of the Mishnaic Law of Purities*, xxi, 191ff.

(iii) If a minor separates a heave offering,
his separation is invalid.
(iv) If a person separating from what is not his separates a heave offering,
his separation is invalid.
(v) If a non-Jew...separates a heave offering,
his separation is invalid.

So the list in mTer. 1:1 can quite easily be transformed into a cluster of five case schemata, *all of which have the same apodosis*. For such a grouping textual coherence would reside primarily in the apodoses, not in the mutual relationship of the the protases. As we said in section 2 above this is one theoretical option open to the Mishnah; but the list is a wholly different form from the case schema, singly or in groups. Also, it must be stressed that there are different types of list in the Mishnah. Far from all of them lend themselves to this transformation. Yet the question of the textual interaction between lists and case schemata seems a useful one to pursue.

In cases where an identical apodosis is used as the focal point of a cluster of case schemata there is nothing further in the apodosis to distinguish them from each other and no principle of serialization can arise from the apodosis – it merely provides identity, no differentiation or progression. A further principle, linked to the theme of the protases, is necessary if any further order is to be created in the material sharing the same apodosis. An example of this in list-form is provided by mMak. 3. This passage starts with the list heading: 'These are those that are lashed',[70] followed by an enumeration of more than fifty transgressions. The sequence of these transgressions, each representing the sort of information which could also be found in a protasis, follows a secondary, internal order. So we can understand a certain type of Mishnaic list as a very *economic* device for conveying information that could also be presented as a cluster of case schemata with the same apodosis.[71] It should here be mentioned that our main example for a series of case schemata mYev. 3 might be interpreted as unified by a *near-identical apodosis*. This is how Jacob Neusner explains the relationship between chapter 3 of Yevamot and its surrounding larger textual units. He groups the material in terms of the following *apodosis*-clusters: 'neither levirate marriage nor *Ḥalitsah*', '*Ḥalitsah* but no levirate marriage' (= mYev. 3), and 'levirate marriage'.[72]

70 This is the halakhic evaluation which corresponds to the apodosis.

71 Since at least the one-sentence list is one grammatical unit (not several), it does not offer the correspondence of thematic and textual proximity which is our theme in this paper. Also, the function of such a list is clearly different from that of a 'pair' or 'series' of case schemata as here defined (i.e. the exhibition of a legal principle), which is why we speak instead of clusters or groups of case schemata. It is also clear that the protasis-type information must be capable of very brief expression in order to become an item in a list; at least some of the protases cited in this paper would be extremely difficult to sum up in a word or even a short clause.

72 *History of the Mishnaic Law of Women*, i, 6ff.

9 The implicitness of universal principles in the Mishnah

We have spoken about the 'logic' or progression of the case schemata and we have tried to show what mechanisms allow their textual arrangement to exhibit underlying legal principles. We now have to address the question: what do the regularities of textual coherence tell us about the substantive nature of the halakhah? First we need to say that the principles of law are only rarely articulated in the Mishnah, but of the apparent exceptions a considerable proportion is found at the end of series of case schemata (in particular shorter series). Here is an example:

> mNed. 11:9
> 'And the vow of a widow and a divorced woman, all that she has imposed on herself, it shall stand against her' (Num. 30:10). How? (i) If she said, Behold I shall be a Nazir after thirty days have passed, even if she was married [again] within thirty days, he [the new husband] cannot revoke her vow. (ii) If she vowed while under the authority of her husband he can revoke it: If she said, Behold, I shall be a Nazir after thirty days have passed, even if she was widowed or divorced within thirty days, behold her vow remains revoked. (iii) If she vowed, was divorced, and received back [by her husband] all on the same day, he cannot revoke it. This is the general rule: If she went out to be under her own authority [even] for one hour [while her vow is still operative], he cannot revoke her vow.

The case schemata are clearly selected and arranged so as to form a series: the *content* of the vow is so chosen that the time of making it is separated from the time of its coming into effect. The contrast between cases (i) and (ii) can thus be used to show that it is the woman's status at the former time, not at the latter which is decisive. Case (iii) shows that even a period of the woman's independence intervening between two spells of being under the authority of the *same* husband on the *same* day (cf. Num. 30:6 and mNed. 10:8) has the effect of making revocation impossible in the second spell. It is at this is the point at which we find the 'general rule' (כלל), speaking of 'an hour'. This rule points to the principle behind each of the three cases and thus explicates why they are selected and arranged as they are. This rule could also be used as an introduction to this series of case schemata. In that case they would function as *illustrations* of the rule. Even coming *after* the series the 'general rule' can have the effect of turning them into illustrations. But the real question is: what if the sentence containing the 'general rule' were absent from the text? Would we, despite this absence, understand that some such principle is in fact implied in the *series* of case schemata simply by considering them in their interdependence? I think the answer is yes. And it is probably fair to say that the cumulative effect of pairs and series of case schemata in the Mishnah is to encourage the reader to look always beyond the actual case to the principle behind it. And in many cases like in our main example mYev. 3:1–7 the Mishnah itself gives no statement of that principle. In the course of discussing the logic of the series from section 3 above onwards, we made several suggestions as what that principle is. We said, for example, that the series embodies 'the principle that the incest laws take priority over the obligation of levirate marriage' (in section 7). But that is *our* formulation; the Mishnah does not enunciate the principle that drives the series. This absence of an articulation of principles of law is very common and not restricted to case schemata. Even where seemingly comprehensive principles or reasons for halakhic evaluations are given they may not in fact be comprehensive at all, but only valid for some segment of halakhah whose limits are left undefined.[73] Let us look again at one apparently universal 'reason' encountered in the course of our series in mYev. 3. It appears in case (xvii), which addresses the situation of the widowed brother of one sister after the second sister has twice been widowed. Can he take her in levirate marriage? The answer is negative:

> behold this woman [the surviving sister] is forbidden to him [the only surviving brother] for ever,
> since she was forbidden to him for an hour.

This reason 'since she was forbidden to him for an hour' strongly resembles what is called a 'general rule' in the passage we have quoted from mNed. 11:9. It is certainly formulated without any restriction. But the woman in question was 'forbidden' in two quite different halakhic contexts. As the wife of his brother she was already forbidden to him 'for an hour', namely when her husband was still alive. As his 'brother's wife' she falls under a basic biblical prohibition.[74] That is obviously not what our reason-clause in (xvii) intends for that would remove the possibility of levirate marriage as such. The Mishnah has in view a much more specific circumstance which could only arise *after* the death of the brother, namely that both the man's own wife and her sister (as widow) are alive at the same time. That is the 'hour' in which the widow was forbidden to him and that is the prohibition whose effect is declared to be eternal.[75] The formulation of the reason, if taken in isolation, is ambiguous and can thus be *false*. Its intent can therefore not be 'absolute' or 'general' but needs to be taken in its narrower halakhic context. But how is that thematic context known? By the position of this reason-clause in the *text* of the Mishnah, namely appended to a case schemata which is part of a series concerned with what happens after the sister has been widowed. The ambiguity causing the problem only arises when the reason-clause is separated from the surrounding text, the co-text. Its formulation does not cater for that

[73] See also my "Delaying the Progress from Case to Case".

[74] Lev. 18:16: 'Do not uncover the nakedness of your brother's wife; it is the nakedness of your brother.' The validity of this norm is presupposed in rabbinic family halakhah in various places in the Mishnah.

[75] Such an understanding is expressed, for example, in Rashi's talmudic commentary (mYev. 30a), addressing precisely this question: which is the 'hour' talked about here? The fundamental tension between the prohibition 'brother's wife' and the commandment of levirate marriage is indirectly addressed in a number of rabbinic passages, for example yNed. 3:2 (ed. Krotoshin, 37d) and *Mekhilta de-Rabbi Ishmael* ad Ex. 20:8 (ed. J. Z. Lauterbach, Philadelphia 1933, ii, 252).

eventuality: not all information necessary to take the rule in isolation is verbalized despite the fact that the unrestricted formulation suggests just that. No attempt is made to ensure that the formulation is accurate regardless of context, i.e. general. It cannot be separated safely from the case schema (or a series of case schemata) to which it is attached and for which it provides a principle. Such dependency on the co-text can be observed for many apparently general reasons or principles in the Mishnah. Without any express restriction they are in fact limited in their validity by local halakhic structures or contexts. There can even be something of a conflict between the formulation and the actual scope of the principle, namely when the principle is *declared* to be a 'general rule' (זה הכלל) while its validity is known to be limited from other Mishnaic passages. Thus textual coherence in a sense takes priority over express surface meaning in the Mishnah, because the former can turn out to *limit* the latter at any time.

We need to see this phenomenon in the context of the overall weakness or absence of universal principles in the Mishnah. There is no part of the document (or of each tractate) devoted to collecting and articulating all the legal principles relevant to a halakhic theme.[76] This means that case schemata, insofar as they are selected and arranged into series and thus have a 'logic' are not an additional, redundant treatment of the principles. They are *the only* such treatment for considerable parts of the halakhic material. The textual arrangement of case schemata thus becomes *primary* evidence for quite a large number of the abstract underlying principles of halakhah. But this evidence does not consist of their verbalization. Instead it lies in the coherence relationships of pairs or series of case schemata. Where the Mishnah chooses not to articulate the legal principle which informs a series of case schemata it prefers *textual structures* of conveyance to *verbal formulation*. Why this should be so is a question of great importance for an historical understanding of early rabbinic Judaism, but I cannot answer it.[77] One point however needs to be stressed. If there is no verbal formulation then any articulation of the principle is *not Mishnaic*. Responsibility for its accuracy rests with the reader and user of the Mishnah, not with the Mishnah itself. The Mishnah itself provides a dynamic structure, a complex textual interdependence. That interplay is open to different interpretations and thus to different verbal articulations of the underlying legal principle. The hermeneutic work which the Mishnah thus requires for core aspects of halakhah introduces a dynamic

[76] The opening sections of Maimonides *Commentary on the Mishnah* (note 28 above) for each of the tractates show what it is that the Mishnah itself does *not* provide. Maimonides often – and his commentary on mYev. 1:1 illustrates this – formulates the legal principles which he considers to be basic to the understanding of the tractate and to which he can make reference throughout the commentary proper. Most modern commentators do the same.

[77] I have made some tentative suggestions in "Delaying the Progress from Case to Case", and also in *Rabbinic Interpretation of Scripture in the Mishnah*, chapter 15. While unable to improve on these suggestions, I have become even more acutely aware of their inadequacy.

element[78] into the halakhic discourse as such. And the hermeneutic process itself can be kept open because no result of its interpretation can ever receive the Mishnah's own seal of approval. It is precisely the absence of formulations which requires the readers to provide their own formulations.

This leads us to a central tension in the rabbinic cultural activity called 'halakhah'. On the one hand halakhah is the work of imposing conceptual order on a multi-faceted world (our topic in section 6) and that work has far-reaching effects of reduction, rigidity and exclusion. On the other hand there is something of a refusal or reluctance to place a cap on this work or to perform the task *once and for all*. The Mishnah makes no attempt to present or to claim to have presented the comprehensive, exhaustive, total picture of the world reduced to its halakhic order. The choice of a contextual, 'casuistic' approach to law is a manifestation of this because it is combined with an absence of reliably universal principles. The case schema is always, by its very nature, partial, limited, local, conditional. That is the price which it pays for bearing an authoritative decision for the small area of halakhah that it covers. And pairs or series of concrete case schemata may well be *mere* illustrations. But where the Mishnah gives no authoritative fixed formulation of what they are illustrations of, it denies the reader the right to leave the concrete case behind in favour of abstractions and absolute formulations. It seems that any historical appreciation of rabbinic halakhah as a whole must assign importance to this open-ended nature of its discourse.

78 There is some overlap between what I mean by 'dynamic' and what Max Kadushin characterized as the 'organic' nature of rabbinic thought. See his *The Rabbinic Mind*, 3rd edn, New York 1972; *Organic Thinking: A Study in Rabbinic Thought*, New York 1938. See more recently the work of Peter Ochs, for example "Rabbinic Process Theology", *JJTP*, 1 (1991), 141–77.

Appendix: The text of mYev. 3:1–7

(**i**) [In the case of] four brothers, two of them married to two [women who are] sisters [to each other]: [if] the two married to the sisters died [childless],

behold these [widows and siblings] perform *Ḥalitsah* and are not taken in levirate marriage [by the two surviving brothers].

(**ii**) If they [the surviving brothers] had already consummated [levirate marriage],

they must send [the women] away.

R. Eliezer says: As far as the House of Shammai is concerned, they can continue [the marriage]; and the House of Hillel say: They must send [them] away.

[3:2] (**iii**) If one of them [the widows] was forbidden to one [of the surviving brothers] by reason of the biblical norms of incest,

he is forbidden to her but allowed to her sister,

and the second [brother] is forbidden to both of them.

(**iv**) [If by reason of] the rabbinic norms of incest or priestly marriage constraints,

they [the widows] perform *Ḥalitsah*, and are not taken in levirate marriage.

[3:3] (**v**) If one of them [the widows] was forbidden to one [of the surviving brothers] by reason of the biblical norms of incest, and the second [widow] was forbidden to the other [surviving brother] by reason of the biblical norms of incest,

the one forbidden to the first is allowed to the second,

and the one forbidden to the second is allowed to the first.

This is what they have said (cf. mYev. 2:3): If the sister is [also] her sister-in-law, she may either perform *Ḥalitsah* or be taken in levirate marriage.

[3:4] (**vi**) [In the case of] **three** brothers, two of them married to two [women who are] sisters, (**vii**) or to a woman and her daughter, (**viii**) or to a woman and her daughter's daughter, (**ix**) or to a woman and her son's daughter, and [if] the two who were married to the sisters died [childless],

behold, they must perform *Ḥalitsah* with him [the surviving brother] and are not taken in levirate marriage.

R. Shim'on exempts [them, even from performing *Ḥalitsah*].

(**x**) If one of them was forbidden to him by reason of the biblical norms of incest,

he is forbidden to her and allowed to her sister.

(**xi**) If forbidden by reason of the rabbinic norms of incest or priestly marriage constraints,

they perform *Ḥalitsah* and are not taken in levirate marriage.

[3:5] (**xii**) [In the case of] three brothers, two of them married to two [women who are] sisters, and one [brother] unmarried: [if] one of the husbands of the sisters died [childless], and the unmarried brother betrothed her, and thereafter his second brother died,

the House of Shammai say: his wife remains with him and the other one is released by reason of the 'sister of his wife' (משום אחות אשה);

and the House of Hillel say: He sends away his wife by bill of divorce and *Ḥalitsah*, and the wife of his [deceased] brother by *Ḥalitsah*.

This is the one about whom they have said (cf. mYev. 13:7): Woe to him because of his wife, and woe to him because of the wife of his brother.

[3:6] (**xiii**) [In the case of] three brothers, two of them married to two [women who are] sisters and one [brother] married to a woman who is not related [to the two sisters]: [if] one of the husbands of the sisters died [childless] and the one married to the woman who is not related consummated marriage with his [deceased brother's] wife and [then] died,

> the second [wife] is released by reason of the 'sister of his wife', and the first [unrelated wife] [is released] by reason of [having been] her 'co-wife'.

(**xiv**) If he [only] betrothed her and [then] died,

> the woman who is not related performs *Ḥalitsah* and is not taken in levirate marriage [by the surviving brother].

[3:7] (**xv**) [In the case of] three brothers, two of them married to two [women who are] sisters and one [brother] married to a woman who is not related: [if] the one married to the woman who is not related died [childless] and one of the husbands of the sisters consummated marriage with his wife and died,

> the first wife [of the latter] is released by reason of the 'sister of his wife', and the second by reason of [having been] her 'co-wife'.

(**xvi**) If he [only] betrothed her and [then] died,

> the woman who is not related performs *Ḥalitsah* and is not taken in levirate marriage.

(**xvii**) [In the case of] three brothers, two of them married to two sisters and one married to a woman who is not related: if one of the husbands of the sisters died and the one who is married to the unrelated woman consummated marriage with his widow, and the wife of the other brother [i.e. the second sister] died and afterwards the [brother] married to the unrelated woman died,

> behold this woman [the surviving sister] is forbidden to him [the only surviving brother] for ever,
>
> since she was forbidden to him for one hour.

(**xviii**) [In the case of] three brothers, two of them married to two sisters and one married to a woman who is not related: if one of the husbands of the sisters divorced his wife, and the one married to the woman who is not related died, and the divorced man consummated marriage with her [the unrelated woman] and died,

> this is the [woman] about whom they have said (cf. mYev. 1:1): And all of them, if they died (or exercised their right of refusal) or were divorced, their co-wives are permitted [to be taken in levirate marriage].

The defective marriage in classical Ḥanafī law
Issues of form and validity

Mona Siddiqui (University of Glasgow)

In the classical *fiqh* tradition, marriage laws are some of the most detailed examples of juristic reflection and ingenuity. Marriage is the only relationship sanctioned by the Qur'ān conferring mutual rights of sexual enjoyment between a man and woman where the financial obligations of dower, maintenance, and inheritance become binding. The marital relationship is viewed primarily as a contract between two parties and thus marriage in the classical *fiqh* tradition is defined for the most part using contract terminology. The word *'aqd* assumes the concept of the contract in *fiqh* works, although literally it means an obligation or an agreement binding two parties. It does not exist in this form in the Qur'ān, which, when it wishes to evoke the idea of a contract, uses the term *'ahd* for engagement, and *'uqda* for marriage. Chehata has pointed out that any theoretical discussion of the word 'contract' is absent from *fiqh* works in general.[1] The closest we arrive at a definition of the word *'aqd* and the purpose behind contracts in general, is contained in the *Fatḥ al-Qadīr*:

> The intention of a contract (*al-murād bi'l-'aqd*) is completion whether it be a marriage contract or otherwise comprising the offer of one of the two speakers followed by the acceptance of the other.[2]

As has been mentioned above, contract terminology defines much of the discussion around the legal institution of marriage. Many scholars have established that it is the contract of sale as elaborated within the classical texts, from which all other contracts in the classical tradition have drawn analogies and borrowed vocabulary. Joseph Schacht claims quite categorically:

> The core of the Islamic law of obligations ... [a]nd other contracts although regarded as legal institutions in their own rights are construed on the model of *bai'* or sale.[3]

Sale, according to the thirteenth-century jurist 'Abdallāh Mawṣilī, has the literal meaning of 'exchange' (*al-muṭlaq al-mubādala*). In a specifically *shar'ī* context, it means an exchange of *mutaqawwim* goods for *mutaqawwim* goods by way of transferring ownership (*tamlīk*) and taking possession (*tamalluk*).[4] That is to say, the

[1] C. Chehata, *Études de droit musulman*, Paris 1971, 157.
[2] Ibn al Humām, *al-Fatḥ al-Qadīr*, Cairo 1970, iii, 187.
[3] J. Schacht, *An Introduction to Islamic Law*, Oxford 1964, 151.
[4] 'Abdallah (b. Maḥmūd b. Mawdūd) al-Mawṣilī, *al-Ikhtiyār li-Ta'līl al-Mukhtār*, (repr.) Beirut 1975, 3.

goods must be capable of legal ownership and legal transfer. It is these very concepts of ownership and assumption of rights over a person which the author of the *Hidāya* takes to be key ones in defining marriage laws, and where the fundamental parallels lie:

> Marriage may be contracted by the use of the term *beeya*, or sale as if a woman were to say to a man, 'I have sold myself unto your hands', and this is approved because sale operates on the principle of a right to a person and a right in the person is the principle of a right to carnal conjunction.[5]
>
> And the contract is binding with words implying transfer of ownership, gift or sale; this is according to the *Hidāya*. And in like words implying purchase according to the *Fatāwā al-Qāḍī-Khān*.[6]

The sense of ownership would appear to be the fundamental basis of the contract:

> It is reported from Abū Ḥanīfa that whatever word creates ownership of person if applied to the case of a female slave, creates ownership of *nikāḥ* when applied to a free woman.[7]

It is primarily because the two concepts of transfer and possession are so intrinsic to the classical definition of the marriage contract, that marriage laws would be construed on principles analogous to the law of sale. Thus in many areas of discussion it is logical that the outward form and language used to bring into effect a valid sale is identical with that bringing into effect a valid marriage. For example, if we compare how the two contracts are formalized legally, we see that a verbal bilateral proposition and ratification are what lie at the basis of the contract:

> Sale is completed by declaration and acceptance, the speech of the first speaker of the contracting parties, being termed the declaration and that of the last speaker, the acceptance.[8]
>
> Marriage takes effect with offer and acceptance where both are expressed in the past or where one of them is expressed in the past and the other in another tense in the future.[9]

Within this bilateral agreement, the issue of intention also plays a role in defining the nature of the language used to bring about a marriage. Ḥanafī law claims that a marriage contract becomes valid whether the words express clearly (*ṣarīḥ*) or obliquely (*kināya*) an offer of marriage. If a man uses expressions that are *kināya* in a contract then his intention to marry the girl must be present for the contract to be valid. However, if he

---

[5] Burhān al-Dīn al-Marghinānī, *The Hedaya* (tr. Charles Hamilton), (repr.) Karachi 1989, 73.

[6] N. Burhānpūr, *al-Fatāwā ʿĀlamgīrī*, 3rd edn, 6 vols, Beirut 1973, 271. This text (also known as *Fatāwā Hindiyya*) was compiled in India during the years 1664–72 under the patronage of the Mughal emperor, ʿAwrangzib ʿĀlamgīr. Although several jurists were involved in the compilation of the text, Shaykh Niẓām Burhānpūr is credited with being the main jurist; thus he will be quoted henceforth as the 'author'. All references to this text in the article will take the form: Niẓām, *al-Fatāwā*.

[7] (Fakhr al-Dīn al-Ḥasan b. Manṣūr) Qāḍī-Khān al-Awzajandī, *Fatāwā al-Qāḍī-Khān*, Calcutta 1835, 904. Text and translation of volume i by M. Bahadur and W. Hussein, Lahore 1977.

[8] Hamilton, *Hedaya*, 361.

[9] Niẓām, *al-Fatāwā*, 270.

uses terms which are *ṣarīḥ*, then intention is irrelevant.[10] In the law of marriage vocabulary, that is, *kināya* is based largely on the concept of transfer of ownership and thus the general terminology used for transactions could constitute much of the necessary vocabulary. An interesting debate between the Shāfiʿī and Ḥanafī schools on this point is mentioned in the *Fatāwā al-Qāḍī-Khān*:

> And in the same way in which marriage is constituted by the use of the words *nikāḥ* [marriage] and *tazwīj* [giving in marriage], so it is constituted by the use of words which denote the creation of immediate ownership in the substance of a thing according to us, the Ḥanafites, as distinguished from the followers of Shāfiʿī (as for instance, words denoting gift or *hiba* or sale or *bayʿa*, which create ownership in the substance of the thing, as contra-distinguished from words which indicate ownership not in the substance of the thing but in the profits such as *ijāra* or lease).[11]

The sense of ownership based on bilateral agreement may come into effect through a variety of expressions as long as these words imply completion of the contract. A marriage contract is therefore not valid through words implying mere intention, and thus any sense of future time in the agreement would render the contract ineffective. An example of a valid contract would be:

> If a man said to her, 'I marry you for such and such', and she replied, 'I have accepted', the marriage is complete.[12]

Contracts that imply future time or insert conditions in the contract making it dependent on future events are known as *muḍāf* and *muʿallaq*, respectively. An example of a *muḍāf* contract is:

> The *muḍāf* contract is where a person should say, 'I have married you to her tomorrow', [and this] is not valid.[13]

Authoritative texts such as the *Fatāwā al-ʿĀlamgīrī* demonstrate the importance of choosing the right words to effect a valid contract of marriage, not only by providing examples in Arabic but also in Persian. Compare the following two phrases:

> Become mine! [And the woman replies], I have become [yours].
> Become my wife (*zan*)! I have become [your wife].[14]

Whereas the first phrase does not constitute a valid contract, the use of the word *zan* in the second phrase qualifies the contract. In this case, the man is seen to have specified the relationship he desires (i.e. to make the woman his wife). Again consider the following:

---

[10] Schacht, *Introduction*, 166.
[11] al-Awzajandī, *Fatāwā al-Qāḍī-Khan*, i, 904.
[12] N. Baillie, *A Digest of Muhammedan Law*, Lahore 1965, i, 14.
[13] *Ibid.*, 17.
[14] Niẓām, *al-Fatāwā*, 271.

> If a man should say to another, 'Give me your daughter', and he reply, 'I have given [her]', the contract is valid, even though the proposer has not actually said, 'I have accepted'.[15]

Since there is no word of acceptance, difference of opinion arose as to whether the above construction was too vague and that some reference to the word 'wife' (*zan*) should be obligatory:

> He must say '*as a wife*' and the other must say, 'I have given [her] *as a wife*'.[16]

If the word for 'wife' is not mentioned, then extra words must be added to the contract to carry explicit recognition of the man's intention to make the woman his wife. The sense of transfer of possession or status must also be implied using the Persian vocabulary:

> A man and a woman say in front of two witnesses in Persian, 'we are husband and wife'; the *nikāḥ* is not valid. If he says, 'This is my wife', and she says, 'This is my husband', and there has not actually been a *nikāḥ* preceding this, then the learned are disagreed upon the matter ... what is correct is that no marriage will take place.[17]

Dispute arises because in the first phrase there is no sense of a bilateral agreement even though the words 'husband' and 'wife' fully indicate the status that each person wishes to assume or has assumed. In the second phrase there is a slightly greater emphasis on a verbal agreement by each of the two parties. On this basis there are two ways of confirming the *nikāḥ*: the decision of the *qāḍī* is the first and secondly, if the man and the woman both answer in the affirmative to the following question by the witnesses, 'Did you make this contract?' This reveals that a mutual agreement expressed in front of witnesses has the force of transforming an assumed marital status into a legal marital contract; the *qāḍī*'s authority or presence at a marriage contract is therefore only optional, not indispensable.

It was stated at the outset of this article that when we compare contracts of marriage with those of sale there are various conceptual similarities. Certain concepts, however, occur in one contract and not in the other. One of them is that of option (*khiyār*). Options are an important part of the law of sale designed to enforce good faith between the two parties:

> Option is a power of cancellation, which may be reserved to either party in a contract of sale by express stipulation, and is allowed without stipulation to a

[15] *Ibid.*, 271.
[16] *Ibid.*, 271.
[17] *Ibid.*, 272.

> purchaser [of something] which he has not seen or which proves to be defective.[18]

Options have no place in marriage laws as they imply a sort of condition:

> There is no option of inspection, defect or approval in the contract of marriage whether the option is made by the man or the woman.[19]

What is implied is that neither a man nor a woman has the right to put forward conditions in the marriage contract with the assumption that if the conditions are not met, they have the option of rescinding the contract. If a condition is stated the contract is still valid, while the condition is regarded as null and void:

> If he does that, the contract is permitted and the condition is void.[20]

It is a curious phenomenon of the marriage contract that despite the intense verbal formalism, the addition of words that imply a condition does not affect the validity of the declaration; the conditional element is quite simply ignored. The conditions that one can make but which would bear no effect on the validity of the contract may be with reference to physical defects or concerned with physical attraction; all these conditions are void and the contract would still be operative:

> If one of the parties makes a condition regarding the other concerning freedom from blindness or paralysis or old age, or concerning the presence of beauty, or if the husband makes a condition of virginity in his wife, and it proves to be the opposite of that, no option is confirmed for either party according to the *Tatarkhāniyya*.[21]

The only exception which allows a woman to exercise a right of option is when the husband is physically incapable of consummating the marriage (i.e. he is either impotent or a eunuch). Since the legitimization of sexual intercourse is the principle upon which the whole contract rests, any impediment to this provides adequate grounds for rescission of the contract.

One significant area where the laws of marriage and sale share mutual terminology is in the division and assessment of contracts. Contracts may be categorized within a scale of legal validity. Of these categories, *ṣaḥīḥ* meaning valid, *fāsid* meaning defective or irregular and *bāṭil* meaning void are the most common. When these terms are applied to a contract, they indicate the two aspects of a transaction: its nature (*aṣl*) and the circumstances (*waṣf*). Ḥanafī law determines that a *ṣaḥīḥ* contract is one where both the nature and the circumstances correspond to the

---

18 Baillie, *Digest*, 184. Baillie explains the three options in the classical law of sale: option of inspection (*khiyār al-ru'ya*), option of defect (*khiyār al-ʿayb*) and the option of approval (*khiyār al-sharṭ*).

19 Niẓām, *al-Fatāwā*, 273 and Baillie, *Digest*, 21.

20 Niẓām, *al-Fatāwā*, 273.

21 *Ibid.*, 273.

law, a *bāṭil* contract is one where neither the nature nor circumstances correspond to the law and a *fāsid* contract is one where the nature corresponds to the law but not the circumstances.[22] In other words, different factors affect the nature of a contract which seemingly comes into effect through offer (*ijāb*) and acceptance (*qabūl*). A valid contract is relatively straightforward, for it is one which is fully operative with respect to its legal consequences when a bilateral agreement is reached by both parties. It is the void and defective contracts that are problematic, and perhaps nowhere more so than in marriage laws. Generally speaking, the following scale of legal validity regarding marriage contracts represents broadly the framework in which the legal discussions take place. A marriage contract which is valid gives full recognition to the rights and duties of both husband and wife during the actual marriage itself and upon death or divorce. In other words, sexual intercourse is legitimized, the wife becomes entitled to her dower (*mahr*) and maintenance (*nafaqa*), the children born of such a marriage are legitimate, mutual rights of inheritance are established, and the wife is expected to observe the necessary *ʿidda*[23] upon the death of her husband or divorce. A defective contract results in no mutual rights and duties unless consummation has occurred. Even after sexual intercourse has taken place, the rights of both partners are restricted, for the contract is never rendered valid by consummation alone. The woman is not entitled to maintenance nor are there mutual rights of inheritance. However, the woman is entitled to her dower, she must observe an *ʿidda* of three months on either divorce, cancellation, or the death of her husband, and the children of such a union are considered legitimate. A void contract is usually defined as an unlawful connexion *ab initio*, and results in no civil rights at all between the two parties. Ameer Ali states that 'the illegality of such unions commences from the date when the contracts are entered into, and the marriage is considered as totally non-existing *in fact as well as in law*'.[24] If consummation has occurred, the woman will be entitled to her customary dower (*mahr al-mithl*) or her specified dower (*mahr al-musammā*) whichever is less. Furthermore, if it is established that the couple were in *bona fide* ignorance of the impediments to the marriage, any children born of such a union will be regarded as legitimate. The difficulty lies in establishing the exact nature of the defect or irregularity that distinguishes between a void contract and one that is merely defective and thus in theory has the potential of being regularized in some way.[25] The primary sources often

---

22 J. N. D. Anderson, "Invalid and Void Marriages in Ḥanafī Law", *BSOAS*, 12 (1950), 357–66.

23 *ʿIdda* refers to the waiting period a woman must observe in case of a dissolution of the marriage or the death of her husband.

24 Ameer Ali, *Mahommedan Law* (ed. Raja S. A. Khan), 7th edn, Lahore 1979, 312.

25 Tabiu has correctly pointed out that much of the modern discussion of unlawful marriages and their effects in Islamic law is to be found in the writings on 'Anglo-Muslim' law, as applied in the Indian subcontinent, and which are therefore mainly Ḥanafī. See M. Tabiu, "Unlawful Marriages and their Effects in Islamic Law of the Maliki School", *Islamic Studies*, 13 (1992), 318ff. He also argues in the same article that 'irregular' marriages are actually void, and that in fact there is no way of regularizing them (p. 322).

conflict in their approach towards these distinctions, leading to great confusion in analysis. Problems occur quite simply because, though sexual intercourse is legitimized in a valid contract, sexual intercourse may still occur within a defective or void contract, thus allowing for the possibility of pregnancy and also threatening punishment for *zinā* (fornication). As the classical tradition endeavours to confer some kind of legitimacy upon the offspring of most unions and makes every effort to avert the punishment for illicit fornication, the jurists are forced to resolve the complexities of a contract that is not valid, but can nevertheless produce results similar to one that is.

J. Anderson has tried to show how Abū Ḥanīfa's logical approach to the whole issue of contract and competency leads him to arrive at some unusual conclusions that are for the most part in conflict with those held by his two companions. He draws upon Ḥanafī works like *Iṣtilāḥāt al-ʿUlūm* to summarize Abū Ḥanīfa's view of assessing the nature and scale of legal validity:

> Arguing that the constituent parts of most contracts are four in number, namely two considerations and two contracting parties, he [Abū Ḥanīfa] held that if a Divine prohibition made either consideration unlawful in nature or either party incompetent to act, then one of the constituent parts of the contract was lacking and the whole vitiated in its very essence; it was therefore void (*bāṭil*) and of no legal effect, just as though no agreement had been reached between the parties. If on the other hand, the Divine prohibition affected not the nature or the essence of the consideration but only one of its qualities or attributes, then the contract concerned was valid in essence and only vitiated in an 'extraneous element'; it was therefore irregular (*fāsid*) but not wholly void.[26]

Anderson continues to explain how this logical approach by Abū Ḥanīfa led to rather curious conclusions and conflicted with the opinions of his two companions, Abū Yūsuf and al-Shaybānī. For in actual fact, this approach sees two separate issues within the marriage union – the legal right to contract and the permissibility to contract. Abū Ḥanīfa's logic concludes that as long as the two people are legally competent to act (*mukallaf*) – being sane (*ʿāqil*), free (*ḥurr*) and mature (*bāligh*), any marriage concluded between them could never be void. It is the legal competency to contract rather than the bar to their union that makes the ensuing contract always a 'semblance' of a marriage, rendering it only ever defective and never void. This is the case irrespective of whether the two people concerned know or do not know of any bar to their union (either through affinity, fosterage or kindred, or any other temporary bar). It is this bar that is seen to be the 'extraneous' element in Abū Ḥanīfa's argument and should be set aside where possible. The marriage in all these cases is only ever deemed *fāsid* or defective. The contract is 'vitiated' and rendered *bāṭil* only if the couple or even one of them is not competent to act.

[26] Anderson, "Invalid and Void marriages", 359.

The two companions differ fundamentally in their perception of what constitutes a valid contract. For in their view, if the legal effect (*ḥukm*) of a marriage, principally sexual intercourse, should not have been realized because the subjects were barred to each other, the contract was not a proper contract irrespective of the fact that the couple may have been legally competent to contract. Furthermore, where the marriage was entered into with full knowledge of any permanent bar, the contract could not be regarded as a 'semblance' of marriage either. Thus consummation would not lead to the payment of dower nor would paternity be established and the couple would be liable to the punishment for *zinā*.[27] Ameer Ali cites the *Radd al-Mukhtar*:

> According to the Imams Abu Yusuf and Mohammed, if the marriage is contracted in good faith and in ignorance of the cause which renders the parties unlawful (*haram*) to each other and is followed by cohabitation, the issue would be affiliated to the father and *nasab* (i.e. descent) would be established. But if it is entered into with a knowledge of its illegality the offspring, if any, would not acquire the status of legitimacy, though the woman would have to observe the '*iddut* or prescribed probation before she can marry again.[28]

Separation and the defective contract

A valid marriage remains in existence until there is a formal dissolution by the judge or the husband's pronouncement of *ṭalāq* or repudiation. In marriages that are not valid for some reason, separation of the couple can take various forms, but is never tantamount to repudiation (as with a valid marriage). Ḥanafi works that present a more developed view of the law are generally concerned with the rules pertaining to this separation between the two parties in a 'defective' (*fāsid*) marriage. In both the *ʿInāya* and the *Fatāwā al-ʿĀlamgīrī*, we see a primary insistence on the duties of the *qāḍī* to terminate such a contract. The *Fatāwā al-ʿĀlamgīrī* even contains a short chapter on such contracts, with emphasis not on the definition of a *fāsid* contract but the consequences of such a contract. It states that separation of the couple must be effected immediately and gives an explanation of three different types of separation, beginning with *tafrīq*, the one that is subject to the *qāḍī*'s authority and jurisdiction. On the authority of the *Muḥīṭ*:

> When a defective marriage has taken place, the *qāḍī* may cause separation between the husband and wife.[29]

---

[27] Anderson, "Invalid and Void Marriages", 361. Professor Anderson's article provides a good analysis of the differences in opinion between Abū Ḥanīfa and his two companions. *Zinā* here refers to illicit sexual intercourse between two consenting adults resulting in the prescribed *ḥadd* punishment of 100 lashes.

[28] Ali, *Mahommedan Law*, 312. The complexities surrounding the various distinctions and the issue of 'semblance' will be dealt with below.

[29] Niẓām, *al-Fatāwā*, 330. The implication is that it is the duty of the judge to separate the two.

As the defective element of such a contract could be due to a variety of reasons, none of which may preclude the couple from having intercourse, the second consideration of such a contract is the consequences of possible consummation:

> When a defective marriage has taken place, if the husband has not had intercourse with her, no *mahr* is due to her, nor must she observe *ʿidda*. If he has had intercourse, she is entitled to whichever is less of the specified *mahr* or her standard *mahr*.[30]

It is important to understand that the *qāḍī*'s judicial separation (i.e. *tafrīq*) is tantamount to a real dissolution of the marriage. It is to be distinguished from divorce or (*ṭalāq*) which may only be pronounced by the husband. The distinction is not purely formal; it is a real dissolution of the contract making the husband liable for *zinā* were he to have intercourse with the woman after the *qāḍī*'s decree for separation.

The second type of separation is the *mutāraka* or 'relinquishment':

> In the *Majmūʿa al-Nawāzil*, divorce in a defective contract is a relinquishment and does not fail by falling short than the number in a divorce according to the *Khalasa*.[31]

This relinquishment is a type of divorce but is not actually *ṭalāq* since *ṭalāq* requires the presence of true ownership (*milk*) and a defective contract results only in a bad ownership (*milk khabīth*).[32] Separation in a *mutāraka* takes effect by a verbal declaration, whether or not the marriage has been consummated; simply to deny the marriage is not sufficient for bringing an end to the contract.

> Relinquishment in a defective contract after consummation can take place only by the use of words such as, 'I have set your way free', or 'I have left you'. The author of the *Muḥīṭ* says that before consummation also, a relinquishment cannot be effected without the use of such words.[33]

However, knowledge of this relinquishment is an issue of *ikhtilāf*:

> Knowledge of the relinquishment is a condition of the validity of the relinquishment; this is the valid view. Thus, if someone does not know, *ʿidda* is not completed according to the *Qunya*. The truth is that knowledge of the relinquishment is not a condition in the same way as it is not a condition in divorce.[34]

The third form of separation is by cancellation or *faskh*:

> Each reserves the right of cancellation without the other being present but after [consummation] only when the other is present.[35]

---

30 Niẓām, *al-Fatāwā*, 330.
31 *Ibid.*, 330
32 Schacht, *Introduction*, 152.
33 Niẓām, *al-Fatāwā*, 330.
34 *Ibid.*, 330.
35 *Ibid.*, 330.

Though *faskh* actually implies cancellation of the contract, it is necessary for the parties to know whether it has been carried out, if the marriage has been consummated owing to the issues of *mahr* and *ʿidda*.

These three forms of separation can take place before or after intercourse. However, after intercourse, a woman's right to her *mahr* is fully established. In a defective contract, the *mahr* becomes obligatory as a result of consummation only as opposed to a valid contract where *mahr* is due as a result of both the contract or consummation.[36] The jurists explain this legal ruling by stating that in a defective contract, it is solely the enjoyment of the wife that necessitates payment of the *mahr*; the contract itself makes no obligation on the man for the contract is essentially not valid:

> If the kazee separate a man from his wife before cohabitation on account of their marriage being invalid, the woman is not entitled to any part of her dower, because where the marriage is invalid, no obligation with respect to dower is involved in the contract as that in such a case, is also null; nor is the dower held to be due on any other ground than the fruition of the connubial enjoyment, which is not found in the present instance.[37]

As demonstrated above, the paternity of a child born in a defective contract is established, giving the woman two of the most important rights of a fully valid contract. Yet, irrespective of children and the length of time ensued, a defective contract remains defective until the element rendering it *fāsid* is removed. One area which again highlights this issue is valid privacy (*al-khalwa al-ṣaḥīḥa*). In a valid contract, *khalwa* (privacy) implies that the man and woman were together in such circumstances as allowed intercourse to take place; thus the woman becomes entitle to her *mahr*, etc. In a contract that is *fāsid*, however, *khalwa* does not imply a presumption of intercourse and therefore the subsequent rights to *mahr*, etc. do not apply. Al-Maydānī explains:

> A defective marriage has no legal consequences before intercourse nor after privacy. This is because the privacy is defective by reason of the marriage being defective. Privacy in a defective marriage does not establish possibility and so it does not take the place of intercourse.[38]

The issue of *khalwa* in a defective contract is again problematic because irrespective of whether or not the marriage contract is legally defined as valid, defective or void, the possibility that intercourse may have taken place remains. The following example illustrates that the classical jurists were well aware of this problem but faced difficulty in resolving it:

---

[36] In a valid marriage, if divorce occurs before consummation, the wife becomes entitled to half of her *mahr*. For a detailed discussion of *mahr*, see Mona Siddiqui, "Mahr: Legal Obligation or Rightful Demand?", *Journal of Islamic Studies*, 6 (1995), 14.

[37] Hamilton, *Hedaya*, 52.

[38] al-Sayyid ʿAbd al-Ghanī al-Maydānī, known as Ghānimī al-Maydānī, *al-Lubāb Sharḥ Mukhtaṣar al-Qudūrī*, in the margins of Abū Bakr b. ʿAlī al-Ḥaddādī, *al-Jawhara al-Nayyira*, Istanbul 1315 (repr. 1978), 24.

> If a man enters into a defective contract, has privacy with his wife and a child is born, then if the husband denies consummation, according to Abū Yūsuf there are two traditions. In one tradition he says that paternity is established and so is the obligation of *mahr* and *ʿidda*. In the other tradition, he claims that paternity is not established nor the obligation of *mahr* and *ʿidda*, according to the *Muḥīṭ*.[39]

The concept of shubha

Much of the complexity surrounding unlawful marriages in Islamic law arises from the importance that Islam attaches to the marital union and from its basic rejection of sexual relationships outside marriage (with the notable exception of concubinage). As a faith, it is not alone in taking this stand, but its penal laws which prescribe a *ḥadd* punishment for illicit fornication are witness to a religion determined at least in theory to delineate parameters of behaviour for the faithful. The marriage contract is one way of ensuring that personal ties are structured sexually, financially and socially. The following quotation from the *ʿInāya* sums up neatly all the different aspects of a marriage contract:

> *Nikah* according to the dictionary means sexual intercourse; then it is used for a marriage, as a metaphor, because a marriage is a means for effecting sexual intercourse. Some have said that it is a word which comprises both meanings; and according to its ordinary acceptation, it means a contract designed for the purpose of creating ownership in the enjoyment of the private parts of the woman.
>
> The general condition of marriage is competency in matters of sanity and majority, and a *mahal* or fitting subject, and this *mahal* is a woman to whose marriage there is no legal bar; and the pillar (*rukn*) of marriage consists of proposal and acceptance, from whichever side it may emanate. And the effect or *hukm* of the marriage is (1) the establishment of the lawfulness of the woman, (2) the liability of the man to pay dower, (3) the establishment of the unlawfulness of affinity and (4) the unlawfulness of joining two sisters.[40]

The two parties to the marriage are again defined in more technical terms:

> The contract of marriage (*nikah*) is completed by a proposal and acceptance by the parties competent for it. It cannot be effected except by its constituent pillars emanating from an *ahal* (one who is competent to contract) and in reference to one who is *mahal* (fitting subject) as in the case of other legal contracts. The *ahal* (person competent to contract marriage) is one who is *ahal* (competent) for all contracts. The *mahal* is the one who is the fit subject for the effects of it. Similarly, the basic condition of marriage is competency (*ahliyat*) in the matter of sanity and majority and a *mahal (*fitting subject). This *mahal* is a woman to whose marriage there is no legal bar. In a valid marriage the husband is *ahal*, possessed of the capacity and the woman is *mahal*, a fit subject to contract a marriage in accordance with the *shari'ah*.[41]

---

39 Niẓām, *al-Fatāwā*, 331.

40 The *ʿInāya* quoted in N. U. A. Siddiqui, *Studies in Muslim Law*, Dacca 1955, 126.

41 Tanzilur Rahman, *A Code of Muslim Personal Law*, Karachi 1978, 113.

These two definitions of *nikāḥ* illustrate the importance of the appropriateness of the contract (i.e. whether the two people concerned are both competent and suitable to be married to each other). As we have established above, it is the sense of possession or ownership (*milk*), implied both in the relationship between a man and his female slave and a man and his wife, that makes cohabitation between the two lawful. Certain women however are considered unfitting subjects for marriage to a man. The prohibition on marriage to these women is dealt with from a particular angle in the classical texts, one which focuses less on the inappropriateness of two people entering a contract unlawful for whatever reason, and more on the classification of the contracts themselves. The principal reasoning is that though marriage between two who are prohibited to each other for some reason is unlawful in itself, once a contract takes place, it must be legally acknowledged. The contract always exists irrespective of how grave the prohibition. Writers on Anglo-Muslim law have used the terms 'relative' and 'absolute' to define the two types of prohibition, as well as the words 'temporary' or 'perpetual'. In the former case, we have examples such as marriage to a widow who is still observing her *ʿidda* or marriage to two sisters by one contract[42] and marriage without witnesses. A man may not have the legal right to marry in such circumstances, but if he does, the contract must be made valid in all respects. Such marriages are defective (*fāsid*) only insofar as the 'extraneous' element (i.e. the temporary nature of the impediment) exists or that the circumstances in which the contract took place were lacking in some external requirement but can be rectified. In the latter case, however, the nature of the prohibition is permanent and absolute; a man can never lawfully marry those women who are prohibited to him on the grounds of kindred or consanguinity or fosterage (for example his sister, his mother, another man's wife). Such a marriage must be legally annulled even though the contract is recognized as null and void (*bāṭil*).[43] Again however, if a contract has taken place, even though it may be classified as null and void, it can still bring about some of the effects of a valid contract. The act of consummation is the one single factor that brings about some of the obligations of a valid contract without actually changing the essence of the contractual status between the man and woman.[44]

It is the definition of consummation in such marriages which is problematic and why the whole concept of semblance or doubt (*shubha*)[45] was developed. Theoretically

[42] The marriage of two sisters by one contract or with two separate contracts is a much debated issue in Ḥanafī texts. The *Radd al-Mukhtār* and the *Kanz al-Daqāʾiq* both agree that the second marriage would only ever be *fāsid* and the man would be liable to pay the dower but not liable for the prescribed *ḥadd*.

[43] A comprehensive list of those marriages that are considered *fāsid* and those that are *bāṭil* can be found in most of the standard texts on Muslim personal law (e.g. Fitzgerald, Schacht, Ameer Ali and A. A. A. Fyzee, *Outlines of Muhammadan Law*, 3rd edn, London 1964). A close reading of these texts shows however the difficulty of such classification.

[44] These issues are all raised in varying level of detail in Ali, *Mahommedan Law*, Fyzee, *Outlines*, Anderson, "Invalid and Void Marriages".

[45] Also defined as 'error'.

a *bāṭil* contract does not result in any real ownership (*milk*), and therefore sexual intercourse within such a contract could be tantamount to constituting the criminal offence of *zinā* for which a *ḥadd* punishment was prescribed. The doctrine of *shubha* essentially implies that cohabitation took place on the grounds that the man and woman were not aware of the bar to their union and it acts in most cases of void marriages as a deterrent against inflicting the punishment for *zinā*. It is based primarily on the Prophetic *ḥadīth*, 'Avoid punishment in cases of doubt (*shubh*) as far as possible', and is a significant development within the law, pertaining mainly to contracts which are void and not just defective:

> Where the prohibition is relative or temporary or the illegality springs from an accidental circumstance such as the absence of witnesses, the position is quite different. Although the doctrine of *shubh* was sometimes brought to bear on these unions, as they were not inherently or radically unlawful the question of knowledge of their relative illegality did not enter into consideration – for under no circumstance, by consensus, the parties contracting such marriages were liable to *hadd*.[46]

It is the issue of knowledge of the bar to the union upon which the Ḥanafi school is divided. The *Hidāya* explains the different categories of 'error'.

> (a) *Shubha ishtibah* – Where the man and woman are unaware of any impediment, cohabitation between them is called *shubha ishtibah* or error of misconception. In this case, the man who has sexual intercourse with a woman is under the impression that she is lawful to him and this does not make him liable for *hadd*.
>
> (b) *Shubha hukmia* – this is the doubt that pertains to the subject (*mahal*) herself, i.e. there is some doubt or dispute as to whether the woman is lawful to the man or not. In such an event, if the man has intercourse, he is again not liable.
>
> (c) *Shubha fi'l 'aqd* – doubt in the contract. According to Abu Hanifa, doubt becomes established by virtue of the contract itself so that even if a person cohabits with a woman whom he knows is not permitted to him, the notion of error or doubt is established and the *hadd* punishment drops. The Hedaya explains: 'According to Hanifa, a contract of marriage is a sufficient ground of error, although the illegality of such marriage be universally allowed and the man entering into such a contract be sensible of this illegality. With our other doctors, on the contrary, a contract of marriage is not admitted as a legal ground of error, if the man be sensible of the illegality'.[47] Furthermore, if this marriage took place with one of the *maharim* (i.e. women who are perpetually forbidden on the grounds of affinity, consanguinity or fosterage), then if the marriage was contracted with knowledge of its illegality, the two companions consider this liaison as tantamount to *zina* with the applicability of the *hadd* punishment. Abu Hanifa however does not consider this as *zina* but recognises that some *ta'zir* punishment could be implemented by the *qadi*.[48]

46 Ali, *Mahommedan Law*, 300.
47 Hamilton, *Hedaya*, 21.
48 Hamilton, *Hedaya*, 25.

Abū Ḥanīfa's consistency in seeing every contract of marriage which was not a totally valid contract as representing at least a semblance of a contract means that the *ḥadd* penalty is always dropped and a financial compensation or *mahr* must be paid; for him knowledge or ignorance of the impediment does not come into the equation. His stance is always based on the logic that every woman may be a proper subject of marriage because the end of marriage is the procreation of children, and to this 'every daughter of Adam is competent'.[49] It is because the Qur'ān forbids certain unions that some unions cannot continue; the Qur'ān does not however prescribe a punishment for such unions and thus a discretionary punishment by the *qāḍī* must be effected.

Miscellaneous cases of unlawful marriages

The following example is usually cited as the most common illustration of a *fāsid* or defective marriage:

> (a) One of the conditions relating to the validity of the marriage is that, according to us, there should be witnesses to the marriage. But Mālik says that the condition regarding the validity of marriage is giving publicity to it, not that there should be witnesses to the marriage: so that if a man marries a woman in the presence of witnesses, and has stipulated for concealment, the marriage is not valid; but if he has married without witnesses, with the stipulation that he will give publicity, the marriage is valid.[50]

The issue of witnesses features in most Ḥanafī texts as an extraneous element, the absence of which renders the marriage *fāsid* but not *bāṭil*.

> (b) A male minor and a female minor are so that between them there is doubt of fosterage, but the reality of this is not known. The learned have said that there is no fear in the marriage between them: the validity of the marriage is when no man gives any information about it [i.e. the fosterage]: but if information of it is given by a just and righteous man, so that his word can be acted on, then the marriage between them is not valid. And if information about the fosterage is received after the marriage, when they have grown up, then it is safe that the man [i.e. the husband] should be separated from her: it is reported from the Prophet of God that he directed separation [in such a case].[51]

The above case demonstrates that the unlawful element in a marriage remains unlawful however much time elapses: where the defect can be removed, it should be removed, where it cannot be removed, the couple should separate. However, where this unlawful element cannot be proven or remains unknown, the marriage is treated as valid as confirmed by the following example:

---

[49] *Ibid.*, 25.
[50] al-Awzajandī, *Fatāwā Qāḍī-Khan*, 129.
[51] *Ibid.*, 129

(c) A girl has been suckled by a large number of the tribe of a village, whether those who suckled her might form a large or a small portion of the people of the village, and it cannot be known who suckled her; one of the villagers contemplates marrying her. Abū Qāsim Saffār has said that if he can find no trace as to who suckled her, and no person bears witness before him as to who suckled her, he shall be at liberty to marry her.[52]

Declaration of suspected relationships or deliberately false declaration can also have an impact on the contract:

(d) A man admits that this woman is his mother, or his foster sister, or his daughter: the man then contemplates marrying the woman and says 'I [merely] suspected so or made a slip of the tongue (*khaṭāʾ*) or made a mistake [when making the above admission]', and the woman bears out to the claim of the man, that he made the mistake, then he shall be entitled to marry her; but if the man remains fixed in his admission and says, 'what I stated is true', it is not acceptable for him to marry her [even if in reality the woman might be a stranger to him]. But if his admission takes place after the marriage, separation shall be effected between them, if he continues to be determined in his admission.[53]

This shows the importance of rectifying what is considered an unlawful union, even if in fact it might not actually be so. The man's insistence that the woman belongs to the class of *maḥārim* (i.e. perpetually prohibited to him), raises the presumption of truth in his favour, thus in effect rendering the contract unlawful. Some forms of ignorance however are not recognized as sufficient to prevent the punishment of *zinā*:

(e) If a man have carnal connection with a woman whom he finds in his own bed, punishment is incurred by him, because there can be no error where he passes any length of time in the company of his wife and thus his apprehension of this woman being his wife, from the circumstances of finding her in bed is not regarded, so as to prevent punishment. The reason of this is that sometimes a relation of the wife, residing in the house with her, may sleep upon her bed. And the law is the same where the man is blind, because it is always in his power to ask and discover who the woman is and he may also discover this by the sound of her voice. But yet if he invite the woman to the act, and she consent, signifying that 'she is his wife', and he copulate with her, in this case, he does not incur punishment, as he is deceived by the woman's declaration and behaviour.[54]

The onus appears to be on the man to ensure that he does not have intercourse with a woman in whom he has no right; in this case the man cannot pretend to be unaware of his real wife in any way. However, where he has been deceived by the woman, he does not incur punishment as it is presumed that he was in *bona fide* ignorance.

---

52 *Ibid.*, 129.
53 *Ibid.*, 125.
54 Hamilton, *Hedaya*, 25.

Conclusion

The above discussion reflects on some of the issues regarding the form of marriage contracts. It shows that despite the form and logic upon which contracts of marriage are assessed and divided, consummation in any contract almost always brings about some mutual rights, namely the payment of dower and the establishment of paternity (*nasab*). The law can be seen to be 'generous' in that it is sensitive to the faithful, allowing for genuine, as well as deliberate, mistakes. Though the distinctions between *fāsid* and *bāṭil* are sometimes blurred, the distinctions have to remain; they are necessary in a legal structure which attempts to accommodate diverse human and social relationships, and in which the jurists are constantly determined to avert punishment for *zinā* wherever possible.

In celebration of spring
A poem by al-Ṣanawbarī

Stefan Sperl (School of Oriental and African Studies)

In the preface to his *Studies in Early Muslim Jurisprudence* Norman Calder expresses his gratitude to the rabbinical scholar Jacob Neusner for 'his demonstration that ... an adequate marking of subdivisions is part of a method of analysis, at least for the type of texts represented for him in Mishnah and Talmud, and for me in early Muslim jurisprudence'.[1] This principle can be said to apply also to classical Arabic poetic texts which consist of a greatly varying number of lines whose subdivision is often far from obvious. While in certain poems the sequence of lines and the length of the subdivisions appear to follow a strict compositional plan, more detailed evidence is needed in order to substantiate such observations and come to a better understanding of the different types of patterns involved.

The following brief analysis is an attempt to gain insight into the compositional structure of an Arabic poem by putting Calder's (and Neusner's) methodological principle to test. The work involved, an Ode to Spring by the Syrian poet al-Ṣanawbarī (d. 334/945), was selected to honour the dedicatee of this volume whose birthday fell on the first day of spring; for analytical purposes it can, therefore, be considered a random specimen.[2] It is not unknown, however, and has been examined in some detail by Gregor Schoeler, whose observations supply the point of departure for this discussion.[3] We must begin with the Arabic text and a translation.

1. In Summer fragrant herbs and fruit abound
   But the earth's a fireplace and the air a furnace.

2. In Autumn the palm trees ripen for harvest
   But the earth is bare and the air is cold.

3. In Winter rainfalls are copious and plenty
   But the earth's under siege and so is the air.

---

[1] Oxford 1993, x.

[2] See al-Ṣanawbarī, *Dīwān* (ed. Iḥsān ʿAbbās), Beirut 1970, 42–3.

[3] G. Schoeler, *Arabische Naturdichtung: die Zahrīyāt, Rabīʿiyāt und Rawḍiyāt von ihren Anfängen bis aṣ-Ṣanawbarī, eine gattungs-, motiv- und stilgeschichtliche Untersuchung*, Beirut 1974, 302–11.

4. Bright Spring is Time at its best; when
Spring comes it brings you blossoms and light!

5. Then the earth's an emerald and the air a pearl
The plants are turquoise and the water's crystal.

6. Not short of a goblet from its clouds, the plants
Are then of only two kinds: tipsy and fully drunk.

7. Then we have roses neatly set out and displayed
Between gatherings, and wallflowers scattered all over,

8. And narcissus with bewitching glances – nay, rather:
As if bewitched by the onlookers' blinded gaze.

9. And these violets, this jasmin, these jonquils
And lilies famed for their beauty.

10. Then the clouds keep scattering their pearls,
So the earth is all smiles and the birds delighted.

11. Wherever you turn there are doves and turtle doves
Singing then, and collared doves and starlings.

12. When two nightingales raise their voices then,
They are flute and pipe, nay, lute and mandolin.

13. God be blessed, how wonderful is Spring! So don't be
Deceived; whoever thinks it's like summer is a fool.

14. The deserts are just as pleasing for their dwellers then
As are in other seasons the palaces.

15. In every valley we descend there is a tavern then,
And on every hill we mount there is an inn.

16. Whoever smells the scent of Spring's greeting will say
Musk isn't musk nor is camphor camphor.

١ ان كان في الصيفِ ريحانٌ وفاكهةٌ   فالأرضُ مستوقَدٌ والجوُّ تَنّورُ
٢ وان يكنْ في الخريفِ النخلُ مخْترَفاً   فالأرضُ عرْيانَةٌ والجوُّ مَقْرُورُ
٣ وان يكنْ في الشتاءِ الغيثُ متّصلاً   فالأرضُ محصورةٌ والجوُّ محصورُ
٤ ما الدهرُ الا الربيعُ المستنيرُ إذا   اتى الربيعُ أتاكَ النَّورُ النُورُ
٥ الأرضُ ياقوتةٌ ، والجوُّ لؤلؤةٌ   والنبتُ فيروزجٌ ، الماءُ بَلّورُ
٦ ما يعدمُ النبتُ كأساً من سحائبِهِ   فالنبتُ ضربان : سكرانٌ ومَخمورُ
٧ فيه لنا الوردُ منضودٌ مُؤزَّرُ ما   بين المجالسِ ، والمنثورُ منثورُ
٨ ونرجسٌ ساحرُ الأبصارِ ليس كما   كأنه مِن عَمَى الأبصارِ مَسْحورُ
٩ هذا البنفسجُ ، هذا الياسمينُ ، وذا الـ   ـنِّسرينُ ، ذا سوسنٌ في الحُسْنِ مشهورُ
١٠ تظلُّ تنثرُ فيه السُّحْبُ لؤلؤَها   فالأرضُ ضاحكةٌ ، والطيرُ مسرورُ
١١ حيث التفتَّ فقمريٌّ وفاختةٌ   فيه تُغَنّي وشفنينٌ وَزَرْزُورُ
١٢ اذا الهزارانِ فيه صَوَّتا فهما السُّـ   ـرْنايُ والنايُ ، بل عودٌ وطنبورُ
١٣ تبارك اللّهُ ما أَحلى الربيعَ فلا   تُغْرَرْ فقائسُهُ بالصيفِ مَغرورُ
١٤ تطيبُ فيه الصحاري للمقيم بها   كما تطيبُ له في غيرِهِ الدورُ
١٥ في كلِّ أرضٍ هبطنا فيه دَسْكَرَةٌ   في كلِّ ظهرٍ علَوْنا فيه ماخورُ
١٦ مَن شَمَّ ريحَ تحيّاتِ الربيع يَقُلْ   لا المسكُ مسكٌ ولا الكافورُ كافورُ

While Schoeler's analysis is principally concerned with situating the work in the tradition of classical Arabic garden and nature poetry he also comments upon its compositional structure. He identifies a first section of five lines which presents the argument in favour of Spring and is characterized by a high degree of coherence, a fact he deems unusual for al-Ṣanawbarī. This is followed by a flower description of five lines (6–10), which he views as rather more disjointed (*mehr sprunghaft)*, and a further two lines on the motif of bird song (11–12).[4] The poem concludes with four more lines on the general merits of Spring (13–16). This subdivision does indeed appear to reflect the thematic sequence at hand, but the overall picture it gives of the poem's development seems somewhat questionable. Why only two lines on birds and five lines on flowers, and why conclude the poem with four lines after having introduced it with five? One is tempted to conclude that this seemingly haphazard sequence reflects no more than the lose structure of al-Ṣanawbarī's verse which not only Schoeler but also the Arab critic F. A. Tūqān have remarked upon. When studying al-Ṣanawbarī's nature descriptions the latter found the poet's images and themes to be independent entities 'which can succeed or precede each other without harming the overall sense' of the poem concerned.[5]

Making the 'adequate marking of subdivisions' into a methodological principle requires Schoeler's view of the poem's structure to be examined more closely. There is no doubt that the first four lines which dwell on the four seasons constitute a tightly woven rhetorical entity which leads up to the climax of line 4 where Spring emerges triumphant. Line 5 does indeed follow on by resuming, in its first hemistich, the themes of earth and air which figure in each of the preceding lines; the second hemistich, however, introduces the themes of water and vegetation which then become the subject of line 6. The link between lines 5 and 6 is emphasized further by the word *nabt* ('plants'): introduced in line 5, it occurs twice more in line 6.

The question then arises: if we wish to mark subdivisions, does line 5 belong to the introductory section of the poem as suggested by Schoeler or does it belong to the ensuing flower description? So far, there are clearly arguments in favour of both points of view. A more definitive answer, however, may be found by examining the nature of the relationship between lines 5 and 6. It appears to be based on a contrast: while the former presents the reader with a static display of elements ennobled by the touch of Spring, the latter focuses on a dynamic interrelationship *between* elements (water and vegetation) and its felicitous results.

If we read on we find that the contrasting sequence between static and dynamic forms of description is not limited to lines 5 and 6 but appears to underlie also the

---

[4] Schoeler, *Naturdichtung*, 306–7.

[5] F. A. Tūqān, "*Waṣf al-ṭabīʿa fī shiʿr al-Ṣanawbarī* (2)", *Revue de l'Académie Arabe de Damas*, 44 (1969), 575.

following three couplets of verses. Line 7 dwells on a (static) display of roses and wallflowers while line 8 depicts a rather remarkable instance of dynamic interaction: the eye of the narcissus and the eye of the beholder are gazing at each other in a state of mutual rapture.[6] Line 9 presents once more a static display of flowers, this time involving four distinct entities, just as in the enumerative sequence of line 5. This is followed by another case of dynamic interaction in line 10 as the pearl-like scattering of raindrops in Spring brings about smiles and delight on the part of the earth and the birds. A further static display of four distinct entities ensues in line 11; this time it is different species of birds. In line 12, interaction follows once more as two birds are singing harmoniously together.

The regularity of this sequence suggests that line 5, while developing themes from the poem's introduction, is in fact the beginning of a new subsection which occupies the following eight lines (5–12). If this observation is correct the poem assumes a highly symmetrical form comprising an introduction of four lines, a middle section consisting of four structurally analogous couplets, and a conclusion of four lines. Is this balance purely coincidental or can it be corroborated in further detail?

The answer may be found by returning to the central section of the poem in order to examine if the contrasting sequence observed above can be seen to hold any particular significance for the overall meaning of the work. The couplets are clearly meant to depict the essence of the qualities that make Spring superior to all other seasons, but why such emphasis on static display and dynamic interaction? Looking further at the four 'static' lines (5, 7, 9 and 11) one senses that each is meant to convey an impression of the wondrous plenitude engendered by Spring, a plenitude emphasized by the repeated fourfold enumeration of natural elements, flowers and birds. There is a certain logic to the sequence as the scene shifts from the general panorama of earth and air in line 5, via the contemplation of flowers (fruits of the earth) in lines 7 and 9, to the contemplation of birds (dwellers of the air) in line 11.

The 'dynamic' lines (6, 8, 10 and 12) make a very different point. They portray Spring not only as a wondrous display, but also as a blissful and unimpeded coming together. The sequence of elements in interaction once again appears to follow a certain pattern. Lines 6 and 10 focus on nature as the Spring rains bring about blossoms and delight the birds, while lines 8 and 12 concern man's reaction as he is enchanted by the beauty of the blossoms and the song of the birds.

Lines 6 and 10 are, moreover, linked by the similarity of their structure as the second hemistich of both shows the rain to have a dual consequence: in one case, two kinds of plants result, the intoxicated and the drunk (*sakrān/makhmūr*); in the other, joy

---

6 For a detailed analysis of this striking image, see Schoeler, *Naturdichtung*, 307; further examples of narcissus descriptions by al-Ṣanawbarī are discussed by Tūqān,"*Waṣf al-ṭabīʿa fī shiʿr al-Ṣanawbarī* (1)", *Revue de l'Académie Arabe de Damas*, 43 (1968), 820–1, and A. Hamori, *On the Art of Medieval Arabic Literature*, Princeton 1974, 78–87.

is brought to two elements, the earth and the birds (*ḍāḥika/masrūr*). While the lines are thus close in meaning and structure the imagery employed evokes quite distinct associations in the context of the poetic tradition. In line 6 the rain cloud appears in the guise of the boon-companion familiar from Arabic wine poetry who, in many instances, dispenses more than just liquor, as in the following verse by Abū Nuwās:[7]

tasqīka min ʿaynihā khamran wa-min yadihā
khamran fa-mā laka min sukrayni min buddi

She gives you wine to drink with her eye and wine
With her hand so you can't but be drunk twice over.

In line 10, on the other hand, the rain cloud is portrayed as a generous source of wealth, scattering 'pearls' in abundance, not unlike the sovereign of Arabic panegyric poetry whose generosity is traditionally likened to clouds heavily pregnant with rain. The analogy between Spring and righteous kingship has, indeed, been explored quite explicitly by Abū Tammām in a poem which ends by giving precedence to the virtues of the latter;[8] in this poem by al-Ṣanawbarī, on the other hand, Spring appears as the ultimate sovereign, the donor of life and joy; simultaneously it is also the ultimate ganymede, rendering the whole of nature drunk with wine and, we may surmise, also with love.

The meaning and associations of the other two 'dynamic' lines, 8 and 12, give further grounds for the speculation that love may be the secret force underlying the spectacle depicted by the poet. Duality and mutuality figure also in these two lines which dwell on the captivating effect of beauty, first in the visual, then in the aural sphere. Here, however, duality is even more pronounced: narcissus and onlooker are both bewitching and bewitched as they gaze at each other (*sāḥir/masḥūr*); and the harmonious sound of two nightingales is likened to that of two closely related pairs of musical instruments. Both images have distinctly amorous overtones. Magic (*siḥr*) and bewitching glances are, not unexpectedly, conventional attributes of the beloved in the poetic tradition,[9] and it is hard not to see the two singing nightingales as a pair engaged in courtship.

The wider associations of the four 'dynamic' lines lead us, I believe, to identify the one quality which makes the season of Spring truly outstanding: it permits, at the level of the natural world, the togetherness of lovers, a state of bliss which Arabic

[7]See Abū Nuwās, *Dīwān* (ed. A. ʿA. al-Ghazzālī), Beirut n. d., 27.

[8] Abū Tammām, *Dīwān* (ed. M. A. Azzām), Cairo 1969, 191–7. For translations and discussions of this poem see Schoeler, *Naturdichtung*, 95–106, J. Ashtiany (Bray), "Abū Tammām's 'Spring' *Qaṣīda*: *raqqat ḥawāshī ʾl-dahri*", *JAL*, 25 (1994), 213–9, and S. Sperl and C. Shackle (eds), *Qaṣīda Poetry in Islamic Asia and Africa*, Leiden 1996, ii, 80–5, 418–9.

[9] For an example see Abū Nuwās' verse *Yā sāḥir al-ṭarfi anta ʾl-dahra wasnānu / sirru ʾl-qulūbi ladā ʿaynayka iʿlānu* ('You with the magic gaze, eternally languid, secrets held close in the heart are drawn out by your eyes'; for text and translation see P. F. Kennedy, *The Wine Song in Classical Arabic Poetry: Abū Nuwās and the Literary Tradition*, Oxford 1997, 263, 272).

poetry describes as *waṣl* (or *wiṣāl*). The term is appropriate here because at a deeper, metaphorical level it refers to all instances where disintegration has been overcome and togetherness, and with it fulfilment, have been attained – the very state al-Ṣanawbarī describes.

To appreciate Spring's achievement fully, however, we must remember that in the poetic orb (and not only there) *waṣl* is notoriously difficult to achieve since it is in the nature of the world (*al-dunyā*) to impede it and, even when it has been secured, to expose it to the destructive forces of Time (*al-dahr*). Numerous verses could be cited to illustrate this theme, which figures in virtually all classical Arabic poetic genres. In the *nasīb*, for instance, the recalcitrance of the beloved often renders *waṣl* impossible and exposes the poet to despair. In the following verse the victim is al-Ṣanawbarī's contemporary Abū Firās (d. 357/968):[10]

Muʿallilatī biʾl-waṣli waʾl-mawtu dūnahu
Idhā muttu ẓamʾānan fa-lā nazala ʾl-qaṭru

She gives me hopes of union but death is more easily attained;
Should I die of thirst not a droplet would fall.

Al-Mutanabbī, another contemporary (d. 354/965), draws the ultimate conclusion in the elegy he composed for the mother of his patron Sayf al-Dawla:[11]

Wa-man lam yaʿshaqi ʾl-dunyā qadīman
Wa-lākin lā sabīla ilā ʾl-wiṣāli

Who has not loved this world in times gone by,
But there is no way to union.

To make such union possible, even for one season, therein lies the glory of Spring. It is only then that man's old enemy, *al-dahr* (Time), shows itself to be beneficent as the poet states in line 4. This line, as is now quite clear I believe, concludes the poem's introduction, a fact with can be rendered even more plausible if we read it in relation to its symmetrical homologue, line 13, which marks the beginning of the poem's conclusion. While line 4 relates Spring (*al-rabīʿ*) to Time (*al-dahr*), line 13 relates Spring to God (*Allāh*), an association which cannot go unnoticed, especially as these lines are, together with the last line, the only ones in which the word for Spring is explicitly mentioned.

Moreover, the relation (and distinction) between *Allāh* and *al-dahr* is a much debated topic[12] and the strategic placement of these two words in the poem must invite

10 Abū Firās, *Dīwān* (ed. S. al-Dahhān), Beirut 1944, ii, 210.
11 *Dīwān al-Mutanabbī bi-sharḥ Abī ʾl-Baqāʾ al-ʿUqbarī*, Cairo 1956, iii, 8.
12 For a detailed discussion of God and *al-dahr* as themes in early Abbasid poetry see Kennedy, *The Wine Song*, 127–32; on the debate whether *al-dahr* could legitimately be one of the names of God see I. Goldziher, *Die Ẓāhiriten, ihr Lehrsystem und ihre Geschichte*, Leipzig 1884, 153–5.

reflection. Line 4 in fact describes Spring as nothing less than a manifestation of *al-dahr* which brings about *nawr* and *nūr*, 'blossoms and light'. *Nūr* presumably refers to the brightness of the sky, but the word also evokes the famous Qur'ānic verse which describes God as *nūr al-samawāti wa 'l-arḍ*, 'the light of the Heavens and the Earth' (24:35). This association is not without relevance here if we consider that earth and air (*al-jaww/al-arḍ*) are very much the focus of the poem's opening lines.

If line 4 links *al-dahr* with the luminosity of Spring (*al-nūr*), its homologue, line 13, links the exclamation *tabāraka Allāh* with a warning not to be taken in by the apparent similarity of spring and summer: *lā tughrar/maghrūr*. Here too, Qur'ānic verses springs to mind: *fa-lā taghrurannakumu 'l-ḥayātu 'l-dunyā wa-lā yaghrurannakum bi-'llāhi 'l-gharūr* ('let not this life deceive you and let not the deceiver deceive you about God', 31:33, 57:14). Bringing into play this grave Qur'ānic admonition against the wiles of Satan lends al-Ṣanawbarī's playful warning against summer a touch of irony. However, the Qur'ānic echoes in lines 4 and 13 may also convey a more serious meaning which is no less appropriate. It is underlined by a rather striking inversion, for Time (*al-dahr*) and deception (*ghurūr*) are, in classical Arabic literary convention, as closely associated as God (*Allāh*) and light (*al-nūr*). The unexpected, 'crosswise', collocation of these four terms in lines 4 and 13 confirms the architectural linkage between the lines and places the poem as a whole into a wider, metaphysical context: for those who can see and are not deceived, God's light becomes tangible in the light of Spring and, we may surmise, it is that which allows love to prosper and union, *waṣl*, to take place.[13]

A more overt variant of the same theme leads the poem to its conclusion: it is the harmonious union between man and nature brought about by the influence of Spring. The very deserts are now palaces of bounty for their inhabitants (14), the hills and valleys have turned into taverns of delight for the travellers (15).[14] The poem ends on a humorous counterpoint achieved through the sudden reversal of a stylistic feature which dominates much of the poem, namely the numerous statements of equivalence highlighted by synthetic parallelism and/or paronomasia. The most notable examples are those involving the rhyme word:

3	*maḥṣūra – maḥṣūru*
4	*al-nawru – al-nūru*
6	*sakrānun – makhmūru*
7	*al-manthūru manthūru*

[13] Ibn al-Rūmī (d. 283/896) quite explicitly attributes the beauty of Spring to the grace of God and Schoeler considers al-Ṣanawbarī's version of this theme inferior by comparison. When viewed in the context of the poem's overall structure, however, al-Ṣanawbari's reference to God becomes more than just a 'formulaic phrase' ('*formelhafte Wendung*', *Naturdichtung*, 309).

[14] Note here once more the static/dynamic contrast, as line 14 refers to stillness (*muqīm*) and line 15 to movement (*habaṭnā/ʿalawnā*).

8 *sāḥiru ʾl-abṣāri – al-abṣāri masḥūru*
10 *ḍāḥikatun – masrūru*
11 *shafnīnun – zarzūru*
12 *ʿūdun – ṭanbūru*
13 *tughrar – maghrūru*

What these lines have in common is that each one of them affirms the equivalence, or near-equivalence, of the two entities cited above with respect to sound (7), meaning (6, 10, 11, 12) or both (3, 4, 8, 13). Heightened by the refrain of the rhyme, these equivalences appear like affirmations of the underlying theme of *waṣl* and generate a rhythm which is not broken until the end of the very last line. Here the sudden occurrence of a double negative brings the poem to an unexpected conclusion: compared to the scent of Spring, 'musk is *not* musk and camphor *not* camphor'. It is as if the union Spring brings to man and nature is so wondrous it can, in the end, sever the union between meaning and words.

The discussion of this poem shows, I believe, that the Neusner/Calder principle outlined at the beginning of this article has a bearing also on the analysis of Arabic poetic texts. The search for a meaningful subdivision which began with the simple question of the status of one line has led to an interpretation of the poem which appears to make sense of its constituent parts. Three findings in particular are worthy of note.

Firstly, the ordering principle which governs the eight lines in the middle section of the poem is not narrative nor even primarily thematic but abstract and conceptual: it is the interplay between static and dynamic forms of portrayal. Interestingly, the latter appear to correspond to two descriptive styles Tūqān identified in al-Ṣanawbarī's verse.[15] Having analysed only single lines and extracts, however, he failed to comment on the structural function of these, and presumably other, descriptive techniques.

Secondly, the identification of this ordering principle reveals the poem to be a tightly woven, symmetrically composed miniature in which the number four determines both the number of lines in the individual subsections (4 + 4 x 2 + 4 = 16) and the enumerative sequences that figure in several verses (5, 9, 11 and 12). The emphasis on the number four appears to derive quite naturally from the four seasons introduced at the beginning of the work. While the evidence gathered from a single poem cannot be conclusive, these findings do cast some doubt on Schoeler's and Tūqān's verdict on al-

[15] He called the first 'animated description' (*waṣf wijdānī*) and found it to be characterized by images in motion (*ṣuwar mutaḥarrika*), while the other, called 'factual description' (*waṣf mawḍūʿī*), he saw as marked by images that are largely static (*lā ḥarakata fīhi*); see Tūqān, "*Waṣf* (1)", 813–4. Hamori also made a similar observation when he noted in one of al-Ṣanawbarī's poems 'a vacillation between comparison with the fixed or fantastic on the one hand, and with the natural or mutable on the other' (*Art*, 86).

Ṣanawbarī's poetic structure. Moreover, the existence of classical Arabic poems exhibiting comparable degrees of symmetry has also been confirmed by other studies.[16]

Thirdly, and perhaps most importantly, attempting to understand the significance of the static/dynamic interplay in the middle section has led us to examine key images of the poem in the wider context of its poetic tradition and to identify a single, underlying theme which appears to govern the work as whole in a meaningful way. Called *fikrat waṣl al-riyāḍ* ('the thought of union with gardens') by Tūqān, it is, in fact, one of the the leitmotifs of al-Ṣanawbarī's verse. Other poems of his state quite explicitly what this ode in celebration of Spring subtly implies: that the bliss of *waṣl* can be found in the manifestations of nature:[17]

Ḥuththi ʾl-kuʾūsa fa-inna hādha waqtuhā
Wa-ṣili ʾl-riyāḍa fa-inna dhā ibbānuhā

Spur on the cups, this is their moment
And seek union with the gardens, this is their time.

[16] See, e.g., A. Hamori, *The Composition of Mutanabbī's Panegyrics to Sayf al-Dawla*, Leiden 1992, 62; S. Sperl, *Mannerism in Arabic Poetry: A Structural Analysis of Selected Texts (3rd Century AH/9th Century AD–5th Century AH/11th Century AD)*, Cambridge 1989, 28–9, 49–50, 85 ; J. S. Meisami, "Unsquaring the Circle: Rereading a Poem by al-Muʿtamid Ibn ʿAbbād", *JAL*, 35 (1988), 294–310.

[17] See Tūqān, "*Waṣf* (1)", 819 and al-Ṣanawbarī, *Dīwān*, 500.

The medieval Kārim
An ancient near eastern paradigm?

John Wansbrough

The topic examined here is the organization of the Kārim, a company of merchants operating in the Red Sea and Indian Ocean in the later Middle Ages (*c.* 1100–1500).[1] For over fifty years now their activities have been extensively depicted, drawn from the standard Arabic sources and from the not yet exhausted mine of the Cairo Geniza.[2] Though one has a fairly vivid impression of persons and their movements, several areas of obscurity persist. These have to do largely with the internal structure of the company, its relation to regalian authority, its concept of economic motivation, and even the origin of its name. While the last mentioned might seem trivial, I intend to pursue that as well, since the term was never identified, neither during the period of its efflorescence nor in subsequent exegesis.

Now, historical reconstruction requires a cadre, and that is invariably a product of analogy. In this instance also of etymology. The danger of circular argument is never absent, nor the tantalizing tension between polygenesis and historical diffusion. For even the fastidious there are traps, and it is unlikely that I have managed to avoid all of them. In a much longer, and rather broader, framework I set out a similar problem some years ago, and cannot be sure it was even partially solved.[3]

Here, incidence of *kārim* is of course determined by context. Owing to the bias of political records (e.g. court reports and fiscal receipts), mercantile activity in the late medieval period of Middle Eastern history is generally interpreted on the paradigm of a 'palace economy'. The dominant parameter is regalian control of commerce, of its commodities, its agents and its revenues. That such ought also to involve its modes of production and of investment was observed, but seldom logically calculated by analysts of the process. Straightforward and relatively simple data like supply and demand with ensuing price fluctuation, cost of labour, transport, and fiscal imposition, tend to be ascribed to the manipulation of political privilege and as though regulated by mere fiat. But even in the presence of centralized authority, these factors have got to

---

[1] Earlier versions of this exercise were proposed at seminars in Leeds and Manchester some fifteen years ago. Norman Calder was present on both occasions and offered helpful advice.

[2] E.g. W. Fischel, "Über die Gruppe der Kārimī Kaufleute", *Studia Arabica*, 1 (1937); G. Wiet, "Les marchands d'épices sous les sultans mamlouks", *Cahiers d'Histoire Egyptienne*, Cairo 1955; E. Ashtor, "The Kārimī Merchants", *JRAS*, 1956; S. Goitein, "New Light on the Beginnings of the Kārim Merchants", *JESHO*, 1 (1958) (amplified *idem*, *Studies in Islamic History and Institutions*, Leiden 1966, 351–60, with outline of earlier scholarship); S. Labib, "Geld und Kredit", *JESHO*, 2 (1959); *idem*, *EI2*, s.v. 'Kārimī' (with further bibliography).

[3] J. Wansbrough, *Lingua Franca in the Mediterranean*, London 1996, see esp. 47–52.

be granted a degree of variability dependent upon circumstances far beyond the control of a single centre, however autocratic. One need only consider the trajectory of spice trade from South Asia via Egypt to Venice to recognize that imposition of political control (as monopoly) could be nothing but destructive.

That strategy led to rejection of a Suez canal project as early as 1504 and subsequent loss of the market to Portugal.[4] What we know is this: the Kārim in Egypt disappeared in the late fifteenth century owing to political rather than economic factors. The spice trade to Europe continued, in other hands and at more or less the same profit margin.[5]

Unlike the Baltic Hansa, the Egyptian Kārim has not bequeathed a self-generated record of its activities.[6] Instead, one must make do with external and/or casual witness: that consists of chronicle and state archives (e.g. Maqrīzī and Qalqashandī), or the memoranda and correspondence of observers and participants (e.g. Geniza). Material so far recovered extends from the early twelfth to the mid-fifteenth century. From this we learn the names of individual merchants, but also of merchant families with widespread connexions, their area of operation (Egypt, South Arabia and India, but also occasionally China and the western Mediterranean),[7] their commodity specialization (spices, but also textiles, metals, lacquer, precious stones and woods), their investments (sugar and grain, but also ships), and their very seldom harmonious relationship to political authority. As may be guessed, the interest of business and fiscality rarely coincided, save in money-lending and tax-farming contracts. The fate of these merchants is not unfamiliar: businessmen become wealthy within the framework of a market economy, eventually perceived, employed, and exploited by autocratic and arbitrary rule.

Their origins are obscure. At some as yet undefined point during their two-century regime in Egypt (969–1169) the Fāṭimid caliphs stationed a fleet in the Red Sea with the general aim of facilitating trade at the expense of their ʿAbbāsid rivals in the Persian Gulf, and more specifically, to protect the Kārim, then operating between ʿAydhāb and Suwakin, from piracy.[8] By 1181 these merchants attracted the attention of Saladin, founder of the succeeding dynasty in Egypt (Ayyūbid 1169–1249), probably for fiscal purposes (i.e. a customs levy on shipping from Aden).[9] Their destiny might seem to have been thereby sealed. Once perceived as source of treasury

[4] W. Heyd, *Histoire du commerce du Levant au moyen-âge,* Leipzig 1885–6, ii, 552; R. Fulin, "Il canale di Suez e Venezia", *Archivio Veneto*, 1873; cf. M. de Mas Latrie, *Traités de paix et de commerce*, Paris 1866, ii, 259–63.

[5] S. Labib, *Handelsgeschichte Ägyptens im Spätmittelalter (1171–1517)*, Wiesbaden 1965, 444–80.

[6] P. Dollinger, *The German Hansa*, London 1970; cf. Wansbrough, *op. cit*., 52–4.

[7] R. di Miglio, "Il commercio arabo con la Cina...", *AIUON*, 15 (1965) and 16 (1966); R. Naura, "Les Kārimīs aux archives de Venise", *JESHO*, 1 (1958); (both *apud* Labib, *EI2*, s.v. 'Kārimī').

[8] al-Qalqashandī, *K. Ṣubḥ al-Aʿshā fī ṣināʿat al-inshā*, Cairo 1913–19, iii, 520; B. Lewis, "The Fatimids and the Route to India", *RFSEI*, 11 (1949).

[9] al-Maqrīzī, *K. al-Sulūk li-maʿrifat duwal al-mulūk*, Cairo 1934f., i, 72–3; Labib, *Handelsgeschichte*, 60–1.

revenue, the movements of the Kārim had to reflect an accommodation between free enterprise and the exigencies of mercantilism. On the other hand, their prosperity had also to be assured, precisely for fiscal motives. So much is clear from the original Fāṭimid protective measure, a policy perpetuated by Saladin in his 'open door' strategy with regard to Mediterranean commerce, and that during the most intensive period of his campaigns against the Crusading states of the Levant (e.g. his correspondence with Pisa 1173–80; and his celebrated letter to the ʿAbbāsid caliph in 1183).[10]

For approximately three and a half centuries merchants of the Kārim are amply and ubiquitously attested: the families of Ibn Kuwayk and al-Kharrūbī, Ibn Musallam and al-Maḥallī, Ibn Muzalliq and al-Ghilanī, together with such Andalusian interlopers as Rufāʾil and Barantishī. Appearance of all these names in the Egyptian court chronicles signifies, of course, not so much commercial expertise as accumulated wealth and political influence. It is to the Geniza and other archival evidence that one must turn in order to assess the role of the Kārim in the actual production of capital. There, the requisite information emerges from such data as frequency of voyages, amount of cargo shipped, market prices sought, found, often rejected in favour of better prospects, and naturally, incessant confrontation with the fisc. While the prosopographical data are not without interest (to calculate for example that the average life of a merchant dynasty was three generations, before either liquidation or absorption into the state bureaucracy), the historical profile of the Kārim is a matter of extrapolation.

The name itself is a little more accessible. Without very much effort one finds that the term *kārim* can refer to a merchant fleet or convoy ('goods arriving with this *kārim*'), a company of merchants (*tujjār kārim*), a trading station (*matjar kārim*), an entrepot or caravansarai (*funduq kārim*), a commercial firm or banking institution (PN with the *nisba*: *kārimī*). In addition to these concrete referents, the image of 'market network' (in relation to named ports) and the more abstract concept of 'market' itself (in relation to commodities, tariffs, price fluctuations: e.g. 'the *kārim* is unchanged') emerge from the several contexts in which the word occurs. From these it would not be rash to infer that *kārim*, mostly but not always provided with the Arabic definite article (*al-*), was, at least in origin, a proper name (or toponym?).[11]

Its generic extension, linguistically attested by both definite article and relative/gentilic adjective (*-ī*), includes so far some fifty names of participants in the enterprise, but that number can hardly comprehend its membership in over three centuries of activity.[12] While it is not perverse to suppose from their names and their

[10] M. Amari, *I diplomi del r. archivio fiorentino*, Florence 1863, nos 7–12; al-Qalqashandī, *Ṣubḥ*, xiii, 81–90; cf. S. Goitein, *A Mediterranean Society*, i, Berkeley–Los Angeles 1967, 266–72.

[11] But cf. Goitein, *Studies*, 356–60; and also biblical Hebrew *(ha)-Pelishtīm*?; *idem*, *Letters of Medieval Jewish Traders*, Princeton 1973, 214, 226, 250.

[12] E. Ashtor, *Levant Trade in the Later Middle Ages*, Princeton 1983, 281.

area of operation that the traders of the Kārim were predominantly Muslim, some evidence of Jewish and Christian participation is available.[13] We are thus confronted with the tip of an iceberg, and it is appropriate to guess that random mention of persons is nothing more than arbitrary and discrete witness to the general phenomenon. Furthermore, since the linguistic medium of these data is Arabic, and because it is well known that both Jews and Christians bore or adopted Muslim names (e.g. Simkhā = Faraj, Kaleb = Khulayf, Yoḥannā = Yaḥyā, etc.), it is almost impossible to argue for a single confessional status. And that particularly under the Fāṭimids, whose regime afforded nearly unlimited opportunity to members of the *dhimmī* communities for self-expression and advancement. It seems not unlikely that this generosity persisted with the succeeding Ayyūbid dynasty, and was only curtailed in the later period of Mamlūk rule (1250–1516), not, incidentally, for confessional reasons.

Now, from its first appearance in Arabic the etymology of *kārim* posed a problem. Even the erudite director of the Mamlūk chancery had to guess that the name was somehow derived from Kanem in West Africa.[14] Orientalist scholarship since then has indulged in conjecture both ingenious and extravagant: *kārim* = 'amber' (Blochet, who also proposed Akkadian/Persian *kurkum* = 'saffron', incidentally a Biblical Hebrew *hapax*); Amharic *kuararima* = 'cardamom' (Littmann); Tamil *karyam* = 'business' (Goitein via Basham).[15] Derivation of the appellative from a single exotic commodity is of course possible but eccentric. Amber was anyway of Baltic origin (already in the Bronze Age); Arabic *ʿanbar* refers to 'ambergris', and there is a common Arabic term for cardamom (*ḥabbhān*). In favour of the Tamil origin, Iranian philology might have been, but in the event was not, pressed into service: cf. Avestan/Pahlavi *kar* = 'work'/'business', *kardak* = 'merchant', *karavan* = 'travelling merchants'/'caravan', modern Persian *karkhana* = 'factory', etc.[16] Admittedly, the parameters of linguistic transfer, whether of loanwords, loan translations (calques), or cognate adaptations, are complex in the extreme, and the traffic between contiguous cultures and languages usually a product of more or less unpredictable sociolinguistic factors.[17]

None of the solutions so far proposed has involved a Semitic etymology or a semantic field in which *kārim* might find a history. Both Hebrew and Arabic exhibit a root *KRH/KRY* in the sense respectively of 'buy' and 'hire', but no trace of a Qal

---

13 *Ibid*, 272 n. 15.

14 al-Qalqashandī, *Ḍauʾ al-ṣubḥ al-musfir*, Cairo 1906, 253; R. Dozy, *Supplément aux dictionnaires arabes*, (repr.) Leiden 1967, ii, 460 s.v.

15 For all this, see *EI2*, s.v. 'Kārimī'.

16 F. Steingass, *Persian–English Dictionary*, (repr.) London 1947, 1001–4 s.vv.; Bartholomae, *Wörterbuch*, 444–8 s.vv.; Nyberg, *Manual*, ii, 112–15 s.vv.; Dozy, *Suppl.*, ii, 434, 454 s.vv. (Persian loanword).

17 Cf. Wansbrough, *Lingua Franca*, 150–61, 184–90.

participle.[18] In fact, only the first vowel *of kārim*, written plene, is certain, the second supplied by analogy to the agent morpheme (*fā'il*) of a root *KRM*. That the latter does not, in either Hebrew (*kōrem*) or Arabic (*karrām*: sic), offer a valid meaning requires no further argument.

What I should like here to suggest, in despite of certain phonetic and morphological difficulties (examined *infra*), is an Akkadian (*ab ovo* Sumerian) paradigm for both the sound and the substance of medieval Arabic *kārim*. The notion of a lexical trajectory spanning three millennia is of course audacious, but not quite impossible.[19] My proposal is, or could have been, secondarily complicated by a question of the value of Sumerian *KAR* in a Semitic context. Akkadian *kārum* is now assured, and the residual problem one of historical exegesis.[20] What exactly is the referent? Is 'market' attested either physically (marketplace) or conceptually (economic behaviour) in the ancient Near East? Arguments *pro et contra* are fascinating, in the end frustrated by a theoretical postulate: what constitutes plausible transaction in the framework of Bronze Age society as portrayed in the extant records?[21] For my purpose here, it is first of all necessary to recall the semantic sector of Akkadian *kārum*; secondly, to ask whether *kārum* and Arabic *kārim* designate comparable phenomena; finally, to examine the linguistic obstacles that block the route to a simple equation.

To Akkadian *kārum* textual evidence attributes an abundant range of referents: dike/embankment → quay; mooring-place/marina → harbour district; entrepot/trading station → marketplace; fiscal perception → douane/customs; joint-stock company → community of merchants with shared assets and liability; commodity unit price → market exchange.[22] It seems clear that lexical usage comprehends both concrete and abstract notions of commercial transaction, i.e. from the physical site of such to the mode of conduct necessary for its completion. The term was productive. While extension from canal or river embankment to mooring-place, hence harbour, is reasonable, especially in Babylonia, application to localities where there is no evidence of a waterway, e.g. Kaniš in Anatolia, must depend upon a metaphor. It could be a transfer like that exhibited in Arabic *sāḥil* (coast → perimeter). Or a metonymy derived from some other and primary feature. From the available documentation, that would of course be 'commerce'. References are to payment (barley, silver), purchase and delivery of commodities (red wool, dates, barley) 'in the harbour → trading station'

[18] W. Gesenius, *Handwörterbuch...Alten Testament*, (repr.) Berlin 1962, 361 s.v.; Dozy, *Suppl.*, ii, 461–2 s.v.

[19] Cf. Wansbrough, "Gentilics and Appellatives: Notes on Aḥābiš Qurayš", *BSOAS*, 49 (1986); and *idem*, *Lingua Franca*, 140–5.

[20] Sign 376* in R. Labat, *Manuel* (= quai, digue, entrepôt, centre commercial), and in R. Borger, *Zeichenliste* (= Kai).

[21] Cf. Wansbrough, "Ugarit: A Bronze Age Hansa?", in K. Haellquist (ed.), *Asian Trade Routes*, London 1991, 21–6, references at 278–81.

[22] *AHw* (W. von Soden, *Akkadisches Handwörterbuch*, Wiesbaden 1958–81) s.v.; *CAD* (*Assyrian Dictionary University of Chicago*, 1956f.) s.v.; cf. W. Röllig, "Der altmesopotamische Markt", *WO*, 8 (1976).

(*ina kārim*). The corporate nature of *kārum* emerges from such contexts as correspondence to and from the trading station, debts and credits accruing thereto, admission or non-admission of merchants into its precinct. Frequent is reference to its 'full assembly' (*kārum ṣaḫir rabi*), settlement therein of disputes (*awat*), and rendering of verdicts (*din kārim, ṭuppum dannum*). The *kārum* could fix dates, keep accounts, control movement of commodities and caravans. Its personnel included a president (*ākil, rabi*), a clerk (*tupšarrum*), and janitor (*maṣṣarum*). It could levy dues and taxes (*miksum, šaddu'tum, datum*) calculated by a revenue officer (*šaqil datim*), demand interest (*ṣibtum*). From this usage must have been extrapolated the locution 'market price' (*kīma KAR ibaššu*) according to current and variable turnover. A complement is also evident in the spatial designation (*bīt kārim*), by which the locus of transaction became concrete and specific. It is probably in this way that the term survived, as affix (determinative) to a toponym, e.g. Kār-Nippur, Kār-Sippar, Kār-Kaniš. These were stations in a network of long-distance trade, not merely 'ports' for trans-shipment, but 'markets', i.e. 'spot' or 'forward', for storage, freight, information about supply and demand. The 'palace', when and where one can be ascertained, does not dictate but rather, subsists in a state of parity composed of mutual recognition. There can be no doubt that the medieval Kārim operated in the same manner. The very fact of conflict with regalian authority and ultimate demise in the face of Mamlūk fiscal pressure (monopoly) would suggest that the ethos of the Kārim was free enterprise, the standard goal-motivated behaviour of businessmen.

The most comprehensive data on the Akkadian *kārum* come from Sippar and Kaniš. Of crucial interest for this material is the fact that a Kār-Sippar is attested at Mari about 300 miles up the Euphrates; and that so far all information about the organization of merchants from Aššur was discovered at Kültepe (Kaniš) some 600 miles away by an overland route.[23] Prosopographically, the documentation is comparable to that of the Arabic Kārim: many names of individual participants in the trade are attested in the extensive correspondence between Aššur and Kaniš (covering a period of *c.* 70 years), and especially of large merchant families (e.g. Pušu-ken, Aššur-idi, Amur-ili). In these we may observe the actual structure of the trade: base of operations in a family firm at Aššur, provision of operating capital for younger members despatched as representatives to the Anatolian *kārum*, informal agreements and legal contracts with other families, development of a differentiated terminology, such as *naruqqum* = 'investment contract', *šazzuztum* = 'agency', *ša kīma* PN = 'representative', *ša barini* = 'common property', *šamalla'um* = 'employee', *be'ulātum* = 'working capital' (cf. *kīsum* = 'purse'), *nēmulum* = 'profit', etc. As in the Kārim and

[23] K. Veenhof, *Aspects of Old Assyrian Trade and its Terminology*, Leiden 1972; M. Larsen, *The Old Assyrian City-State and its Colonies*, Copenhagen 1976.

Geniza records, it is possible here to trace the fortunes over two or three generations of a particular family.

Whether or not this juxtaposition of structural and sociological data be thought acceptable, the proposed link between *kārum* and Kārim will probably founder on a lengthy series of linguistic obstacles:

(1) The Sumerian logogram is *KAR*, and its Akkadian reading in stat. const., hence in toponyms, is also *kār*-GN.

(2) While fixed phrases like *ina/ana kārim, bīt kārim, ša kārim* (all genitive) are, as also nom. *kārum* and acc. *kāram*, mostly spelled with mimation (= determinate?), the final consonant is of course not part of the root, nor is it consistently written in later sources.

(3) The Arabic term does at least exhibit the indispensable Akkadian long vowel /*ā*/ but is orthographically neutral in its second syllable.

(4) Arabic *kārim*, even though occasionally written without the definite article /*al-*/ (suggesting a PN/GN), has mostly been assimilated to the Arabic lexicon, confirmed by production of a gentilic (*nisba*) form *kārimī*. I have alluded to the failure of the Semitic root *KRM* to provide either a satisfactory etymology or, in Arabic, a plausible morphology for the appellative. While the gentilic would appear to make of the third consonant /*m*/ a root constituent, this is possibly nothing more than a backformation elicited from standard Semitic structure.

(5) That it is /*m*/ may be significant. In Semitic morphology final /*m*/ (or /*n*/) has several functions, which could be depicted as either (a) phonetic or (b) phonemic:

(a) includes extension of biconsonantal roots to the triconsonantal standard; enclisis; 'ballast' in poetic structure.[24] These phenomena would seem quite arbitrary unless /*m*/ or /*n*/ had also achieved marked/phonemic status in Semitic.

(b) includes adverbial function; determinate value (with generic and indeterminate); number (plural and dual).[25] Here, too, a relationship is not clear, unless the phonetic value of /*m*/ or /*n*/ had already become general.

Both sets are widely, and randomly, exhibited, the number class more consistently, and rigorously, than the others. Though it would be unwise to exclude any of these phenomena from an explanation of /*m*/ in Arabic *kārim*, I am inclined to favour the determinate/generic array. An evolution of mimation/nunation from designation of the defined (individual) to the generic (categorial) to the undefined

---

[24] See J. Blau, *The Emergence and Linguistic Background of Judaeo-Arabic*, Oxford 1965, 171 n. 2 (*ad* Nöldeke, *NBSS* and Brockelmann, *GVG*); C. Gordon, *Ugaritic Textbook*, Rome 1965, paras 11.6–7, 13.99–102 and 116; H. Hummel, "Enclitic mem in Early Northwest Semitic", *JBL*, 76 (1957); G. Rendsburg, "Eblaite U-MA and Hebrew WM-", *Eblaitica*, 1 (1987).

[25] Gordon, *op. cit.* paras 11.4–5; Brockelmann, *GVG* 473–4; S. Moscati *et al.*, *Comparative Grammar of the Semitic Languages*, Wiesbaden 1964, paras 12.36–63, 70–79; A. Beeston, *Sabaic Grammar* (JSS Monographs), Manchester 1984, paras 12–15; J. Nougayrol *et al.*, *GLECS*, 5 (1948/51), 73–82, 88–90; J. Kurylowicz, "La mimation et l'article en arabe", *AO*, 18 (1950); W. Diem, "Zur Frage der Mimation und Nunation in den semitischen Sprachen", *ZDMG*, 125 (1975).

(random) substantive is hypothetically possible and had been more than once proposed. The intrusive element, and hence catalyst of the evolution would be the emergence of a new morpheme for the defined (determinate) state, e.g. *'a + l* or gemination (Arabic), *h* + gemination (Hebrew), final *alef* (Aramaic).[26] That such should have entailed a shift in the semantic function of mimation/nunation is plausible but difficult to pinpoint. And impossible, within the diachronic witness of Classical Arabic. One would be compelled to postulate, say, *(ša) kārim* = 'the collectivity of the *kār*' as a pre-CA formation.

(6) Existence in Akkadian of a convergent term for 'price', 'transaction', even 'marketplace', must be mentioned but not allowed to mislead. *Maḫirum* has, admittedly, the advantage of a cognate in Hebrew (*meḥīr*) and elsewhere in West Semitic, but in neither Sumerian (*KAR* vs *KI.LAM/GAN.BA*) nor Akkadian are the terms confused.[27]

(7) In a quadrilingual wordlist from Ras Shamra the Sumerogram *KAR* is rendered *ka-a-ru* (Akkadian), *ma-ḫa-zi* (Hurrian), and *ma-aḫ-ḫa-zu* (Ugaritic).[28] The Ugaritic word is mḫd, attested also in Aramaic (*māḥōzā*), Hebrew (*meḥōz*), Arabic (*māḥūz*: rare), with the several by now familiar meanings 'harbour', 'city', 'commercial transaction'. This could suggest either a Hurrian loanword or a North-West Semitic translation of *kāru(m)*, were it not for Akkadian *maḫazu* = 'city', 'holy city', 'holy precinct'. While *mḫz* is rendered 'forum' in a bilingual (Punic/Latin) inscription from Leptis Magna,[29] it would seem that *KAR* remained an East Semitic property.

Now, all this must appear to make at least arduous if not impossible the passage of Akkadian *kāru(m)* into medieval Arabic. Toponyms compounded with *kār-* (stat. const.) might, especially in their Neo-Assyrian proliferation, furnish a clue. In the most recent collections one finds, in addition to the well known Kār-Duniaš (= Kassite Babylon) and Kār-Kemoš (Carchemish), such entries as Kār-Esarhaddon (= Sidon), Kār-Šalmaneser (= Til Barsip), Kār-Banīti and Kār-Muṣur (in Egypt).[30] It would of course be helpful if the Arabic toponymy of the Middle East could yield compounds of Kār-, but Yāqūt's geographical dictionary (thirteenth century) provides only examples from the regions of Ispahan and Mosul, of which the latter might be of mild documentary value.[31] One would need a more explicit array of evidence.

---

26 See T. Lamdin, "The Junctural Origin of the West Semitic Definite Article", in H. Goedicke, *Festschrift Albright*, Baltimore 1971.

27 *AHw* s.v.; *CAD* s.v.; Gesenius, *Handwörterbuch*, 413.

28 *RS* 20.123 = *Ugaritica*, v, Paris 1968, 420–3 and 240–3 (no. 137); to the references cited *apud* Wansbrough, *Lingua Franca*, ch. 1 n. 150 add Dozy, *Suppl.*, ii, 570 s.v.

29 See I. Eph'al, *The Ancient Arabs*, Jerusalem 1984, 102 n. 340 *ad* H. Donner and W. Röllig, *Kanaanäische und aramäische Inschriften*, Wiesbaden 1962–4, 124.2.

30 S. Parpola, "Neo-Assyrian Toponyms", *AOAT* 6, Kevelaer/Neukirchen-Vluyn 1970, 195–201; G. Bunnens, "Considérations géographiques sur la place occupée par la Phénicie dans l'expansion de l'Empire assyrien", in *Studia Phoenicia*, *OLA* 15, Leuven 1983, esp. 179; Eph'al, *op. cit.*, 101–2 nn. 339–41.

31 Yāqūt al-Ḥamawī, *K. Muʿjam al-Buldān*, Leipzig 1866–70, iv, 223.

I should like now to revert to the structural implications of Kārim and *kārum*. It ought to be clear that from these may be extrapolated an economic paradigm enabling the trace of 'market economy'. While it is true that much of this exegesis depends upon a definition of trade as egocentric and entrepreneurial behaviour, it is difficult to discover in the sources any other motive for the production and accumulation of investment capital.[32] The paradigm is approximately as follows: a supply of luxury goods (e.g. spices, textiles, temple and funerary ornament) evolves into provision of raw materials (e.g. dyes, lacquer, ivory, gems) to feed a home industry. While these may be cheaper to acquire than manufactures, they also tend to be bulkier and require more elaborate transport arrangements, a technology that can be costed and hence converted into a tangible asset. A noteworthy example of the process is furnished by the Phoenicians, whose Iron Age expansion marked a significant change in the pattern of Mediterranean commerce. Establishment of 'factories' as far west as the Atlantic coast involved not merely shipment of finished products but also intervention in local extraction of raw materials destined to supply a Levantine work force. In other words, Phoenician presence on the Quadalquivir and Rio Tinto attests a concern with long-distance industry as well as long-distance trade.[33] But the Phoenicians owned their ships, a fact that generated the notion of transport as calculable gain.

Five or six centuries earlier, the commercial viability of Ugarit rested upon acknowledgement of the same fact. There, of course, documentary evidence of an 'imperial context' is exiguous (as I think it is also in the case of Phoenicia), and the impression is one of a market economy hardly affected by fiscal pressure. There, too, the *kārum* is attested, both in the wordlist mentioned above and in a number of Akkadian chancery instruments.[34] It might seem that the term was there consciously applied to a mode of economic activity corresponding approximately to the parameters of the marketplace, both spatial (venue of commodity, seller, buyer) and temporal (season, supply, demand).

Now, that usage exhibits a notion of commerce quite independent of both its local machinery and identifiable agents. While the Akkadian term has long since been seen to include this concept, Arabic Kārim is mostly read as designating a corporeal formation, i.e. a recognizable company of men engaged in the long-distance transfer and exchange of specific commodities. That the appellative Kārimī has that reference may be conceded (with the plural forms *kārim/kārimiyyūn/akārim*, the latter only *apud*

---

32 Wansbrough, *Lingua Franca*, 3–4, 20–2, references at nn. 4, 57–62.
33 Bunnens, *art. cit.* (note 30 above); *idem*, "Tyr et la mer", *ibid.* 7–21; but also the 'interstitial' models (i.e. Phoenician expansion as direct result of Neo-Assyrian economic strategy) adumbrated by G. Kestemont, "Tyr et les Assyriens", *ibid.* 53–78; exaggerated by S. Frankenstein, "The Phoenicians in the Far West: A Function of Neo-Assyrian Imperialism", *apud* M. Larsen, *Power and Propaganda: A Symposium on Ancient Empires*, Copenhagen, 1979, 263–94. Cf. Wansbrough, *op. cit.*, 13–7, references at nn. 26–35, 44.
34 E.g. *PRU*, iv, 119.8; *Ugaritica*, iv, Paris 1962, 219.10; *Ugaritica*, v, 13.4; see Wansbrough, *art. cit.* (*supra* note 21).

Ibn Baṭṭūṭa). So far as I know, the corresponding *nisba* formation (*-ay*/*-ī*) is not attested for the Akkadian word. But where Arabic Kārim is not obviously the plural of Kārimī, the abstract meaning is possible and even probable. On present evidence, however, further speculation would be futile. The Arabic term enjoyed only a limited life in the vast lexicon of that language: some three and a half centuries and with reference to a particular, though very important, sector of the economy. When, in the second half of the fifteenth century, the Kārim vanished from Egyptian history, so did also the structure of a market economy, to be succeeded by an organization of commerce subservient to state control and political imperative.